COMPUTATIONAL GEOMETRY IN C

COMPUTATIONAL GEOMETRY IN C

JOSEPH O'ROURKE

The Spencer T. and Ann W. Olin Professor of Computer Science
Smith College

CAMBRIDGE
UNIVERSITY PRESS

PUBLISHED BY THE PRESS SYNDICATE OF THE UNIVERSITY OF CAMBRIDGE
The Pitt Building, Trumpington Street, Cambridge CB2 1RP, United Kingdom

CAMBRIDGE UNIVERSITY PRESS
The Edinburgh Building, Cambridge CB2 2RU, United Kingdom
40 West 20th Street, New York, NY 10011-4211, USA
10 Stamford Road, Oakleigh, Melbourne 3166, Australia

First published 1993
Reprinted with corrections 1994
Reprinted 1995, 1996

Printed in the United States of America

Typeset in Times

A catalogue record for this book is available from the British Library

Library of Congess Cataloguing-in-Publication Data is available

ISBN 0-521-44034-3 hardback
ISBN 0-521-44592-2 paperback

To Marylynn, Nell, and Russell

Contents

Preface

Computational geometry broadly construed is the study of algorithms for solving geometric problems on a computer. The emphasis in this text is on the design of such algorithms, with somewhat less attention paid to analysis of performance. I have in several cases carried out the design to the level of working C programs, which are discussed in detail.

There are many brands of geometry, and what has become known as "computational geometry," covered in this book, is primarily discrete and combinatorial geometry. Thus polygons play a much larger role in this book than do regions with curved boundaries. Much of the work on continuous curves and surfaces falls under the rubrics of "geometric modeling" or "solid modeling," a field with its own conferences and texts,[1] distinct from computational geometry. Of course there is substantial overlap, and there is no fundamental reason for the fields to be partitioned this way; indeed they seem to be merging to some extent.

The field of computational geometry is a mere 15 years old at this writing, if one takes M. I. Shamos's thesis (Shamos, 1978) as its inception. Now there are annual conferences, journals, texts, and a thriving community of researchers with common interests.

TOPICS COVERED

I consider the "core" concerns of computational geometry to be polygon partitioning, convex hulls, Voronoi diagrams, arrangements of lines, geometric searching, and motion planning. These topics form the chapters of this book. The field is not so settled that this list can be considered a consensus; other researchers would define the core differently.

It has become the fashion for textbooks to include far more material than can be covered in one semester. This is not such a text. Rather it is a written record of what I cover with undergraduates in one 40 class-hour semester. In order to touch on each of the core topics, I find it necessary to oscillate the level of detail, only sketching some algorithms while detailing others. Which ones are sketched and which are detailed is a personal choice that I can only justify by my classroom experiences.

---

[1] e.g., Mortenson (1985) and Hoffmann (1989).

PREREQUISITES

The material in this text should be accessible to students with only minimal preparation. Discrete mathematics, calculus, and linear algebra suffice for mathematics. In fact, very little calculus or linear algebra is used in the text, and the enterprising student can learn the little needed on the fly. In computer science, a course in programming and exposure to data structures is enough (Computer Science I and II at many schools). In particular, I do not presume a course in algorithms, although that would certainly enhance the reader's appreciation. I teach this material to college juniors and seniors, mostly computer science and mathematics majors.

I hasten to add that the book can be fruitfully studied by those who have no programming experience at all, simply by skipping all the implementation sections. Those who know some programming language, but not C, can easily appreciate the implementation discussions even if they cannot read the code.

When teaching this material to both computer science and mathematics majors, I offer them a choice of projects that permits those with programming skills to write code, and those with theoretical inclinations to avoid programming.

Although written to be accessible to undergraduates, my experience is that the material can form the basis of a challenging graduate course as well. I have tried to mix elementary explanations with references to the latest literature. Footnotes provide technical details and citations. A number of the exercises pose open problems. It is not difficult to supplement the text with a few research articles, effectively upgrading the material to the graduate level.

IMPLEMENTATIONS

Not all algorithms discussed in the book are provided with implementations. In fact, full code for only nine algorithms is included.[2] Researchers in industry coming to this book for working code for their favorite algorithms will likely be disappointed: they may seek an algorithm to find the minimum spanning circle for a set of points and find it as an exercise.[3]

The presented code should be viewed as samples of geometry programs. I hope I have chosen a representative set of algorithms to implement; I have left much room for student projects.

All the C code in the book is available by anonymous ftp from grendel.csc.smith.edu (131.229.64.23), in the directory /pub/compgeom. I will update the files in this directory to correct errors and incorporate improvements. An errata file for the text will also be included.

---

[2]Area of a polygon, triangulating a polygon, convex hull in two dimensions, convex hull in three dimensions, Delaunay triangulation, point in polygon, extreme point of convex polygon, intersecting convex polygons, and multi-link robot arm reachability.
[3]Exercise 5.5.6[12].

EXERCISES

There are approximately 200 exercises sprinkled throughout the text. They range from easy extensions of the text to quite difficult problems to "open" problems. These latter are an exciting feature of such a fresh field; students can reach the frontier of knowledge so quickly that even undergraduates can hope to solve problems that no one has managed to crack yet. Indeed I have written several papers with undergraduates as a result of their work on homework problems I posed.[4] Not all open problems are necessarily difficult; some are simply awaiting the requisite attention. Exercises are sporadically marked "[easy]" or "[difficult]," but the lack of these notations should not be read to imply that neither apply. Those marked "[programming]" require programming skills, and those marked "[open]" are unsolved problems as far as I know at this writing. I have tried to credit authors of individual problems where appropriate.

ACKNOWLEDGEMENTS

I thank the many people who read various portions of the text in draft and provided useful advice: Herbert Edelsbrunner, Steve Fortune, Daniel Halperin, Paul Heffernan, Chun-hsiung Huang, Michael McKenna, Peter Schorn, Thomas Shermer, Steve Skiena, Sharon Solms, Seth Teller, Godfried Toussaint, and several sage, anonymous referees. Special thanks to Stacia Wyman, who read a complete draft in a matter of weeks, and to Joseph Mitchell, whose steady stream of corrections to various drafts nearly kept pace with the rate at which I introduced new errors during revisions. Lauren Cowles at Cambridge has been the ideal editor.

I have received generous support from the National Science Foundation for my research in computational geometry, most recently under grant CCR-9122169.

Joseph O'Rourke
orourke@cs.smith.edu
Smith College, Massachusetts
August 17, 1993

---

[4]The material from one paper is incorporated into Section 7.4.

1

Polygon Triangulation

1.1. ART GALLERY THEOREMS

1.1.1. Polygons

Much of computational geometry performs its computations on geometrical objects known as polygons. Polygons are a convenient representation for many real-world objects: convenient both in that an abstract polygon is often an accurate model of real objects and in that it is easily manipulated computationally. Examples of their use include representing shapes of individual letters for automatic character recognition, of an obstacle to be avoided in a robot's environment, or of a piece of a solid object to be displayed on a graphics screen. However, polygons can be rather complicated objects, and often a need arises to view them as composed of simpler pieces. This leads to the topic of this and the next chapter: partitioning polygons.

Definition of a Polygon
A *polygon* is the region of a plane bounded by a finite collection of line segments[1] forming a simple closed curve. Pinning down a precise meaning for the phrase "simple closed curve" is unfortunately a bit difficult. A topologist would say that it is the homeomorphic image of a circle,[2] meaning that it is a certain deformation of a circle. We will avoid topology for now and approach a definition in a more pedestrian manner, as follows.

Let $v_0, v_1, v_2, \ldots, v_{n-1}$ be n points in the plane. Here and throughout the book, all index arithmetic will be mod n, implying a cyclic ordering of the points, with v_0 following v_{n-1}, since $(n-1)+1 \equiv n \equiv 0 \pmod{n}$. Let $e_0 = v_0 v_1$, $e_1 = v_1 v_2, \ldots, e_i = v_i v_{i+1}, \ldots, e_{n-1} = v_{n-1} v_0$ be n segments connecting the points. Then these segments bound a polygon iff[3]   *or* $e_0 = v_0 \cup v_1$

1. The intersection of each pair of segments adjacent in the cyclic ordering is the single point shared between them: $e_i \cap e_{i+1} = v_{i+1}$, for all $i = 0, \ldots, n-1$.

2. Nonadjacent segments do not intersect: $e_i \cap e_j = \emptyset$, for all $j \neq i + 1$.

[1] A *line segment* is a closed subset of a line contained between two points, which are called its *endpoints*. The subset is closed in the sense that it includes the endpoints.
[2] A *circle* is a one-dimensional set of points. We reserve the term *disk* to mean the two-dimensional region bounded by a circle.
[3] "Iff" means "if and only if," an extremely convenient abbreviation introduced by Halmos. See (Halmos 1985, p. 403).

Handwritten margin notes: homeo-morphic; e for edge; v for vertex; $(n-1)+1 \equiv n$ is an identity; ∩ for Meet; ∪ for Union; Why not $e_i \cap e_{i+1} = v_i$? Ans: Convention. The words. The corresponding symbols.

Handwritten note at bottom: Note added 21 March. If you use ∩ for Meet of intersection & ∪ for Union or Join, then with these 2 dual symbols the equivalent of De Morgan's Laws for Boolean algebra fall out quite naturally by becoming visually self evident.

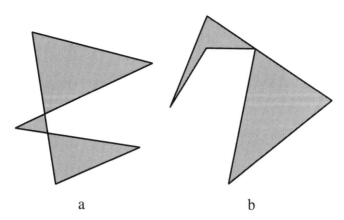

FIGURE 1.1   Nonsimple polygons.

The reason these segments define a *curve* is that they are connected end-to-end; the reason the curve is *closed* is that they form a cycle; the reason the closed curve is *simple* is that nonadjacent segments do not intersect.

The points v_i are called the *vertices* of the polygon, and the segments e_i are called its *edges*. Note that a polygon of n vertices has n edges.

An important theorem of topology is the Jordan Curve Theorem:

Theorem 1.1.1   (Jordan Curve Theorem).   *Every simple closed plane curve divides the plane into two parts.*

This strikes most as so obvious as not to require a proof; but in fact, a precise proof is quite difficult.[4] We will take it as given. The two parts of the plane are called the *interior* and *exterior* of the curve. The exterior is unbounded, the interior bounded. This justifies our definition of a polygon as the region bounded by the collection of segments. Note that we define a polygon P as a closed region of the plane. Often a polygon is considered to be just the segments bounding the region, and not the region itself. We will use the notation ∂P to mean the boundary of P; this is notation borrowed from topology.[5] By our definition $\partial P \subseteq P$.

Figure 1.1 illustrates two nonsimple polygons. For both objects in the figure, the segments satisfy condition (1) above (adjacent segments share a common point) but not condition (2): nonadjacent segments intersect. Such objects are often called polygons, with those polygons satisfying (2) called *simple polygons*. As we will have little use for nonsimple polygons in this book, we will drop the redundant modifier.

We will follow the convention of listing the vertices of a polygon in counterclockwise order, so that if you walked along the boundary visiting the vertices in

---

[4] See Henle (1979, p. 100–103). The theorem dates back to 1877.
[5] There is a sense in which the boundary of a region is like a derivative, so it makes sense to use the partial derivative symbol ∂.

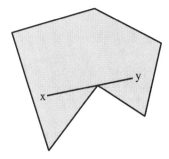

FIGURE 1.2   Grazing contact of line-of-sight.

that order (a *boundary traversal*), the interior of the polygon would be always to your left.

1.1.2. The Art Gallery Theorem

Problem Definition

We will study a fascinating problem posed by Klee[6] that will lead us naturally into the issue of triangulation, the most important polygon partitioning. Imagine an art gallery room whose floor plan can be modeled by a polygon of n vertices. Klee asked: How many stationary guards are needed to guard the room? Each guard is considered a fixed point that can see in every direction, that is, has a   *circular* 2π range of visibility.[7] Of course a guard cannot see through a wall of the room. We will make Klee's problem rigorous before attempting an answer.

Visibility

To make the notion of visibility precise, we say that point x can *see* point y (or y is *visible* to x) iff the closed segment[8] xy is nowhere exterior to the polygon P: $xy \subseteq P$. Note that this definition permits the line-of-sight to have grazing contact with a vertex, as shown in Figure 1.2. An alternative, equally reasonable definition would say that a vertex can block vision: say that x has *clear visibility* to y if $\overline{xy} \subseteq P$ and $\overline{xy} \cap \partial P \subseteq \{x, y\}$. We will occasionally use this alternative definition in exercises (Exercises 1.1.4[2] and [3]).

HA!   A guard is a point. A set of guards is said to *cover* a polygon if every point in the polygon is visible to some guard. Guards themselves do not block each other's visibility. Note that we could require the guards to see only points of ∂P, for presumably that is where the paintings are! This is an interesting variant, explored in Exercise 1.1.4[1].

---

[6] Posed in 1973, as reported by Honsberger (1976). The material in this section (and more on the topic) may be found in O'Rourke (1987).

[7] We will use radians throughout to represent angles. π radians = 180°.   *radians*

[8] Many authors use $\overline{xy}$ to indicate this segment.

As sides flex around watch the guard pts move. And fuse & split. This would make a nice animation.

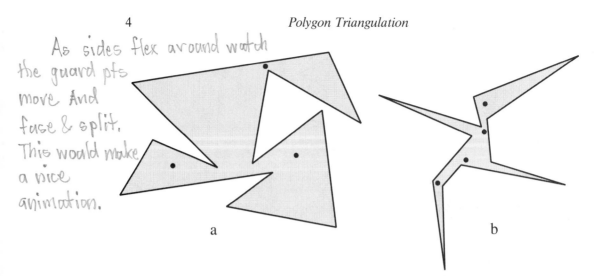

a   b

FIGURE 1.3 Two polygons of $n = 12$ vertices: (*a*) requires 3 guards; (*b*) requires 4 guards.

Max over Min Formulation

We have now made most of Klee's problem precise, except for the phrase "How many." Succinctly put, the problem is to find the maximum over all polygons of n vertices, of the minimum number of guards needed to cover the polygon. This max-over-min formulation is confusing to novices, but it is used quite frequently in mathematics, so we will take time to explain it carefully.

For any given fixed polygon, there is some minimum number of guards that are *necessary* for complete coverage. Thus, in Figure 1.3*a*, it is clear that three guards are needed to cover this polygon of 12 vertices, although there is considerable freedom in the location of the three guards; but is three the most that is ever needed for all possible polygons of 12 vertices? No. The polygon in Figure 1.3*b*, also with 12 vertices, requires four guards. What is the largest number of guards that any polygon of 12 vertices needs? We will show eventually that four guards always *suffice* for any polygon of 12 vertices. This is what Klee's question seeks: Express as a function of n, the smallest number of guards that suffice to cover any polygon of n vertices. Sometimes this number of guards is said to be necessary and sufficient for coverage: necessary in that at least that many are needed for *some* polygons, and sufficient in that that many always suffice for *any* polygon.   *I would write* $\min g(P)$.

We formalize the problem before exploring it further. Let $g(P)$ be the smallest number of guards needed to cover polygon P: $g(P) = \min_S |\{S : S$ covers $P\}|$, where S is a set of points, and $|S|$ is the cardinality[9] of S. Let P_n be a polygon of n vertices. $G(n)$ is the maximum of $g(P_n)$ over all polygons of n vertices: $G(n) = \max_{P_n} g(P_n)$. Klee's problem is to determine the function $G(n)$. It may not be immediately evident that $G(n)$ is defined for each n: it is at least conceivable that for some polygon, no finite number of guards suffice. Fortu-

little g is min big G is max Ugh!

[9]The *cardinality* of a set is its number of elements.

nately, $G(n)$ is finite for all n, as we will see, but whether it can be expressed as a simple formula or must be represented by an infinite table of values is less clear.

Empirical Exploration

Sufficiency of n. Certainly at least one guard is always necessary. In terms of our notation, this provides a lower bound on $G(n)$: $1 \leq G(n)$. It seems obvious that n guards suffice for any polygon: stationing a guard at every vertex will certainly cover the polygon. This provides an upper bound: $G(n) \leq n$. However, it is not even so clear that n guards suffice. At the least it demands a proof. It turns out to be true, justifying intuition, but this success of intuition is tempered by the fact that the same intuition fails in three dimensions: guards placed at every vertex of a polyhedron do not necessarily cover the polyhedron! (See Exercise 1.1.4[6]).

There are many art-gallery-like problems, and for most, it is easiest to first establish a lower bound on $G(n)$ by finding generic examples showing that a large number of guards are sometimes necessary. When it seems that no amount of ingenuity can increase the number necessary, then it is time to turn to proving that that number is also sufficient. This is how we will proceed.

Necessity for Small n. For small values of n, it is possible to guess the value of $G(n)$ with a little exploration. Clearly every triangle requires just one guard, so $G(3) = 1$.

Quadrilaterals may be divided into two groups: convex quadrilaterals and quadrilaterals with a reflex vertex. Intuitively a polygon is convex if it has no dents. This important concept will be explored in detail in Chapter 3. A vertex is called *reflex*[10] if its internal angle is strictly greater than π; otherwise a vertex is called *convex*[11]. A convex quadrilateral has four convex vertices. A quadrilateral can have at most one reflex vertex, for reasons that will become apparent in Section 1.2. As Figure 1.4*a* makes evident, even quadrilaterals with a reflex vertex can be covered by a single guard placed near that vertex. Thus, $G(4) = 1$.

For pentagons the situation is less clear. Certainly a convex pentagon needs just one guard, and a pentagon with one reflex vertex needs only one guard for the same reason as in a quadrilateral. A pentagon can have two reflex vertices. They may be either adjacent or separated by a convex vertex, as in Figure 1.4*c* and *d*; in each case one guard suffices. Therefore, $G(5) = 1$. Hexagons may require two guards, as shown in Figure 1.4*e* and *f*. A little experimentation can lead to a conviction that no more than two are ever needed, so that $G(6) = 2$.

Necessity of $\lfloor n/3 \rfloor$

At this point, the reader might be able to leap to a generalization of Figure 1.4*f* for larger values of n. Figure 1.5 illustrates the design for $n = 12$; note the

---

[10] Often called *concave*, but the similarity of "concave" and "convex" invites confusion, so I will use "reflex."

[11] Sometimes the term "convex" is used to indicate strict convexity, an interior angle strictly less than π.

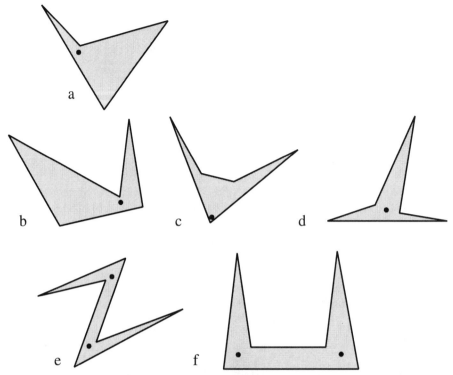

a

b   c   d

e   f

FIGURE 1.4   Polygons of $n = 4, 5, 6$ vertices.

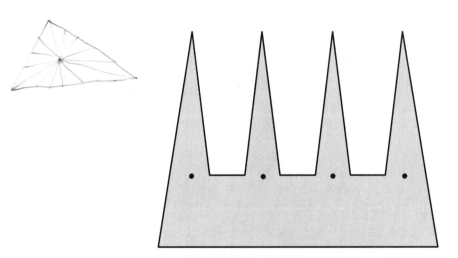

FIGURE 1.5   Chvátal's Comb for $n = 12$.

relation to Figure 1.3*b*. This "comb" shape consists of k prongs, with each prong composed of two edges, and adjacent prongs separated by an edge. Associating each prong with the separating edge to its right and the bottom edge with the rightmost prong, we see that a comb of k prongs has $n = 3k$ edges (and therefore vertices). Since each prong requires its own guard, we establish with this one example that $n/3 \le G(n)$ for $n = 3k$. This is what I meant earlier by saying that a generic example can be used to establish a lower bound on $G(n)$.

Noticing that $G(3) = G(4) = G(5)$ might lead one to conjecture that $G(n) = \lfloor n/3 \rfloor$,[12] and in fact this conjecture turns out to be true. This is the usual way that such mathematical questions are answered: first the answer is conjectured after empirical exploration, and only then, with a definite goal in mind, is the result proven. We now turn to a proof.

1.1.3. Fisk's Proof of Sufficiency

The first proof that $G(n) = \lfloor n/3 \rfloor$ was due to Chvátal (1975). His proof is by induction: assuming that $\lfloor n/3 \rfloor$ guards are needed for all $n < N$, he proves the same formula for $n = N$ by carefully removing part of the polygon so that its number of vertices is reduced, applying the induction hypothesis, and then reattaching the removed portion. The proof splinters into a number of cases, and is quite delicate. Three years later, Fisk found a very simple proof, occupying just a single journal page (Fisk, 1978). We will present Fisk's proof here.

Diagonals and Triangulation

Fisk's proof depends crucially on partitioning a polygon into triangles with diagonals. A *diagonal* of a polygon P is a line segment between two of its vertices a and b that are clearly visible to one another. Recall that this means the intersection of the closed segment ab with ∂P is exactly the set $\{a, b\}$. Another way to say this is that the open segment from a to b does not intersect ∂P; thus, a diagonal cannot make grazing contact with the boundary.

Let us call two diagonals *noncrossing* if their intersection is a subset of their endpoints: they share no interior points. If we add as many noncrossing diagonals to a polygon as possible, the interior is partitioned into triangles. Such a partition is called a *triangulation* of a polygon. The diagonals may be added in arbitrary order, as long as they are legal diagonals and noncrossing. In general, there are many ways to triangulate a given polygon. Figure 1.6 shows two triangulations of a polygon of $n = 14$ vertices.

We will defer a proof that every polygon can be triangulated to Section 1.2, and for now just assume the existence of a triangulation.

Floor: [12] $\lfloor x \rfloor$ is the *floor* of x: the largest integer less than or equal to x. The floor function has the effect of discarding the fractional portion of a positive real number.

Their is also ceiling $\lceil \ \rceil$.

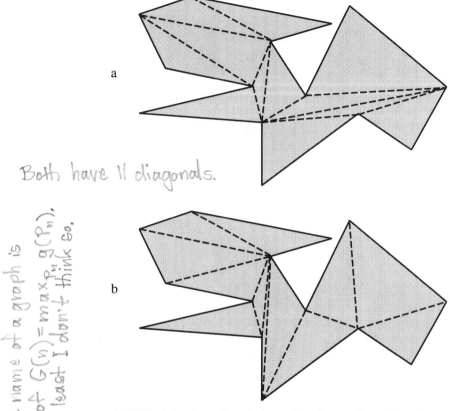

a

b

FIGURE 1.6   Two triangulations of a polygon of $n = 14$ vertices.

Both have 11 diagonals.

Here big G as the name of a graph is not the big G of $G(n) = \max_{P_n} g(P_n)$. At least I don't think so.

Three Coloring

To prove sufficiency of $\lfloor n/3 \rfloor$ guards for *any* polygon, the proof must work for an arbitrary polygon. So assume an arbitrary polygon P of n vertices is given. The first step of Fisk's proof is to triangulate P. The second step is to "recall" that the resulting graph may be three-colored. We need to explain what this graph is, and what three-coloring means.

Let G be a graph associated with a triangulation, whose arcs are the edges of the polygon and the diagonals of the triangulation, and whose nodes are the vertices of the polygon. This is the graph used by Fisk. A *k-coloring* of a graph is an assignment of colors to the nodes of the graph, such that no two nodes connected by an arc are assigned the same color. Fisk claims that every triangulation graph may be three-colored. We will again defer a proof of this claim, but a little experimentation should make it plausible. Three-colorings of the triangulations in Figure 1.6 are shown in Figure 1.7. Starting at, say, the vertex indicated by the arrow, and coloring its triangle arbitrarily with three colors, the remainder of the coloring is completely forced: there are no other free choices. Roughly, the reason this always works is that the forced choices

I would have preferred K, or W, since we have k-coloring.

"The remainder of the coloring is completely forced." I love it! Now, do this on the surface of a sphere or a torus & see what happens.

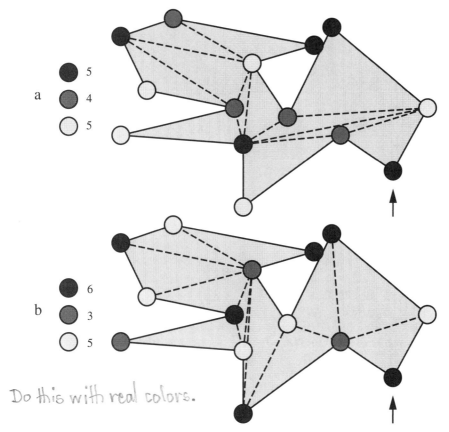

a

5
4
5

b

6
3
5

Do this with real colors.

FIGURE 1.7 Two three-colorings of a polygon of $n = 14$ vertices, based on the triangulations shown in Figure 1.6.

never double back on an earlier choice; and the reason this never happens is that the underlying figure is a polygon (with no holes by definition).

The third step of Fisk's proof is the observation that placing guards at all the vertices assigned one particular color guarantees visibility coverage of the polygon. His reasoning is as follows. Let red, green, and blue be the colors used in the three-coloring. Each triangle must have each of the three colors at its three corners. Thus, every triangle has a red node at one corner. Suppose guards are placed at every red node; then every triangle has a guard in one corner. Clearly a triangle is covered by a guard at one of its corners. Thus, every triangle is covered. Finally, the collection of triangles in a triangulation completely covers the polygon. Thus, the entire polygon is covered if guards are placed at red nodes. Similarly, the entire polygon is covered if guards are placed at green nodes or at blue nodes. *But similarly the entire polygon is covered it*

The fourth and final step of Fisk's proof applies the "pigeon-hole principle": *a guard is*
if n objects are placed into k pigeon holes, at least one hole must contain no *placed at the*

1 March 2002

center of each triangle, so why bother with the coloring? Why not just triangulate?

more than n/k objects. Because if every one of the k holes contained more than n/k objects, the total number of objects would exceed n. In our case, the n objects are the n nodes of the triangulation graph, and the k holes are the 3 colors. The principle says that one color must be used no more than $n/3$ times. Since n is an integer, we can conclude that one color is used no more than $\lfloor n/3 \rfloor$ times. We now have our sufficiency proof: just place guards at nodes colored with the least-frequently used color in the three-coloring. We are guaranteed that this will cover the polygon with no more than $G(n) = \lfloor n/3 \rfloor$ colors. If you don't find this argument beautiful (or at least charming), you will not enjoy much in this book!

In Figure 1.7, $n = 14$, so $\lfloor n/3 \rfloor = 4$. In (1.7a) of the figure the second color is used four times; in (1.7b), the same color is used only three times. Note that the three-coloring argument does not always lead to the most efficient use of guards.

1.1.4. Exercises

1. *Guarding the walls.* Construct a polygon P and a placement of guards such that the guards see every point of ∂P, but there is at least one point interior to P not seen by any guard.

2. *Clear visibility, point guards.* What is the answer to Klee's question for clear visibility (Section 1.1.2)? More specifically, let $G'(n)$ be the smallest number of *point guards* that suffice to see clearly every point in any polygon of n vertices. Point guards are guards who may stand at any point of P; these are distinguished from *vertex guards* who may be stationed only at vertices. Are clearly-seeing guards stronger or weaker than usual guards? What relationship between $G'(n)$ and $G(n)$ follows from their relative strength? ($G(n)$ is defined on p. 4.) Does Fisk's proof establish $\lfloor n/3 \rfloor$ sufficiency for clear visibility? Try to determine $G'(n)$ exactly.

3. *Clear visibility, vertex guards* (Shermer). Answer question 2 but for *vertex* guards: guards restricted to vertices.

4. *Edge guards* [open]. An *edge guard* is a guard who may patrol one edge e of a polygon. A point $y \in P$ is covered by the guard, if there is some point $x \in e$ such that x can see y. Another way to view this is to imagine a florescent light whose extent matches e. The portion of P that is illuminated by this light is the set of points covered by the edge guard.

    Toussaint showed that $\lfloor n/4 \rfloor$ edge guards are sometimes necessary, as demonstrated by the "half-swastika" polygon shown in Figure 1.8 (O'Rourke, 1987, p. 83) He conjectured that $\lfloor n/4 \rfloor$ suffice except for a few small values of n. This odd exception is necessitated by the two "arrowhead" polygons shown in Figure 1.9, which do not seem to generalize. These examples are taken from Shermer (1992).
    Prove or disprove Toussaint's conjecture.

5. *Edge guards in star polygons* [open]. A *star polygon* is one that can be covered by a single (point) guard. Toussaint proved that $\lfloor n/5 \rfloor$ edge guards are sometimes necessary to cover a star polygon with the example shown in Figure 1.10 (O'Rourke, 1987, p. 119). The conjecture that $\lfloor n/5 \rfloor$ always suffice was recently shown to be false for $n = 14$ (Subramaniyam and Diwan, 1991), but otherwise little is known. Prove or disprove that $\lfloor n/5 \rfloor$ suffice for sufficiently large n.

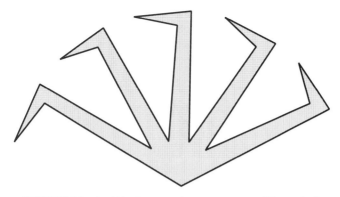

FIGURE 1.8 $\lfloor n/4 \rfloor$ edge guards are necessary (Toussaint).

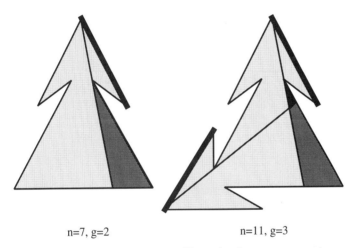

n=7, g=2   n=11, g=3

FIGURE 1.9   Two polygons that require $\lfloor (n+1)/4 \rfloor$ edge guards (shown as heavy edges).

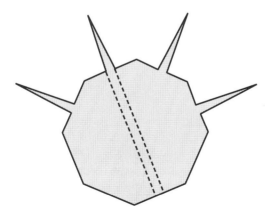

FIGURE 1.10 $\lfloor n/5 \rfloor$ edge guards are necessary (Toussaint).

6. *Guards in polyhedra.* Design a polyhedron such that guards placed at every vertex fail to cover completely the interior. A polyhedron is a three-dimensional version of a polygon, composed of polygonal faces, and enclosing a volume. A precise definition is offered in Chapter 4 (Section 4.1).

I've already got one. A 3 stick tensegrity.

1.2. TRIANGULATION: THEORY

In this section, we prove that every polygon has a triangulation, and establish some basic properties of triangulations. In later sections (1.3–1.6.4), we will discuss algorithms for constructing triangulations.

A natural reaction on being presented with the question, "Must every polygon have a triangulation," is to respond with another question: "How could a polygon *not* have a triangulation?" Indeed, it cannot not have one! However, if you feel this is too obvious for a proof, consider the equivalent question in three dimensions: there the natural generalization is false! See O'Rourke, 1987 (p. 253–254).

1.2.1. Existence of a Diagonal

The key to proving the existence of a triangulation is proving the existence of a diagonal. Once we have that, the rest will follow easily. For the proof, we need one other even more obvious fact: every polygon must have at least one convex vertex.[13]

Lemma 1.2.1.   *Every polygon must have at least one strictly convex vertex.*

Proof. If the edges of a polygon are oriented so that their direction indicates a counterclockwise traversal, a strictly convex vertex is a left turn for someone walking around the boundary, and a reflex vertex is a right turn. The interior of the polygon is always to the left of this hypothetical walker. Let L be a line through a lowest vertex v of P, lowest in having minimum y coordinate with respect to a coordinate system; if there are several lowest vertices, let v be the rightmost. The interior of P must be above L. The edge following v must lie above L. See Figure 1.11. Together, these conditions imply that the walker makes a left turn at v and therefore that v is a strictly convex vertex.   □

Lemma 1.2.2 (Meister).   *Every polygon of $n \geq 4$ vertices has a diagonal.*

Proof. Let v be a strictly convex vertex, whose existence is guaranteed by Lemma 1.2.1. Let a and b the vertices adjacent to v. If ab is a diagonal, we are finished. So suppose ab is not a diagonal; then either ab is exterior to P, or it intersects ∂P. In either case, since $n > 3$, the closed triangle $\triangle avb$ contains at least one vertex of P other than a, v, b. Let x be the vertex of P in $\triangle avb$ that

---

[13] In my proof in (O'Rourke 1987, p. 12) I just said "We take it as obvious ... ."

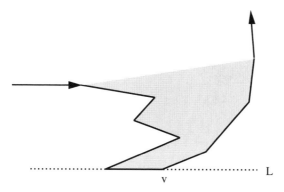

FIGURE 1.11   The rightmost lowest vertex must be strictly convex.

is closest to v, where distance is measured orthogonal to the line through ab. Thus, x is the first vertex in $\triangle avb$ hit by a line L parallel to ab moving from v toward ab. See Figure 1.12.

Now we claim that vx is a diagonal of P. For it is clear that the interior of $\triangle avb$ intersected with the halfplane bounded by L that includes v (the shaded region in the figure), is empty of points of ∂P. Therefore vx cannot intersect ∂P except at v and x, and so is a diagonal.   □

Theorem 1.2.3 (Triangulation).   *Every polygon P of n vertices may be partitioned into triangles by the addition of (zero or more) diagonals.*

Proof. The proof is by induction. If $n = 3$, the polygon is a triangle, and the theorem holds trivially.

Let $n \geq 4$. Let $d = ab$ be a diagonal of P, as guaranteed by Lemma 1.2.2. Because d by definition only intersects ∂P at its endpoints, it partitions P into

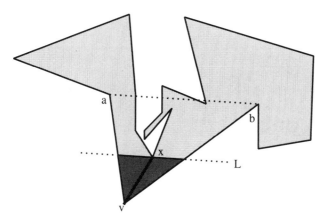

FIGURE 1.12 vx must be a diagonal.

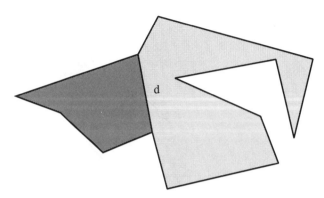

FIGURE 1.13   A diagonal partitions a polygon into two smaller polygons.

two polygons, each using d as an edge, and each of fewer than n vertices; see Figure 1.13. The reason each has fewer vertices is that no vertices are added by this process, and clearly there is at least one vertex in each part in addition to a and b. Applying the induction hypothesis to the two subpolygons completes the proof.   □

1.2.2. Properties of Triangulations

Although in general there can be a large number of different ways to triangulate a given polygon (Exercise 1.2.5[4]), they all have the same number of diagonals and triangles, as is easily established by the same argument as used in Theorem 1.2.3:

Lemma 1.2.4 (Number of Diagonals).   *Every triangulation of a polygon P of n vertices uses $n - 3$ diagonals and consists of $n - 2$ triangles.*

Proof. The proof is by induction. Both claims are trivially true for $n = 3$.

Let $n \geq 4$. Partition P into two polygons P_1 and P_2 with a diagonal $d = ab$. Let the two polygons have n_1 and n_2 vertices respectively. We have that $n_1 + n_2 = n + 2$, since a and b are counted in both n_1 and n_2. Applying the induction hypothesis to the subpolygons, we see that altogether there are $(n_1 - 3) + (n_2 - 3) + 1 = n - 3$ diagonals, with the final $+1$ term counting d, and there are $(n_1 - 2)(n_2 - 2) = n - 2$ triangles.   □

Corollary 1.2.5 (Sum of Angles).   *The sum of the internal angles of a polygon of n vertices is $(n - 2)\pi$.*

Proof. There are $n - 2$ triangles by Lemma 1.2.4, and each contributes π to the internal angles.   □

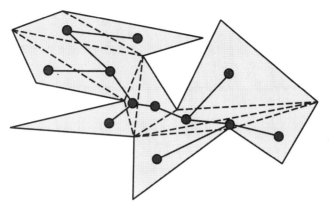

FIGURE 1.14   Triangulation dual.

1.2.3. Triangulation Dual

An important concept in graph theory is the "dual" of a graph. We will not need this concept in its full generality, but rather we will define specific dual graphs as the need arises. In particular, studying the triangulation dual reveals useful structure in the triangulation.

The *dual T* of a triangulation of a polygon is a graph with a node associated with each triangle, and an arc between two nodes iff their triangles share a diagonal. See Figure 1.14.

Lemma 1.2.6.   *The dual T of a triangulation is a tree,*[14] *with each node of degree at most three.*

Proof. That each node has degree at most three is immediate from the fact that a triangle has at most three sides to share.

Suppose T is not a tree; then it must have a cycle C. If this cycle is drawn as a path π in the plane, connecting with straight segments the midpoints of the diagonals shared by the triangles whose nodes comprise C (to make the path specific), it must enclose some polygon vertices: namely one endpoint of each diagonal crossed by π. However, then π must also enclose points exterior to the polygon, for these enclosed vertices are on ∂P. This contradicts the simplicity of the polygon.   □

The nodes of degree one are leaves of T; nodes of degree two lie on paths of the tree; nodes of degree three are branch points. Note that T is a binary tree when rooted at any node of degree one or two! Given the ubiquity of binary trees in computer science, this correspondence between triangulation duals and binary trees is fortunate, and may often be exploited (Exercise 1.2.5[6]).

---

[14] A *tree* is a connected graph with no cycles.

Lemma 1.2.6 leads to an easy proof of Meister's "Two Ears Theorem" (Meister, 1975), which, although simple, is quite useful. Three consecutive vertices of a polygon a, b, c form an *ear* of the polygon if ac is a diagonal; b is the ear *tip*. Two ears are *nonoverlapping* if their triangle interiors are disjoint.

Theorem 1.2.7 (Meister's Two Ears Theorem). *Every polygon of $n \geq 4$ vertices has at least two nonoverlapping ears.*

Proof. A leaf node in a triangulation dual corresponds to an ear. A tree of two or more nodes (by Lemma 1.2.4 the tree has $(n - 2) \geq 2$ nodes) must have at least two leaves.   □

1.2.4. Three-coloring Proof

This theorem in turn leads to an easy proof of the three-colorability of triangulation graphs. The idea is to remove an ear for induction, which, because it only "interfaces" at its one diagonal, can be colored consistently.

Theorem 1.2.8 (Three-coloring). *The triangulation graph of a polygon P may be three-colored.*

Proof. The proof is by induction on the number of vertices n. Clearly, a triangle can be three-colored.

Assume therefore that $n \geq 4$. By Theorem 1.2.7, P has an ear $\triangle abc$, with ear tip b. Form a new polygon P' by cutting off the ear: that is, replace the sequence abc in ∂P with ac in $\partial P'$. P' has $n - 1$ vertices: it is missing only b. Apply the induction hypothesis to three-color P'. Now put the ear back, coloring b with the color not used to color a and c. This is a three-coloring of P.   □

1.2.5. Exercises

1. *Exterior angles* [easy]. What is the sum of the exterior angles of a polygon of n vertices?
2. *Realization of triangulations.* Prove or disprove: Every binary tree is realizable as a triangulation dual of a polygon.
3. *Extreme triangulations.* Which polygons have the fewest number of distinct triangulations? Can polygons have unique triangulations? Which polygons have the largest number of distinct triangulations?
4. *Number of triangulations* [difficult]. How many distinct triangulations are there of a convex polygon of n vertices?
5. *Boxed ears.* An *orthogonal polygon* is one composed entirely of edges that meet orthogonally, e.g., horizontal and vertical edges. Define a notion of a "boxed ear" of an orthogonal polygon, a four-sided version of an ear, and answer the question of whether every orthogonal polygon has a boxed ear under your definition.

6. *Tree rotations.* For those who know tree rotations used to balance binary trees:[15] interpret tree rotations in terms of polygon triangulations.

7. *Diagonals $\Rightarrow$ triangulation.* Given an unordered collection of diagonals of a polygon forming a triangulation, design an algorithm to build the triangulation dual tree in $O(n)$ time.

1.3. IMPLEMENTATION ISSUES

The remainder of the chapter takes a rather long "digression" into implementation issues. The goal is to present code to compute a triangulation. This hinges on detecting intersection between two segments, a seemingly trivial task that often is implemented incorrectly. We will approach segment intersection via computation of areas in Section 1.4. We start with a few representation issues.

1.3.1. Representation of a Point

Arrays versus Records

All points will be represented by arrays of the appropriate number of coordinates. It is common practice to represent a point by a record with fields named x and y, but this precludes the use of for-loops to iterate over the coordinates.[16] There may seem little need to write a for-loop to iterate over only two indices, but:

- Sometimes there are as many as four coordinates, for "homogeneous" coordinates in three dimensions;

- Code written with a loop more easily generalizes to higher dimensions;

- A loop is easier to read and understand than nearly identical copies of the same statements; and

- Nearly identical copies of the same statements are fertile environments for the spontaneous generation of difficult-to-eradicate bugs.

Integers versus Reals

We will represent the coordinates with integers rather than with floating-point numbers wherever possible. This will permit us to avoid the issue of floating-point roundoff error, and write code that is verifiably correct within a range of coordinate values. Roundoff error is an important topic and will be discussed at various points throughout the book (although never confronted as directly as the topic deserves). Obviously, this habit of using integers will have to be relaxed when we compute, for example, the intersection of two line segments. The type definitions will be isolated so that modification of the code to handle different varieties of coordinate datatypes can be made in one location.

---

[15] See, e.g., Cormen, Leiserson, and Rivest (1990, pp. 265–267).

[16] That is, precludes in most programming languages.

Point Type Definition

All type identifiers will begin with lowercase t. All defined constants will appear entirely in uppercase. The suffixes i and d indicate integer and double types respectively. See Code 1.1.

```
#define X          0
#define Y          1
typedef enum       { FALSE, TRUE }      bool;

#define DIM        2                    /* Dimension of points */
typedef int        tPointi[DIM];        /* type integer point */
typedef double     tPointd[DIM];        /* type double point */
```

Code 1.1 typedefs.

In mathematical expressions, we will write p_0 and p_1 for p[0] and p[1]. We will freely add and subtract indices, with the implicit assumption that all arithmetic is mod n. Of course, in the code this wraparound must be made explicit by using % n.

1.3.2. Representation of a Polygon

The main options here are whether to use an array or a list, and if the latter, whether singly or doubly linked, and whether linear or circular.

There are obvious reasons for using lists: memory need not be preallocated; and lists support easy insertion and deletion of points. However we will opt for arrays (see Code 1.2), just for the clarity it makes in the code: the structure of loops and index increments are somewhat clearer with arrays than with lists. In addition it is useful to separate the basic algorithm structure from the details of data structure manipulation. The places where this decision causes inefficiencies will be mentioned.

```
#define PMAX        1000                /* Max # of pts in polygon */
typedef tPointi     tPolygoni[PMAX];    /* type integer polygon */
```

Code 1.2 Polygon type.

These conventions will be first employed in Code 1.3, which computes the area of a polygon.

1.4. AREA OF POLYGON

In this section, we explore the question of how to compute the area of a polygon. Although this is an interesting question in its own right, our objective is

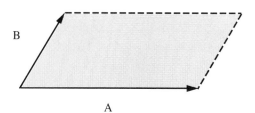

B

A

FIGURE 1.15   Cross product parallelogram.

to prepare the way for calculation of containment in halfplanes, the intersection between line segments, visibility relations, and ultimately leading to a triangulation algorithm in Section 1.6.4.

1.4.1. Area of a Triangle

The area of a triangle is $1/2$ the base times the altitude. However, this formula is not directly useful if we want the area of a triangle T whose three vertices are arbitrary points a, b, c. Let us denote this area as $\mathscr{A}(T)$. The base is easy: $|a - b|$.[17] However, the altitude is not so immediately available from the coordinates, unless the triangle happens to be oriented with one side parallel to one of the axes.

1.4.2. Cross Product

From linear algebra, we know that the magnitude of the cross product of two vectors is the area of the parallelogram they determine: if A and B are vectors, then $|A \times B|$ is the area of the parallelogram with sides A and B, as shown in Figure 1.15. Since any triangle can be viewed as half of a parallelogram, this gives an immediate method of computing the area from coordinates. Just let $A = b - a$ and $B = c - a$; then the area is half the length of $A \times B$. Recall that the cross product can be computed from the following determinant:

$$\begin{vmatrix} \hat{i} & \hat{j} & \hat{k} \\ A_0 & A_1 & A_2 \\ B_0 & B_1 & B_2 \end{vmatrix} = (A_1 B_2 - A_2 B_1)\hat{i} + (A_2 B_0 - A_0 B_2)\hat{j} + (A_0 B_1 - A_1 B_0)\hat{k}$$

$$(1.1)$$

Here $\hat{i}$, $\hat{j}$, and $\hat{k}$ are unit vectors in the x, y, and z directions respectively. For two-dimensional vectors, $A_2 = B_2 = 0$, so the above calculation reduces to $(A_0 B_1 - A_1 B_0)\hat{k}$: the cross product is a vector normal to the plane of the

---

[17]$|a - b|$ is the length of the vector $a - b$, sometimes written $\|a - b\|$.

triangle. Thus the area is given by

$$\mathscr{A}(T) = \tfrac{1}{2}(A_0 B_1 - A_1 B_0). \tag{1.2}$$

Substitution of $A = b - a$ and $B = c - a$ yields

$$2\mathscr{A}(T) = a_0 b_1 - a_1 b_0 + a_1 c_0 - a_0 c_1 + b_0 c_1 - c_0 b_1. \tag{1.3}$$

This achieves our immediate goal: an expression for the area of the triangle as a function of the coordinates of its vertices.

1.4.3. Determinant Form

There is another way to represent the calculation of the cross product that is formally identical but generalizes more easily to higher dimensions.[18]

The expression obtained above (Equation 1.3) is the value of the 3×3 determinant of the three point coordinates, with the third coordinate replaced by 1:

$$\begin{vmatrix} a_0 & a_1 & 1 \\ b_0 & b_1 & 1 \\ c_0 & c_1 & 1 \end{vmatrix} = a_0 b_1 - a_1 b_0 + a_1 c_0 - a_0 c_1 + b_0 c_1 - c_0 b_1 = 2\mathscr{A}(T). \tag{1.4}$$

This determinant is explored in Exercise 1.6.8[1]. We summarize in a lemma.

Lemma 1.4.1. *Twice the area of a triangle $T = (a, b, c)$ is given by*

$$2\mathscr{A}(T) = \begin{vmatrix} a_0 & a_1 & 1 \\ b_0 & b_1 & 1 \\ c_0 & c_1 & 1 \end{vmatrix} = a_0 b_1 - a_1 b_0 + a_1 c_0 - a_0 c_1 + b_0 c_1 - c_0 b_1. \tag{1.5}$$

1.4.4. Area of a Convex Polygon

Now that we have an expression for the area of a triangle, it is easy to find the area of any polygon by first triangulating it, and then summing the triangle areas. However, it would be pleasing to avoid the rather complex step of triangulation, and indeed this is possible. Before turning to that issue, we consider convex polygons, where triangulation is trivial.

Every convex polygon may be triangulated as a "fan," with all diagonals incident to a common vertex; and this may be done with any vertex serving as

---

[18] Note that the operation of cross product is restricted to three-dimensional vectors (or two-dimensional vectors with a zero third coordinate). It is more accurate to view the cross product as an exterior product producing, not another vector, but a "bivector." See Koenderink (1990).

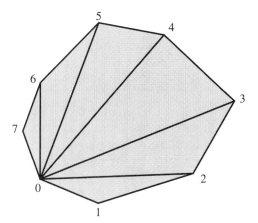

FIGURE 1.16   Triangulation of a convex polygon. The fan center is at 0.

the fan "center." See Figure 1.16. Therefore, the area of a polygon with vertices $v_0, v_1, \ldots, v_{n-1}$ labeled counterclockwise can be calculated as

$$\mathscr{A}(P) = \mathscr{A}(v_0, v_1, v_2) + \mathscr{A}(v_0, v_2, v_3) + \cdots + \mathscr{A}(v_0, v_{n-2}, v_{n-1}). \quad (1.6)$$

Here, v_0 is the fan center.

We will warm up to the result we will prove in Theorem 1.4.3 below by examining convex and nonconvex quadrilaterals, where the relevant relationships are obvious.

1.4.5. Area of a Convex Quadrilateral

The area of a convex quadrilateral $Q = (a, b, c, d)$ may be written in two ways, depending on the two different triangulations (see Figure 1.17):

$$\mathscr{A}(Q) = \mathscr{A}(a, b, c) + \mathscr{A}(a, c, d) = \mathscr{A}(d, a, b) + \mathscr{A}(d, b, c) \quad (1.7)$$

Writing out the expressions for the areas from Lemma 1.4.1 for the two terms of

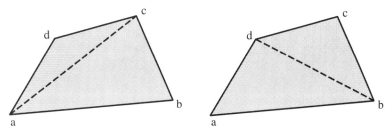

FIGURE 1.17   The two triangulations of a convex quadrilateral.

the first triangulation, we get

$$2\mathscr{A}(Q) = a_0 b_1 - a_1 b_0 + a_1 c_0 - a_0 c_1 + b_0 c_1 - c_0 b_1$$

$$+ a_0 c_1 - a_1 c_0 + a_1 d_0 - a_0 d_1 + c_0 d_1 - d_0 c_1. \qquad (1.8)$$

Note that the terms $a_1 c_0 - a_0 c_1$ appear in $\mathscr{A}(a,b,c)$ and in $\mathscr{A}(a,c,d)$ with opposite signs, and so cancel. Thus, the terms "corresponding" to the diagonal ac cancel; similarly the terms corresponding to the diagonal db in the second triangulation cancel. Thus, we arrive at the exact same expression independent of the triangulation, as of course we must.

Generalizing, we see we get two terms per polygon edge, and none for internal diagonals. So if the coordinates of vertex v_i are x_i and y_i, twice the area of a convex polygon is given by

$$2\mathscr{A}(P) = \sum_{i=0}^{n-1} (x_i y_{i+1} - y_i x_{i+1}). \qquad (1.9)$$

We will soon see that this equation holds for nonconvex polygons as well.

1.4.6. Area of a Nonconvex Quadrilateral

Now suppose we have a nonconvex quadrilateral $Q = (a,b,c,d)$ as shown in Figure 1.18. Then there is only one triangulation, using the diagonal db. However, we just showed that the algebraic expression obtained is independent of the diagonal chosen, so it must be the case that the equation

$$\mathscr{A}(Q) = \mathscr{A}(a,b,c) + \mathscr{A}(a,c,d) \qquad (1.10)$$

is still true, even though the diagonal ac is external to Q. This equation has an obvious interpretation: $A(a,c,d)$ is negative, and is therefore subtracted from

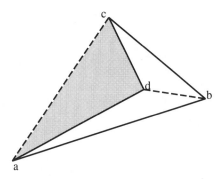

FIGURE 1.18   Triangulations of a nonconvex quadrilateral. The shaded area $\mathscr{A}(a,c,d)$ is negative.

the surrounding triangle (a, b, c). Note that (a, c, d) is a clockwise path, so the cross product formulation shows that the area will be negative.

The phenomenon observed with a nonconvex quadrilateral is general, as we now proceed to demonstrate.

1.4.7. Area from an Arbitrary Center

We now formalize the observations in the preceding paragraphs, which we will then use to obtain the area of general nonconvex polygons. Let us generalize the method of summing the areas of the triangles in a triangulation to summing areas based on an arbitrary, perhaps external, point p. Let $T = (a, b, c)$ be a triangle, with the vertices oriented counterclockwise, and let p be any point in the plane. Then we claim that

$$\mathscr{A}(T) = \mathscr{A}(p, a, b) + \mathscr{A}(p, b, c) + \mathscr{A}(p, c, a). \qquad (1.11)$$

Consider Figure 1.19. With $p = p_1$, the first term of Equation 1.11, $\mathscr{A}(p_1, a, b)$, is negative because clockwise, whereas the remaining two terms are positive because counterclockwise. Now note that $\mathscr{A}(p_1, a, b)$ subtracts exactly that portion of the quadrilateral (p_1, b, c, a) that is outside T, leaving the total sum to be precisely $\mathscr{A}(T)$ as claimed. Similarly, from $p = p_2$, both $\mathscr{A}(p_2, a, b)$ and $\mathscr{A}(p_2, b, c)$ are negative because clockwise, and they remove from $\mathscr{A}(p_2, c, a)$, which is positive, precisely the amount needed to leave $\mathscr{A}(T)$.

All other positions for p in the plane not internal to T are equivalent to either p_1 or p_2 by symmetry; and of course the equation holds when p is internal, as we argued in Section 1.4.4. Therefore, we have established the following lemma.

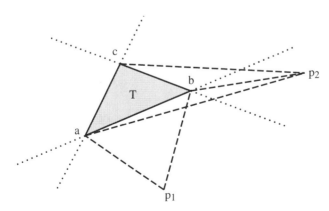

FIGURE 1.19   Area of T based on various external points p_1, p_2.

Lemma 1.4.2. *If $T = (a, b, c)$ is a triangle, with vertices oriented counterclockwise, and p is any point in the plane. Then*

$$\mathcal{A}(T) = \mathcal{A}(p, a, b) + \mathcal{A}(p, b, c) + \mathcal{A}(p, c, a). \tag{1.12}$$

We may now generalize the preceding lemma to establish the same equation (generalized) for arbitrary polygons.

Theorem 1.4.3 (Area of Polygon)[19]. *Let a polygon (convex or nonconvex) P have vertices $v_0, v_1, \ldots, v_{n-1}$ labeled counterclockwise, and let p be any point in the plane. Then*

$$\mathcal{A}(P) = \mathcal{A}(p, v_0, v_1) + \mathcal{A}(p, v_1, v_2) + \mathcal{A}(p, v_2, v_3)$$

$$+ \cdots + \mathcal{A}(p, v_{n-2}, v_{n-1}) + \mathcal{A}(p, v_{n-1}, v_0). \tag{1.13}$$

If $v_i = (x_i, y_i)$, this expression is equivalent to the equation

$$2\mathcal{A}(P) = \sum_{i=0}^{n-1} (x_i y_{i+1} - y_i x_{i+1}). \tag{1.14}$$

Proof. We prove the area sum equation by induction on the number of vertices n of P. The base case, $n = 3$, is established by Lemma 1.4.2.

Suppose then that equation Equation 1.13 is true for all polygons with $n - 1$ vertices, and let P be a polygon of n vertices. By Theorem 1.2.7, P has an "ear." Renumber the vertices of P so that $E = (v_{n-2}, v_{n-1}, v_0)$ is an ear. Let P_{n-1} be the polygon obtained by removing E. By the induction hypothesis,

$$\mathcal{A}(P_{n-1}) = \mathcal{A}(p, v_0 v_1) + \cdots + \mathcal{A}(p, v_{n-3}, v_{n-2}) + \mathcal{A}(p, v_{n-2}, v_0). \tag{1.15}$$

By Lemma 1.4.2,

$$\mathcal{A}(E) = \mathcal{A}(p, v_{n-2}, v_{n-1}) + \mathcal{A}(p, v_{n-1}, v_0) + \mathcal{A}(p, v_0, v_{n-2}). \tag{1.16}$$

Since $\mathcal{A}(P) = \mathcal{A}(P_{n-1}) + \mathcal{A}(E)$, we have

$$\mathcal{A}(P) = \mathcal{A}(p, v_0, v_1) + \cdots + \mathcal{A}(p, v_{n-3}, v_{n-2}) + \mathcal{A}(p, v_{n-2}, v_0)$$

$$+ \mathcal{A}(p, v_{n-2}, v_{n-1}) + \mathcal{A}(p, v_{n-1}, v_0) + \mathcal{A}(p, v_0, v_{n-2}). \tag{1.17}$$

---

[19] This theorem can be viewed as a discrete version of Green's theorem, which relates an integral around the boundary of a region, with an integral over the interior of the region: $\int_{\partial P} \omega = \int\int_P d\omega$ where ω is a "1-form" (see, e.g., Buck and Buck, 1965, p. 406).

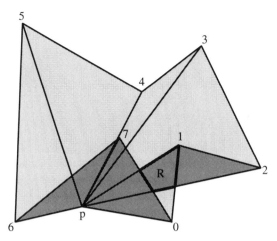

FIGURE 1.20 Computation of the area of a nonconvex polygon from point p. The darker triangles are orientated clockwise and so have negative area.

However, note that $\mathscr{A}(p, v_0, v_{n-2}) = -\mathscr{A}(p, v_{n-2}, v_0)$. Canceling these terms leads to the claimed equation.

The summation formula Equation 1.14 is obtained by expansion of the determinants and cancelling terms, as explained in Section 1.4.5. □

In Figure 1.20 the triangles $(p,1,2)$, $(p,6,7)$, and $(p,7,0)$ are oriented clockwise, and the remainder are counterclockwise. One can think of the counterclockwise triangles as attaching to each point they cover a $+1$ charge, and the clockwise triangles a -1 charge. Then the points R of $(p,1,2)$ that fall inside the polygon (labeled in the figure) are given a -1 charge by this clockwise triangle; but R is also covered by two counterclockwise triangles, $(p,0,1)$ and $(p,2,3)$. So R has net $+1$ charge. Similarly every point inside P is assigned a net $+1$ charge, and every point outside is assigned a net 0 charge.

1.4.8. Code for Area

Computing the area of a polygon is now a straightforward implementation of Equation 1.13, with $p = v_0$; see Code 1.3. The conventions discussed in Section 1.3 are used.

There is an interesting potential problem with `Area2`: if the coordinates are large, the multiplications of coordinates could cause integer word overflow, which is unfortunately not reported by most C implementations. We will revisit this point in Section 4.2.4. See Exercise 1.6.8[2].

```
/ *
            Returns twice the signed area of the triangle determined by
            a,b,c, positive if a,b,c are oriented ccw, and negative if cw.
* /
int     Area2( tPointi a, b, c)
{
        return
                a[0] * b[1] - a[1] * b[0] +
                a[1] * c[0] - a[0] * c[1] +
                b[0] * c[1] - c[0] * b[1];
}
/ *
            Returns twice the area of polygon P.
* /
int     AreaPoly2( int n, tPolygoni P )
{
        int      i;
        int      sum = 0;                  / * Partial area sum * /

        for (i = 1; i < n-1; i++)
                sum += Area2( P[0], P[i], P[i+1] );
        return  sum;
}
```

Code 1.3   `Area2` and `AreaPoly2`.

1.4.9. Volume in Three and Higher Dimensions

One of the benefits of the determinant formulation of the area of a triangle in Lemma 1.4.1 is that it extends directly into higher dimensions. In three dimensions, the volume of a tetrahedron T with vertices a, b, c, d is

$$\begin{vmatrix} a_0 & a_1 & a_2 & 1 \\ b_0 & b_1 & b_2 & 1 \\ c_0 & c_1 & c_2 & 1 \\ d_0 & d_1 & d_2 & 1 \end{vmatrix} = 6\mathcal{V}(T) \tag{1.18}$$

$$= -b_0 c_1 d_2 + a_0 c_1 d_2 + b_1 c_0 d_2 - a_1 c_0 d_2 - a_0 b_1 d_2$$

$$+ a_1 b_0 d_2 + b_0 c_2 d_1 - a_0 c_2 d_1 - b_2 c_0 d_1 + a_2 c_0 d_1$$

$$+ a_0 b_2 d_1 - a_2 b_0 d_1 - b_1 c_2 d_0 + a_1 c_2 d_0 + b_2 c_1 d_0$$

$$- a_2 c_1 d_0 - a_1 b_2 d_0 + a_2 b_1 d_0 + a_0 b_1 c_2 - a_1 b_0 c_2$$

$$- a_0 b_2 c_1 + a_2 b_0 c_1 + a_1 b_2 c_0 - a_2 b_1 c_0. \tag{1.19}$$

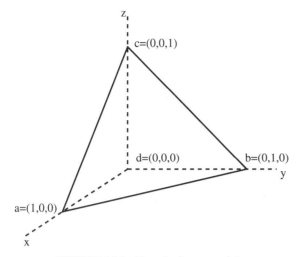

FIGURE 1.21 Tetrahedron at origin.

This volume is signed and is positive if (a, b, c) form a counterclockwise circuit when viewed from the side away from d, so that the face normal determined by the right-hand rule points toward the outside. For example, let $a = (1, 0, 0)$, $b = (0, 1, 0)$, $c = (0, 0, 1)$, and $d = (0, 0, 0)$ Then (a, b, c) is counterclockwise from outside; see Figure 1.21. Substitution into Equation 1.18 yields a determinant of 1, so $\mathscr{V}(T) = 1/6$. This accords with the 1/3 base area times height rule: $1/3 \cdot 1/2 \cdot 1$. We will make use of this volume formula later to compute the "convex hull" of points in three dimensions (Chapter 4).

Remarkably, Theorem 1.4.3 generalizes directly also: the volume of a polyhedron may be computed by summing the (signed) volumes of tetrahedra formed by an arbitrary point and each triangular face of the polyhedron. Here all the faces must be oriented counterclockwise from outside.

Moreover, Equation 1.18 generalizes to higher dimensions d, yielding the volume of the d-dimensional "simplex" (the generalization of a tetrahedron to higher dimensions) times the constant $d!$.

1.5. SEGMENT INTERSECTION

1.5.1. Diagonals

Our goal is to develop code to triangulate a polygon. The key step will be finding a diagonal of the polygon, a direct line of sight between two vertices v_i and v_j. The segment $v_i v_j$ will not be a diagonal if it is blocked by a portion of the polygon's boundary. To be blocked, $v_i v_j$ must intersect an edge of the polygon. Note that if $v_i v_j$ only intersects an edge e at its endpoint, perhaps only grazing contact with the boundary, it is still effectively blocked, because diagonals must have clear visibility.

The following is an immediate consequence of the definition of a diagonal (Section 1.1.3).

Lemma 1.5.1. *The segment $s = v_i v_j$ is a diagonal of P iff*

1. *for all edges e of P that are not incident to either v_i or v_j, s and e do not intersect: $s \cap e = \varnothing$;*
2. *s is internal to P in a neighborhood of v_i and v_j.*

Condition 1 of this lemma has been phrased so that the "diagonalhood" of a segment can be determined without finding the actual point of intersection between s and each e: only a boolean segment intersection predicate is required. Note this would not be the case with the more direct implementation of the definition: a diagonal only intersects polygon edges at the diagonal endpoints. This phrasing would require computation of the intersection points, and subsequent comparison to the endpoints. The purpose of condition 2 is to distinguish internal from external diagonals. We will revisit this condition in Section 1.6.2. We now turn our attention to developing code to check the non-intersection condition.

1.5.2. Problems with Slopes

Let $v_i v_j = ab$ and $e = cd$. A common first inclination when faced with the task of deciding whether ab and cd intersect, is to find the point of intersection between the lines L_1 and L_2 containing the segments by solving the two linear equations in slope/intercept form, and checking that the point falls inside the segments. This method will clearly work and is not all that difficult to code. However, the code is messy and error-prone; it takes a surprising amount of diligence to get it exactly right. It is difficult to appreciate the beauty of the signed-area approach described in the next section without considering this slopes-based alternative. So in this section, I explore this alternative far enough to illustrate its inferiority.

Slope Equations

The equation of a straight line in slope/intercept form is $y = mx + b$. The straight line through the two points (x_1, y_1) and (x_2, y_2) can be found by setting the slopes determined by these two points and a generic third point on the line (x, y) equal:

$$\frac{y - y_1}{x - x_1} = \frac{y_2 - y_1}{x_2 - x_1}. \qquad (1.20)$$

From this, the slope and intercept may be derived:

$$m = \frac{y_2 - y_1}{x_2 - x_1} \tag{1.21}$$

$$b = (1 - m) x_1. \tag{1.22}$$

Here, we see the first difficulty: for vertical line segments, the denominator of Equation 1.21 is zero, the slope is infinite, there is no y-intercept, and the code will have to treat this as a special case.

However, let us plow ahead. Suppose we have obtained equations for L_1 and L_2:

$$y = m_1 x + b_1 \tag{1.23}$$

$$y = m_2 x + b_2 \tag{1.24}$$

Solving for the point of intersection (x, y) yields

$$y = \frac{b_1 m_2 - b_2 m_1}{m_2 - m_1}$$

$$x = \frac{b_1 - b_2}{m_2 - m_1}. \tag{1.25}$$

These equations show the second difficulty: their denominators are zero when $m_1 = m_2$, that is, when L_1 and L_2 are parallel. Note this does not mean that the lines do not intersect: they could overlap collinearly. This will require the code to have further special cases.

Special Cases Philosophy
There is a distinction between the two division-by-zero special cases in Equations 1.21 and 1.25: parallel lines are a true geometric special case,[20] whereas vertical lines are only special because of the chosen line representation. Rotating the coordinate system would leave the segment's point of intersection invariant, but change the vertical special case.

Four methods for dealing with special cases may be distinguished:

1. Rule them out by fiat: require that the input be restricted such that the special cases never arise.
2. Write code that handles the special cases properly.
3. Find a different geometrical system in which the special cases disappear.
4. Find another computer representation of the same geometrical ideas that avoids the special cases.

---

[20] At least in Euclidean geometry. In projective geometry, they are not special; see next page.

Ruling out the special cases 1 is a time-honored tradition in computational geometry, and is difficult to avoid entirely. Indeed, we will resort to this at various locations throughout the book. In our example above, these could be accomplished by restricting the input so that no parallel lines can occur (Equation 1.25), and that no vertical lines can occur (Equation 1.21). Although the former is less reprehensible than the latter, neither restriction is very satisfying. In addition, either one would greatly reduce the code's true applicability because real-world polygons often are derived from some underlying grid, which lends itself to precisely these special cases.

Writing the special case code 2 is tedious and error-prone. Finding a different geometrical system 3 would of course be wonderful, but it is not always possible, or only possible with accompanying major revision of other dependent sections of code. In the instance we are considering, it so happens that projective geometry is highly appropriate, because parallel lines intersect "at infinity." Most computations in computer graphics code use "homogeneous coordinates," implementing the projective viewpoint. However often this solution is simply not available, and in this particular instance it is more than is needed.

Which leaves us with 4: find another representation that avoids the special cases. This is the subject of the next section.

1.5.3. Left

Whether two segments intersect can be decided by using a `Left` predicate, which determines whether or not a point is to the left of a directed line. How `Left` is used to decide intersection will be shown in the next section. Here we concentrate on `Left` itself.

A directed line is determined by two points given in a particular order (a, b) If a point c is to the left of the line determined by (a, b), the triple (a, b, c) forms a counterclockwise circuit: this is what it means to be to the left of a line. See Figure 1.22.

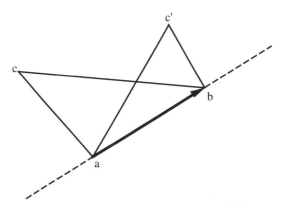

FIGURE 1.22 c is left of ab iff the triangle abc has positive area; abc' also has positive area.

Now the connection to signed-area is finally revealed: c is to the left of (a, b) iff the area of the counterclockwise triangle, $\mathscr{A}(a, b, c)$, is positive. Therefore, we may implement the `Left` predicate by a single call to `Area2` (Code 1.4).

```
bool    Left( tPointi a, b, c )
{
        return  Area2( a, b, c ) > 0;
}
```

Code 1.4 `Left`.

Note that `Left` could be implemented by finding the equation of the line through a and b, and substituting the coordinates of point c into the equation. This method would be straightforward, but subject to the special case objections raised in the previous section. The area code in contrast has no special cases.

What happens when c is collinear with ab? Then the determined triangle has zero area. Thus, we have the happy circumstance that the exceptional geometric situation corresponds to the exceptional numerical result. Because it will sometimes be useful to distinguish collinearity, we write a separate `Collinear` predicate[21] for this, as well as `LeftOn`, giving us the equivalent of $=$, $<$, and $\leq$; see Code 1.5.

```
bool    LeftOn( tPointi a, b, c )
{
        return  Area2( a, b, c ) >= 0;
}
bool    Collinear( tPointi a, b, c )
{
        return  Area2( a, b, c ) == 0;
}
```

Code 1.5 `LeftOn` and `Collinear`.

Note that we are comparing twice the area against zero in these routines: we are not comparing the area itself. The reason is that the area might not be an integer, and we would therefore be forced to leave the comfortable domain of the integers.

---

[21] If floating-point coordinates are demanded by a particular application, this predicate would need modification, as it depends on exact equality with zero.

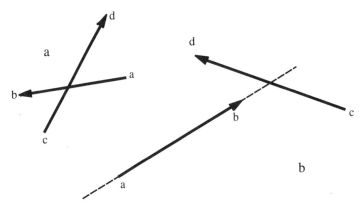

FIGURE 1.23 Two segments intersect (*a*) iff their endpoints are split by their determined lines; both pair of endpoints must be split (*b*).

1.5.4. Boolean Intersection

If the two segments *ab* and *cd* intersect in their interiors, *c* and *d* are split by the line L_1 containing *ab*: *c* is to one side and *d* to the other. Likewise, *a* and *b* are split by L_2, the line containing *cd*. See Figure 1.23(*a*). Neither one of these conditions is alone sufficient to guarantee intersection, as Figure 1.23(*b*) shows, but it is clear that both together are sufficient. This leads to straightforward code to determine *proper* intersection, when two segments intersect at a point interior to both, if it is known that no three of the four endpoints are collinear. We can enforce this non-collinearity condition by explicit check; see Code 1.6.

```
/*      Returns true iff ab properly intersects cd: they share
        a point interior to both segments.  The properness of the
        intersection is ensured by using strict leftness.
*/
bool    IntersectProp( tPointi a, b, c, d )
{
        /* Eliminate improper cases. */
        if (
            Collinear(a,b,c) ||
            Collinear(a,b,d) ||
            Collinear(c,d,a) ||
            Collinear(c,d,b)
            )
            return FALSE;

        return
                Xor( Left(a,b,c), Left(a,b,d) )
        &&      Xor( Left(c,d,a), Left(c,d,b) );
}
```

Code 1.6 IntersectProp.

The code for `Xor` is in the appendix to this chapter (Code 1.18).

There is unfortunate redundancy in the above code, in that the four relevant triangle areas are being computed twice each. This redundancy could be removed by computing the areas and storing them in local variables, or by designing other primitives that fit the problem better. I would argue against storing the areas, as then the code would not be transparent. However, it may be that the code can be designed around other primitives more naturally. It turns out that the first `if`-statement may be removed entirely for the purposes of triangulation, although then the routine no longer computes proper intersection (nor does it compute improper intersection). This is explored in Exercise 1.6.8[3]. I prefer to sacrifice efficiency for clarity, and leave `IntersectProp` as is. For it is useful to look beyond the immediate programming task to possible other uses. In this instance, `IntersectProp` is precisely the function needed to compute clear visibility (Section 1.1.2).

One subtlety here: it might be tempting to implement the exclusive-or by requiring that the products of the relevant areas be strictly negative, thus assuring that they are of opposite sign, and neither is zero (see Code 1.7):

```
                    Area2(a,b,c)  *  Area2(a,b,d) < 0
        &&          Area2(c,d,a)  *  Area2(c,d,b) < 0;
```

Code 1.7   Area products.

The flaw in this is that the product of the areas might cause integer word overflow! Thus a clever coding trick to save a few lines could hide a pernicious bug.[22]

Improper Intersection

Finally, we must deal with the "special case" of improper intersection between the two segments, as Lemma 1.5.1 requires that the intersection be completely empty for a segment to be a diagonal. Improper intersection occurs precisely when an endpoint of one segment (say c) lies somewhere on the other (closed) segment ab. See Figure 1.24a. This can only happen if a, b, c are collinear. However, collinearity is not a sufficient condition for intersection, as Figure 1.24b makes clear. What we need to decide is if c is *between* a and b.

Betweenness

We would like to compute this "betweenness" predicate without resorting to slope, which would require special-case handling. As we will only check betweenness of c when we know it lies on the line containing ab, we may exploit this knowledge. If ab is not vertical, c lies on ab iff the x-coordinate of c falls

---

[22] This overflow problem could be avoided by having `Area2` return $+1$, 0, or -1 rather than the true area (Sedgewick 1992, p. 350). I prefer to return the area, as this is useful in other contexts.

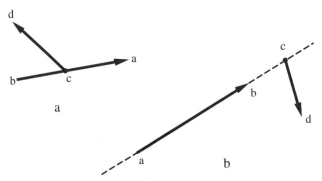

FIGURE 1.24   Improper intersection between two segments (*a*); collinearity is not sufficient (*b*).

```
/ *
            Returns T iff (a,b,c) are collinear and point c lies
            on the closed segment ab.
* /
bool    Between( tPointi a, tPointi b, tPointi c )
{
            tPointi ba, ca;
            if ( ! Collinear( a, b, c ) )
                    return  FALSE;

            / * If ab not vertical, check betweenness on x; else on y. * /
            if ( a[X] != b[X] )
                    return  ((a[X] <= c[X]) &&
                            (c[X]<= b[X])) ||
                            ((a[X] >= c[X]) &&
                            (c[X]>= b[X]));
            else
                    return  ((a[Y] <= c[Y]) &&
                            (c[Y]<= b[Y])) ||
                            ((a[Y] >= c[Y]) &&
                            (c[Y]>= b[Y]));
}
```

Code 1.8 Between.

in the interval determined by the *x*-coordinates of *a* and *b*. If *ab* is vertical, then a similar check on *y*-coordinates determines betweenness. See Code 1.8.

1.5.5. Segment Intersection Code

We finally can present code for computing segment intersection. Two segments intersect iff they intersect properly or one endpoint of one segment lies between the two endpoints of the other segment. The check for improper intersection is therefore implemented by four calls to `Between`: see Code 1.9. Exercise 1.6.8[4] asks for an analysis of the inefficiencies of this routine.

1.6. TRIANGULATION: IMPLEMENTATION

1.6.1. Diagonals, Internal or External

Having developed segment intersection code, we are nearly prepared to write (inefficient) code for triangulating a polygon. Our first goal is to find a diagonal of the polygon, then we will cut the polygon in two and recursively triangulate the pieces.

Recall that Lemma 1.5.1 characterized diagonals by two conditions: noninter-section with polygon edges, and being interior. If we ignore the distinction between internal and external diagonals, finding diagonals is a straightforward repeated application of `Intersect`: for every edge e of the polygon not incident to either end of the potential diagonal s, see if e intersects s. As soon as an intersection is detected, it is known that s is not a diagonal. If no such edge intersects s, then s is a diagonal. See Code 1.10.

Although this seems straightforward, there is a subtlety to this code stemming from a "degenerate" case: it is possible for a polygon edge adjacent to i or j to block visibility! This is illustrated in Figure 1.25: if an edge incident to i is collinear with ij, then ij is not a diagonal. So skipping edges incident to i or j in the code is not justified. Or is it? Let $e = (i - 1, i)$ be a polygon edge collinear

```
/*
        Returns true iff segments ab and cd intersect, properly or
        improperly.
*/
bool    Intersect( tPointi a, b, c, d )
{
        if ( IntersectProp( a, b, c, d ) )
                return  TRUE;
        else if (       Between( a, b, c )
                     || Between( a, b, d )
                     || Between( c, d, a )
                     || Between( c, d, b )
                )
                return  TRUE;
        else    return  FALSE;
}
```

Code 1.9 `Intersect`.

```
/*
        Returns T if (vi, vj) is a proper internal * or * external
        diagonal of P, or |i − j| = 2 and i and j are collinear
        with the middle vertex: only checks nonblocked condition.
*/
bool    Diagonalie( int i, int j, int n, tPolygoni P )
{

        int     k;
        int     k1;     /* k + 1 */

        /* For each edge (k,k + 1) of P */
        for ( k = 0; k < n; k++ ) {
                k1 = (k+1) % n;
                /* Skip edges incident to i or j */
                if ( ! (
                             ( k == i ) || ( k1 == i )
                     ||      ( k == j ) || ( k1 == j )
                     )                          )
                        if ( Intersect( P[i], P[j],
                            P[k], P[k1] ) )
                                return  FALSE;
        }
        return  TRUE;
}
```

Code 1.10 `Diagonalie`.

with *ij*. Consider two cases: *ij* is longer than *e*, or *ij* is shorter than *e*; clearly *j ≠ i − 1* so they cannot be the same length. Figure 1.25*a* shows that when *ij* is longer, it must be that $(i − 2, i − 1)$ intersects *ij*, and Figure 1.25*b* shows that when *ij* is shorter, *P* is not a polygon. If $j = i − 2$ in Fig. 1.25*a*, then the collinearity with $i − 1$ will never be detected, and `Diagonalie` with return `TRUE`. Fortunately, `InCone` in the next section will prevent `Diagonalie` from being called in this case. So skipping $(i − 1, i)$ in the code is justified after all!

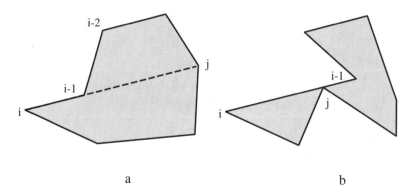

a   b

FIGURE 1.25 Edge incident to *i* collinear with *ij*.

1.6.2. InCone

Now we turn to the second condition of Lemma 1.5.1: we must distinguish the internal from the external diagonals. The first point to notice on this problem is that this is a local, constant-time check: if the diagonal $s = v_i v_j$ is interior to the polygon P in the neighborhood of v_i and v_j, it is interior throughout its length. This is because we have already established that s does not intersect any polygon edge. So the check for "interiorness" may be restricted to neighborhoods of the endpoints of s. Moreover, since these neighborhoods may be arbitrarily small, the interiorness depends on only the edges of P incident to the endpoints: no other edges need be involved in the decision. Thus, the check will be constant-time: it will not require time proportional to any function of n.

The second relevant observation is that only one of the two endpoints need be examined: if s is interior to P in the neighborhood of v_i, it must be interior to P in the neighborhood of v_j, and similarly for exterior. Again, this follows from our knowledge that s does not touch the boundary of P, so that its interior/exterior status is the same throughout its length. We have therefore reduced the problem to determining whether s is interior in a neighborhood of v_i. We partition this check into two cases: v_i is convex, or v_i is reflex.

The convex case is illustrated in Figure 1.26a. The actual output produced by the code is as follows. It is clear from this figure that s is internal to P iff it is internal to the cone whose apex is v_i, and whose sides pass through v_{i-1} and v_{i+1}. This can be easily determined via our **Left** function: v_{i-1} must be left of $v_i v_j$, and v_{i+1} must be left of $v_j v_i$. Both left-of's should be strict for $v_i v_j$ to agree with the definition of a diagonal.

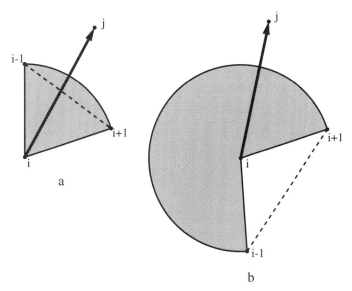

FIGURE 1.26   Diagonal $s = ij$ is in the cone determined by v_{i-1}, v_i, v_{i+1}: (a) convex; (b) reflex. In (b), both v_{i-1} and v_{i+1} are right of ij.

Figure 1.26*b* shows that these conditions do not suffice to characterize internal diagonals when v_i is reflex: v_{i-1} and v_{i+1} could be both left of, or both right of, or one could be left and the other right of, an internal diagonal. However, note that the *exterior* of a neighborhood of v_i is now a cone as in the convex case, for the simple reason that a reflex vertex looks like a convex vertex if interior and exterior are interchanged. So it is easiest in this case to characterize *s* as internal iff it is not external: it is not the case that both v_{i+1} is left or on $v_i v_j$, and v_{i-1} is left or on $v_j v_i$. Note that this time the left-of's must be improper, permitting collinearity, as we are rejecting diagonals that satisfy these conditions.

Finally, distinguishing between the convex and reflex cases is easily accomplished with one invocation of `Left`: v_i is convex iff v_{i+1} is left or on $v_{i-1} v_i$. Note that if (v_{i-1}, v_i, v_{i+1}) are collinear, the internal angle at v_i is π, which we defined as convex (p. 5).

The code in Code 1.11 implements the above ideas in a straightforward manner.

Although this `InCone` test is simple, there are many opportunities to implement it incorrectly. Note that the entire function consists of five signed-area calculations, illustrating the utility of that calculation.

```
/*
          Returns true iff the diagonal (i,j) is strictly internal to the
          polygon P in the neighborhood of the i endpoint.
*/
bool    InCone( int i, int j, int n, tPolygoni P )
{
        int       i1;        /* i + 1 */
        int       in1;       /* i - 1 */

        i1  = (i + 1)        % n;
        in1 = (i + n - 1) % n;

        /* If P[i] is a convex vertex [ i + 1 left or on (i-1,i) ]. */
        if ( LeftOn( P[in1], P[i], P[i1] ) )
                return  Left( P[i], P[j], P[in1] )
                     && Left( P[j], P[i], P[i1]  );

        /* Assume (i-1,i,i + 1) not collinear. */
        /* else P[i] is reflex. */
        else
                return  !(    LeftOn( P[i], P[j], P[i1]  )
                           && LeftOn( P[j], P[i], P[in1] ) );
}
```

Code 1.11 `InCone`.

1.6.3. Diagonal

We now have developed code to determine if (i, j) is a diagonal: iff both
`Diagonalie(i,j)` and `InCone(i,j)` are true. There would seem to be
little more to say on this topic, but in fact there is a choice of which of the two
function calls to make first. Once the question is asked, the answer is immediate: `InCone` should be first, because it is a constant-time calculation (it contains
no loop), whereas `Diagonalie` includes a loop over all n polygon edges. If
`InCone` is false, the (potentially) expensive `Diagonalie` check will not be
executed. See Code 1.12.

```
/*
            Returns T iff (i, j) is a proper internal diagonal of P.
*/
bool    Diagonal( int i, int j, int n, tPolygoni P)
{
        return  InCone( i, j, n, P ) &&
                Diagonalie( i, j, n, P );
}
```

Code 1.12 `Diagonal`.

1.6.4. Triangulation by Otectomy [23]

A triangulation algorithm and code may now be developed by mimicking the
proof of the triangulation theorem (Theorem 1.2.3): find a diagonal, cut the
polygon into two pieces, and recurse on each. To discuss the speed of this (or
any) algorithm, it is useful to use the so-called "big-Oh" notation, so we make a
brief digression.

Big-Oh

Throughout the book we will be measuring the performance of algorithms by
their "worst-case asymptotic time complexity" as a function of the input size.
For triangulation, the input size is measured by n, the number of vertices of the
input polygon. A typical complexity assessment would be, "Algorithm A has
time complexity $O(n^3)$." This is a judgment about the eventual growth rate of
the algorithm's time consumption with respect to n. It means that its growth,
even for the "worst" possible inputs, is bounded above by cn^3, where c is some
constant, for all n beyond a certain point. Whether c is $1/10$ or 10^{10} is not
relevant for this notation; this is where differences in machines and implementation details are absorbed. All that matters is the eventual (asymptotic) growth
rate of the algorithm.

The notation $O(f(n))$ sets an upper bound on the algorithm's performance.
Lower bounds are described with the notation $\Omega(f(n))$, which we will not

---

[23] Otectomy: ear excision.

```
Triangulation
if n > 3 then
    for each potential ear diagonal (i, i + 2) do
        if Diagonal (i, i + 2) then
            Print diagonal.
            Remove ear at v_i.
            Recurse on remainder of polygon.
```

Algorithm 1.1   Triangulation algorithm.

employ until Chapter 3 (Section 3.6). When matching lower and upper bounds are known, the notation is $\Theta(f(n))$. Since we will use these concepts somewhat loosely, I will not duplicate the more precise definitions found in algorithms texts.[24]

Pseudocode
We return to consideration of our first algorithm attempt: find a diagonal, cut the polygon into two pieces, and recurse on each. A rough analysis shows this is an $O(n^4)$ algorithm: there are $\binom{n}{2} = O(n^2)$ diagonal candidates, and testing each for diagonalhood costs $O(n)$. Repeating this $O(n^3)$ computation for each of the $n - 3$ diagonals yields $O(n^4)$.

We can speed this up by a factor of n by exploiting the two ears theorem (Theorem 1.2.7): not only do we know there must be an internal diagonal, we know there must be an internal diagonal that separates off an ear. There are only $O(n)$ "ear diagonal" candidates: $(i, i + 2)$ for $i = 0, \ldots, n - 1$. This also makes the recursion simpler, as there is only one piece on which to recurse: the other is the ear, a triangle, which is of course already triangulated.

This leads to the pseudocode shown in Algorithm 1.1 for constructing a triangulation.

Note that we are interpreting the task "triangulate a polygon" as "print out, in arbitrary order, diagonals which form a triangulation." This is primarily for ease of presentation. Often a more structured output is required by a particular application: for example, the triangle adjacency information in the dual graph might be required. It turns out that obtaining more structured output is no more difficult in terms of asymptotic time complexity, but often complicates the code considerably. We will not pursue further these alternative triangulation outputs.

Data Structures
In refining the above pseudocode into real C code, we face some resistance from the choice to represent a polygon as an array of vertices. The problem is

---

[24] See, e.g., Cormen et al. (1990, Chapter 2), Albertson and Hutchinson (1988, Section 2.8), Rawlins (1992, Section 1.4).

that clipping off an ear puts a gap into the array, and either this hole must be flagged, or the gap bridged, or the array squashed. All of these choices are unpleasant. Clearly, it would be more natural were the polygon represented as a linked list, so that excision of the ear would be simple deletion of a cell from a linked list.

I have chosen to stick to arrays in spite of their inappropriateness, for ease of presentation. The code is shown in Code 1.13. The two utility functions `PrintPoint` and `PointAssign` do exactly what one might guess from their names; see the appendix to this chapter (Section 1.7: Code1.20 and Code 1.19).

The recursion is terminated when $n = 3$ by the leading `if`-statement. Note the `break` immediately after the recursive call: there is no need to return to the partially executed loop at the higher level. This shows that in fact the recursion

```
/*
         Triangulates polygon P with n − 3 diagonals.
         Prints out coordinates of diagonal endpoints.
         Side effect: destroys the data in P.
*/
void     Triangulate( int n, tPolygoni P )
{
         int       i, i1, i2;

         if ( n > 3 )
                 for ( i = 0; i < n; i++ ) {
                         i1 = (i+1) % n;
                         i2 = (i+2) % n;
                         if ( Diagonal( i, i2, n, P ) ) {
                                 PrintPoint( P[i]  );
                                 putchar( '\t' );
                                 PrintPoint( P[i2] );
                                 putchar( '\n' );
                                 ClipEar( i1, n, P );
                                 Triangulate( n-1, P );
                                 break;
                         }
                 }
}

void     ClipEar( int i, int n, tPolygoni P )
{
         int       k;

         for ( k = i; k < n-1; k++ )
                 PointAssign( P[k], P[k+1] );
}
```

Code 1.13   Triangulate.

is entirely unnecessary, and could be replaced by a suitable loop. I found the recursive formulation somewhat cleaner to write, however.

Several critical remarks about this code are in order.

1. `ClipEar` is implemented by copying polygon array locations $[i + 1, n - 1]$ into locations $[i, n - 2]$, thereby overwriting location i. This means that `ClipEar` is $O(n)$, but of course this cost could be $O(1)$ (i.e., constant time) if linked lists were used.

2. Another data structure awkwardness crops up here: because points are defined as arrays, assignment between points must be done with a loop. (See Code 1.19 in the Appendix [Section 1.7] for `PointAssign`.) Were points defined as structures, then a single structure assignment would suffice. Again the choice of data structure is guided by ease of presentation.

3. Note that the coordinates of the diagonal endpoints are printed, rather than their indices.

4. And note that the original polygon data are destroyed by the time the program finishes.

Although I will reply to the first two criticisms by claiming pedagogical license, the third and fourth are more serious drawbacks: usually the endpoint indices are more useful than the coordinates, and we certainly don't want

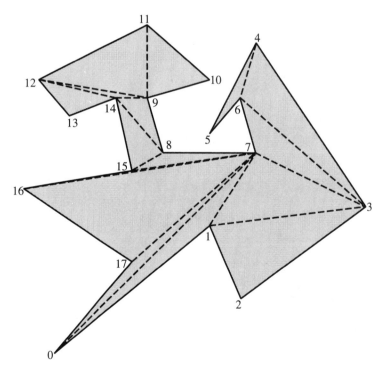

FIGURE 1.27 A polygon of 18 vertices and the triangulation produced by Triangulate.

triangulation to literally cut up and destroy the polygon. An easy fix to 4 is to make a copy of the polygon before commencing triangulation. A fix to 3 is to maintain an array of the vertex labels. Both of these fixes uglify the code without changing the essential structure and are relegated to the appendix to this chapter to avoid distraction.

1.6.5. Examples

Figure 1.27 shows a polygon and the triangulation produced by the simple main program (Code 1.14).

```
main( )
{
        int        n;
        tPolygoni                    P;

        n = ReadPoints( P );
        Triangulate1( n, P );
}
```

Code 1.14 `main`.

The actual output produced by the code is as follows (shown in two columns)

	Polygon		Triangulation diagonals	
i	x	y	1	3
0	0	0	4	6
1	10	7	3	6
2	12	3	3	7
3	20	8	1	7
4	13	17	0	7
5	10	12	9	11
6	12	14	9	12
7	13	11	12	14
8	7	11	9	14
9	6	14	8	14
10	10	15	8	15
11	6	18	7	15
12	-1	15	7	16
13	1	13	7	17
14	4	14		
15	5	10		
16	-2	9		
17	5	5		

n=18 vertices read

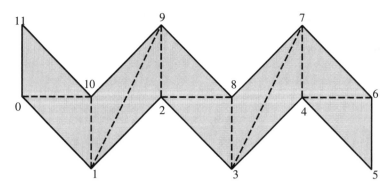

FIGURE 1.28 A polygon with six collinear vertices, and the triangulation produced by
Triangulate.

Here, I am showing only the output of `Triangulate1` (Code 1.15), the one
that prints diagonal endpoint indices rather than coordinates. Note that vertices
7, 15, and 16 are just barely non-collinear.

A somewhat more stringent test is a polygon containing collinear degeneracies, as in Figure 1.28. Here all 6 vertices with even indices are collinear. The
output of the code (again in two columns) is:

			Triangulation diagonals	
	Polygon			
i	x	y	4	6
0	0	10	4	7
1	10	0	3	7
2	20	10	3	8
3	30	0	2	8
4	40	10	2	9
5	50	0	1	9
6	50	10	1	10
7	40	20	0	10
8	30	10		
9	20	20		
10	10	10		
11	0	20		

n = 12 vertices read

Note that segments $(0, 2)$ and $(2, 4)$ are rejected as diagonals, because they are
degenerately blocked by vertices 10 and 8 respectively. Thus $(4, 6)$ is the first ear
diagonal found.

1.6.6. Analysis

We now analyze the time complexity of the triangulation algorithm we have
implemented. Let $T(n)$ be the time complexity of the algorithm operating on a

---

Triangulation $[T(n)]$
if $n > 3$ then
      for each potential ear diagonal $(i, i + 2)$ do $[\leq n \text{ iter}]$
          if Diagonal $(i, i + 2)$ then $[O(n)]$
             Print diagonal. $[O(1)]$
             Remove ear at v_i. $[O(n)]$
             Recurse on remainder of polygon. $[T(n-1)]$
          break

Algorithm 1.2   The algorithm from Algorithm 1.1 annotated with time complexities.

polygon of n vertices. Algorithm 1.2 shows the pseudocode annotated with time complexities and iterations in brackets.

The worst case occurs when the for-loop runs its full course before finding a diagonal, and each diagonal test runs its full course before rejecting the potential diagonal. Note that once a diagonal is found, the ear is clipped, and the reduced polygon is triangulated with one recursive call, and the for-loop is abandoned. To emphasize this structure, I have added the C break statement to the pseudocode above. Thus, even though the recursive call is nested in a loop that can iterate n times, it is only called once. Therefore,

$$T(n) = O(n) \times O(n) + O(1) + O(n) + T(n-1). \tag{1.26}$$

Note that the $O(n)$ term contributed by our inefficient implementation of ear removal gets absorbed in the asymptotic analysis by the quadratic search for a diagonal:

$$T(n) = O(n^2) + T(n-1). \tag{1.27}$$

This elementary recurrence relation has a solution $T(n) = O(n^3)$. This can be seen by repeatedly expanding the relation:

$$T(n) = O(n^2) + T(n-1) \tag{1.28}$$

$$T(n) = O(n^2) + O\big((n-1)^2\big) + T(n-2) \tag{1.29}$$

$$T(n) = O(n^2) + O\big((n-1)^2\big) + O\big((n-2)^2\big) + T(n-3) \tag{1.30}$$

$$T(n) = O(n^2) + O\big((n-1)^2\big) + O\big((n-2)^2\big) + \cdots + T(3). \tag{1.31}$$

Thus,

$$T(n) = \sum_{k=3}^{n} O(k^2) \tag{1.32}$$

and such a sum of n quadratics is a cubic:[25] $O(n^3)$.

---

[25] Specifically, $1 + 2^2 + 3^2 + \cdots + n^2 = (2n^3 + 3n^2 + n)/6$.

1.6.7. Speedups

Do we really need to spend $O(n^2)$ time to find just one ear? Certainly we might have to look at every potential ear diagonal $(i, i + 2)$, so the cost must be $O(n) \times E(n)$, where $E(n)$ is the cost of determining whether a potential ear is truly an ear. Our implementation checked all possible segments for intersection, and so $E(n) = O(n)$.

Short of a major reorganization of the computation employing efficient data structures, it does seem to require quadratic time to find one ear. However, a bit of cleverness permits all subsequent ears to be found quickly, resulting in an $O(n^2)$ algorithm based on ear removal (Exercise 1.6.8[10]). Further improvements require rather different approaches, to be explored in Chapter 2.

1.6.8. Exercises

1. *Triple Product.* Interpret the determinant expression (Equation 1.4) for the area of a triangle in terms of the triple vector product.

   If A, B, and C are three-dimensional vectors, their triple product is $A \cdot (B \times C)$. This is a scalar with value equal to the volume of the parallelepiped determined by the three vectors, determined in the same sense that two vectors determine a parallelogram. The value is the same as that of the determinant

$$A \cdot (B \times C) = \begin{vmatrix} A_0 & A_1 & A_2 \\ B_0 & B_1 & B_2 \\ C_0 & C_1 & C_2 \end{vmatrix}. \tag{1.33}$$

   Assuming this determinant is the parallelepiped volume, argue that Equation 1.4 is twice the area of the indicated triangle.

2. *Integer overflow.* On a machine that restricts int's to $\pm 2^{31}$, how large can the coordinates of a, b, and c be to guarantee no integer overflow in the computation of `Area2` (Code 1.3)?

3. `IntersectProp`. Detail exactly what `IntersectProp` (Code 1.6) computes if the `if`-statement is deleted. Argue that after this deletion, `Intersect` (Code 1.9) still works properly.

4. *Inefficiencies in* `Intersect`. Trace out (by hand) `Intersect` (Code 1.9) and determine the largest number of calls to `Area2` (Code 1.3) it might induce. Design a new version that avoids duplicate calls.

5. *Repeated intersection tests* [programming]. The algorithm often checks for the same segment/segment intersections. Modify the code so that you can determine how many unnecessary segment/segment intersection tests are made in the example of Figure 1.27.

6. *Saving intersection information.* Work out a scheme to avoid testing the same two segments for intersection twice. Analyze the time and space complexity of the new algorithm.

7. *Polygon as linked list* [programming]. Revise the triangulation code so that the data structure for a polygon is a linked list. Decide between singly or doubly linked lists,

and linear or circular. Test your code on the example of Figure 1.27, and make certain your output is identical.

8. *Convex polygons* [easy]. Analyze the performance of Triangulate (Code 1.13) when run on a convex polygon.

9. *Worst case.* Find a generic polygon that forces the triangulation code to use $\Theta(n^3)$ time.

10. *$O(n^2)$ triangulation algorithm.* Code based on ear removal has worst-case complexity $O(n^3)$. In this exercise, you are to develop an algorithm that has worst-case complexity $O(n^2)$, but uses the same data structures and Diagonal (Code 1.12) function and does not sort.

One call to Diagonal costs $O(n)$. So to achieve $O(n^2)$, Diagonal can only be called $O(n)$ times. Imagine that you first determine whether each potential ear diagonal is in fact a diagonal on the original polygon P, and mark vertex i as "ear" if $(i-1, i+1)$ is a diagonal. This already uses $O(n^2)$.

Let P' be a polygon of $n-1$ vertices that results from clipping off one ear. Is it true that if j is marked "ear" in P, it remains an ear in P'? If ear $\Delta(i-1, i, i+1)$ is removed, which values of j might be affected? How many new diagonals need to be checked? Under what conditions can a non-ear in P become an ear in P'? Can these conditions be recognized so that the "earity" of all vertices can be updated in time that does not exceed $O(n)$ at each iteration? If so, an $O(n^2)$ algorithm can be achieved simply by maintaining earity for all vertices, and at each step choosing an ear to remove.

Formulate a precise statement of which vertex-vertex segments of P' need to be checked to result in all the ears of P' marked. Prove this lemma and analyze the time complexity of the resulting algorithm.

11. *$O(n^2)$ Triangulation code* [programming]. Implement the algorithm you designed in the previous exercise, using as much of the code and conventions from the text as possible.

12. *Center of gravity.* Design an algorithm to compute the center of gravity of a polygon, assuming that it is cut from a material of uniform density. The center of gravity is a point, which can be treated as a vector. The center of gravity of a triangle is at its *centroid*: the point common to lines from each corner to the midpoint of the opposite side. The center of gravity $\gamma(S)$ of any set S that is the disjoint union of sets A and B, is the weighted sum of the centers of gravity of the two pieces. Let $w(S) = w(A) + w(B)$ be the weight of S. Then,

$$\gamma(S) = \frac{w(A)\gamma(A) + w(B)\gamma(B)}{w(S)}.$$

1.7. APPENDIX

1.7.1. Triangulate1: Prints Indices

Code 1.15–1.17 modifies Triangulate (Code 1.13) so that it prints diagonal endpoint indices rather than coordinates. This is accomplished by maintaining an array labels that records, for each polygon point, its *original* label.

```
/*
        Prints out n − 3 diagonals (as pairs of integer indices)
        which form a triangulation of P.
*/
void    Triangulate1( int n, tPolygoni P )
{
        tPolygoni               Pt;
        int     labels[PMAX];
        int     i;

        /* Initialize arrays. */
        for ( i = 0; i < n; i++ ){
                PointAssign( Pt[i], P[i] );
                labels[i] = i;
        }

        printf("Triangulation diagonals:\n");
        TriRecurse( n, Pt, labels );
}
```

Code 1.15 `Triangulate`

```
void    TriRecurse( int n, tPolygoni P, int labels[] )
{
        int     i, i1, i2;

        if ( n > 3 )
                for ( i = 0; i < n; i++ ) {
                        i1 = (i+1) % n;
                        i2 = (i+2) % n;
                        if ( Diagonal( i, i2, n, P ) ) {
                                printf("%d %d\n",
                                        labels[i],
                                        labels[i2]);
                                ClipEar1( i1, n, P,
                                        labels );
                                TriRecurse( n-1, P,
                                        labels );
                                break;
                        }
                }
}
```

Code 1.16 `TriRecurse`.

```
/*
            Removes P[i] by copying P[i + 1]...P[n-1] left one index.
*/
void    ClipEar1( int i, int n, tPolygoni P, int labels[]
){

    int     k;

    for ( k = i; k < n-1; k++ ) {
            PointAssign( P[k], P[k+1] );
            labels[k] = labels[k+1];
    }
}
```

Code 1.17 `ClipEar1`.

Whenever a point is deleted from the polygon by squashing out one element, a parallel squashing is performed on `labels`. Thus at all times, `labels` contains the original indices. When a diagonal is found, the appropriate entry of `labels` is printed.

1.7.2. Common Code

Codes 1.18–1.22 are various utility functions that perform simple operations and I/O routines.

```
/*
            Exclusive or: true iff exactly one argument is true.
            The arguments are negated to ensure that they are 0 / 1
            values.  Then the bitwise xor operator may apply.
            (This idea is due to Michael Baldwin.)
*/
bool    Xor( bool x, bool y )
{
    return  !x ^ !y;
}
```

Code 1.18 `Xor`.

```
/*
        Implements a = b, assignment of points / vectors.
        Assignment between arrays is not possible in C.
*/
void    PointAssign( tPointi a, tPointi b )
{
        int     i;

        for ( i = 0; i < DIM; i++ )
                a[i] = b[i];
}
```

Code 1.19 PointAssign.

```
void    PrintPoint( tPointi p )
{
        int     i;

        putchar( '( ');
        for ( i = 0; i < DIM; i++ ) {
                printf("%d", p[i]);
                if ( i != DIM-1 ) putchar( ', ');
        }
        putchar( ') ');
}
```

Code 1.20 PrintPoint.

```
int     ReadPoints( tPolygoni P )
/ *
        Reads in the coordinates of the vertices of a polygon from
        stdin, puts them into P, and returns n, the number of vertices.
        The input is assumed to be pairs of whitespace-separated
        coordinates, one pair per line.  The number of points is not part
        of the input.
* /
{
        int     n = 0;

        printf("Polygon:\n");
        printf("  i    x    y\n");
        while ( (n < PMAX) &&
                (scanf("%d %d",&P[n][0],&P[n][1]) != EOF) ) {
                printf("%3d%4d%4d\n", n, P[n][0], P[n][1]);
                ++n;
        }
        if (n < PMAX)
                printf("n = %3d vertices read\n",n);
        else    printf("Error in ReadPoints:\
                        too many points; max is %d\n",
                        PMAX);
        putchar( '\n ');

        return  n;
}
```

Code 1.21 `ReadPoints`.

```
void    PrintPoly( int n, tPolygoni P, int labels[] )
{
        int     i;

        printf("Polygon:\n");
        printf("  i   l    x    y\n");
        for( i = 0; i < n; i++ )
                printf("%3d%4d%4d%4d\n",
                        i, labels[i], P[i][0], P[i][1]);
}
```

Code 1.22 `PrintPoly`.

2

Polygon Partitioning

In this short chapter, we explore other types of polygon partitions: partitions into monotone polygons (Section 2.1), into trapezoids (Section 2.2) and into convex polygons (Section 2.4) Our primary motivation is to speed up the triangulation algorithm presented in the previous chapter, but these partitions have many applications and are of interest in their own right. One application of convex partitions is character recognition: optically-scanned characters can be represented as polygons (sometimes with polygonal holes), partitioned into convex pieces, and the resulting structures matched against a database of shapes to identify the characters (Feng and Pavlidis, 1975). In addition, since so many computations are easier on convex polygons (intersection with obstacles or with light rays, finding the distance to a line, determining if a point is inside), it often pays to partition a complex shape into convex pieces first. This chapter contains no implementations.

2.1. MONOTONE PARTITIONING

We presented an $O(n^3)$ triangulation algorithm in Section 1.3, and this is improved to $O(n^2)$ in Exercise 1.6.8[10]. Further improvements require organizing the computation more intelligently, so that each diagonal can be found in sublinear time.[1] There are now many algorithms that achieve $O(n \log n)$ time, averaging $O(\log n)$ work per diagonal.[2] The first was due to Garey, Johnson, Preparata and Tarjan (1978). Although one might expect an $O(n \log n)$ algorithm to find each diagonal by an $O(\log n)$ binary search, that is not in fact the way their algorithm works. Rather they first partition the polygon into simpler pieces, in $O(n \log n)$ time, and then triangulate the pieces in linear time. The pieces are called "monotone," a concept first introduced and exploited by Lee and Preparata (1977). It develops that partitions into monotone polygons have several other uses aside from triangulation, so we will study them in some detail. We first define monotonicity, then show how to triangulate monotone polygons in linear time, and finally describe how to partition a polygon into monotone pieces.

---

[1] The technical notation for sublinear time is $o(n)$ time.

[2] Throughout the text, all logarithms are to the base 2; so $\log 1000 \approx 10$ because $2^{10} = 1024$. However, since the big-Oh notation (Section 1.6.4) absorbs constants, the base of the logarithm is irrelevant when inside an $O(\ )$ expression.

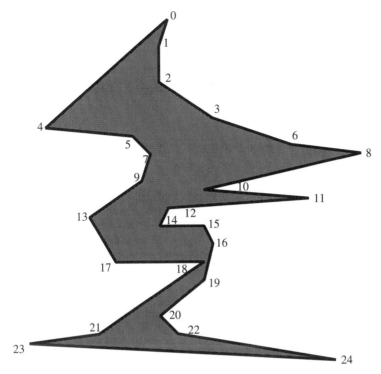

FIGURE 2.1 A polygon monotone with respect to the vertical.

2.1.1. Monotone Polygons

Monotonicity is defined with respect to a line. First, we define monotonicity of polygonal chains. A polygonal chain C is *strictly monotonic* with respect to L if every line L' orthogonal to L meets C in at most one point, i.e., $L' \cap C$ is either empty or a single point. A chain is *monotonic* if $L' \cap C$ has at most one connected component: it is either empty, a single point, or a single line segment.[3] These chains are "monotonic" in the sense that a traversal of C projects to a monotone sequence on L: no reversals occur.

A polygon P is said to be *monotone* with respect to a line L if ∂P can be split into two polygonal chains A and B such that each chain is monotonic with respect to L. The two chains share a vertex at either end. A polygon monotone with respect to the vertical is shown in Figure 2.1. The two monotone chains are $A = (0, 4, 5, 7, 9, 13, 17, 18, 21, 23, 24)$ and $B = (0, 1, 2, 3, 6, 8, 10, 11, 12, 14, 15, 16, 19, 20, 22, 24)$. Neither chain is strictly monotonic because edges $(17, 18)$ and $(14, 15)$ are horizontal. Some polygons are monotone with respect to several lines; and some polygons are not monotone with respect to any line.

---

[3] This definition differs from some others in the literature (e.g., from that of Preparata and Shamos [1985, p. 49]) in that here monotonic chains need not be strictly monotonic.

Properties of Monotone Polygons

Many algorithms that are difficult for general polygons are easy for monotone polygons, primarily because of this key property: the vertices in each chain of a monotone polygon are sorted with respect to the line of monotonicity. Let us fix the line of monotonicity to be the y-axis, here and henceforth. Then the vertices can be sorted by y-coordinate in linear time: find a highest vertex, find a lowest, and partition the boundary into two chains. The vertices in each chain are sorted with respect to y. Two sorted lists of vertices can be merged in linear time to produce one list sorted by y.

We now establish a simple local structural feature that characterizes monotonicity. Essentially, it says that a polygon is monotone, if it is monotone in the neighborhood of every vertex. This will be used later to partition a polygon into monotone pieces, by cutting at the local non-monotonicities.

Define an *interior cusp* of a polygon as a reflex vertex v whose adjacent vertices v_- and v_+ are either both at or above, or both at or below v. See Figure 2.2. Recall that a reflex vertex has internal angle strictly greater than π, so it is not possible for an interior cusp to have both adjacent vertices with the same y-coordinate as v. Thus d in Figure 2.2b is not an interior cusp.

Lemma 2.1.1. *If a polygon P has no interior cusps, then it is monotone.*

Proof. We prove the lemma in the contrapositive: if P is not monotone, it must have an interior cusp. Partition ∂P into two polygonal chains A and B sharing a lowest and a highest vertex. If P is not monotone, then one of these chains is not monotone, say the left chain A. Since A is not monotone, some horizontal line L meets A in two or more connected pieces. The points on L strictly between these pieces are either interior or exterior to P. Let S and T be two adjacent connected components of $L \cap A$, with S left of T: each is either a point or a segment. Let s be the rightmost point of S, and t the leftmost point of T. See Figure 2.3. We now consider two cases depending on whether or not there is an S and T such that the open segment (s, t) is exterior.

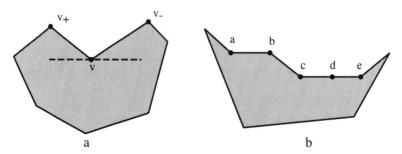

FIGURE 2.2 Interior cusps: (*a*) v_+ and v_- are both above v; (*b*) a, c, and e are interior cusps; b and d are not.

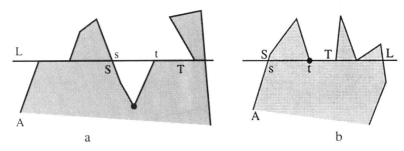

FIGURE 2.3 Monotone if no interior cusp. (*a*) The chain [*s,t*] contains an interior cusp; (*b*) *t* is an interior cusp.

1. There is an S and T such that (s, t) is exterior to P; see Figure 2.3*a*. Then somewhere on the subchain of A from s to t there must lie an interior cusp. If that subchain lies below L as illustrated in the figure, it must have lowest points, among which must be a reflex vertex satisfying the definition of interior cusp. A similar claim holds if the subchain lies above L.

2. (s,t) is interior to P ro all S and T. Suppose first that L intersects A in exactly two components. Then [s,t] contains a highest or lowest point, contradicting the assumption that A's endpoints are highest and lowest. Next suppose that L intersects A in more than two components, with S and T leftmost (Fig. 2.3b). Then t is an interior cusp: it must be a reflex vertex, and if it were not an interior cusp L would be exterior to the right of T.   □

This lemma cannot be strengthened to the claim that the lack of interior cusps implies strict monotonicity (Exercise 2.2.4[2]).

We will employ this lemma in Section 2.2 partition a polygon into monotone pieces.

2.1.2. Triangulating a Monotone Polygon

Our discussion of triangulation of monotone polygons will skim one level above details, and accordingly we will assume throughout that our polygon is strictly monotonic. Extension to monotonic polygons is left as an exercise (Exercise 2.2.4[3]).

Algorithm Idea

The main idea behind triangulating a monotone polygon is quite simple. First sort the vertices from top to bottom (in linear time), then cut off triangles from the top in a "greedy" fashion; this is a technical algorithms term indicating in this instance that at each step the first available triangle removed. The algorithm is, therefore, for each vertex v, connect v to all the vertices above it and visible via a diagonal, and remove the top portion of the polygon thereby triangulated; continue with the next vertex below v.

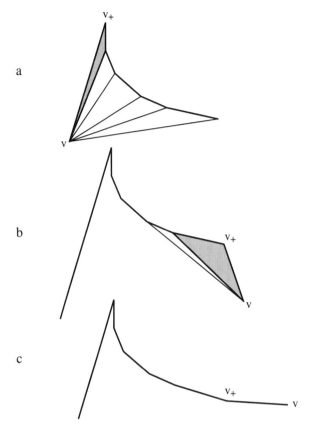

FIGURE 2.4 Algorithm cases: (*a*) v on opposite chain; (*b*) v on same chain, strictly convex angle; (*c*) v on same chain, reflex or flat angle.

There are two issues to address. Does this work? If so, can it be done in linear time? We examine these questions prior to detailing the algorithm further.

Why Does This Work?

The key is establishing properties of the structure of the top portion of the polygon at an arbitrary step of the algorithm. Suppose at some point v can be connected to several vertices above it via diagonals. Then the claim is that if all these vertices are in one chain, the chain is a *reflex chain* in the sense that all vertices have internal angle $\geq \pi$.[4] The generic situations are illustrated in Figure 2.4; this figure will be discussed further below.

---

[4]Note this is a slight abuse of notation: we have defined a reflex vertex to have internal angle $> \pi$, so a vertex with angle exactly π is not reflex; but we include it as part of a "reflex chain."

Lemma 2.1.2. *The vertices above v at the start of a new iteration of the monotone triangulation algorithm:*

1. *are all in one chain (where the topmost vertex is a member of both chains); and*

2. *the chain is reflex: all internal angles are $\geq \pi$.*

Proof. First suppose they are not all in one chain, contradicting (1). Let a be in the left chain, and let b be the vertex just above a in the right chain. We can find an a and b such that b is not the highest vertex, which is counted as part of both chains. Then ab is a diagonal, and would have been found earlier by the algorithm.

Next suppose the chain is not reflex, contradicting (2). Let c be a strictly convex vertex, and c_+ and c_- its adjacent vertices. Then c_+c_- is a diagonal, and would have been found earlier by the algorithm.   □

This then leaves only two situations: either v is in the chain opposite the vertices above it, or it is in the same chain. Within the latter case, two further situations may be distinguished: v_+, the vertex adjacent to and above v, is strictly convex, or v_+ is reflex or flat. These cases are illustrated in Figure 2.4.

Linear Time?

The structure established by Lemma 2.1.2 obviates the potentially expensive test for visibility: we know that certain segments must be diagonals without checking.

Simply keep the reflex chain in a double-ended queue, whose first (top) element is highest in y-coordinate, and whose last (bottom) element is lowest. If

---

Algorithm: MONOTONE TRIANGULATION
Sort vertices by y-coordinate.
Initialize *reflex chain* to be two top vertices.
Let v be the third-highest vertex.
while $v \neq$ lowest vertex do
    Case 1: v is on chain opposite to reflex chain.
        Draw diagonal from v to second vertex from top of chain.
        and remove top of chain.
        if chain has one element **then** add v and advance v.
    Case 2: v is adjacent to bottom of reflex chain.
        Case 2a: v_+ is strictly convex.
            Draw diagonal from v to second vertex from
            bottom of chain, and remove bottom of chain.
            if chain has one element **then** add v and advance v.
        Case 2b: v_+ is reflex or flat.
            Add v to bottom of reflex chain.
            Advance v.

Algorithm 2.1 Triangulating a monotone polygon.

v is on the opposite chain (Figure 2.4*a*), draw a diagonal from v to the top element and remove the triangle (shaded in the figure). If v is on the same chain and v_+ is strictly convex (Figure 2.4*b*) draw a diagonal from v to the bottom element and remove the triangle (shaded in the figure). If v is on the same chain and v_+ is reflex or flat (Figure 2.4*c*), add it to the bottom of the queue, since v cannot clearly see any vertices above it, and advance v to the next lowest vertex. If the queue is empty, advance v to the next lowest vertex. Clearly the work per diagonal is constant, implying linear time for the whole algorithm: $O(n)$ The algorithm is summarized in pseudocode in Algorithm 2.1.

Example

An example is shown in Figure 2.5. In Figure 2.5*a*, when $v = 4$, the reflex chain is $(0, 1, 2, 3)$. In Figure 2.5*b*, when $v = 11$, the reflex chain is $(9, 10)$. Since 10 is

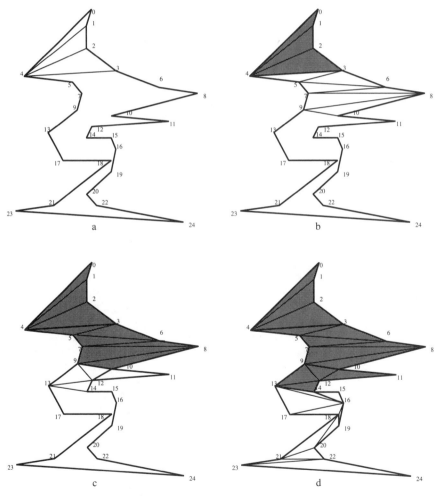

FIGURE 2.5   Monotone triangulation.

reflex, the chain is extended to $(9, 10, 11)$. Then when $v = 12$, the diagonals $(12, 10)$ and $(12, 9)$ are drawn in that order; see Figure 2.5*b* and *c*. The complete triangulation is shown in Figure 2.5*d*.

2.2. TRAPEZOIDALIZATION

Now that we see that monotone polygons may be triangulated quickly, it becomes an interesting problem to partition a polygon into monotone pieces quickly. We do this via yet another intermediate partition, which is itself of considerable interest: a partition into trapezoids. This partition was introduced by Chazelle and Incerpi (1984) and Fournier and Montuno (1984) as the key to triangulation. This partition will differ from those considered previously in that we will not restrict the partitioning segments to be diagonals.

A *horizontal trapezoidalization* of a polygon is obtained by drawing a horizontal line through every vertex of the polygon. More precisely, pass through each vertex v the maximal (open) horizontal segment s such that $s \subset P$ and $s \cap \partial P = v$. Thus, s represents clear lines-of-sight from v left and right. It may be that s is entirely to one side or the other of v; and it may be that $s = v$. An example is shown in Figure 2.6. We will only consider polygons whose vertices have unique y-coordinates to simplify the exposition: no two vertices lie on a horizontal line.

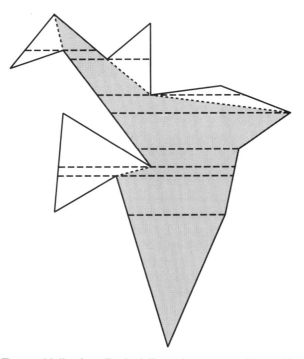

FIGURE 2.6 Trapezoidalization. Dashed lines show trapezoid partition lines; dotted diagonals resolve interior cusps. The shaded polygon is one of the resulting monotone pieces.

A *trapezoid* is a quadrilateral with two parallel edges. One can view a triangle as a degenerate trapezoid, with one of the two parallel edges of zero length. Call the vertices through which the horizontal lines are drawn *supporting vertices.*

Let P be a polygon with no two vertices on a horizontal line. Then in a horizontal trapezoidalization, every trapezoid has a exactly two supporting vertices: one on its top edge and one on its bottom edge. The connection between trapezoid partitions and monotone polygons is this: if a supporting vertex is on the interior of a trapezoid edge, it is an interior cusp. If every interior supporting vertex is connected to the "opposite" supporting vertex, downward for a "downward" cusp and upward for an "upward" cusp, these diagonals partition P into pieces monotone with respect to the vertical. This follows from Lemma 2.1.1, since every interior cusp is removed by these diagonals. These diagonals are shown dotted in Figure 2.6. Now that we see that a trapezoidalization yields a monotone partition directly, we concentrate on drawing horizontal chords through every vertex of a polygon.

2.2.1. Plane Sweep

The algorithm we use to construct a trapezoidalization depends on a technique called a "plane sweep" (or "sweep line"), which is useful in many geometric algorithms (Nievergelt and Preparata, 1982). The main idea is to "sweep" a line over the plane, maintaining some type of data structure along the line. The sweep stops at discrete "events" where processing occurs and the data structure is updated. For our particular problem, we sweep a horizontal line L over the polygon, stopping at each vertex. This requires sorting the vertices by y-coordinate, and since the polygon is general, this requires $O(n \log n)$ time.[5]

The processing required at each event vertex v is finding the edge immediately to the left and immediately to the right of v. To do this efficiently, a sorted list of polygon edges pierced by L is maintained at all times. For example, for the sweep line in the position shown in Figure 2.7, this list is $(e_{19}, e_{18}, e_{17}, e_6, e_8, e_{10})$.

Suppose this list is available. How can we determine that v lies between e_{17} and e_6 in the figure? Let us assume that e_i is a pointer to an edge of the polygon, from which the coordinates of its endpoints can be retrieved easily. Suppose the vertical coordinate of v (and therefore L) is y. Knowing the endpoints of e_i and y, we can compute the x coordinate of the intersection between L and e_i. So we can determine v's position in the list by computing the x-coordinates of where L pierces each edge at height y.

This would take time proportional to the length of the list [which is $O(n)$] if done by a naive search from left to right, but if we store the list in an efficient data structure, such as a height-balanced tree, the search will only require

---

[5]Sorting has time complexity $\Theta(n \log n)$: it can be accomplished in $O(n \log n)$ time, but no faster. See Knuth (1973).

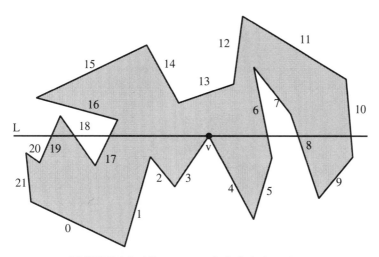

FIGURE 2.7 Plane sweep. Labels index edges.

$O(\log n)$ time. Since this search will be done at each event, the total cost over the entire plane sweep is $O(n \log n)$.

It remains to show that it is possible to maintain the data structure at all times, and in time $O(n \log n)$. This is easy as long as the data structure supports $O(\log n)$-time insertions and deletions, as do, for example, height-balanced or 2–3 trees.[6] We now detail the updates at each event. There are three possible types of event, illustrated in Figure 2.8. Let v fall between edges a and b on L, and let v be shared by edges c and d.

1. c is above L and d below. Then delete c and insert d:

$$(\ldots, a, c, b, \ldots) \Longrightarrow (\ldots, a, d, b, \ldots).$$

2. Both c and d are above L. Then delete both c and d:

$$(\ldots, a, c, d, b, \ldots) \Longrightarrow (\ldots, a, b, \ldots).$$

3. Both c and d are below L. Then insert both c and d:

$$(\ldots, a, b, \ldots) \Longrightarrow (\ldots, a, c, d, b, \ldots).$$

---

[6]See, e.g., Aho, Hopcroft, and Ullman (1983, pp. 169–180).

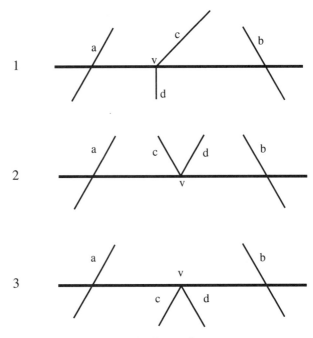

FIGURE 2.8   Sweep line events.

2.2.2. Example of Plane Sweep

Returning to Figure 2.7, the list of edges pierced by L is initially empty, when L is above the polygon, and follows this sequence as it passes each event vertex:

$$(e_{12}, e_{11})$$
$$(e_{15}, e_{14}, e_{12}, e_{11})$$
$$(e_{15}, e_{14}, e_{12}, e_6, e_7, e_{11})$$
$$(e_{15}, e_{14}, e_{13}, e_6, e_7, e_{10})$$
$$(e_{16}, e_{14}, e_{13}, e_6, e_7, e_{10})$$
$$(e_{16}, e_6, e_7, e_{10})$$
$$(e_{16}, e_6, e_8, e_{10})$$
$$(e_{19}, e_{18}, e_{16}, e_6, e_8, e_{10})$$
$$(e_{19}, e_{18}, e_{17}, e_6, e_8, e_{10}).$$

The final list corresponds to the position of L shown in the figure.

2.2.3. Triangulation in $O(n \log n)$

We summarize the $O(n \log n)$ algorithm for triangulating a polygon in Algorithm 2.2. There are still a few details we have not discussed, most involving data structures (Exercise 2.2.4[4]), but the overall design should now be clear.

Algorithm: POLYGON TRIANGULATION
Sort vertices by *y*-coordinate.
Perform plane sweep to construct trapezoidalization.
Partition into monotone polygons by connecting from interior cusps:
      Connect each upward cusp to trapezoid support vertex above,
      and each downward cusp to trapezoid support below.
      (See dotted connections in Figure 2.6.)
Triangulate each monotone polygon in linear time.

Algorithm 2.2 $O(n \log n)$ polygon triangulation.

2.2.4. Exercises

1. *Monotone with respect to a unique line.* Can a polygon be monotone with respect to precisely one line?

2. *Interior cusps.* Construct a monotone but not strictly monotone polygon that has no interior cusps, thereby showing that Lemma 2.1.1 cannot be strengthened to the claim that the lack of interior cusps implies strict monotonicity.

3. *Trapezoids when several vertices on a horizontal.* Extend the trapezoid partition algorithm to polygons that may have several vertices on a horizontal line.

4. *Trapezoid data structures.* Discuss the data structures and algorithm needed to extract lists of monotone polygons from a trapezoidalization.

5. *Polygon $\implies$ convex quadrilaterals.* Prove or disprove: Every polygon with an even number of vertices may be partitioned by diagonals into convex quadrilaterals.

6. *Polygon $\implies$ quadrilaterals.* Prove or disprove: Every polygon with an even number of vertices may be partitioned by diagonals into quadrilaterals.

7. *Orthogonal Pyramid $\implies$ convex quadrilaterals.* An *orthogonal polygon* is a polygon in which each pair of adjacent edges meets orthogonally (Exercise 1.2.5[5]). Without loss of generality, one may assume that the edges alternate between horizontal and vertical.
   An *orthogonal pyramid P* is an orthogonal polygon monotone with respect to the vertical, that contains one horizontal edge *h* whose length is the sum of the lengths of all the other horizontal edges. *P* consists of two "staircases" connected to *h*, as shown in Figure 2.9.

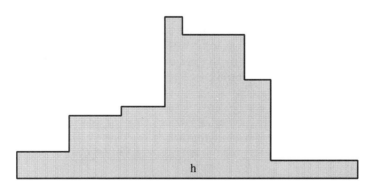

FIGURE 2.9 Orthogonal pyramid.

Table 2.1. History of Triangulation Algorithms

Year	Complexity	Reference
1911	$O(n^2)$	Lennes (1911)
1978	$O(n \log n)$	Garey et al. (1978)
1983	$O(n \log r)$, r reflex	Hertel and Mehlhorn (1983)
1984	$O(n \log s)$, s sinuosity	Chazelle and Incerpi (1984)
1988	$O(n + nt_0)$, t_0 int. triangs.	Toussaint (1990)
1988	$O(n \log\log n)$	Tarjan and VanWyk (1988)
1989	$O(n \log^* n)$, randomized	Clarkson, Tarjan, and VanWyk (1989)
1990	$O(n \log^* n)$, bnded. ints.	Kirkpatrick, Klawe, and Tarjan (1990)
1991	$O(n)$	Chazelle (1991)

a. Prove that an orthogonal pyramid may be partitioned by diagonals into *convex* quadrilaterals.

b. Design an algorithm for finding such a partition. Try for linear-time complexity. Describe your algorithm in pseudocode, at a high level, ignoring data structure details and manipulations.

8. *Orthogonal polygon* $\Longrightarrow$ *convex quadrilaterals.* Can every orthogonal polygon be partitioned into convex quadrilaterals? Explore this question enough to form a conjecture.

2.3. LINEAR-TIME TRIANGULATION

Quadratic triangulation algorithms have been implicit in proofs since at least 1911 (Lennes 1911).[7] The $O(n \log n)$ algorithm described in the previous section was one of the early achievements of computational geometry, having been published in 1978, just three years after Shamos named the field in his thesis. Soon the question of whether $O(n \log n)$ is optimal for triangulation became the outstanding open problem in computational geometry, fueling an amazing variety of clever algorithms. Algorithms were found that succeeded in breaking the $n \log n$ barrier, but only in special cases; see Table 2.1 for a sampling. The worst case remained $O(n \log n)$.

Finally, after a decade of effort, Tarjan and VanWyk (1988) discovered an $O(n \log\log n)$ algorithm. This breakthrough lead to a flurry of activity, including two $O(n \log^* n)$ algorithms:[8] one "randomized," [9] and one for polygons with appropriately bounded integer coordinates.

Finally, Chazelle constructed a remarkable $O(n)$ worst-case algorithm in 1991, ending a 13-year pursuit by the community. It would take us too far afield to describe the algorithm in detail, but I will offer a rough sketch.

[7] I depend here on the historical research of Toussaint (1985a).

[8] $\log^* n$ is the number of times the log must be iterated to reduce n to 1 or less. Thus for $n = 2^{(2^{16})} \approx 10^{19,728}$, $\log^* 2^{(2^{16})} = 5$, because $\log 2^{(2^{16})} = 2^{16}$, $\log 2^{16} = 16$, $\log 2^4 = 4$, $\log 2^2 = 2$, and $\log 2 = 1$. Note that $\log\log 2^{(2^{16})} = \log 2^{16} = 16$; for sufficiently large n, $\log^* n \ll \log\log n$.

[9] Randomized algorithms are discussed briefly in Chapter 9.

The main structure computed by the algorithm is a *visibility map*, which is a generalization of a trapezoidalization to drawing horizontal chords towards both sides of each vertex in a polygonal chain. As Chazelle explains it, his algorithm mimics merge sort, a common technique for sorting by divide-and-conquer. The polygon of n vertices is partitioned into chains of with $n/2$ vertices, and these into chains of $n/4$ vertices, and so on. The visibility map of a chain is found by merging the maps of its subchains. This leads to an $O(n \log n)$ time complexity.

Chazelle improves on this by dividing the process into two phases. In the first phase, only coarse approximations of the visibility maps are computed, coarse enough so that the merging can be accomplished in linear time. These maps are coarse in the sense that they are missing some chords. A second phase then refines the coarse map into a complete visibility map, again in linear time. A triangulation is then produced from the trapezoidalization defined by the visibility map as before. The details are formidable. Although the longstanding open problem is finally closed, it remains open to find a simple, fast, practical algorithm for triangulating a polygon.

2.4. CONVEX PARTITIONING

A partition into triangles can be viewed as a special case of a partition into convex polygons. Since there is an optimal-time triangulation algorithm, there is an optimal-time convex partitioning algorithm. However, triangulation is by no means optimal in the number of convex pieces.

There are two goals of partitions into convex pieces: (1) partition a polygon into as few convex pieces as possible, and (2) as quickly as possible. The goals conflict of course. There are two main approaches. First, compromise on the number of pieces: find a quick algorithm whose inefficiency in terms of the number of pieces is bounded with respect to the optimum. Second, compromise on the time complexity: find an algorithm that produces an optimal partition, as quickly as possible. We will only discuss the first approach in any detail but will mention results on the second approach.

Two types of partition of a polygon P may be distinguished: a partition by diagonals, or a partition by segments. The distinction is that diagonal endpoints must be vertices, whereas segment endpoints need only lie on ∂P. Partitions by segments are in general more complicated in that their endpoints must be computed somehow, but the freedom to look beyond the set of vertices often results in more efficient partitions.

2.4.1. Optimum Partition

To evaluate the efficiency of partitions, it is useful to have bounds on the best possible partition.

Theorem 2.4.1 (Chazelle).   *Let Φ be the fewest number of convex pieces into which a polygon may be partitioned. For a polygon of r reflex vertices, $\lceil r/2 \rceil + 1 \le \Phi \le r + 1$.*

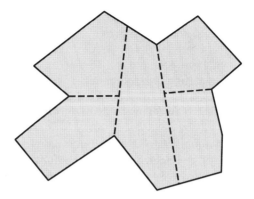

FIGURE 2.10 $r + 1$ convex pieces: $r = 4$; 5 pieces.

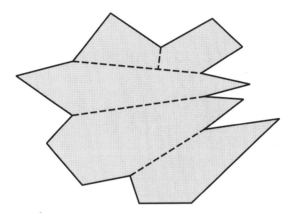

FIGURE 2.11 $\lceil r/2 \rceil + 1$ convex pieces: $r = 7$; 5 pieces.

Proof. Drawing a segment that bisects each reflex angle removes all reflex angles, and therefore results in a convex partition. The number of pieces is $r + 1$. See Figure 2.10.

All reflex angles must be resolved to produce a convex partition. At most two reflex angles can be resolved by a single partition segment. This results in $\lceil r/2 \rceil + 1$ convex pieces. See Figure 2.11.   □

2.4.2. Hertel and Mehlhorn Algorithm

Hertel and Mehlhorn (1983) found a very clean algorithm that partitions with diagonals quickly and has bounded "badness" in terms of the number of convex pieces.

In some convex partition of a polygon by diagonals, call a diagonal d *essential for vertex* v if removal of d creates a piece that is nonconvex at v. Clearly, if d is essential it must be incident to v, and v must be reflex. A diagonal that is not essential for any vertex is called *inessential*.

Hertel and Mehlhorn's algorithm is simply this: start with a triangulation of P; remove an inessential diagonal; repeat. Clearly this algorithm results in a partition of P by diagonals into convex pieces. Just as clearly it can be done in linear time. The only issue is how far from the optimum might it be.

Lemma 2.4.2. *There can be at most two diagonals essential for any reflex vertex.*

Proof. Let v be a reflex vertex, and v_+ and v_- its adjacent vertices. There can be at most one essential diagonal in the halfplane H_+ to the left of (v, v_+); for if there were two, the one closest to (v, v_+) could be removed without creating a nonconvexity at v. See Figure 2.12. Similarly, there can be at most one essential diagonal in the halfplane H_- to the left of (v_-, v). Together these halfplanes cover the interior angle at v, and so there are at most two diagonals essential for v. $\square$

Theorem 2.4.3. *The Hertel-Mehlhorn algorithm is never worse than four-times optimal in the number of convex pieces.*

Proof. When the algorithm stops, every diagonal is essential for some (reflex) vertex. By Lemma 2.4.2, each reflex vertex can be "responsible for" at most two essential diagonals. Thus, the number of essential diagonals can be no more than $2r$, where r is the number of reflex vertices (and it can be less if some diagonals are essential for the vertices at both of its endpoints). Thus the number of convex pieces M produced by the algorithm satisfies $2r + 1 \geq M$. Since $\Phi \geq \lceil r/2 \rceil + 1$ by Lemma 2.4.1, $4\Phi \geq 2r + 4 > 2r + 1 \geq M$.

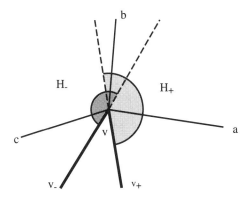

FIGURE 2.12 Essential diagonals. Diagonal a is not essential because b is also in H_+. Similarly c is not essential.

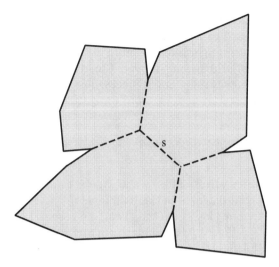

FIGURE 2.13   An optimal convex partition. Segment s does not touch ∂P.

2.4.3. Optimal Convex Partitions

As might be expected, finding a convex partition optimal in the number of pieces is much more time-consuming than finding a suboptimal one. The first algorithm for finding an optimal convex partition of a polygon with diagonals was due to Greene (1983): his algorithm runs in $O(r^2 n^2) = O(n^4)$ time. This was subsequently improved by Keil (1985) to $O(r^2 n \log n) = O(n^3 \log n)$ time. Both employ dynamic programming, a particular algorithm technique.

If the partition may be formed with arbitrary segments, then the problem is even more difficult, as it might be necessary to employ partition segments that do not touch the polygon boundary, as shown in Figure 2.13. Nevertheless, Chazelle (1980) solved this problem in his thesis with an intricate $O(n + r^3) = O(n^3)$ algorithm (see also, Chazelle and Dobkin [1985]).

2.4.4. Exercises

1. *Worst case number of pieces.*   Find a generic polygon that can lead to the worst case of the Hertel-Mehlhorn (H-M) algorithm: there is a triangulation, and an order of inessential diagonal removal, that leads to $2r$ convex pieces.

2. *Worst case with respect to optimum.*   Find a generic polygon that can lead to the worst-case behavior in the H-M algorithm with respect to the optimum: H-M produces $2r$ pieces, but $\lceil r/2 \rceil + 1$ pieces are possible.

3. *Better optimality constant?*   Is there any hope of improving the optimality constant of H-M below 4? Suppose the choice of diagonals was made more intelligently. Is a constant of, say, 3 possible?

4. *Better approximate algorithm (diagonals)* [open].   Find a "fast" algorithm that achieves an optimality constant less than 4. By fast I mean $O(n \text{ polylog } n)$, where polylog n is some polynomial in $\log n$, such as $\log^3 n$.

5. *Better approximate algorithm (segments)* [open]. Find a fast approximation algorithm using segments rather than diagonals.

6. *Partition into rectangles.* Design an algorithm to partition an orthogonal polygon (Exercise 2.2.4[7]) into rectangles. Use only horizontal and vertical partition segments, collinear with some polygon edge. Try to achieve as few pieces as possible, as quickly as possible.

7. *Cover with rectangles.* Design an algorithm to *cover* an orthogonal polygon P with rectangles whose sides are horizontal and vertical. Each rectangle should fall inside P, and their union should be exactly P. In a partition, the rectangle interiors are pairwise disjoint, but in a cover they may overlap. Try to achieve as few pieces as possible, as quickly as possible.

Convex Hulls in Two Dimensions

The most ubiquitous structure in computational geometry is the convex hull (sometimes shortened to just "the hull"). It is useful in its own right and useful as a tool for constructing other structures in a wide variety of circumstances. Finally, it is an austerely beautiful object playing a central role in pure mathematics.

It also represents something of a success story in computational geometry. One of the first papers identifiably in the area of computational geometry concerned the computation of the convex hull, as will be discussed in Section 3.5. Since then there has been an amazing variety of research on hulls, ultimately leading to optimal algorithms for most natural problems. We will necessarily select a small thread through this work for this chapter, partially compensating with a series of exercises on related topics (Section 3.9).

Before plunging into the geometry, we briefly mention a few applications.

1. *Collision avoidance.* If the convex hull of a robot avoids collision with obstacles, so does the robot. Since the computation of paths that avoid collision is much easier with a convex robot than with a nonconvex one, this is often used to plan paths. This will be discussed in Chapter 8 (Section 8.4).

2. *Fitting ranges with a line.* Finding a straight line that fits between a collection of data ranges maps[1] to finding the convex region common to a collection of halfplanes (O'Rourke, 1981).

3. *Smallest box.* The smallest area rectangle that encloses a polygon has at least one side flush with the convex hull of the polygon and so the hull is computed at the first step of minimum rectangle algorithms (Toussaint, 1983*b*). Similarly finding the smallest three-dimensional box surrounding an object in space depends crucially on the convex hull of the object (O'Rourke, 1985*a*).

4. *Shape analysis.* Shapes may be classified for the purposes of matching by their "convex deficiency trees," structures which depend for their computation on convex hulls. This will be explored in Exercise 3.2.3[2].

The importance of the topic demands not only formal definition of a convex hull, but a thorough intuitive appreciation. The convex hull of a set of points in the plane is the shape taken by a rubber band stretched around nails pounded into the plane at each point. The boundary of the convex hull of points in three

---

[1]Maps via a duality relation to be studied in Chapter 6 (Section 6.5).

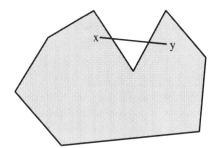

FIGURE 3.1 Any dent implies nonconvexity.

dimensions is the shape taken by plastic wrap stretched tightly around the points. We now examine a series of more formal definitions and approaches to convexity concepts. The remainder of the chapter is devoted to algorithms for constructing the hull.

3.1. DEFINITIONS OF CONVEXITY AND CONVEX HULLS

1. A set S is *convex* if $x \in S$ and $y \in S$ implies that the (closed) segment $xy \subseteq S$. This can be taken as the primary definition of convexity. Note that this definition does not specify any particular dimension for the points, whether S is connected, bounded or unbounded, closed or open. It should be clear from Figure 3.1. that any region with a "dent" is not convex, since two points straddling the dent can be found such that the segment they determine contains points exterior to the region. So, in particular any polygon with a reflex vertex[2] is not convex.

2. The *segment xy* is the set of all points of the form $\alpha x + \beta y$ with $\alpha \geq 0$, $\beta \geq 0$, and $\alpha + \beta = 1$.[3] For example, the midpoint $\frac{1}{2}(x + y)$ is realized with equal weights: $\alpha = \frac{1}{2}$ and $\beta = \frac{1}{2}$; the endpoints are achieved with one of the two weights zero. This algebraic view of a segment is quite useful both in mathematics and for computation. As an example of the latter, we will use it as the basis for finding the intersection point between two segments (Section 7.4.2).

3. A *convex combination* of points $x_1, \ldots, x_k$ is a sum of the form $\alpha_1 x_1 + \cdots + \alpha_k x_k$, with $\alpha_i \geq 0$ for all i and $\alpha_1 + \cdots + \alpha_k = 1$. So, a line segment consists of all convex combinations of its endpoints, and a triangle consists of all convex combinations of its three corners. In three dimensions, a tetrahedron is the convex combinations of its four corners. Note that all of these objects are themselves convex.

---

[2] Recall a vertex is reflex if its interior angle is $> \pi$.
[3] In the expression $\alpha x + \beta y$, α and β are scalar real numbers, while x and y are points or (equivalently) vectors.

4. The *convex hull* of a set of points S is the set of all convex combinations of points of S. In the mathematics literature, the convex hull of S is denoted by conv S. We will sometimes also use the notation $\mathcal{H}(S)$. Although it should be intuitively clear that the hull defined this way cannot have a dent, a proof is not immediate (Exercise 3.2.3[1]).

5. The convex hull of a set of points S in d dimensions is the set of all convex combinations of $d + 1$ (or fewer points) of S. The distinction between this and the previous definition is that here only $d + 1$ points need be used. Thus, the hull of a two-dimensional set is the convex combinations of its subsets of three points, which as we saw in (3) above, each determine a triangle. That the $(d + 1)$-points definition is equivalent to the all-points definition (4) is known as Caratheodory's Theorem (Lay 1982, p. 17).

6. The convex hull of a set of points S is the intersection of all convex sets that contain S. This definition is perhaps clearer than the previous two because it does not depend on the notion of convex combination. However, the notion of "all convex sets" is not easily grasped.

7. The convex hull of a set of points S is the intersection of all halfspaces that contain S. This is perhaps the clearest definition, equivalent (although not trivially) to all the others. A halfspace in two dimensions is a *halfplane*: is the set of points on or to one side of a line. This notion generalizes to higher dimensions: a *halfspace* is the set of points on or to one side of a plane, and so on. Note that the convex hull of a set is a closed "solid" region, including all the points inside. Often the term is used more loosely in computational geometry to mean the boundary of this region, since it is the boundary we compute, and that implies the region. Usually confusion can be avoided.

8. The convex hull of a set of points S in the plane is the smallest convex polygon P that encloses S, smallest in the sense that there is no other polygon P' such that $P \supset P' \supseteq S$.

9. The convex hull of a set of points S in the plane is the enclosing convex polygon P with smallest area.

10. The convex hull of a set of points S in the plane is the enclosing convex polygon P with smallest perimeter. The equivalence of these last two definitions (9 and 10) with smallest in terms of subset nesting (8), is intuitively but not mathematically obvious (Exercise 3.2.3[6]). However, none of these three definitions of the boundary suggest an easy algorithm.

11. The convex hull of a set of points S in the plane is the union of all the triangles determined by points in S. This is just a restatement of 5 above, but in a form that hints at a method of computation.

The remainder of this chapter concentrates on algorithms for constructing the boundary of the convex hull of a finite set of points in two dimensions. We start with rather inefficient algorithms (Sections 3.2, 3.3, and 3.4) gradually working toward an optimal algorithm (Section 3.5) and finally examining algorithms that extend to three dimensions (Sections 3.7 and 3.8). The only algorithm we exhibit in full detail, and for which code is provided, is Graham's (Section 3.5).

3.1.1. Extreme Points

Before studying algorithms, we must first address the question of what output we desire from the algorithms: in particular, what constitutes constructing the boundary. Let us keep attention fixed to two dimensions until Chapter 4, with S a finite set of n points. There are two, perhaps distinct problems: compute the "extreme" points, and compute the boundary polygon. The extreme points are the vertices of the convex hull. The boundary polygon is the convex polygon bounding the hull. The difference is that a representation of the convex polygon includes linking the vertices in order around the boundary, whereas the extreme points could be treated as an unordered set, and identified in arbitrary order. It is conceivable that finding just the extreme points is easier. We will see in Section 3.6 that in fact it is no easier (under the big-Oh measure), but it remains conceptually simpler.

We first formally define the notion of "extreme." The *extreme points* of a set S of points in the plane are the vertices of the convex hull at which the interior angle is strictly convex, less than π. Thus, we only want to count "real" vertices as extreme: points in the interior of a segment of the hull are not considered extreme.[4]

Given a set of S points in the plane, how can the extreme points be identified computationally? First, note that the highest point of S, the one with the largest y-coordinate, is extreme if it is unique, or even if there are exactly two equally highest vertices (both are then extreme). The same is of course true of the lowest points, the rightmost points, and the leftmost points. It should be clear that a point is extreme iff there exists a line through that point that otherwise does not touch the convex hull. Such "there exists" formulations, however, do not immediately suggest a method of computation.

Let us therefore look at the other side of the coin, the nonextreme points.

3.2. NAIVE ALGORITHMS FOR EXTREME POINTS

This section is a bit of a digression in that it leads only to rather slow algorithms, but they serve as useful foils for the faster algorithms to follow.

3.2.1. Nonextreme Points

Clearly, identifying the nonextreme points is enough to identify the extreme points.

---

[4]The definition used by mathematicians is that "a point x in S is extreme if there is no nondegenerate line segment in S that contains x in its relative interior" (Lay 1982, p. 42).

Algorithm: INTERIOR POINTS
for each i do
for each $j \neq i$ do
for each $k \neq i \neq j$ do
    for each $l \neq i \neq j \neq k$ do
        if p_l is left or on (p_i, p_j) and
           p_l is left or on (p_j, p_k) and
           p_l is left or on (p_k, p_i)
           then p_l is nonextreme

Algorithm 3.1 Interior points.

Lemma 3.2.1. *A point is nonextreme iff it is inside some (closed) triangle whose vertices are points of the set, and is not itself a corner of that triangle.*

Proof. The basis of this lemma is the final characterization of the hull, 11 in the list in Section 3.1. Assuming that, it is clear that if a point is interior to a triangle, it is nonextreme, and it is also evident that corners of a triangle might be extreme. A point that lies on the boundary of a triangle but not at a corner, is not extreme. This accounts for all possibilities.   □

On the basis of this lemma, Algorithm 3.1 is immediate. Let $S = \{p_0, p_1, \ldots, p_{n-1}\}$, with all points distinct. Note that it is unnecessary to check the second clause of the lemma, that p_l not be a corner of the triangle: by our assumption that the points of S are distinct, and our exclusion of i, j, and k as indices in the l loop, this condition is guaranteed.

   This algorithm clearly runs in $O(n^4)$ time because there are four nested loops, each $O(n)$: for each of the n^3 triangles, the test for extremeness costs n. It would be a challenge to find a slower algorithm!

3.2.2. Extreme Edges

It is somewhat easier to identify extreme edges, edges of the convex hull. An edge is extreme if every point of S is on or to one side of the line determined by the edge. It seems easiest to detect this by treating the edge as directed and specifying one of the two possible directions as determining the "side." Let the left side of a directed edge be the inside. Phrased negatively, a directed edge is not extreme if there is some point that is not left or on. This is the formulation we use in the code below.

   There is unfortunately an inaccuracy in our characterization of extreme edges. Suppose xy is an extreme edge, and z lies on the interior of the segment xy. Then xz and zy will both have the property that there is no point strictly to their rights—no point that is not left of or on. However, it makes sense to say that neither of these counts as an extreme edge, and to demand that both endpoints of an *extreme edge* be extreme vertices.

```
Algorithm: EXTREME EDGES
for each i do
for each j ≠ i do
    for each k ≠ i ≠ j do
        if p_k is not left or on (p_i, p_j)
            then (p_i, p_j) is not extreme
```

Algorithm 3.2   Extreme edges

We opt not to check this precise condition (since we are only sketching this algorithm in order to improve upon it), so Algorithm 3.2 works only for point sets "in general position": no three points collinear.

This algorithm clearly runs in $O(n^3)$ time because there are three nested loops, each $O(n)$: for each of the n^2 pairs of points, the test for extremeness costs n. Which vertices are extreme can be found easily now (under the general position assumption), since an extreme point is an endpoint of two extreme edges.

3.2.3. Exercises

1. *Convexity of the convex hull.* Starting from the definition of the convex hull of S as the set of all convex combinations of points from S, prove that conv S is in fact convex, in that the segment connecting any two points is in conv S.

2. *Extreme point implementation* [programming]. Write code to take a list of points as input, and to print the extreme points in arbitrary order. Try to write the shortest, simplest code you can think of, without regard to running time. Make use of the functions in the triangulation code from Chapter 1: `ReadPoints` (Code 1.21) to read in the points (that they do not necessarily form a polygon is irrelevant), `Left` and `LeftOn` (Code 1.4), and so on.

3. *Min supporting line* (Modayur 1991). Design an algorithm to find a line L that

   a. has all the points of a given set to one side,

   b. minimizes the sum of the perpendicular distances of the points to L.

   Assume a hull algorithm is available.

4. *Affine hulls* [easy]. An *affine combination* of points $x_1, \ldots, x_k$ is a sum of the form $\alpha_1 x_1 + \cdots + \alpha_k x_k$, with $\alpha_1 + \cdots + \alpha_k = 1$. Note this differs from the definition of a convex combination in that the condition $\alpha_i \geq 0$ is dropped. In two dimensions, what is the affine hull of two points? Three points? $n > 3$ points? In three dimensions, what is the affine hull of two points? Three points? Four points? $n > 4$ points?

5. *Extreme edges.* Modify Algorithm 3.2 so that it works correctly without the general position assumption.

6. *Minimum area, convex.* Prove characterization 9 of Section 3.1: the minimum area convex polygon enclosing a set of points is the convex hull of the points.

7. *Minimum area, nonconvex* [easy]. Show by explicit example that the minimum area polygon (perhaps nonconvex) enclosing a set of points might not be the convex hull of the points.

8. *Shortest path below.* Let a set of points S and two additional points a and b be given, with a left of S and b right of S. Develop an algorithm to find the shortest path from a to b that goes below S. Assume a convex hull algorithm is available.

3.3. GIFT WRAPPING

We now move to more realistic hull algorithms. A minor variation on the Extreme Edge algorithm (Algorithm 3.2) will both accelerate it by a factor of n, and at the same time output the extreme points in the order in which they occur around the hull boundary. The idea is to use one extreme edge as an anchor for finding the next. This works because we know that the extreme edges are linked into a convex polygon. Since the most vertices this polygon can have is n, the number of extreme edges is $O(n)$. The anchored search will only explore $O(n)$ candidates, rather than the $O(n^2)$ candidates in Algorithm 3.2. This saves a factor of n and reduces the complexity to $O(n^2)$.

Now let's examine how this anchored search can be accomplished. Assume general position of the points for clarity: no three points in S are collinear. Suppose the algorithm last found an extreme edge whose unlinked endpoint is x; see Figure 3.2. We know there must be another extreme edge e sharing endpoint x. Draw a directed line L from x to another point y of the set. L includes e only if all other points are to the left, or alternatively, only if there are no points to the right. However, if we check for each y whether all other points are to the left, we will be back to an n^3 calculation: for each x, for each y, check all other points.

The key observation to reducing the complexity is that, as can be seen from Figure 3.2, the line L that includes e also has the property of making the smallest counterclockwise angle with respect to the previous hull edge. This implies that it is not necessary to check whether all points are to the left: this can be *inferred* from the angle. So for each point y, compute that angle; call it θ. The point that yields the smallest θ must determine an extreme edge (under the general position assumption).

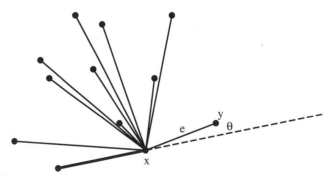

FIGURE 3.2 The next edge e makes the smallest angle with respect to the previous edge.

Algorithm: GIFT WRAPPING
Find the lowest point (smallest y-coordinate).
Let i_0 be its index, and set $i \leftarrow i_0$.
repeat
    for each $j \neq i$ do
        Compute counterclockwise angle θ from previous hull edge.
    Let k be the index of the point with the smallest θ.
    Output (p_i, p_k) as a hull edge.
    $i \leftarrow k$
until $i = i_0$

Algorithm 3.3   Gift wrapping.

The reason this algorithm is called the "gift wrapping" algorithm should now be clear: one can view it as wrapping the point set with a string that bends the minimal angle from the previous hull edge until the set is hit. This algorithm was first suggested by Chand and Kapur (1970) as a method for finding hulls in arbitrary dimensions. We will see that it can be surpassed in two dimensions, but for many years it was the primary algorithm for higher dimensions. One nice feature is that it is "output-size sensitive," in that it runs faster when the hull is small: its complexity is $O(nh)$ if the hull has h edges (Exercise 3.4.1[1]).

Again, we would need to modify the algorithm to remove the general position assumption, and again we will not bother. There remains one minor detail: how to start the algorithm. We can use the lowest point of the set as the first anchor, treating the "previous" hull edge as horizontal. Pseudocode is shown in Algorithm 3.3 This algorithm runs in $O(n^2)$ time: $O(n)$ work for each hull edge.

3.4.   QUICKHULL

We continue our catalog of hull algorithms with one that was suggested independently by several researchers in the late 1970s. It was dubbed the "QuickHull" algorithm in (Preparata and Shamos, 1985) because of its similarity to the QuickSort algorithm (Knuth, 1973).[5] The basic intuition is as simple as it is sound: for "most" sets of points, it is easy to discard many points as definitely interior to the hull, and then concentrate on those closer to the hull boundary. The first step of the QuickHull algorithm is to find the points extreme in the four compass directions: highest, lowest, leftmost, and rightmost points. Let us assume for ease of presentation that all four of these extremes are unique. Connect these four extreme points into a quadrilateral; then all points on the boundary or inside this quadrilateral may be discarded from further consideration. See Figure 3.3. Now our problem is reduced to four separate problems of finding the hulls in each of the four triangular regions exterior to the quadrilateral. QuickHull finds these by finding an extreme point in the

---

[5]The presentation here is based on that in Preparata and Shamos (1985, pp. 112–114).

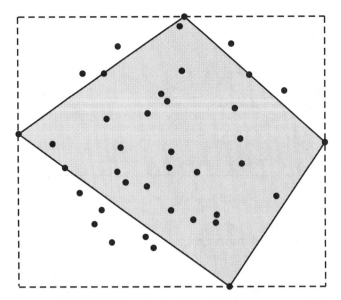

FIGURE 3.3   QuickHull discards the points in the extreme quadrilateral.

triangle, discarding points, and recursing on two smaller sets of points, as follows.

At any stage, we will know two points on the hull a and b, and there will be a set of points S strictly to the right of ab. The task is to find the chain of the convex hull from a to b encompassing S. See Figure 3.4. Initially a and b are two of the four extreme points. The key idea is that a point $c \in S$ that is furthest away from ab must be on the hull: it is extreme in the direction orthogonal to ab. Therefore, we can discard all points on or in the triangle abc (except for a,

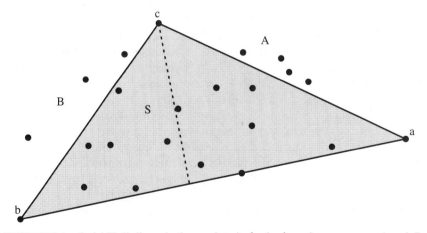

FIGURE 3.4   QuickHull discards thee points in (a, b, c), and recurses on A and B.

Algorithm: QUICKHULL
function *QuickHull* (a, b, S)
    if $S = \{a, b\}$ then return (a, b)
    else
        $c \leftarrow$ index of point with max distance from ab.
        $A \leftarrow$ points right of (a, c).
        $B \leftarrow$ points right of (c, b).
        return *QuickHull* $(a\,c\,A)$ concatenated with *QuickHull* $(c\,b\,B)$

Algorithm 3.4 QuickHull.

b, and c themselves) and repeat the same procedure on the points A right of ac and the points B right of cb (again see Figure 3.4). The essence of this algorithm can be embodied in a recursive function that takes as input a, b, and a list of the points in S: See Algorithm 3.4.

Many details are missing from our description; we will leave those for Exercise 3.4.1[3]. Instead we turn to an analysis of the time complexity of QuickHull.

Forming the initial quadrilateral can be accomplished in $O(n)$ time. For the recursive function, suppose $|S| = n$. Then it takes n steps to determine the extreme point c, but the cost of the recursive calls depends on the sizes of A and B. Let $|A| = \alpha$ and $|B| = \beta$ with $\alpha + \beta = n - 1 = O(n)$. If the time complexity for calling QuickHull with $|S| = n$ is $T(n)$, we can express T recursively in terms of itself: $T(n) = O(n) + T(\alpha) + T(\beta)$. It is not possible to solve this equation without expressing α and β in terms of n.

Consider the best possible case, when each division is as balanced as possible: $\alpha = \beta = n/2$ (it is safe to ignore the minor discrepancy that $\alpha + \beta$ should sum to $n - 1$ in this rough analysis). Then, we have $T(n) = 2T(n/2) + O(n)$. This is a familiar recurrence relation, whose solution is $T(n) = O(n \log n)$.[6] Therefore $T(n) = O(n \log n)$ in the "best" case, which would occur with randomly distributed point sets.

The worst case occurs when each division is as skewed as possible: $\alpha = 1$ and $\beta = n - 1$. Then, we arrive at the recurrence relation $T(n) = T(n - 1) + O(n) = T(n - 1) + cn$. If we repeatedly expand this we get

$$T(n) = cn + c(n - 1) + c(n - 2) + \cdots + c = O(n^2).$$

Thus, although QuickHull is indeed generally quick, it is still quadratic in the worst case.

In the next section, we culminate our progression of ever-faster algorithms with a worst-case optimal $O(n \log n)$ algorithm.

---

[6]We will analyze this recurrence in Section 3.8 below, where it plays a crucial role.

3.4.1. Exercises

1. *Best case?* Find the best case for the gift wrapping algorithm (Algorithm 3.3): sets of n points such that the algorithm's asymptotic time complexity is as small as possible as a function of n. What is this time complexity?

2. *Improving gift wrapping.* During the course of gift wrapping (Algorithm 3.3), it is sometimes possible to identify points that can not be on the convex hull and eliminate them from the set "on the fly." Work out rules to accomplish this. What is a worst-case set of points for your improved algorithm?

3. *QuickHull details.* Provide more details for the QuickHull algorithm. In particular, specify how the point c with maximum distance from ab can be found. In addition, consider "degenerate" cases: when the four compass extremes are not unique, when the point c is not uniquely maximal, when there are points lying on ab, when there are less than four compass extremes (if e.g. leftmost and highest are the same point), and so on.

4. *QuickHull worst case.* Construct a generic point set that forces QuickHull to its worst-case quadratic behavior. By "generic" is meant a construction that works for arbitrarily large values of n, i.e., "general" n.

5. *Akl and Toussaint algorithm.* Rather than using the recursive QuickHull function in Algorithm 3.4, compute the hull chain in each of the four triangles outside the original quadrilateral as follows. Sort the points left to right in each region. For each region, find the convex chain from one extremal point to the other by processing the points in some manner left to right.

   Work out a method for finding these convex chains in time linear in the cardinality of the point sets. What is the final time complexity of your algorithm?[7]

6. *Implementation of QuickHull* [programming]. Implement QuickHull, and measure its performance on points uniformly distributed within a square.

3.5. GRAHAM'S ALGORITHM

Perhaps the honor of the first paper published in the field of computational geometry should be accorded to Graham's algorithm for finding the hull of points in two dimensions in $O(n \log n)$ time (Graham, 1972)[8] In the late 1960s, an application at Bell Labs required the hull of $n \approx 10,000$ points, and they found the $O(n^2)$ algorithm in use too slow. Graham developed his simple algorithm in response to this need (Graham, 1992).

3.5.1. Top Level Description

The basic idea of his algorithm is simple. We will first explain it with an example, making several assumptions that will be removed later. Assume we are given a point x interior to the hull, and further assume that no three points of the given set (including x) are collinear. Now sort the points by angle, counter-

---

[7]This algorithm was suggested by Akl and Toussaint (1978).

[8]I say "perhaps" because Toussaint (1985*a*) found an earlier paper that contained many ideas that appeared in later hull algorithms. (See Bass and Schubert, 1967.)

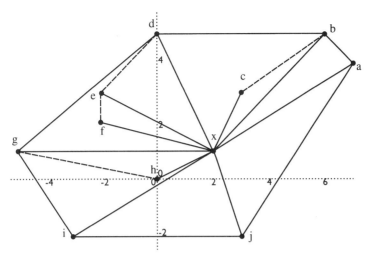

FIGURE 3.5   Example for Graham's algorithm: $x = (2, 1)$;
$S = \{(7, 4), (6, 5), (3, 3), (0, 5), (-2, 3), (-2, 2), (-5, 1), (0, 0), (-3, -2), (3, -2)\}$.

clockwise about x. For the example shown in Figure 3.5, the sorted points are labeled $a, b, \ldots, j$. The points are now processed in their sorted order, and the hull grown incrementally around the set. At any step, the hull will be correct for the points examined so far, but of course points encountered later will cause earlier decisions to be reevaluated.

The hull-so-far is maintained in a stack S of points. Initially, the stack contains the first two points, $S = (a, b)$ in our example, with b on top. Point c is added because (a, b, c) forms a left turn at b, the previous stack top. Note that $S = (a, b, c)$ is a convex chain, a condition that will be maintained throughout. Next point d is considered, but since (b, c, d) forms a right turn at the stack top c, the chain is not extended, but rather the last decision, to add c, is revoked by popping c from the stack, which then becomes $S = (a, b)$. Now d is added, because (a, b, d) forms a left turn at b.

Continuing in this manner, e and f are added, after which the stack is $S = (a, b, d, e, f)$. Point g causes f and then e to be deleted, since both (e, f, g) and (d, e, g) are right turns. Then g can be added, and the stack is $S = (a, b, d, g)$, and so on.

If we are as fortunate as in the considered example and our first point a is on the hull, the convex chain will close naturally, resulting in the final hull $S = (a, b, d, g, i, j, a)$. If a were not on the hull, the head of the chain would start to consume the tail (so to speak), and the algorithm analysis would be more difficult. We will see that this can be avoided.

3.5.2. Pseudocode, Version A

Before proceeding to a more careful presentation, we summarize the rough algorithm in pseudocode in Algorithm 3.5. We assume stack primitives

---

Algorithm: GRAHAM SCAN, VERSION A
Find the interior point x; label it p_0.
Sort all other points angularly about x; label $p_1, \ldots, p_{n-1}$.
Stack $S = (p_1, p_2) = (p_{t-1}, p_t)$; t indexes top.
$i \to 3$
while $i < n$ do
    if p_i is left of (p_{t-1}, p_t)
        then Push(S, i) and increment i.
        else Pop(S).

Algorithm 3.5   Graham Scan, Version A.

Push(S, p) and Pop(S), which push p onto the top of the stack S, and pop the top off, respectively. We use t to index the stack top, and i the angularly-sorted points. Many issues remain to be examined (start and termination in particular), but at this coarse level, it should be apparent that the while loop iterates $O(n)$ times: each stack pop permanently removes one point, so the number of backups cannot exceed n. Together with n forward steps, the loop iterates at most $2n$ times. So the algorithm runs in linear time after the sorting step, which takes $O(n \log n)$ time. We will see in Section 3.6 that this is the best for which we can hope for: its time complexity is "worst-case optimal."

3.5.3. Details: Boundary Conditions

A number of details have been ignored in our presentation so far. We will rectify this in two stages. First, various "boundary" conditions are examined in this section. Second, implementation issues are explored in the sections following.

Start and Stop of Loop
Even a simple loop can be difficult to start and stop properly: the algorithm so far presented might have trouble at either end.[9] We already mentioned the termination difficulties that would arise if a, the stack bottom, were not on the hull. Startup difficulties occur when b, the second point pushed on the stack, is not on the hull. Suppose that (a, b, c) is a right turn. Then b would be popped from the stack, and the stack reduced to $S = (a)$. However, at least two points are needed to determine if a third forms a left turn with the stack top.

Clearly, both startup and stopping problems are avoided if both a and b are on the hull. How this can be arranged will be shown in the next subsection.

Sorting Origin
We assumed that the point x, about which all others are sorted, is interior to the hull. Graham provided a careful linear algorithm for computing such an

---

[9]Several early published versions were in error over these difficulties. A short history is presented by Gries and Stojmenović (1987).

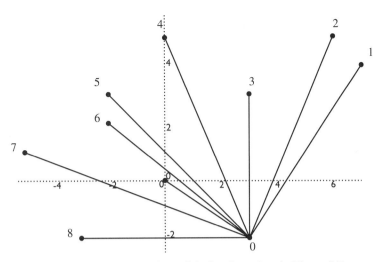

FIGURE 3.6 New sorting origin for the points in Figure 3.5.

interior point.[10] However, not only is this calculation unnecessary, it may force the use of floating-point numbers even when the input coordinates are all integers. We would like to avoid all floating-point calculations to guarantee a correct answer on integer input.

A simplification is to sort with respect to a point of the set, and in particular, with respect to a point on the hull.[11] We will use the lowest point, which is clearly on the hull. In case there are several with the same minimum y-coordinate, we will use the rightmost of the lowest as the sorting origin. This is point j in Figure 3.5. Now the sorting appears as in Figure 3.6. Note all points in the figure have been relabeled with numbers; this is how they will be indexed in the implementation. We will call the points $p_0, p_1, \ldots, p_{n-1}$, with p_0 the sorting origin and p_{n-1} the most counterclockwise point.

Now we are prepared to solve the startup and termination problems discussed above. If we sort points with respect to their counterclockwise angle from the horizontal ray emanating from our sorting origin p_0, p_1 and p_n *must* be on the hull, as they form extreme angles with p_0. For reasons that will become apparent momentarily, we will use p_{n-1}. If we initialize the stack to $S = (p_{n-1}, p_0)$, the stack will always contain at least two points, avoiding startup difficulties, and will never be consumed when the chain wraps around to p_0 again, avoiding termination difficulties.

---

[10]His method may be of interest in its own right (Graham, 1972): "...this can be done...by testing 3 element subsets...for collinearity, discarding middle points of collinear sets, and stopping when the first noncollinear set (if there is one), say x, y, and z, is found. [The point] can be chosen to be the centroid of the triangle formed by x, y, and z." It is notable that he did not assume that the given points are in general position.

[11]This useful idea occurred to several researchers independently, including Akl and Toussaint (1978) and Anderson (1978).

Collinearities

The final "boundary condition" we consider is the possibility that three or more points are collinear, until now a situation conveniently assumed not to occur. This issue affects several aspects of the algorithm. First, we focus on defining precisely what we seek as output.

Hull Collinearities. Should the algorithm output a point interior to a hull edge, one that is not a corner of the hull? One can imagine applications that would require all points on the hull to be output, but here we demand that every point output by the algorithm be an extreme point (Section 3.2): a true corner through which there passes a line that meets the hull in only this point. Thus, if the input consists of the corners of a square, together with points sprinkled around its boundary, the output should consist of just the four corners of the square.

This condition is easily enforced by requiring a *strict* left turn (p_{t-1}, p_t, p_i) to push p_i onto the stack, where p_t and p_{t-1} are the top two points on the stack. Then if p_t is collinear with p_{t-1} and p_i, it will be deleted.

Sorting Collinearities. Collinearities raise another issue: how should we break ties in the angular sorting if both points a and b form the same angle with p_0? One's first inclination is to assume (or hope) it does not matter, but alas the situation is more delicate. Suppose we use this reasonable rule: if angle$(a) =$ angle(b), then define $a < b$ if $|a - p_0| < |b - p_0|$: closer points are treated as earlier in the sorting sequence. With this rule, we obtain the sorting indicated by the indices for the highly degenerate set of points in Figure 3.7. Now it should be clear why we initialized the stack to (p_{n-1}, p_0) rather than to (p_0, p_1). With the sorting convention just chosen, p_{n-1} (p_{18} in the figure) must be a corner of the hull, whereas p_1 might be interior to a hull edge, and therefore subject to deletion. Thus, our choices combine to guarantee that our initial

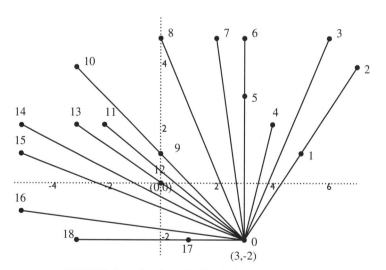

FIGURE 3.7   Sorting of points with collinearities.

Algorithm: GRAHAM SCAN, VERSION B
Find rightmost lowest point; label it p_0.
Sort all other points angularly about p_0,
    break ties in favor of closeness to p_0;
    label $p_1, \ldots, p_{n-1}$.
Stack $S = (p_{n-1}, p_0) = (p_{t-1}, p_t)$; t indexes top.
$i = 1$
while $i < n$ do
    if p_i is strictly left of (p_{t-1}, p_t)
        then Push(S, i) and set $i \leftarrow i + 1$
        else Pop(S).

Algorithm 3.6   Graham Scan, Version B.

stack contains two consecutive hull corners, which guarantee correct operation of the loop.

3.5.4. Pseudocode, Version B

Before proceeding with implementation details, we summarize the preceding discussion with pseudocode in Algorithm 3.6 that incorporates the changes.

Loop Termination.

We have not discussed yet the details of loop termination. Is the condition $i < n$ correct, even when there are collinearities? Should it be $i \leq n$, or $i < n - 1$? First, note that we need to let the algorithm reach $i = n - 1$, so that p_{n-1} can trigger the deletion of any points collinear with the (p_{n-1}, p_0) hull edge, such as p_{17} in Figure 3.7. Note also that our decision on sorting ties implies that all these collinear points will have index smaller than $n - 1$. Once p_{n-1} is pushed on the stack, we are assured of being finished, so the loop stopping condition is indeed $i < n$. However, note that because the bottom element on the stack is p_{n-1}, it appears twice on the final stack. This is easily corrected by one final stack pop.

I hope the reader appreciates the delicacy of making this simple algorithm work correctly in all cases.

3.5.5. Implementation of Graham's Algorithm

We now describe an implementation of Algorithm 3.6. We assume the input points are given with integer coordinates, and we insist on avoiding all floating-point calculations so that a correct output can be guaranteed. We will see that this can only be guaranteed if the coordinates are not too large, but with that caveat aside, the implementation yields the correct hull. We start with data structures, then tackle the sorting step, and finally present the code.

Data Representation

The input points are stored in an integer array P: P[0],...,P[n-1] corresponding to $p_0, \ldots, p_{n-1}$. We can use the data types we defined for polygons in Chapter 1 for this purpose: see Code 3.1. The reason for making P global will be discussed under "Sorting" below.[12]

The stack is most naturally represented by a singly-linked list of cells, each of which "contains" a point. Since the array of points will remain fixed after sorting, we can use array indices to represent points: see Code 3.2.

With these definitions, the stack top can be declared as tStack top; then the point on top of the stack has index top->i, and the element under the top is top->next.

```
#define X           0              /* Coordinate index */
#define Y           1              /* Coordinate index */
#define DIM         2              /* Dimension of points */
#define PMAX        1000           /* Max # of points in polygon */


typedef int        tPointi[DIM];     /* type integer point */
typedef tPointi    tPolygoni[PMAX];  /* type integer polygon */


static  tPolygoni      P;       /* global so Compare can access it. */
```

Code 3.1   Basic type definitions

```
typedef struct tCell *tStack
struct tCell {
        int        i;
        tStack     next;
};
```

Code 3.2   struct tCell

We need four stack manipulation routines: Push, Pop, PrintStack, and GetCell. All are straightforward, but since this is our first use of linked lists in this book, we will discuss them in perhaps more detail than they deserve. The stack top is head of the list, as shown in Figure 3.8a. Push links a new element to the head (Code 3.3), as shown in Figure 3.8b, and Pop removes the top element and returns its storage to the system with the library function free (Code 3.4). Note that Push and Pop return a pointer to the top of the stack, and so are used in assignments: e.g., top=Pop(top). PrintStack prints the top element and recursively the remainder of the stack (Code 3.5). Finally,

[12]The static declaration limits the scope to the use of functions in this file, e.g., Compare below.

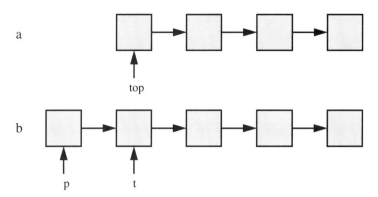

FIGURE 3.8   Stack is implemented as a list of cells.

```
/ *
        Pushes cell p on top of stack t, and returns new top.
* /
tStack   Push( tStack t, tStack p )
{
        p->next = t;
        return p;
}
```

Code 3.3   Push

```
/ *
        Pops off top element of stack p, frees up the cell, and
        returns new top.
* /
tStack   Pop( tStack p )
{
        tStack top;

        top = p->next;
        free( (void *) p );
        return top;
}
```

Code 3.4   Pop

```
/*
                Prints the stack, both point index and point coordinates.
*/
void    PrintStack( tStack t )
{
        if (t)   {
                printf("i=%d:", t->i);
                PrintPoint( P[t->i] );
                putchar( '\n' );
                PrintStack( t->next );
        }
}
```

Code 3.5 `PrintStack`

```
/*
                GetCell returns a pointer to a newly allocated piece of storage
                of type tCell, or exits of no space is available.
*/
tStack  GetCell( void )
{
        tStack p;

        p = (tStack) malloc( sizeof( struct tCell ) );

        if (p == NULL) {
                printf("Error in GetCell: Out of memory!\n");
                exit(1);
        }
        else    return p;
}
```

Code 3.6 `GetCell`

`GetCell` allocates a new piece of storage with the library function `malloc` (Code 3.6).

Sorting

`FindLowest`. We first dispense with the easiest aspect of the sorting step: finding the rightmost lowest point in the set. The function `FindLowest` accomplishes this, and swaps the point into `P[0]`: Code 3.7.

Avoiding Floats. The sorting step seems straightforward, but there are hidden pitfalls if we want to guarantee an accurate sort. First a bit of notation. Let

```
/ *
            FindLowest finds the rightmost lowest point and swaps with 0-th.
            The lowest point has the min y-coord, and amongst those, the
            max x-coord: so it is rightmost among the lowest.
* /
void    FindLowest( int n, tPolygoni P )
{
        int       i;
        int       m;              / * Index of lowest so far. * /
        tPointi   low;            / * To hold point when swapping. * /

        m = 0;
        for ( i = 1; i<n; i++ )
                if ( (P[i][Y] < P[m][Y]) ||
                    ((P[i][Y] == P[m][Y]) &&
                    (P[i][X] > P[m][X]))
                    )
                         m = i
        / * Swap. * /
        PointAssign( low,  P[m] );
        PointAssing( P[m], P[0] );
        PointAssign( P[0], low  );
}
```

Code 3.7 `FindLowest`. `PointAssign` is defined in Code 1.19.

$r_i = p_i - p_0$, the vector from p_0 to p_i. Our goal is to give a precise calculation to determine when $p_i < p_j$, where " $<$ " represents the sorting relation.

Atan2. The obvious choice is to define $p_i < p_j$ if $\text{angle}(r_i) < \text{angle}(r_j)$, where $\text{angle}(r)$ is the counterclockwise angle of r from the positive x-axis. See Figure 3.9. (We will discuss tie breaking later.) Since p_0 is lowest, all these angles are in the range $(0, \pi]$, which is convenient since sorting positive and negative

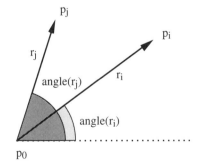

FIGURE 3.9 Notation for sorting angle.

angles can be tricky. C provides precisely the desired function: angle(r) = atan2(r[Y], r[X]). So why not use it?

- It requires a conversion from ints to doubles, as that is the type demanded by atan2. This conversion could be inaccurate if the machine allocates more bits to the int type than it does to the mantissa of the double type. For then several distinct ints would have to map to the same double.

- Even assuming the int to double conversion is accurate, there is no guarantee that the arctangent computation is accurate.

- The arctangent is a complicated function: slopes are simpler and serve the same purpose.

Slopes. For r in the first quadrant (i.e., both coordinates positive), the slope r[Y] / r[X] can substitute for the arctangent, and in the second quadrant, we could use (-r[X]) / r[Y]. Although a simpler calculation than atan2, this approach suffers from several of the same weaknesses. An example should suffice to illustrate the point.

Clearly if $r_i = cr_j$, where c is some positive number, we want to conclude that angle(r_i) = angle(r_j), and then fall into our tie-breaking code. If we are using slopes, this amounts to requiring that $a/b = (ca)/(cb)$, which is of course true mathematically. But it may come as a shock to realize that this equality is not guaranteed to hold for floating-point division in C. It depends on the machine. In particular, on a Cray Y-MP/4, the following evaluates to FALSE: 1.0/1.0 == 3.0/3.0. The reason is that the Cray performs division by reciprocating and multiplying, and the two operations sometimes lead to small errors. Here 3.0/3.0 == 0.999999999999996.[13]

The lesson is clear: any floating-point calculation might be in error on some machine whose C compiler and libraries fully meet specifications. This is why we insist on integer computation whenever possible.

Left. The impatient reader will have realized long ago that the solution is already in hand: Left, the function to determine whether a point is left of a line determined by two other points, is precisely what we need to compare r_i and r_j. In addition we implemented this entirely with integer computations in Chapter 1. Recall that Left was itself a simple test on the value of Area2, which computes the signed area of the triangle determined by three points. We will use this area function rather than Left, as it is then easier to distinguish ties.

As we mentioned before (Section 1.4.8), Area2 itself is "flawed" in that standard C gives no error on integer overflow, which could occur in the calculation if the input coordinates are large with respect to the machine word size. This point will be revisited in Chapter 4, Section 4.3.5, but it is worth

---

[13]I am indebted to Dik T. Winter for this example (Winter, 1991).

noting the nearly scandalous situation faced by almost all existent C code[14] that performs geometric computations: if the code uses floating-point calculations, it may rely on machine-dependent features, whereas if the code uses integer calculations only, it is not guaranteed to work correctly unless the size of the integers is severely restricted. My suspicion is that the vast majority of code for geometric algorithms is faulty for these reasons.

Inherently faulty C algorithms

We first discuss the overall sorting method before showing how `Area2` is employed for comparisons.

Qsort. The standard C library includes a sorting routine `qsort` that is at least as good as most programmers could develop on their own, and it makes sense to use it. Because it is general, however, it takes a bit of effort to set it up properly. The routine requires information on the shape and location of the data, and a comparison function to compare keys. It then uses the provided comparison function to sort the data in place.

Here is the manual entry on `qsort`:

```
Name
    qsort-quicker sort

Syntax
    #include <stdlib.h>

    void qsort(base, nel, width, compar)
    void *base;
    sizet nel, width;
    int (*compar)();

 Description
    The qsort subroutine is an implementation of the
    quicker-sort algorithm. The first argument is a
    pointer to the base of the data; the second is the
    number of elements; the third is the width of an
    element in bytes; the last is the name of the
    comparison routine to be called with two arguments
    which are pointers to the elements being compared.
    The routine must return an integer less than, equal
    to, or greater than 0 according as the first argument
    is to be considered less than, equal to, or greater
    than the second.
```

This entry neglects to mention the routine sorts from smallest to largest.

In our case, the data is stored in the array P, and we want to sort $n-1$ points, from P[1] to P[n-1]. So we call qsort as in Code 3.8.

---

[14]This is true of many other languages as well, including any language that uses a fixed word size to represent either integers or floating-point numbers.

```
qsort(
                (void *) P[1],       /* base: pointer to 1st elem */
                n-1,                 /* count: # of elems */
                sizeof( tPointi ),   /* size of each elem */
                Compare              /* -1, 0, +1 compare fnc */
      );
```

Code 3.8 `qsort`

`Compare`. The comparison function presents a slight technical problem: it is designed to take as input (pointers to) two elements to compare, but we need three inputs: p_0, p_i, and p_j. One way around this difficulty is to compute a separate array filled with the r_i's. Here we opt for another solution:[15] we make P global. Then p_0 can be referenced inside the body of `Compare` without passing it as a parameter.

Finally, we can specify the heart of `Compare`: if p_j is left of the directed line through $p_0 p_i$, then $p_i < p_j$. In other words, $p_i < p_j$ if `Area2( P[0], P[i], P[j] ) > 0`. (See Figure 3.9.) In this case, `qsort` expects a return of −1 to indicate "less than." When the area is 0, we need to compute the lengths of r_i and r_j to determine which is less.

```
/*
             Compare: returns -1, 0, +1 if p1 < p2, =, or > respectively;
             here " < " means smaller angle. Follows the conventions of qsort.
*/
int     Compare( tPointi *p1, tPointi *p2 )
{
        int        a;               /* area */
        tPointi    r1, r2;          /* ri = pi - p0 */
        int        L1, L2;          /* length of r1 & r2 */
        a = Area2( P[0], *p1, *p2 );
        if (a > 0)
                return -1;
        else if (a < 0)
                return 1;
        else{
                SubVec( *p1, P[0], r1 );
                SubVec( *p2, P[0], r2 );
                L1 = Length2( r1 );
                L2 = Length2( r2 );
                return (L1 < L2) ? -1 : (L1 > L2) ? 1 : 0;
        }
}
```

Code 3.9 `Compare`.

[15]I thank Michael Baldwin for this suggestion.

```
main()
{
        int     n;
        tStack  top;

        n = ReadPoints( P );
        FindLowest( n, P );
        qsort(
                (void *) P[1],          / * base: pointer to 1st elem * /
                n-1,                    / * count: # of elems * /
                sizeof( tPointi ),      / * size of each elem * /
                Compare                 / * −1, 0, +1 compare fnc * /
        );

        top = Graham( n, P );
        printf("Hull:\n");
        PrintStack( top );
}
```

Code 3.10 `main`.

The code for `Compare` is in Code 3.9. The vector functions `SubVec` and `Length2` are in the appendix (Section 3.10) to this chapter: Code 3.13 and 3.15.

`main`. Now that we have the low-level details worked out, we can present `main` (Code 3.10). The points are read in with `ReadPoints` (Code 1.21), the lowest point swapped with `P[0]` with `FindLowest`, the other points sorted by angle with `qsort`, and finally, Graham's algorithm is applied with a function `Graham`, which returns the final stack, the hull.

Code for the Graham Scan
The code for the Graham scan is a nearly direct translation of the pseudocode presented earlier (Algorithm 3.6); see Code 3.12. We make one small modular-

```
/ *
        Get a cell, fill it with i, and push it onto the stack.
        Return pointer to stack top.
* /
tStack  GetPush( int i, tStack top )
{
        tStack p;
        p = GetCell();
        p->i = i;
        return Push( top, p );
}
```

Code 3.11 `GetPush`.

```
/ *
            Performs the Graham scan on an array of angularly sorted points P.
* /
tStack   Graham( int n, tPolygoni P )
{
         int      i;                     / * Loop index * /
         tStack   top;                   / * Stack * /

         / * Initialize stack to (P[n – 1], P[0]. * /
         top = NULL;
         top = GetPush ( n-1, top );
         top = GetPush ( 0, top );

         / * Bottom two elements will never be removed. * /
         i=1;

         while (i  < n ) {
                 if ( Left( P[ (top->next)->i],
                         P[ top->i ],P[ i ] ) ) {
                       top = GetPush ( i, top );
                       i++;
                 }
                 else     top = Pop( top );
         }
         / * P[n – 1] pushed twice, so pop it off. * /
         return Pop(top);
}
```

Code 3.12 Graham.

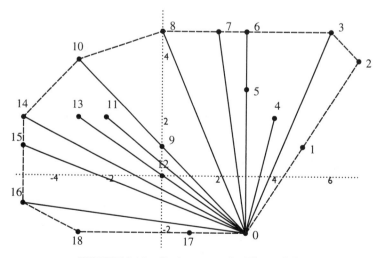

FIGURE 3.10 Graham scan for Figure 3.7.

ity savings with `GetPush` (Code 3.11): since every `Push` is preceded by a call to `GetCell`, they are merged into one function to streamline the code a bit.

Example

The example in Figure 3.10 (a repeat of Figure 3.7) was designed[16] to be a stringent test of the algorithm, as it includes collinearities of all types. The points after angular sorting are as follows (presented in two columns):

i	x	y		i	x	y
0	3	-2		10	-3	4
1	5	1		11	-2	2
2	7	4		12	0	0
3	6	5		13	-3	2
4	4	2		14	-5	2
5	3	3		15	-5	1
6	3	5		16	-5	-1
7	2	5		17	1	-2
8	0	5		18	-3	-2
9	0	1				

The indices shown accord with the labels in Figure 3.10.

Below is shown the stack (point indices only) and the value of i at the top of the `while` loop. The stack is initialized to $(0, 18)$, where the top is shown leftmost (the opposite of our earlier convention). Point p_1 is added to form $(1, 0, 18)$, but then p_2 causes p_1 to be deleted, and so on. Note that p_{18} causes the deletion of p_{17} when $i = 18$, as it should. For this example, the total number of iterations is $29 < 2 \cdot n = 2 \cdot 19 = 38$.

```
i=  1:    0,  18
i=  2:    1,  0,  18
i=  2:    0,  18
i=  3:    2,  0,  18
i=  4:    3,  2,  0,  18
i=  5:    4,  3,  2,  0,  18
i=  5:    3,  2,  0,  18
i=  6:    5,  3,  2,  0,  18
i=  6:    3,  2,  0,  18
i=  7:    6,  3,  2,  0,  18
i=  7:    3,  2,  0,  18
i=  8:    7,  3,  2,  0,  18
i=  8:    3,  2,  0,  18
i=  9:    8,  3,  2,  0,  18
i=10:    9,  8,  3,  2,  0,  18
```

[16]Designed by Jennifer Ripple.

```
i=10:     8,  3,  2,  0,  18
i=11:    10,  8,  3,  2,  0,  18
i=12:    11, 10,  8,  3,  2,  0,  18
i=13:    12, 11, 10,  8,  3,  2,  0,  18
i=13:    11, 10,  8,  3,  2,  0,  18
i=13:    10,  8,  3,  2,  0,  18
i=14:    13, 10,  8,  3,  2,  0,  18
i=14:    10,  8,  3,  2,  0,  18
i=15:    14, 10,  8,  3,  2,  0,  18
i=16:    15, 14, 10,  8,  3,  2,  0,  18
i=16:    14, 10,  8,  3,  2,  0,  18
i=17:    16, 14, 10,  8,  3,  2,  0,  18
i=18:    17, 16, 14, 10,  8,  3,  2,  0,  18
i=18:    16, 14, 10,  8,  3,  2,  0,  18,
i=19:    18, 16, 14, 10,  8,  3,  2,  0,  18
```

After popping off the redundant copy of p_{18}, we have the precise hull we seek: $(0, 2, 3, 8, 10, 14, 16, 18)$.

3.5.6. Conclusion

We summarize in a theorem.

Theorem 3.5.1. *The convex hull of n points in the plane can be found by Graham's algorithm in $O(n \log n)$ time: $O(n \log n)$ for sorting and no more than $2n$ iterations for the scan. His algorithm can be implemented entirely with integer arithmetic.*

3.5.7. Exercises

1. *Not all points distinct.* Will the presented code work if not all input points are distinct?
2. *All points collinear.* What will the code output if all input points are collinear?
3. *Best case.* How many iterations of the scan's `while` loop (in Algorithm 3.6) occur if the input points are all on the hull?
14. *Worst case.* Construct a set of points for each n that causes the largest number of iterations of the `while` loop of the scan (in Algorithm 3.6).

3.6. LOWER BOUND

Having presented an $O(n \log n)$ algorithm to construct the convex hull, the next question is: can we do better? It seems at least feasible that $O(n)$ might be possible. We show in this section that this is in fact *not* possible: $n \log n$ is a "lower bound" on the complexity of any algorithm that finds the hull. This is our first encounter with lower bounds, so we will proceed slowly.

Let us first review the meaning of a time complexity upper bound from Section 1.6.4, adding a bit more technical detail. $O(f(n))$, where $f(n)$ is some function of n (e.g., n^2), is a set of functions whose growth rate is ultimately bound above by some constant times $f(n)$. Formally, the set $O(f(n))$ can be defined as:

$$O(f(n)) = \{g(n)\colon \exists c \text{ and } \exists n_0 \text{ such that } |g(n)| \leq cf(n)\ \forall n > n_0\}.\quad (3.1)$$

In words: $O(f(n))$ is the set of all functions g such that there is a constant c and an integer n_0 so that the absolute value of $g(n)$ is bounded above by c times $f(n)$ for all n larger than n_0.

The concept of a lower bound is very similar, with of course the sense of inequality reversed. $\Omega(f(n))$ is defined to be the set of all functions g such that there is a constant c such that the absolute value of $g(n)$ is bounded below by c times $f(n)$. For technical reasons, that will not concern us, the definition of Ω replaces the $n > n_0$ condition with the weaker requirement that the inequality must hold "infinitely often":

$$\Omega(f(n)) = \{g(n)\colon \exists c \text{ such that } |g(n)| \geq cf(n) \text{ infinitely often}\}.\quad (3.2)$$

What we seek to show is that the time complexity of any algorithm that constructs the convex hull is in the set $\Omega(n \log n)$; this often is abbreviated by saying that hull construction has a lower bound of $\Omega(n \log n)$.

Unfortunately, researchers in computer science have found it fiendishly difficult to establish nontrivial lower bounds for problems. The difficulty is that the lower bound must hold for *any* conceivable algorithm, and it is hard to capture all algorithms in a proof. Nevertheless, this has been accomplished for a few key problems, notably sorting: $\Omega(n \log n)$ is a lower bound for sorting n elements.[17] Once a lower bound for one problem has been established, lower bounds for other problems can be proved via "problem reduction."

Suppose problem A is known to have some particular lower bound. One can view this as knowing that problem A is "hard" to the degree exhibited by the lower bound. So, if A has a lower bound of $\Omega(n^4)$, it is a rather hard problem. Now suppose problem A can be *reduced* to problem B, in the sense that an algorithm for solving problem B can be used to solve problem A (with little additional work). A has been reduced to B in the sense that if we can solve B quickly, we can solve A quickly.[18] This often leads to a lower bound on B, since if we could solve B too quickly, the known lower bound on A would be violated.

This is how we establish a lower bound on constructing the hull: we show that if we had a fast algorithm for the hull, we could sort faster than $O(n \log n)$; but this is known to be impossible.

---

[17]This statement is imprecise as it stands, and it would take us far too far afield to make it airtight. Suffice it to say that the model of computation only permits comparisons between the input numbers, and the lower bound is on the number of such comparisons necessary.

[18]It is a frequent confusion of algorithm novices to assimilate this definition backwards and to say mistakenly that B is reduced to A.

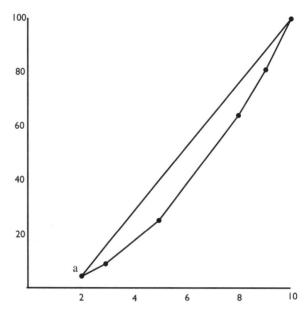

FIGURE 3.11 Parabola construction for sorting $(2, 3, 5, 8, 9, 10)$.

The original method of sorting using the hull is due to Shamos (1978), and is quite simple. Suppose we are given an unsorted list of numbers to be sorted, $(x_1, x_2, \ldots, x_n)$, $x_i \geq 0$ $\forall i$; this is problem A. Second, suppose we have an algorithm B that constructs the convex hull (as a convex polygon) of n points in $T(n)$ time. Now our task is to use B to solve A in time $T(n) + O(n)$, where the additional $O(n)$ represents the time to convert the solution of B to a solution of A.

Form a set of two dimensional points (x_i, x_i^2), as shown in Figure 3.11. These points fall on a parabola. Run algorithm B to construct the hull. Clearly, every point is on the hull. Identify the lowest point a on the hull in $O(n)$ time; this corresponds to the smallest x_i. The order in which the points occur on the hull counterclockwise from a is their sorted order. Thus, we can use a hull algorithm to sort.

Note that it is crucial for this reduction that algorithm B yields the vertices of the hull in order around the boundary. It is not at all clear how to perform a similar reduction from sorting to the problem of identifying the extreme points of the hull, which could be output in arbitrary order. It remained an open problem for several years to determine if finding extreme points was easier, but the work of several researchers finally established that $\Omega(n \log n)$ is a lower bound on this problem also.[19]

---

[19]See (Preparata and Shamos 1985, pp. 101–103).

Algorithm: INCREMENTAL   ALGORITHM
Let $H_2 \leftarrow \text{conv}\{p_0, p_1, p_2\}$.
for $k = 3$ to $n - 1$ do
    $H_k \leftarrow \text{conv}\{H_{k-1} \cup p_k\}$

Algorithm 3.7   Incremental.

3.7.   INCREMENTAL ALGORITHM

Having arrived at an optimal $O(n \log n)$ algorithm (Section 3.5), it may seem there is no point in exploring additional algorithms. However, there is motivation: extension to three (and higher) dimensions. The convex hull is if anything more useful in three dimensions than in two, and we will spend the next chapter exploring two algorithms for constructing three-dimensional hulls. The difficulty is that Graham's algorithm has no obvious extension to three dimensions: it depends crucially on angular sorting, which has no direct counterpart in three dimensions. So we now proceed to describe two further algorithms in two dimensions, each of which extends to three dimensions.

The first algorithm is one of the most straightforward imaginable: the incremental algorithm. Its basic plan is simple: add the points one at a time, at each step constructing the hull of the first k points, and using that hull to incorporate the next point. It turns out that "factoring" the problem this way simplifies it greatly, in that we only have to deal with one very special case: adding a single point to an existing hull.

Let our set of points be $P = \{p_0, p_1, \ldots, p_{n-1}\}$, and assume for simplicity of exposition that the points are in general position: no three are collinear. The high-level structure is shown in Algorithm 3.7.

The first hull is the triangle $\text{conv}\{p_0, p_1, p_2\}$. Let $Q = H_{k-1}$ and $p = p_k$. The problem of computing $\text{conv}\{Q \cup p\}$ naturally falls into two cases, depending on whether $p \in Q$, or $p \notin Q$.[20]

1. $p \in Q$. Of course, once p is determined to be in Q, it can be discarded. Note that we can discard p even if it is on the boundary of Q. Although there are several ways to decide if $p \in Q$, perhaps the most robust is to use LeftOn from Chapter 1 (Code 1.5): $p \in Q$ iff p is left of or on every directed edge.[21] Clearly this test takes time linear in the number of vertices of Q.

2. $p \notin Q$. If any LeftOn test returns false, then $p \notin Q$, and we have to compute $\text{conv}\{Q \cup p\}$. What makes this task relatively easy is that we need only find the two lines of tangency from p to Q, as shown in

---

[20] We could ensure that $p \notin Q$ by presorting the p's by x-coordinate (for example), as suggested by Edelsbrunner (1987, p. 143). See Exercise 3.7.1[3].

[21] Note that this method only works for convex Q, which is all we need. More general point-in-polygon algorithms will be discussed in Section 7.2.

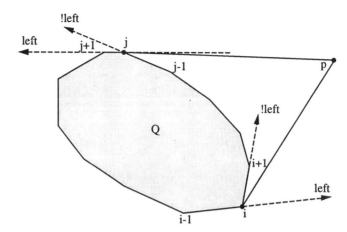

FIGURE 3.12 Tangent lines from p to Q; "left" means that p is left of the indicated directed line, and "!left" means "not left."

Figure 3.12, and modify the hull accordingly. By our general-position assumption, each line of tangency between p and Q touches Q at just one point. Suppose p_i is one such point of tangency. How can we find p_i?

Examination of Figure 3.12 shows that we can use the results of the LeftOn tests to determine tangency: for the lower point of tangency p_i, p is left of $p_{i-1}p_i$ but right of $p_i p_{i+1}$. For the upper point of tangency p_j, the sense is reversed: p is right of $p_{j-1}p_j$ but left of $p_j p_{j+1}$. Both cases can be captured with the exclusive-or (xor) function: p_i is a point of tangency if two successive edges yield different LeftOn results (Algorithm 3.8). Thus the two points of tangency can be identified via the same series of LeftOn tests used to decide if $p \in Q$.

It only remains to form the new hull. In Figure 3.12, the new hull is

$$(p_0, p_1, \ldots, p_{i-1}, p_i, p, p_j, p_{j+1}, \ldots, p_{n-1}).$$

If the hulls are represented by linked lists, this update can be accomplished by a simple sequence of insertions and deletions.

We leave as an exercise (Exercise 3.7.1[2]) exploring how to proceed when a line of tangency from p is flush with an edge of Q.

Algorithm: TANGENT POINTS
for $i = 0$ to $n - 1$ do
    if xor(p left or on (p_{i-1}, p_i), p left or on (p_i, p_{i+1}))
        then p_i is point of tangency

Algorithm 3.8 Tangent Points.

The complexity analysis of this algorithm is simple: the work at each step is $O(n)$; more precisely, it is proportional to the number of vertices of the k-th hull. In the worst case we would have $p \notin Q$ at each step, resulting in total work proportional to $3 + 4 + \cdots + n = O(n^2)$.

It turns out that with only a little more effort, the time complexity can be reduced to $O(n \log n)$ (Exercise 3.7.1[3]).

3.7.1. Exercises

1. *Collinearities.* Modify the incremental algorithm to work with sets of points that may include three or more collinear points.

2. *Degenerate tangents.* Modify the incremental algorithm as presented to output the correct hull when a tangent line from p includes an edge of Q. The "correct" hull should not have three collinear vertices.

3. *Optimal incremental algorithm.* Presort the points by their x-coordinate, so that $p \notin Q$ at each step. Now try to arrange the search for tangent lines in such a manner that the total work over the life of the algorithm is $O(n)$. This then provides an $O(n \log n)$ algorithm.[22]

3.8. DIVIDE AND CONQUER

The final two-dimensional hull algorithm we consider achieves optimal $O(n \log n)$ time by a method completely different than Graham's algorithm: divide and conquer. This is the only technique known to extend to three dimensions and achieve the same asymptotically optimal $O(n \log n)$ time complexity. It is therefore well worth studying, even though in two dimensions it is relatively complicated.

3.8.1. Divide-and-Conquer Recurrence Relation

"Divide and conquer" is a general paradigm for solving problems that has proved very effective in computer science. The essence is to partition the problem into two (nearly) equal halves, solve each half recursively, and create a full solution by "merging" the two half solutions. When the recursion reduces the original problem down to very small subproblems, they are usually quite easy to solve. All the work therefore lies in the merge step.

Let $T(n)$ be the time complexity of a divide and conquer hull algorithm for n points. If the merge step can be accomplished in linear time, we have the recurrence relation $T(n) = 2T(n/2) + O(n)$: the two problems of half size take $2T(n/2)$ time, and the merge takes $O(n)$ time. As we mentioned before, this has solution $O(n \log n)$. Because of the importance of divide and conquer, and this recurrence relation in particular, we will take time out to explain why it has a solution of $O(n \log n)$. Those familiar with this material can skip to Section 3.8.2.

---

[22] This idea is due to Edelsbrunner (1987, p. 144).

The reasoning is easiest to see when n is a power of 2; so let $n = 2^k$, so that $k = \log n$. Now we repeatedly expand $T(n) = T(2^k)$ according to the recurrence relation $T(n) = 2T(n/2) + cn$. Note that $O(n)$ has been replaced by cn for specificity.

$$T(2^k) = 2T(2^{k-1}) + c2^k \tag{3.3}$$

$$T(2^{k-1}) = 2T(2^{k-2}) + c2^{k-1} \tag{3.4}$$

$$T(2^k) = 4T(2^{k-2}) + 2c2^{k-1} + c2^k \tag{3.5}$$

$$= 4T(2^{k-2}) + 2c2^k \tag{3.6}$$

$$T(2^{k-2}) = 2T(2^{k-3}) + c2^{k-2} \tag{3.7}$$

$$T(2^k) = 8T(2^{k-3}) + 4c2^{k-2} + 2c2^k \tag{3.8}$$

$$= 8T(2^{k-3}) + 3c2^k \tag{3.9}$$

$$\cdots \tag{3.10}$$

$$T(2^k) = 2^m(2^{k-m}) + mc2^k. \tag{3.11}$$

Here Equation 3.6 is Equation 3.3 after substitution of Equation 3.4 and simplification from Equation 3.5, and so on. So, if we expand m times, we get Equation 3.11: $T(2^k) = 2^m(2^{k-m}) + mc2^k$. Letting $m = k$, this reduces to $T(2^k) = 2^k + ck2^k$; recalling that $2^k = n$ and $k = \log n$, we have $T(n) = n + cn \log n$, which is $O(n \log n)$.

It is useful to view the repeated expansion of the recurrence formula as the growth of a binary tree, shown in Figure 3.13. Now look at the merge work at

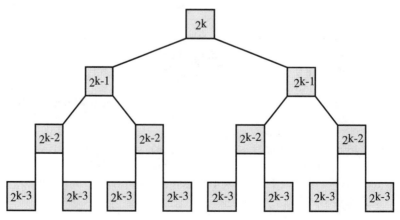

FIGURE 3.13   Divide-and-conquer expansion tree.

each level of the tree. Merging the two children of the root takes time $cn = c2^k$, because the total number of vertices is at most n. Merging to produce those children takes time $c2^{k-1}$ each, because there are at most $n/2$ vertices each; since there are two merges, the total work is $2(c2^{k-1}) = cn$. Merging to get the four children at depth two of the tree takes $4(c2^{k-2}) = cn$. And so on: the merge work at each level is cn independent of the level, since the number of merges is exactly compensated by the reduction in size of each merge. The total number of levels of the tree is $k = \log n$, the number of times n can be halved before reaching 1. So, the total work is the number of levels times the work per level: $(\log n)(cn) = O(n \log n)$. Exercises 3.8.4[1] and [2] ask for exploration of the recurrence relation when the merge step is less efficient; the conclusion is that the merge must be $O(n)$ to achieve optimality.

3.8.2. Algorithm Description

The divide and conquer technique was first applied to the convex hull problem by Preparata and Hong, (1977), whose goal was an efficient algorithm for three dimensions. To keep the explanation simple, we assume two types of nondegeneracy: no three points are collinear, and no two points lie on a vertical line. The outline of their algorithm is as follows:

1. Sort the points by x coordinate.
2. Divide the points into two sets $\mathscr{A}$ and $\mathscr{B}$, $\mathscr{A}$ containing the left $\lceil n/2 \rceil$ points, and $\mathscr{B}$ the right $\lfloor n/2 \rfloor$ points.
3. Compute the convex hulls $A = \mathscr{H}(\mathscr{A})$ and $B = \mathscr{H}(\mathscr{B})$ recursively.
4. Merge A and B: compute conv$\{A \cup B\}$.

The sorting step (1) guarantees the sets $\mathscr{A}$ and $\mathscr{B}$ will be separated by a vertical line (by our assumption that no two points lie on a vertical), which in turn guarantees that A and B will not overlap. This simplifies the merge step. Steps 2, 3, and 4 are repeated at each level of the recursion, stopping when $n \leq 3$; if $n = 3$ the hull is a triangle by our assumption of noncollinearity.

All of the work in this divide-and-conquer algorithm is in the merge step. For this algorithm, it is tricky to merge in linear time: the most naive algorithm would only achieve $O(n^2)$, which as we mentioned is not sufficient to yield $O(n \log n)$ performance overall.

We will use a and b as indices of vertices of A and B respectively, with the vertices of each ordered counterclockwise and numbered from 0. All index arithmetic is modulo the number of vertices in the relevant polygon, so that expressions like $a + 1$ and $a - 1$ can be interpreted as the next and previous vertices around A's boundary, respectively. The goal is to find two tangent lines, one supporting the two hulls from below, and one supporting from above. From these tangents, conv$\{A \cup B\}$ is easily constructed in $O(n)$ time. We will only discuss finding the lower tangent; the upper tangent can be found analogously.

Let the lower tangent be $T = ab$. The difficulty is that neither endpoint of T is known ahead of time, so a search has to move on both A and B. Note that

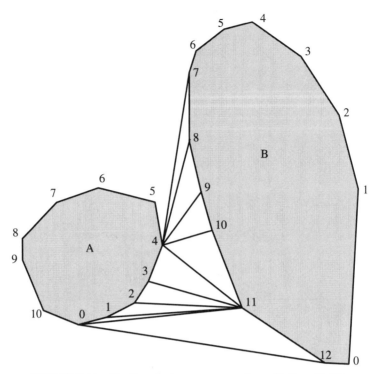

FIGURE 3.14 Finding the lower tangent: from $(4, 7)$ to $(0, 12)$.

the task in the incremental algorithm was considerably easier because only one end of the tangent was unknown, the other being a single point. Now a naive search for all possible a endpoints and all possible b endpoints would result in a worst-case quadratic merge step, which is inadequate. So the search must be more delicate.

The idea of Preparata and Hong is to start T connecting the rightmost point of A to the leftmost point of B, and then to "walk" it downward, first advancing on one hull, then on the other, alternating until the lower tangent is reached. See Figure 3.14. Pseudocode is displayed in Algorithm 3.9. Note that

---

Algorithm: LOWER TANGENT

$a \leftarrow$ rightmost point of A.
$b \leftarrow$ leftmost point of B.
while $T = ab$ not lower tangent to both A and B do
    while T not lower tangent to A do
        $a \leftarrow a - 1$
    while T not lower tangent to B do
        $b \leftarrow b + 1$

Algorithm 3.9 Lower tangent.

$a - 1$ is clockwise on A, and $b + 1$ is counterclockwise on B, both representing downward movements. $T = ab$ is a lower tangent at a if both $a - 1$ and $a + 1$ lie above T; this is equivalent to saying that both of these points are left or on ab. A similar definition holds for lower tangency to B. Again we assume for simplicity of exposition that lines are always tangent at a point, rather than along an edge.

An example is shown in Figure 3.14. Initially, $T = (4, 7)$; note that T is tangent to both A and B, but is only a lower tangent for A. The A loop does not execute, but the B loop increments b to 11, at which time $T = (4, 11)$ is a lower tangent for B. But now T is no longer a lower tangent for A, so the A loop decrements a to 0; now $T = (0, 11)$ is a lower tangent for A. This is not a lower tangent for B, so b is incremented to 12. Now $T = (0, 12)$ is a lower tangent for both A and B, and the algorithm stops. Note that $b = 12$ is not the lowest vertex of B: 0 is slightly lower.

3.8.3. Analysis

Neither the time complexity nor the correctness of the hull-merging algorithm are evident. Certainly when the outermost while loop terminates, T is tangent to both A and B. However, two issues remain:

1. The outer loop must terminate: it is conceivable that establishing tangency at a always breaks tangency at b and vice versa.

2. There are four mutual tangents (see Figure 3.15), and the algorithm as written should only find one, the one that supports both A and B to its left.

Lemma 3.8.1.   *The lower tangent $T = ab$ touches both A and B on their lower halves: both a and b lie on the closed chain from the leftmost vertex counterclockwise to the rightmost vertex, of A and B respectively.*

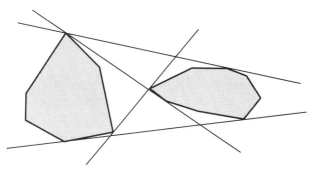

FIGURE 3.15   Four mutual tangents.

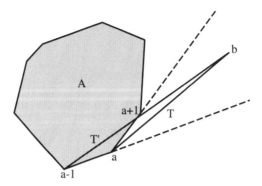

FIGURE 3.16   If T' intersects A, then t must be a lower tangent at a.

Proof. This is a consequence of the horizontal separation of A and B. Let L be a vertical line separating them. Then if B is very high above A, T approaches being parallel to L, and a approaches the rightmost vertex of A. Similarly if B is very low below A, a approaches the leftmost vertex of A. Between these extremes, a lies on the lower half of A.   □

Since a starts at the rightmost vertex, and is only decremented, i.e., moved clockwise, the inner A loop could only iterate infinitely if a could pass the leftmost vertex. However, the next lemma will show this is not possible.

Lemma 3.8.2.   *Throughout the life of Algorithm 3.9, ab does not meet the interior of A or of B.*

Proof. The proof is by induction. The statement is true at the start of the algorithm.

Suppose it is true after some step, and suppose that a is about to be decremented, which only happens when T is not lower tangent to A. The new tangent $T' = (a - 1, b)$ could only intersect the interior of A if b is left of $(a - 1, a)$; see Figure 3.16. But b could not also be left of $(a, a + 1)$, for then T would have intersected A, which we assumed by induction was not the case. So, if the next step would cause intersection, T must be tangent at a, and the next step would not be taken.   □

Now because T does not meet the interior of A, and because b is right of L (the line separating A and B), a cannot advance (clockwise) beyond the leftmost vertex of A. Similar reasoning applies to B. Therefore both loops must terminate eventually, since they each move the indices in one direction only, and there is a limit to how far the indices can move. Now everything we need for correctness follows. Because the loops terminate, they must terminate with double tangency, which clearly must be the lower tangent.

The loops can only take linear time, since they only advance, never back up, and the number of steps is therefore limited by the number of vertices of A and B. Therefore, the merge step is linear, which implies that the entire algorithm is $O(n \log n)$.

3.8.4. Exercises

1. *Recurrence relation with $O(n^2)$ merge.* Solve the recurrence relation $T(n) = 2T(n/2) + O(n^2)$.

2. *Recurrence relation with $O(n \log n)$ merge.* Solve the recurrence relation $T(n) = 2T(n/2) + O(n \log n)$.

3. *Degeneracies.* Remove all assumptions of nondegeneracy from the divide-and-conquer algorithm by considering the following possibilities:

   a. Several points lie on the same vertical line.

   b. A tangent line T is collinear with an edge of A and/or B.

   c. The recursion bottoms out with three collinear points.

4. *Merge without sorting* (Toussaint 1986b). If the sorting step of the divide-and-conquer algorithm is skipped, the hulls to be merged might intersect. Design an algorithm that can merge two arbitrarily located hulls of n and m vertices in $O(n + m)$ time. This then provides an alternative $O(n \log n)$ divide-and-conquer algorithm.

3.9. ADDITIONAL EXERCISES

3.9.1. Polygon Hull

1. *Hull of monotone polygon.* Develop an algorithm to find the convex hull of a monotone polygon in linear time.

2. *Hull of polygon* [difficult]. Develop an algorithm to find the convex hull of an arbitrary polygon in linear time. (Note the lower bound in Section 3.6 holds for sets of unorganized points, not for the vertices of a polygon.) This is quite tricky, and several published algorithms for this problem were later discovered to be flawed.

3.9.2. Orthogonal polygons

1. *Orthogonally convex polygons: characterization.* The standard definition of a convex polygon is a polygon P for which the line segment connecting any two points in P lies entirely within P (Section 3.1[1]). This definition is equivalent to the intersection of P with any (infinite) line L having at most one connected component—it is either empty, a line segment, or a point. The only truly convex orthogonal polygon is a rectangle. However, we can generalize the second definition of convexity in a natural way to define "orthogonally convex" to include more than just the rectangle.

   Define an orthogonal polygon to be *orthogonally convex* if its intersection with any vertical or horizontal line has at most one connected component. Characterize the shape of orthogonal convex polygons. By "characterize the shape" I mean state and prove something like "an orthogonal polygon is orthogonally convex if and only if every two convex vertices have at least one reflex vertex between them, and there is

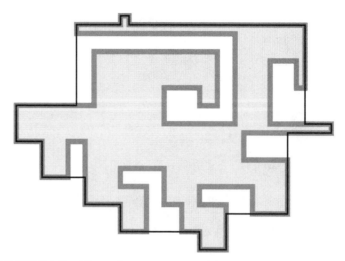

FIGURE 3.17   The orthogonal convex hull of an othogonal polygon.

one vertical edge whose length is the square root of the sum of the lengths of the horizontal edges." This is manifestly false but indicative of my intentions. Of course, the definition of orthogonal convexity itself provides a characterization: "its intersection with any vertical or horizontal line is either empty or a line segment." However, there are other ways to characterize the shape, some of which will help in 2 below.

2. *Orthogonal convex polygons: test algorithm.* Design an algorithm to test whether a given orthogonal polygon is orthogonally convex, based on your characterization in 1 above. Argue for its correctness (perhaps invoking your characterization) and analyze its time complexity as a function of *n*.

3. *Orthogonal convex hull.* Let P be an orthogonal polygon. Define the *orthogonal convex hull* $\overline{\mathscr{H}}(P)$ of an orthogonal polygon P as the smallest orthogonally convex polygon that encloses P. (See 1 above for a definition of orthogonally convex.) If P is already orthogonally convex, then $\overline{\mathscr{H}}(P) = P$. Otherwise, $\overline{\mathscr{H}}(P)$ encloses P. In the example in Figure 3.17, P is shown shaded, and $\overline{\mathscr{H}}(P)$ is shown in dark lines.

   Design an algorithm to compute $\overline{\mathscr{H}}(P)$. Assume as input a list of the coordinates of the vertices of P, given in counterclockwise order around the boundary of P. Produce as output a similar list for $\overline{\mathscr{H}}(P)$. Do *not* assume that no two edges occur on the same vertical or horizontal line: in fact most applications that produce orthogonal polygons select their vertices from an integer grid, and it is quite likely that several lie on the same grid line (as in Figure 3.17).

   Hand-execute your algorithm on at least one non-trivial example.

4. *Orthogonal star polygons: characterization.* A polygon P is *star* if there exists a point $x \in P$ that can see every point in the polygon (Exercise 1.1.4[5]). (The line of sight does not have to be vertical or horizontal: it may be at any angle.) Characterize (state and prove) the shape of *orthogonal* star polygons, star polygons comprised of horizontal and vertical edges.

5. *Orthogonal star kernels: algorithm.* The *kernel* of a star polygon is the set of all points that can see every point in the polygon. Design an algorithm for constructing the kernel of an orthogonal star polygon. Argue for its correctness (perhaps invoking your characterization) and analyze its time complexity as a function of *n*.

6. *Krasnosselsky's theorem.*[23] Characterize (state and prove) the shape of an orthogonal polygon P for which the following holds: for every two points a and b on the boundary of P, there exists a point $x \in P$ that can see both a and b. (Note that x is [or may be] dependent on a and b.)

3.9.3. Miscellaneous Hull-Related

1. *Distance between convex polygons.* Let A and B be two convex polygons. Define two distance concepts as follows:

$$\delta = \min_{x \in A, y \in B} |x - y|$$

$$\Delta = \max_{x \in A, y \in B} |x - y|$$

where $|x - y|$ is the Euclidean distance between the points x and y. Design algorithms to compute both δ and Δ. You may assume that $A \cap B = \varnothing$.

First establish a few geometric lemmas that characterize the type of points that can achieve the minimum or maximum distance. Can the points be interior to A or B, or must they be on the boundary? If the latter, must one or both be vertices, i.e., can either or both lie on the interior of an edge? The answers to these questions are not necessarily the same for both types of distance measures.

Try to achieve $O(n)$ for computing Δ and $O(\log n)$ for computing δ. The former is not that difficult, but the latter is rather tricky (Edelsbrunner, 1985) depending on the fact that the median of n numbers can be found in linear time. It is somewhat surprising that δ can be computed in less than linear time.

2. *Convex deficiency tree.* Let P be a polygon (with no holes) and $\mathscr{H}(P)$ its convex hull, where as usual both are considered closed regions in the plane. Define the *convex deficiency* of P, $D(P)$ to be the set of points $\mathscr{H}(P) - P$, that is, the set difference between the hull and the polygon.[24] In general this set will have several disconnected components, which I will call *bays*. Each of these bays has the shape of a polygon, as shown in Figure 3.18b. Technically these are partially "open" sets, because portions of their boundaries were subtracted away. To clean up this minor blemish, redefine D to fill in the boundaries by taking the *closure*. Let $\overline{Q}$ be the closure of Q. Then,

$$D(P) = \overline{\mathscr{H}(P) - P}.$$

Define the *deficiency tree* $T(P)$ for a polygon P as follows. The root of T is a node associated with P. The children of the root are nodes associated with the distinct connected components of $D(P)$. In general, if P' is the set of points corresponding to a node of T, the children of the node correspond to the distinct connected components of $D(P')$. Define $P(N)$ to be the parent of a node N. Define the depth of a node of T in the usual manner: the depth of the root is 0, and the depth of any node N is 1 greater than the depth of $P(N)$.

---

[23] Krasnosselsky's theorem states that for any compact set S in d dimensions containing at least $d + 1$ points, if each $d + 1$ point of S is visible to one point, then S is star-shaped (Lay 1982, p. 53).

[24] This concept was introduced by Batchelor (1980).

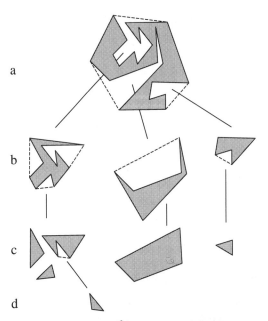

FIGURE 3.18 (*a*) P and $\mathcal{H}(P)$; (*b*) $D(\dot{P})$ and hulls; (*c*) deficiencies of polygons from (*b*); (*d*) deficiency of the one nonconvex piece from (*c*).

These exercises ask you to explore the properties of the convex deficiency tree.

a. Is $T(P)$ a tree in fact? Is it always finite for a polygon P? What if P were permitted to have curved edges?

b. Let us identify a node and its associated region, so that phrases such as "the area of a node" make sense. Is the area of a node N always less than or equal to the area of $P(N)$? Is the sum of the areas of all the children of N less than or equal to the area of N?

c. Is there any relationship between the number of vertices of N and $P(N)$, or between N and the sum of the number of vertices in all the children of N?

d. For a polygon P of n vertices, what is the maximum possible *breadth* of $T(P)$ as a function of n, i.e., what is the largest possible degree of a node? What is the maximum possible depth of $T(P)$ as a function of n? In both cases, show worst-case examples.

e. Can you write one equation that expresses the set of points represented by the root in terms of all of its descendants? Using set unions and differences of regions? Using sums and differences of areas?

f. Do two polygons with the same deficiency tree (viewed as a combinatorial object, i.e., without consideration of the specific regions associated with each node) necessarily have similar shapes? Can you find polygons with identical trees with wildly different shapes? This is an imprecise question because "shape" is left intuitive. So re-ask the questions with shape replaced by "number of vertices": must two polygons with the same deficiency tree have the same number of vertices? Is there any feature shared by the class of polygons with the same deficiency tree?

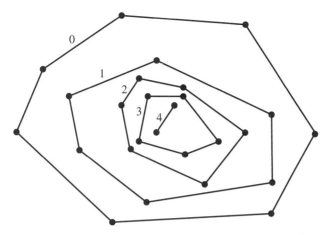

FIGURE 3.19 The onion layers of a set of points, labeled with depth numbers.

g. Can every tree be realized as the convex deficiency tree of some polygon? Given an arbitrary tree, how can you construct a representative "realizing" polygon, a polygon whose convex deficiency tree is the given tree?

h. Can the concept of deficiency tree be extended to include polygons with holes?

i. Does the concept of deficiency tree make sense for three-dimensional polyhedra? Is it a tree? Is it finite?

3. *Diameter and width.* Define the *diameter* of a set of points $\{p_0, p_1, \ldots\}$ to be the largest distance between any two points in the set: $\max_{i,j} |p_i - p_j|$.

a. Prove that the diameter of a set is achieved by two hull vertices.

b. A *line of support* to a set is a line L that touches the hull and has all points on or to one side of L. Prove that the diameter of a set is the same as the maximum distance between parallel lines of support for the set.

c. Two points a and b are called *antipodal* if they admit parallel lines of support: there are parallel lines of support through a and b. Develop an algorithm for enumerating (listing) all antipodal pairs of a set of points in two dimensions. It helps to view the lines of support as jaws of a caliper. An algorithm can be based on the idea of rotating the caliper around the set.[25]

d. Define the *width* as the minimum distance between parallel lines of support. Develop an algorithm for computing the width of a set of points in two dimensions.

4. *Onion Peeling.* Start with a finite set of points $S = S_0$ in the plane, and consider the following iterative process. Let S_1 be the set $S_0 - \partial \mathcal{H}(S_0)$: S minus all the points on the boundary of the hull of S. Similarly, define $S_{i+1} = S_i - \partial \mathcal{H}(S_i)$. The process continues until the empty set is reached. The hulls $H_i = \partial \mathcal{H}(S_i)$ are called the *layers* of the set, and the process of peeling away the layers is called *onion peeling* for obvious reasons. See Figure 3.19. Any point on H_i is said to have *onion depth*, or just *depth*, i. Thus, the points on the hull of the original set have depth 0.

a. For each n, determine the maximum number of layers for any set of n points in two dimensions.

[25]This idea is due to Toussaint (1983*b*).

b. For a polygon *P*, define its *depth sequence* to be the sequence of onion depths of its vertices (a list of integers) in a counterclockwise traversal of the boundary.[26] Express some gross constraints on the form of a depth sequence.

c. Is every sequence that meets your constraints realizable by some polygon? If not, find an unrealizable sequence. If so, provide an argument.

3.10. APPENDIX

```
/*
        Puts a − b into c.
*/
void    SubVec( tPointi a, tPointi b, tPointi c )
{
        int    i;

        for( i = 0; i < DIM; i++ )
                c[i] = a[i]-b[i];
}
```

Code 3.13 `SubVec`.

```
/*
        Returns the dot product of the two input vectors.
*/
int     Dot( tPointi a, tPointi b )
{
        int    i;
        int    sum = 0;
        for( i = 0; i < DIM; i++ )
                sum += a[i] * b[i];
        return sum;
}
```

Code 3.14 `Dot`.

```
/*
        Returns the square of the length of the vector p.
*/
int     Length2( tPointi p )
{
        return Dot( p, p );
}
```

Code 3.15 `Length2`.

---

[26]These sequences were introduced by Hernández and Serra (1992).

4

Convex Hulls in Three Dimensions

The focus of this chapter is algorithms for constructing the convex hull of a set of points in three dimensions (Section 4.2). We also touch on related issues: properties of polyhedra (Section 4.1), how to represent polyhedra (Section 4.4), and a brief exploration of higher dimensions (Section 4.5). Finally, several related topics will be explored via a series of exercises (Section 4.6). The centerpiece of the chapter is the most complex implementation in the book: code for constructing the three-dimensional hull via the incremental algorithm (Section 4.3).

4.1. POLYHEDRA

4.1.1. Introduction

A polyhedron is the natural generalization of a two-dimensional polygon to three-dimensions: it is a region of space whose boundary comprises a finite number of flat polygonal faces, any pair of which are either disjoint or meet at edges and vertices. This description is vague, and it is a surprisingly delicate task to make it capture just the right class of objects. Since our primary concern in this chapter is convex polyhedra, which are simpler than general polyhedra, we could avoid a precise definition of polyhedra, but facing the difficulties helps develop three-dimensional geometric intuition, an invaluable skill for understanding computational geometry.

We concentrate on specifying the boundary or surface of a polyhedron. It comprises three types of geometric objects: zero-dimensional vertices (points), one-dimensional edges (segments), and two-dimensional faces (polygons). It is a useful simplification to demand that the faces be *convex* polygons, which we defined to be bounded (p. 1). This is no loss of generality since any nonconvex face can be partitioned into convex ones, although we must then allow adjacent faces to be coplanar. What constitutes a valid polyhedral surface can be specified by conditions on how the components relate to one another. We impose three types of conditions: the components intersect "properly," the local topology is "proper," and the global topology is "proper." We now expand each of these constraints.

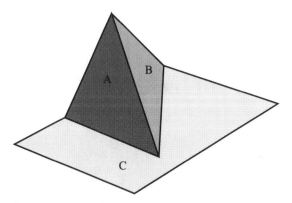

FIGURE 4.1 Faces A and B meet C improperly even though they do not penetrate C.

1. Components intersect "properly."
   For each pair of faces, we require that either

   (a) they are disjoint, or

   (b) they have a single vertex in common, or

   (c) they have two vertices, and the edge joining them, in common.

   This is where the assumption that faces are convex simplifies the conditions. Improper intersections include not only penetrating faces, but also faces touching in the "wrong" way; see Figure 4.1. There is no need to specify conditions on the intersection of edges and vertices, as the condition on faces covers them also: so an improper intersection of a pair of edges implies an improper intersection of faces.

2. Local topology is "proper."
   The local topology is what the surface looks like in the vicinity of a point. This notion has been made precise via the notion of *neighborhoods*: arbitrarily small portions (open regions) of the surface surrounding a point. We seek to exclude the three objects shown in Figure 4.2. In all three examples in that figure, there are points that have neighborhoods that are not topological two-dimensional disks. The technical way to capture the constraint is to require the neighborhoods of every point on the surface to be "homeomorphic" to a disk. A *homeomorphism* between two regions permits stretching and bending, but no tearing.[1] A fly on the surface would find the neighborhood of every point to be topologically like a disk. A surface for which this is true for every point is called a 2-*manifold*, a class more general than the boundaries of polyhedra.

---

[1]Two sets are *homeomorphic* if there is a mapping between them that is one-to-one and continuous, and whose inverse is also continuous. See, e.g., Mendelson (1990, pp. 90–91). This concept is different from a *homomorphism*.

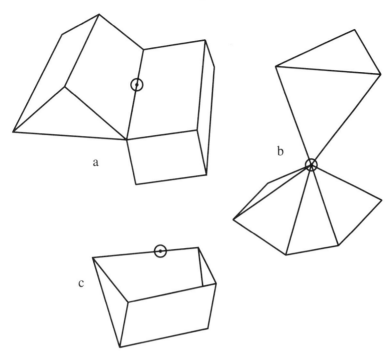

FIGURE 4.2 Three objects that are not polyhedra. In all three cases, a neighborhood of the circled point is not homeomorphic to an open disk. In (*a*) the point lies both on the top surface shown, and on a similar surface underneath. Object (*c*) is not closed, so the indicated point's neighborhood is a half-disk.

We have expressed the condition geometrically, but it is useful to view it combinatorially also. Suppose we triangulate the polygonal faces. Then every vertex is the apex of a number of triangles. Define the *link* of a vertex v to be the collection of edges opposite v in all the triangles incident to v.[2] Thus, the link is in a sense the combinatorial neighborhood of v. For a legal triangulated polyhedron, we require that the link of every vertex be a simple, closed polygonal path. The link for circled vertex in Figure 4.2*b*, for example, is not such a path.

One consequence of this condition is that every edge is shared by exactly two faces.

3. Global topology is "proper."

We would like the surface to be connected, closed, and bounded. So we require that the surface be connected in the sense that from any point, one may walk to any other on the surface. This can be stated combinatorially by requiring that the 1-*skeleton*, the graph of edges and vertices, be connected. Note this excludes, e.g., a cube with a "floating" internal

---

[2] My discussion here is indebted to that of Giblin (1977, pp. 51–53).

cubical cavity. Together with stipulating a finite number of faces, our previous conditions already imply closed and bounded, although this is perhaps not self-evident (Exercise 4.1.6[1]).

One might be inclined to rule out "holes" in the definition of polyhedron, holes in the sense of "channels" from one side of the surface to the other that do not disconnect the exterior (unlike cavities). Should a torus (a shape like a donut) be a polyhedron? We adopt the usual terminology and permit polyhedra to have an arbitrary number of such holes. The number of holes is called the *genus* of the surface. Normally, we will only consider polyhedra with genus zero: those topologically equivalent to the surface of a sphere.

To summarize: the boundary of a polyhedron is a finite collection of planar, bounded convex polygonal faces such that

1. The faces intersect properly (as in [1] above);
2. The neighborhood of every point is topologically an open disk, or (equivalently) the link of every vertex is a simple polygonal chain.
3. The surface is connected, or (equivalently) the one-skeleton is connected.

The boundary is closed and encloses a bounded region of space. Every edge is shared by exactly two faces; these faces are called *adjacent*.

Convex polyhedra are called *polytopes*, or sometimes 3-polytopes to emphasize their three-dimensionality.[3] A polytope is a polyhedron that is convex in that the segment connecting any two of its points is inside. Just as convex polygons can be characterized by a local condition on the vertex angles, polytopes can be specified locally in one of two ways:

1. The *dihedral* angles are convex: $\leq \pi$. These are the internal angles in space at an edge between the planes containing its two incident faces.
2. The sum of the face angles around each vertex are $\leq 2\pi$.

That these conditions are equivalent, and imply convexity, is not self-evident.

It is important for building intuition and testing out ideas to become intimately familiar with a few polyhedra. We therefore take time to discuss the five Platonic solids.

4.1.2. Regular Polytopes

A *regular polygon* is one with equal sides and equal angles: equilateral triangle, square, regular pentagon, regular hexagon, and so on. Clearly, there are an infinite variety of regular polygons, one for each n. It is natural to examine

---

[3]The notation in the literature is unfortunately not standardized. I define a polytope to be convex and bounded, and a polyhedron to be bounded. Some define a polytope to be bounded but permit a polyhedron to be unbounded. Some do not require a polytope to be convex. Often polytopes have arbitrary dimensions.

regular polyhedra; they are convex, so they are often called *regular polytopes*. The greatest regularity one can impose is that all faces are congruent regular polygons, and the number of faces incident to each vertex is the same for all vertices. It turns out that these conditions imply equal dihedral angles, so that need not be included in the definition.

The surprising implication of these regularity conditions is that there are only five distinct types of regular polytopes! These are known as the *Platonic solids*, since they are discussed in Plato's *Timaeus*.[4]

We now prove that there are exactly five regular polytopes. The proof is pleasingly elementary. The intuition is that the internal angles of a regular polygon grow large with the number of vertices of the polygon, but there is only so much room to pack these angles around each vertex.

Let p be the number of vertices per face; so each face is a regular p-gon. The sum of the faces angles for one p-gon is $\pi(p-2)$ (Corollary 1.2.5), so each face angle is $1/p$th of this, $\pi(1 - 2/p)$.

Let v be the number of faces meeting at a vertex. The key constraint is that the sum of the face angles meeting at a vertex is less than 2π, in order for the polyhedron to be convex.[5] This can be seen intuitively by noticing that if the polyhedron surface is flat in the vicinity of a vertex, the sum of the angles is exactly 2π; and the sum of angles at a needle-sharp vertex is quite small. So the angle sum is in the range $(0, 2\pi)$. Thus, we have v angles, each $\pi(1 - 2/p)$, which must sum to less than 2π. We transform this inequality with a series of algebraic manipulations to reach a particularly convenient form:

$$v\pi(1 - 2/p) < 2\pi \tag{4.1}$$

$$1 - 2/p < 2/v$$

$$pv < 2v + 2p$$

$$pv - 2v - 2p + 4 < 4$$

$$(p - 2)(v - 2) < 4. \tag{4.2}$$

Both p and v are of course integers. Because a polygon must have at least three sides, $p \geq 3$. It is perhaps less obvious that $v \geq 3$: at least three faces must meet at each vertex, for no "solid angle" could be formed at v with only two faces. These constraints suffice to limit the possibilities to those listed in Table 4.1 below. For example, $p = 4$ and $v = 4$ leads to $(p - 2)(v - 2) = 4$, violating the inequality: if four squares are pasted at a vertex, they must be coplanar, and this case cannot lead to a polyhedron.

It is not immediately evident why the listed p and v values lead to the objects claimed: these numbers provide local information, from which the global

---

[4]It seems that the constructions in Plato may originate with the Pythagoreans (Heath 1956) [Vol. 2, p. 98]. See Malkevitch (1988) for a history of polyhedra.
[5]We only consider "real" vertices, at which the face angles sum to strictly less than 2π.

Table 4.1: Legal p/v Values

p	v	$(p-2)(v-2)$	Name	Description
3	3	1	tetrahedron	3 triangles at each vertex
4	3	2	cube	3 squares at each vertex
3	4	2	octahedron	4 triangles at each vertex
5	3	3	dodecahedron	3 pentagons at each vertex
3	5	3	icosahedron	5 triangles at each vertex

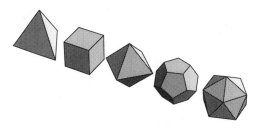

FIGURE 4.3 The five Platonic solids: tetrahedron, cube, octahedron, dodecahedron, icosahedron, left to right.

Table 4.2: Number of Vertices, Edges, and Faces of the Five Regular Polytopes

Name	(p,v)	V	E	F
Tetrahedron	$(3,3)$	4	6	4
Cube	$(4,3)$	8	12	6
Octahedron	$(3,4)$	6	12	8
Dodecahedron	$(3,5)$	20	30	12
Icosahedron	$(5,3)$	12	30	20

structure must be inferred. We will not take the time to perform this deduction; examining the five polytopes in Figure 4.3[6] quickly reveals they realize the (p,v) numbers.[7] Counting vertices, edges, and faces leads to the numbers in Table 4.2.

The Greek prefixes in the names refer to the number of faces: tetra = 4, octa = 8, dodeca = 12, icosa = 20. Sometimes a cube is called a hexahedron!

4.1.3. Euler's Formula

In 1758, Leonard Euler noticed a remarkable regularity in the numbers of vertices, edges, and faces of a polyhedron of genus zero: the number of vertices and faces together is always two more than the number of edges; and this is true for *all* polyhedra. So a cube has eight vertices and six faces, and $8 + 6 = 14$ is

---

[6]This figure and most of the three-dimensional illustrations in the book were generated by Mathematica.

[7]This pair of numbers is called the *Schläfli symbol* for the polyhedron (Coxeter 1973, p. 14).

two more than its 12 edges. The remaining regular polytopes can be seen to satisfy the same relationship. If we let V, E, and F be the number of vertices, edges, and faces respectively of a polyhedron, what is now known as *Euler's formula* is

$$V - E + F = 2. \qquad (4.3)$$

One might think that recognizing this regularity is no great achievement, but Euler had to first "invent" the notions of vertex and edge to formulate his conjecture. It was many years before mathematicians developed a rigorous proof,[8] although with modern methods it is not too difficult. We now turn to a proof.

4.1.4. Proof of Euler's Formula

Unfortunately there are counter examples to this proof.

Our proof is in three parts:

1. Converting the polyhedron surface to a plane graph.
2. The theorem for trees.
3. Proof by induction.

We first "flatten" the polyhedron surface P onto a plane, perhaps with considerable distortion, by the following procedure. Imagine the surface is made of a pliable material. Choose an arbitrary face f of P and remove it, leaving a hole in the surface. Now stretch the hole wider and wider until it becomes much larger than the original size of P. It should be intuitively plausible that one can then flatten the surface onto the plane, resulting in a plane graph G (the 1-skeleton of the polytope):[9] a graph embedded in the plane without edge crossings, whose nodes derive from vertices of P, and whose arcs derive from edges of P. The edges of f become the outer boundary of G. Each face of P except for f becomes a bounded face of G; f becomes the exterior, unbounded face of G. Figure 4.4 illustrates the graph that results from flattening a cube. Thus, if we count this exterior face of G as a true face (which is the usual convention), the vertices, edges, and faces of P are in one-to-one correspondence with those of G. This permits us to concentrate on proving Euler's formula for plane graphs.

The second step is to prove the formula in the highly restricted case where G is a tree. Of course a tree could never result from stretching a polyhedron, but this is a useful tool for the final step of the proof. So suppose G is a tree of V vertices and E edges. It is a property of trees that $V = E + 1$, a fact we assume for the proof. A tree bounds or delimits only one face, the exterior face, so $F = 1$. Now Euler's formula is immediate:

$$V - E + F = (E + 1) - E + 1 = 2$$

---

[8]See Lakatos (1976) for the fascinating history of this theorem.
[9]Note that this flattening would not work for genus greater than zero

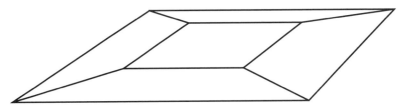

FIGURE 4.4   The 1-skeleton of a cube, obtained by flattening to a plane.

The third and final step of the proof is by induction on the number of edges. Suppose Euler's formula is true for all connected graphs with no more than $E - 1$ edges, and let G be a graph of V, E, and F vertices, edges, and faces. If G is a tree, we are done by the previous argument without even using induction. So suppose G has a cycle, and let e be an edge of G in some cycle. The graph $G' = G - e$ is connected,[10] with V vertices, $E - 1$ edges, and (here is the crux) $F - 1$ faces: removal of e must join two faces into one. By the induction hypothesis,

$$V - (E - 1) + (F - 1) = 2 = V - E + F,$$

and we are finished.

4.1.5. Consequence: Linearity

We now show that Euler's formula implies that the number of vertices, edges, and faces of a polytope are linearly related: if $V = n$, then $E = O(n)$ and $F = O(n)$. This will permit us to use "n" rather loosely in complexity analyses involving polyhedra.

Since we seek to establish an upper bound on E and F as a function of $V = n$, it is safe to triangulate every face of the polytope: for this will only increase E and F without affecting V. So for the remainder of this argument, we assume the polytope is *simplicial*: all of its faces are triangles.[11] If we count the edges face by face, then because each face has three edges, we get $3F$. However, since each edge is shared by two faces, this double-counts the edges. So $3F = 2E$. Now substitution into Euler's formula establishes the linear bounds:

$$V - E + F = 2$$

$$V - E + 2E/3 = 2$$

$$V - 2 = E/3$$

$$E = 3V - 6 < 3V = 3n = O(n) \tag{4.4}$$

$$F = 2E/3 = 2V - 4 < 2V = 2n = O(n). \tag{4.5}$$

---

[10] $G - e$ is the graph G with edge e removed

[11] A triangle is a two-dimensional *simplex*, and thus the name "simplicial."

We summarize in a theorem for later reference:

Theorem 4.1.1. *For a polyhedron with* V = n, E, *and* F *vertices, edges, and faces respectively,* V − E + F = 2, *and both* E *and* F *are* O(n).

4.1.6. Exercises

1. *Closed and bounded.* Argue that the definition of a polyhedron in the text guarantees that it is closed and bounded.

2. *Flawed definition 1.* Here is a "flawed" definition of polyhedron; call the objects so defined polyhedra$_1$. Find objects that are polyhedra$_1$ but are not polyhedra according to the definition in the text.
   A *polyhedron$_1$* is a region of space bounded by a finite set of polygons such that every polygon shares at least one edge with some other polygon, and every edge is shared by exactly two polygons.

3. *Flawed definition 2.* Same as the previous exercise, but with this definition:
   A *polyhedron$_2$* is a region of space bounded by a finite set of polygons such that every edge of a polygon is shared by exactly one other polygon, and no subset of these polygons has the same property.

4. *Cuboctahedron* [easy]. Verify Euler's formula for the *cuboctahedron*: a polytope formed by slicing off each corner of a unit cube in such a fashion that each corner is sliced down to an equilateral triangle of side length $\sqrt{2}/2$, and each face of the cube becomes a diamond: a square again of side length $\sqrt{2}/2$. Make a rough sketch of the polytope first.

5. *Euler's formula for nonzero genus.* There is a version of Euler's Formula for polyhedra of any genus. Guess the formula based on empirical evidence for genus 1: polyhedra topologically equivalent to a torus.

6. *Polyhedral torus* [difficult]. What is the fewest number of triangles needed to build a polyhedral torus? (Certainly four triangles are not enough.) What is the fewest number of vertices? Design a polyhedral torus, attempting to minimize the combinatorial size of the surface measured in these two ways.

7. *Gauss-Bonnet theorem.* Compute the total sum of the face angles at all the vertices of a few polyhedra (of genus 0), and formulate a conjecture.

4.2. HULL ALGORITHMS

Algorithms for constructing the hull in three dimensions are much more complex than two-dimensional algorithms, and the coverage here will be necessarily uneven. We will only mention gift-wrapping, and talk through divide and conquer at a high level. The bulk of this chapter plunges into the incremental algorithm in full detail.

4.2.1. Gift Wrapping

As mentioned previously, the gift-wrapping algorithm was invented to work in arbitrary dimensions (Chand and Kapur, 1970). The three-dimensional version is a direct generalization of the two-dimensional algorithm. At any step, a connected portion of the hull is constructed. A face F on the boundary of this partial hull is selected, and an edge e of this face whose second adjacent face remains to be found, is also selected. The plane π containing F is "bent" over e toward the set until the first point p is encountered. Then conv $\{p, e\}$ is a new triangular face of the hull, and the wrapping can continue. As in two dimensions, p can be characterized by the minimum turning angle from π. A careful implementation can achieve $O(n^2)$ time complexity: $O(n)$ work per face, and as we just saw in Theorem 4.1.1, the number of faces is $O(n)$. As in two dimensions, this algorithm has the advantage of being output-size sensitive: $O(nF)$ for a hull of F faces.

4.2.2. Divide and Conquer

The only lower bound for constructing the hull in three dimensions is the same as for two dimensions: $\Omega(n \log n)$ (Section 3.6). The question then naturally arises, is this complexity achievable in three dimensions, as it is in two dimensions. We mentioned in the previous chapter that although several of the two-dimensional algorithms extend (with complications) to three dimensions, the only one to achieve optimal $O(n \log n)$ time is the divide-and-conquer algorithm of Preparata and Hong (1977).[12] This algorithm is both theoretically important, and quite beautiful. It is, however, rather difficult to implement and seems not used as frequently in practice as other asymptotically slower algorithms, such as the incremental algorithm (Section 4.2.3). In this section, I will describe the algorithm at a level one step above implementation details. Greater detail may be found in Preparata and Shamos (1985), Edelsbrunner (1987) and Day (1990).

The paradigm is the same as in two dimensions: sort the points by their x-coordinate, divide into two sets, recursively construct the hull of each half, and merge. The merge must be accomplished in $O(n)$ time to achieve the desired $O(n \log n)$ bound. All the work is in the merge, and we concentrate solely on this.

Let A and B be the two hulls to be merged. The hull of $A \cup B$ will add a single "band" of faces with the topology of a cylinder without endcaps. See Figure 4.5ab.[13] The number of these faces will be linear in the size of the two polytopes: each face uses at least one edge of either A or B, so the number of faces is no more than the total number of edges. So, it is feasible to perform the merge in linear time, as long as each face can be added in constant time (on average).

Let π be a plane that supports A and B from below, touching A at the vertex a and B at the vertex b. To make the exposition simpler, assume that A and b are the only points of contact. Then π contains the line L determined by

---

[12](Preparata and Shamos, 1985) contains important corrections to the original paper.

[13]These figures, and Figures 4.10 and 4.11, were first prepared by Sharmilli Ghosh and Vinita Subramanian.

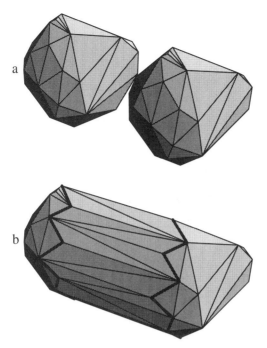

FIGURE 4.5   (*a*) Polytopes prior to merge. In this example, *A* and *B* are congruent, although that will not be true in general. (*b*) conv{*A* ∪ *B*}. The dark edges show the "shadow boundary": the boundary of the newly added faces.

ab. Now "crease" the plane along *L* and rotate half of it about *L* until it bumps into one of the two polytopes. See Figure 4.6. A crucial observation is that if it first bumps into point *c* on polytope *A* (say), *ac* must be an edge of *A*. In other words, the first point *c* hit by π must be a neighbor of either *a* or *b*. This limits the vertices that need to be examined to determine the next to be bumped. We highlight this important fact as a lemma but do not prove it.

Lemma 4.2.1.   *When plane π is rotated about the line through* ab *as described above, the first point* c *to be hit is a vertex adjacent to either* a *or* b.

Once π hits *c*, one triangular face of the merging band has been found: (*a, b, c*). Now the procedure is repeated, but this time around the line through *cb* (if *c* ∈ *A*). The wrapping stops when it closes in on itself. So what needs to be shown is that the point *c* can be found in constant time on average, so that the cost of merging is linear over the entire band.

Let's first examine a naive search of all neighbors of *a* and *b*. We can easily define the "angle" of any candidate *c* as the angle that π must be turned around *ab* from its initial position to hit *c*. Let α be the vertex adjacent to *a* with the smallest angle; α is the "*A*-winner." Let β be the vertex adjacent to *b*

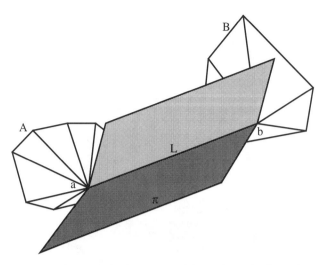

FIGURE 4.6 Plane π is creased along L and bent towards the polytopes A and B (only the faces incident to a and b are shown).

with the smallest angle, the "*B*-winner." The ultimate winner c is either α or β, whichever has the smaller angle. Clearly the winner c can be found in time proportional to the number of neighbors of a and b.

Two difficulties arise immediately. First, finding one winner might require examining $\Omega(n)$ candidate vertices, because a or b might have many neighbors. To completely wrap A and B with a band of faces, $\Omega(n)$ winner computations might be required, leading to a quadratic merge time. Although we cannot circumvent the fact that finding a single winner might cost $\Omega(n)$, this is not as damaging as might first appear because we only need to achieve constant time per winner *on average*, amortized over all winner computations for one merge step. We will see that indeed this can be done.

The second difficulty is that if α is the winner, the work just done to find β might be wasted. Imagine a situation where the candidate on A wins many times in a row, so that b remains fixed. Suppose further that b has many neighbors. Then, if we discard the search that obtains the loser β each time, and repeat it for each A winner, again we will be led to quadratic merge time.

Fortunately, this repeated search can be avoided because of the following monotonicity property. Let α_i and β_i be the A- and B-winners respectively at the ith iteration of the wrapping.

Lemma 4.2.2. *If α_i is the winner, then the B-winner at the next iteration, β_{i+1}, is counterclockwise of β_i around* b.

Of course a symmetric statement holds with the roles of A and B reversed.

This means that each loop either results in the ultimate winner, in which case its work will not have to be repeated, or it advances around the pivoting vertex, an advance that will not have to be retracted and explored again. Therefore, if we "charge" the work to the examined edges, each edge will be charged at most twice (once from each endpoint). Thus, the wrapping can be accomplished in linear time.

Discarding Hidden Faces

After wrapping around A and B with a cylinder of faces, it only remains to discard the faces hidden by the wrapped band to complete the merge. Unfortunately, the wrapping process does not immediately tell us which faces of A are visible from some point of B, and vice versa; it is just these faces that should be deleted. However, the wrapping does discover all the "shadow boundary" edges: those edges of A and B touched by one of the wrapped faces, shown dark in Figure 4.5b. (If all of B were a light source, the shadow boundary on A marks the division between light and dark; and symmetrically the shadow boundary on B separates light from dark when A is luminous.) Intuitively, one could imagine "snipping" along these edges in the data structure and detaching the hidden caps of A and B.

I implemented this procedure in 1980, and it would occasionally fail for reasons that were mysterious to me. It was not until Edelsbrunner (1987, p. 175) examined the algorithm closely that the flaw became evident: contrary to intuition, the shadow boundary edges on A do not necessarily form a simple cycle on A (and similarly for B)! This is illustrated in Figure 4.7. Figure 4.7a shows two polytopes before merging: A is a flat wedge, extending 10 units in the y-dimension; B is a tall box, 6 units in the y-dimension. The coordinates of their vertices are as follows:

```
A: Wedge
 #              x       y       z
 0:           -20      10       5
 1:           -20      20       5
 2:            -5      10       5
 3:            -5      20       5
 4:            -5      10       8
 5:            -5      20       8
B: Block
 #              x       y       z
 6:            10      18      20
 7:            20      18      20
 8:            20      12      20
 9:            10      12      20
10:            10      18     -10
11:            20      18     -10
12:            20      12     -10
13:            10      12     -10
```

The hull conv$\{A \cup B\}$ is shown in Figure 4.7b. The vertices of A on the shadow

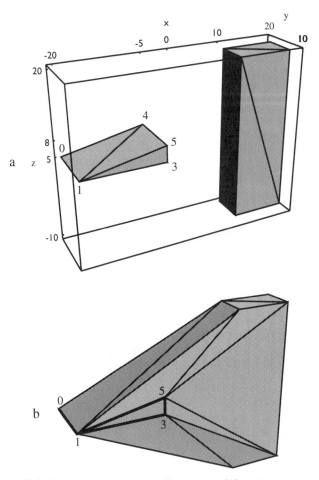

FIGURE 4.7　(*a*) Wedge and block prior to merging; (*b*) Hull of wedge and block.

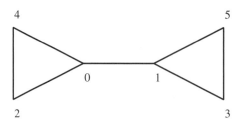

FIGURE 4.8　Topology of shadow boundary edges for Figure 4.7*b*.

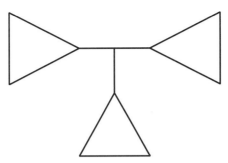

FIGURE 4.9   Can this graph be realized as a shadow boundary?

boundary occur in the order $(0, 2, 4, 0, 1, 3, 5, 1)$ (drawn dark in the figure), forming the topological "barbell" shown in Figure 4.8. Note that this sequence touches p_0 and p_1 twice, and so is not simple.

In spite of this unexpected complication, the hidden faces form a connected cap (Exercise 4.2.2[3]), and can be found by a search from the shadow boundary, for example by depth-first search.

My discussion has been somewhat meandering, but I hope it conveys something of both the delicacy and the beauty of the algorithm. Given the complexity of the task of constructing the three-dimensional hull, I find it delightfully surprising that an $O(n \log n)$ algorithm exists.

Exercises

1. *Winning angle*. Detail the computation of the A-winner. Assume you know a and b, and you have accessible all of a's neighbors on A sorted counterclockwise about a.

2. *Degeneracies*. Discuss some difficulties that might arise for the divide-and-conquer algorithm with points that are not in general position: more than two collinear and/or more than three coplanar.

3. *Deleted faces*. Prove that the faces deleted from A during the merge step form a connected set.

4. *Topology of shadow boundary* (Goodrich). Construct an example of two polytopes A and B such that the shadow boundary on A in $\text{conv}\{A \cup B\}$ has the topology shown in Figure 4.9.

4.2.3. Incremental Algorithm

The overall structure of the three-dimensional incremental algorithm[14] is identical to that of the two-dimensional version (Section 3.7): at the ith iteration, compute $H_i \leftarrow \text{conv}(H_{i-1} \cup p_i)$. Again, the problem of computing the new hull naturally divides into two cases. Let $p = p_i$ and $Q = H_{i-1}$. Decide if $p \in Q$. If

---

[14]This algorithm is sometimes called the "beneath-beyond" method when used to construct the hull in arbitrary dimensions. It seems to have been first discussed in print around 1981: Seidel (1986) and Kallay (1984) (cited by Preparata and Shamos (1985)).

so, discard p; if not, compute the cone tangent to Q whose apex is p, and construct the new hull.

The test $p \in Q$ can be made in the same fashion as in two-dimensions: p is inside Q iff p is to the positive side of every plane determined by a face of Q. The left-of-triangle test is based on the volume of the determined tetrahedron, just as the left-of-segment test is based on the area of the triangle. If all faces are oriented consistently, the volumes must all have the same sign (positive under our conventions). This test clearly can be accomplished in time proportional to the number of faces of Q, which as we saw in the previous section, is $O(n)$.

When p is outside Q, the problem is more difficult, as the hull will be altered. Recall that in the two-dimensional incremental algorithm, the alteration required finding two tangents from p to Q (Figure 3.12). In three dimensions, there are tangent planes rather than tangent lines. These planes bound a *cone* of triangle faces, each of whose apex is p, and whose base is an edge e of Q. An example is shown in Figures 4.10 and 4.11. Figure 4.10ab shows H_{i-1} and H_i from one point of view, and Figure 4.11ab show the same example from a different viewpoint. We now discuss how these cone faces can be constructed.

Imagine standing at p and looking toward Q. Assuming for the moment that no faces are viewed edge-on: the interior of each face of Q is either visible or not visible from p. It should be clear that the visible faces are precisely those that are to be discarded in moving from $Q = H_{i-1}$ to H_i. Moreover, the edges on the border of the visible region are precisely those that become the bases of cone faces apexed at p. For suppose e is an edge of Q such that the plane determined by e and p is tangent to Q. Edge e is adjacent to two faces, one of which is visible from p, and one of which is not. Therefore, e is on the border of the visible region. An equivalent way to view this is to think of a light source placed at p. Then the visible region is that portion of Q illuminated, and the

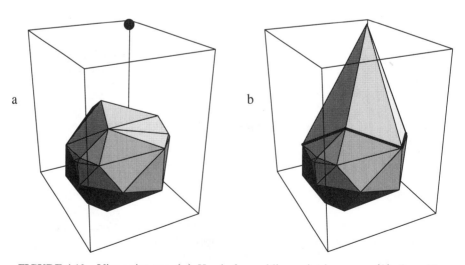

FIGURE 4.10 Viewpoint one: (a) H_{i-1} before adding point in corner; (b) after: H_i.

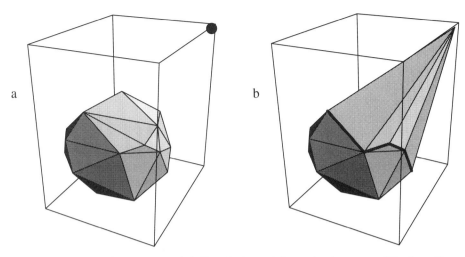

FIGURE 4.11   Viewpont two: (a) H_{i-1} before adding point in corner; (b) after: H_i.

border edges are those between the light and dark regions, analogous to the shadow boundary edges in Section 4.2.2.

From this discussion, it is evident that if we can determine which faces of Q are visible from p and which are not, we will know enough to find the border edges and therefore construct the cone, and we will know which faces to discard. We now need a precise definition of visibility.

Define a face to be *visible* from p iff some point x interior to f is visible from p, that is, px does not intersect Q except at x: $px \cap Q = \{x\}$. Note that under this definition, seeing only an edge of a face does not render the face visible, and faces seen edge-on are also considered invisible. Whether a triangle face (a, b, c) is visible from p can be determined from the signed volume of the tetrahedron (a, b, c, p): it is visible iff the volume is strictly negative. (This sign

---

Algorithm: THREE-DIMENSIONAL INCREMENTAL ALGORITHM
Initialize H_4 to tetrahedron (p_0, p_1, p_2, p_3).
for $i = 4, \ldots, n - 1$ do
    for each face f of H_{i-1} do
        Compute volume of tetrahedron determined by f and p_i.
        Mark f visible iff volume < 0.
    if no faces are visible
        then Discard p_i (it is inside H_{i-1}).
        else
            for each border edge e of H_{i-1} do
                Construct cone face determined by e and p_i.
            for each visible face f do
                Delete f.
        Update H_i.

Algorithm 4.1   Incremental algorithm, three dimensions.

convention will be discussed in Section 4.3.2 below.)

We can now outline the algorithm based on the visibility calculation; see Algorithm 4.1. Of course many details remain to be explained, but the basics of the algorithm should be clear.

Complexity Analysis

Recall by Theorem 4.1.1 that $F = O(n)$ and $E = O(n)$, where n is the number of vertices of the polytope, so the loops over faces and edges are linear. Since these loops are embedded inside a loop that iterates n times, the total complexity is quadratic: $O(n^2)$.

4.3. IMPLEMENTATION OF INCREMENTAL ALGORITHM

Although the incremental algorithm is conceptually clean, an implementation is nontrivial. Nevertheless, in this section we plunge into a complete description of an implementation,[15] the most complex presented in this book. The details left out of our highlevel description above will be included when the code is presented. Those uninterested in the code should skip to the discussion of volume overflow in Section 4.3.5.

4.3.1. Data Structures

It is not obvious how best to represent the surface of a polyhedron, and several sophisticated suggestions have been made in the literature. We will examine a few of these ideas in Section 4.4. Here we will opt for very simple structures, which are limited in their applicability. In particular, we will assume the surface of our polytope is triangulated: every face is a triangle. This will simplify our data structures at the expense of producing an awkward representation for any polytope that is not triangulated, for example, a cube. In addition, our data structure will not possess the symmetry that some others have, and it will force some operations to be a bit awkward. In spite of these various drawbacks, I think it is the easiest to comprehend.

Structure Definitions. There are three primary data types: vertices, edges, and faces. All the vertices are doubly linked into a list, as are all the edges, and all the faces. The ordering of the elements in the list has no significance; so these lists should be thought more as sets than as lists. Each element of these lists is a fixed-size structure containing relevant information, including links into the other lists. The vertex structure contains the (integer) coordinates of the vertex. It contains no pointers to its incident edges nor its incident faces. The edge structure contains pointers to the two vertices that are endpoints of the edge, and pointers to the two adjacent faces. The ordering of both of these pairs is arbitrary; more sophisticated data structures enforce an ordering. The face

---

[15]Carole Gitlin, John Kutcher, Catherine Schevon, and Susan Weller contributed to this implementation.

structure contains pointers to the three vertices forming the corners of the triangular face, as well as pointers to the three edges. Note that it is here that we exploit our assumption that all faces are triangles. The basic fields of the three structures are shown in Code 4.1. The structures will need to contain other miscellaneous fields, which will be discussed shortly.

```
struct tVertexStructure {
        int     v[3];
        tVertex next, prev;
};

struct tEdgeStructure {
        tVertex endpts[2];
        tFace   adjface[2];
        tEdge   next, prev;
};

struct tFaceStructure {
        tVertex vertex[3];
        tEdge   edge[3];
        tFace   next, prev;
};
```

Code 4.1   Three primary `structs`.

Each of the three primary structures has three associated type names, beginning with `t` as per our convention. The vertex structure is `tVertexStructure`; this name is used only in the declarations. The type `struct tVertexStructure` is given the name `tsVertex`; this name is used only when allocating storage, as an argument to `sizeof`. Finally, the type used throughout the code is `tVertex`, a pointer to an element in the vertex list. The edge and face structures have similar associated names. These names are established with `typedef`'s preceding the structure declarations; see Code 4.2.

```
typedef struct tVertexStructure tsVertex;
typedef tsVertex *tVertex;

typedef struct tEdgeStructure tsEdge;
typedef tsEdge *tEdge;

typedef struct tFaceStructure tsFace;
typedef tsFace *tFace;
```

Code 4.2   Structure `typedefs`.

Example of Data Structures. We will illustrate the convex hull code with a running example, constructing the hull of eight points comprising the corners of a cube. One of the polytopes created enroute to the final cube has five vertices, and we use this to illustrate the data structures. We call it P_4 because it is the result of adding v_4 to the base tetrahedron.

The vertex list contains all the input points; not all are referenced by the edge and face lists. The cube has edge length 10, and is in the positive orthant[16] of the coordinate system. The odd indexing chosen for the vertices is an artifact of the read procedure. The indices play no role in the code, as all references are conducted via pointers.

Vertex	Coordinates
v_0	$(0, 0, 0)$
v_7	$(10, 0, 10)$
v_6	$(10, 10, 10)$
v_5	$(0, 10, 10)$
v_4	$(0, 0, 10)$
v_3	$(10, 0, 0)$
v_2	$(10, 10, 0)$
v_1	$(0, 10, 0)$

The polytope P_4 consists of nine edges and six faces.

Edge	Endpoints	Adjacent faces
e_0	(v_0, v_7)	(f_0, f_4)
e_8	(v_5, v_4)	(f_5, f_6)
e_7	(v_7, v_4)	(f_4, f_5)
e_6	(v_0, v_4)	(f_4, f_6)
e_5	(v_6, v_5)	(f_2, f_3)
e_4	(v_7, v_5)	(f_5, f_2)
e_3	(v_0, v_5)	(f_6, f_3)
e_2	(v_6, v_0)	(f_0, f_3)
e_1	(v_7, v_6)	(f_0, f_2)

Face	Vertices	Edges
f_0	(v_0, v_6, v_7)	(e_0, e_2, e_1)
f_6	(v_5, v_0, v_4)	(e_3, e_6, e_8)
f_5	(v_7, v_5, v_4)	(e_4, e_8, e_7)
f_4	(v_0, v_7, v_4)	(e_0, e_7, e_6)
f_3	(v_6, v_0, v_5)	(e_2, e_3, e_5)
f_2	(v_7, v_6, v_5)	(e_1, e_5, e_4)

---

[16]An *orthant* is the intersection of three mutually orthogonal halfspaces, the natural generalization of "quadrant" to three dimensions.

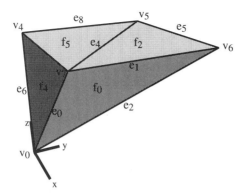

FIGURE 4.12   A view of P_4, with labels.

The three lists above are shown exactly as they are constructed by the code. The indices on the v, e, and f labels indicate the order in which the records were created. Note that the face list contains no f_1; that face was created and deleted before the illustrated snapshot of the data structures.

A view of the polytope is shown in Figure 4.12. Two of the faces, f_2 and f_5, are coplanar, forming the square top of the cube, v_4, v_7, v_6, v_5. Faces f_3 (right face) and f_6 (back face) are hidden in the view shown.

An important property of the face data structure that is maintained at all times is that the vertices in field **vertex** are ordered counterclockwise, so that the right-hand rule yields a normal vector to the face pointing exterior to the polytope. Thus f_0's vertices occur in the order (v_0, v_6, v_7). The same counterclockwise ordering is maintained for the **edge** field. Thus, the ordering of f_2's edges is (e_1, e_5, e_4). The code often exploits the counterclockwise ordering of the vertices, but by happenstance never needs to use the counterclockwise ordering of the edges. The edge ordering is maintained by judicious swaps nevertheless, for aesthetics, and for potential uses beyond those presented here.

Head Pointers. At all times a "head" pointer is maintained to each of the three lists, initialized to NULL. The head pointer of each list is linked to the tail, to facilitate deletion of the head. Thus the lists are actually circular rather than linear lists, but we always process them linearly. These pointers are global to all functions. See Code 4.3. Loops over all vertices, edges, or faces all have the same basic structure, shown in Code 4.4. Note this structure assumes that the lists are nonempty, which is indeed the case. The **prev** pointers are only used for deleting elements.

```
tVertex vertices   = NULL;
tEdge edges        = NULL;
tFace faces        = NULL;
```

Code 4.3   Head pointers.

```
        v = vertices;
        do{
                /* Process v */
                v = v->next;
        } while ( v != vertices )
```

Code 4.4   Typical loop.

Basic List Processing. Four basic list processing routines are needed for each of the three data structures: allocation of a new element (NEW), freeing an element's memory (FREE), adding a new element to the list (ADD), and deleting an old element (DELETE). Because C does not permit manipulation of variables without regard to type, it would be necessary to write separate functions for these tasks for each of the three data structures. To avoid this unpleasant

```
#define NEW(p,type)   if ((p = type *) malloc
                          (sizeof(type))) == NULL) {\
                          printf ("Out of Memory!\n");\
                          exit(0);\
                }
#define FREE(p)       if (p) { free ((char *) p); p = NULL;
}
```

Code 4.5   NEW and FREE macros.

```
#define ADD( head, p )  if ( head ) { \
                            p->next = head->next; \
                            p->prev = head; \
                            head->next = p; \
                            p->next->prev = p; \
                        } \
                        else { \
                            head = p; \
                            head->next = head->prev = p; \
                        }
#define DELETE( head, p )   if ( head ) { \
                            if ( head == head->next ) \
                                    head = NULL; \
                            else if ( p == head ) \
                                    head = head->next; \
                            p->next->prev = p->prev; \
                            p->prev->next = p->next; \
                            FREE( p ); \
                        }
```

Code 4.6   ADD and DELETE macros.

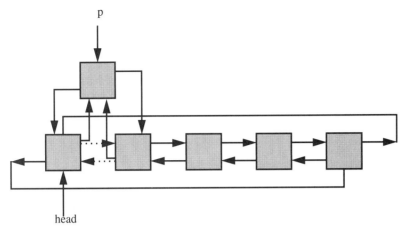

FIGURE 4.13   ADD: *p* is inserted immediately after *head*.

replication, we write the list processing functions as macros. These macros are expanded inline prior to compilation, and so inherit the types of whichever variables are its parameters. Note that we have called the list pointers `prev` and `next` in each of the three data structures, in anticipation of this savings.

The two memory management functions (Code 4.5) allocate and deallocate storage. Note that NEW is passed the type, which will be one of `tsVertex`, `tsEdge`, or `tsFace`.

The addition and deletion macros (Code 4.6) must manage the head pointer, which might, for example, be deleted. Note that `head` is a macro parameter, as it is different for each of the three data structures. ADD always adds the new element between `head` and `head- > next`. See Figure 4.13.

`structs`: *Full Detail.* The fields of the basic data structures are augmented by several flags and auxiliary pointers, presented in Code 4.7 and Code 4.8 with the

```
/ * Define vertex indices. * /
#define X   0
#define Y   1
#define Z   2

/ * Define Boolean type. * /
typedef enum { FALSE, TRUE }   bool;

/ * Define flags. * /
#define ONHULL       TRUE
#define REMOVED      TRUE
#define VISIBLE      TRUE
#define PROCESSED    TRUE
```

Code 4.7   Defines.

```
struct tVertexStructure {
        int      v[3];
        tEdge    duplicate;        / * pointer to incident cone edge
                                       (or NULL) * /
        bool     onhull;           / * T iff point on hull. * /
        bool     mark;             / * T iff point already processed. * /
        tVertex  next, prev;
};

struct tEdgeStructure {
        tFace    adjface[2];
        tVertex  endpts[2];
        tFace    newface;          / * pointer to incident cone face. * /
        bool     delete;           / * T iff edge should be deleted. * /
        tEdge    next, prev;
};
struct tFaceStructure {
        tEdge    edge[3];
        tVertex  vertex[3];
        bool     visible;          / * T iff face visible from new point. * /
        tFace    next, prev;
};
```

Code 4.8   Full vertex, edge, and face structures.

full structure definitions. The additional fields are all commented, and each will be explained further when first used.

4.3.2. Example: Cube

In this section the running of the program is illustrated with the example started in the previous section, with input the eight corners of a cube. We will discuss each section of the code as it becomes relevant.

main. The work is separated into four sections at the top level (Code 4.9): read, create initial tetrahedron, construct the hull, and print.

```
main( int argc, char *argv[] )
{
        / * (Flags etc. not shown here.) * /
        ReadPoints();
        Tetrahedron();
        ConstructHull();
        Print();
}
```

Code 4.9   main.

```
/* 1 */  ReadPoints()
                  MakeVertex()
/* 2 */  Tetrahedron()
                  MakeEdge()
                  MakeFace()
                  MakeStructs()
                          MakeEdge()
                          MakeFace()
                          MakeCcw()
                  Collinear()
/* 3 */           Volume6()
                  Cleanup()
                          CleanEdges()
                          CleanFaces()
                          CleanVertices()
/* 4 */  ConstructHull()
/* 5 */           AddOne()
                  Volume6()
/* 8 */           MakeStructs()
/* 6 */                   MakeEdge()
/* 7 */                   MakeFace()
/* 9 */                   MakeCcw()
/* 10 */          Cleanup()
/* 12 */                  CleanEdges()
/* 11 */                  CleanFaces()
/* 13 */                  CleanVertices()
                  Print()
```

Code 4.10   Who calls whom.

The code will be discussed in as linear an order as is possible. Code 4.10 shows a list of which routine calls which, with a comment number indicating the order in which they are discussed.

Read. The input file for the cube example is:

0	0	0
0	10	0
10	10	0
10	0	0
0	0	10
0	10	10
10	10	10
10	0	10

The vertices are labeled $v_0, \ldots, v_7$ in the above order. They are read in and formed into the vertex list with the straightforward procedures Code 4.11 and Code 4.12.

```
void     ReadVertices( void )
{
        tVertex  v;
        int      x, y, z;
        int      vnum = 0;

        while ( scanf ("%d %d %d", &x, &y, &z ) != EOF ) {
                v = MakeVertex();
                v->v[X] = x;
                v->v[Y] = y;
                v->v[Z] = z;
                v->vnum = vnum++;
        }
}
```

Code 4.11 ReadVertices.

```
tVertex MakeVertex( void )
{
        tVertex v;

        NEW( v, tsVertex );
        v->duplicate = NULL;
        v->onhull = !ONHULL;
        v->mark = !PROCESSED;
        ADD( vertices, v );

        return v;
}
```

Code 4.12 MakeVertex.

The meaning of the various fields of each vertex record will be explained later. One artifact of the ADD macro is that after reading v_0 and making that the head of the list, all subsequent elements are inserted immediately after the head. The result is the ordering that was remarked on earlier.

Tetrahedron. The next step is to create the initial tetrahedron, accomplished by a procedure Tetrahedron, shown in Code 4.13 and Code 4.14. One might think this task is trivial, but in fact the code is complicated and messy, for several reasons. First, it is not adequate to use simply the first four points in the vertex list, as those four points might be "degenerate" and not determine a tetrahedron of positive volume. This is an unavoidable complication without an assumption of general position. Second, the data structures need to be constructed to have the appropriate properties. In particular, the counterclockwise

```
void Tetrahedron( void )
{
    tVertex   v1;              /* first point of tetrahedron, in base */
    tVertex   v4;              /* fourth point of tetrahedron, apex */
    tVertex   t;               /* temp vertex for swapping */
    tFace     f;               /* base triangle of tetrahedron */
    tEdge     e1, e2, e3;      /* edges of base triangle */
    tEdge     s;               /* temp edge for swapping */
    tEdge     MakeEdge();
    tFace     MakeFace(), MakeStructs();
    int            vol;        /* volume for ccw test */

    /* Find 3 non-collinear points. */
    v1 = vertices;
    while ( collinear( v1, v1->next, v1->next->next ) )
            if ( ( v1 = v1->next ) == vertices ) {
                    printf("All points are collinear!\n");
                    exit(0);
            }

    /* Mark the vertices as processed. */
    v1->mark = PROCESSED;
    v1->next->mark = PROCESSED;
    v1->next->next->mark = PROCESSED;

    /* Create edges of the initial triangle. */
    e1 = MakeEdge();
    e2 = MakeEdge();
    e3 = MakeEdge();
    e1->endpts[0] = v1; e1->endpts[1] = v1->next;
    e2->endpts[0] = v1->next; e2->endpts[1] = v1->next->next;
    e3->endpts[0] = v1->next->next; e3->endpts[1] = v1;

    /* Create face for triangle. */
    f = MakeFace();
    f->edge[0] = e1; f->edge[1] = e2; f->edge[2] = e3;
    f->vertex[0] = v1; f->vertex[1] = v1->next;
    f->vertex[2] = v1->next->next;

    /* Link edges to face. */
    e1->adjface[0] = e2->adjface[0] = e3->adjface[0] = f;
    /* continued ... */
```

Code 4.13 Tetrahedron, part a.

```
/ * ... continued  * /

/ * Find a fourth, non-coplanar point to form tetrahedron. * /
v4 = v1->next->next->next;
vol = Volume6( f, v4 );
while ( !vol ) {
        if ( ( v4 = v4->next )  == v1 ) {
                printf("All points are coplanar!\n");
                exit(0);
        }
        vol = Volume6( f, v4 );
}
v4->mark = PROCESSED;

/ * Store vertices in ccw order. * /
if( vol < 0 ) {
    SWAP( t, f->vertex[1], f->vertex[2] );
    SWAP( s, f->edge[1], f->edge[2] );
}

/ * Construct the faces and edges between the original
   triangle and the fourth point. * /
e1->adjface[1] = MakeStructs( e1, v4 );
e2->adjface[1] = MakeStructs( e2, v4 );
e3->adjface[1] = MakeStructs( e3, v4 );

CleanUp();
}
```

Code 4.14 Tetrahedron, part b.

ordering of the vertices in each face record must be ensured. This also seems unavoidable. Third, the data structures are somewhat unwieldy. I have no doubt this *is* avoidable with more sophisticated data structures.

The tetrahedron is constructed in four stages:

1. Three non-collinear points are found and formed into a base triangle face f.
2. A fourth point v4 not coplanar with f is found.
3. The counterclockwise ordering of f's vertices (and edges) is enforced.
4. The remaining faces of the tetrahedron are added.

We now discuss each stage in more detail.

1. Three non-collinear points. It suffices to check all triples of three consecutive points in the vertex list. For if not all points are collinear, at least one of these triples must be non-collinear. Collinearity is checked

with the triangle area function `Area2` discussed in Chapter 1 (Code 1.5).

2. Fourth noncoplanar point. Coplanarity is checked by computing the volume of the tetrahedron: `Volume6( f, v4 )` is zero iff `v4` is coplanar with `f`.

3. Counterclockwise ordering. This is ensured by requiring that the volume be negative. If it is not, two vertices and edges are swapped.

4. Remaining faces. Most of the work here is handled by a routine `MakeStructs`, which in turn invokes a function to enforce counter-clockwise ordering. This will be discussed later (Code 4.20).

When `Tetrahedron` is run on our cube example, the first three vertices tried are noncollinear: v_0, v_7, v_6. These then form face `f`, f_0 in the face list. The first candidate tried for `v4` is v_5, and the volume of the determined tetrahedron is calculated.

`Volume`. Recall from Section 1.4.9 that the volume of the tetrahedron whose vertices are (a, b, c, d) is $1/6$ of the determinant

$$\begin{vmatrix} a_x & a_y & a_z & 1 \\ b_x & b_y & b_z & 1 \\ c_x & c_y & c_z & 1 \\ d_x & d_y & d_z & 1 \end{vmatrix} \tag{4.6}$$

We compute the volume with a straightforward integer function `Volume6` (Code 4.15). The equation for the determinant was computed in Mathematica. The individual coordinates are tediously assigned to many distinct variables to make it easier to write the volume equation.

We will have more to say about this volume calculation later (Section 4.3.5), but for now we just recall that the volume is positive when p is on the negative side of f, with the positive side determined by the right-hand rule. In the particular case at hand, the determinant of f_0 and v_5 is:

$$\begin{vmatrix} 0 & 0 & 0 & 1 \\ 10 & 0 & 10 & 1 \\ 10 & 10 & 10 & 1 \\ 0 & 10 & 10 & 1 \end{vmatrix} = -1000 < 0. \tag{4.7}$$

This indicates that v_5 is on the positive side of f_0, which implies that the ordering of the vertices in f_0, (v_0, v_7, v_6) is clockwise "from the outside"; see Figure 4.12. Therefore, the code swaps v_7 and v_6 in f_0's `vertex` list (and also swaps in the `edge` list), resulting in the counterclockwise orientation (v_0, v_6, v_7). As we will see, establishing the correct orientation for f_0 is crucial, as all other face orientations are propagated from this first face.

```
int Volume6(tFace f, tVertex p)
{
    int  vol;
    int  ax, ay, az, bx, by, bz, cx, cy, cz, dx, dy, dz;

    ax = f -> vertex[0] -> v[X];
    ay = f -> vertex[0] -> v[Y];
    az = f -> vertex[0] -> v[Z];
    bx = f -> vertex[1] -> v[X];
    by = f -> vertex[1] -> v[Y];
    bz = f -> vertex[1] -> v[Z];
    cx = f -> vertex[2] -> v[X];
    cy = f -> vertex[2] -> v[Y];
    cz = f -> vertex[2] -> v[Z];
    dx = p -> v[X];
    dy = p -> v[Y];
    dz = p -> v[Z];

    vol =
    - az * by * cx+ay * bz * cx+az * bx * cy - ax * bz * cy
    - ay * bx * cz+ax * by * cz+az * by * dx - ay * bz * dx
    - az * cy * dx+bz * cy * dx+ay * cz * dx - by * cz * dx
    - az * bx * dy+ax * bz * dy+az * cx * dy - bz * cx * dy
    - ax * cz * dy+bx * cz * dy+ay * bx * dz - ax * by * dz
    - ay * cx * dz+by * cx * dz+ax * cy * dz - bx * cy * dz;

    return vol;
}
```

Code 4.15 Volume6.

ConstructHull. We now come to the heart of the algorithm. It is instructive to note how much "peripheral" code is needed to reach this point. The routine ConstructHull (Code 4.16) is called by main after the initial tetrahedron is constructed, and simply adds each point one at a time with the function AddOne. One minor feature to note: the entire list of vertices is processed, using the field v- >mark to avoid points already processed. It would not be possible to simply pick up in the vertex list where the initial tetrahedron computation left off, since the vertices comprising that tetrahedron might be spread out in the list.

After each point is added to the previous hull, an important routine CleanUp is called. This deletes superfluous parts of the data structure and prepares for the next iteration. We discuss this in detail below.

AddOne. The primary work of the algorithm is accomplished in the procedure AddOne (Code 4.17), which adds a single point p to the hull, constructing the

```
void ConstructHull( void )
{
    tVertex     v;
    bool        changed;

    v = vertices;
    do {
        if ( !v->mark ) {
            v->mark = PROCESSED;
            changed = AddOne( v );
            CleanUp( );
        }
        v = v->next;
    } while ( v != vertices );
}
```

Code 4.16 ConstructHull. (The changed flag is not used in this version.)

new cone of faces if p is exterior. There are two steps to this procedure:

1. Determine which faces of the previously constructed hull are "visible" to *p*. Recall that face *f* is visible to *p* iff *p* lies strictly in the positive halfspace determined by *f*, where, as usual, the positive side is determined by the counterclockwise orientation of *f*. The strictness condition is a crucial subtlety: we do not consider a face visible if *p* illuminates it edge-on.

   The visibility condition is determined by a volume calculation: *f* is visible from *p* iff the volume of the tetrahedron determined by *f* and *p* is negative. Recall that a negative volume results from *p* lying on the positive side of *f*.

   If no face is visible from *p*, then *p* must lie inside the hull, and it is marked for subsequent deletion.

2. Add a cone of faces to *p*. The portion of the polytope visible from *p* forms a connected region on the surface. The interior of this region must be deleted, and the cone connected to its boundary. Each edge of the hull is examined in turn.[17] Those edges whose two adjacent faces are both marked visible are known to be interior to the visible region. They are marked for subsequent deletion (but are not deleted yet). Edges with just one adjacent visible face are known to be on the border of the visible region. These are precisely the ones that form the base of a new triangle face apexed at *p*. The (considerable) work of constructing this new face is handled by MakeStructs.

   One tricky aspect of this code is that we are looping over all edges at the same time as new edges are being added to the list by MakeStructs

---

[17]One could imagine representing this region then it is marked, and then only looping over the appropriate edges. See Exercise 4.3.5[6].

```
bool AddOne( tVertex p )
{
    tFace       f;
    tEdge       e;
    int         vol;
    bool        vis;        /* t if some face visible */

    /* Mark faces visible from p. */
    f = faces;
    do {
            vol = Volume6( f, p );
            if ( vol < 0 ) {
                    f->visible = VISIBLE;
                    vis = TRUE;
            }
            f = f->next;
    } while ( f != faces );

    /* If no faces are visible from p, then p is inside the hull. */
    if ( !vis ) {
            p->onhull = !ONHULL;
            return FALSE;
    }

    /* Mark edges in interior of visible region for deletion.
       Erect a newface based on each border edge. */
    e = edges;
    do {
            tEdge temp;
            temp = e->next;
            if ( e->adjface[0]->visible
              && e->adjface[1]->visible )
                    /* e interior: mark for deletion. */
                    e->deleted = REMOVED;
            else if ( e->adjface[0]->visible ||
                    e->adjface[1]->visible )
                    /* e border: make a new face. */
                    e->newface = MakeStructs( e, p );
            e = temp;
    } while ( e != edges );
    return TRUE;
}
```

Code 4.17 AddOne.

(as we will see). Recall that all edges are inserted immediately after the head of the list, edges. So by storing e->next at the top of the loop, these new edges are skipped over. This is a minor efficiency, as even if those edges were processed by the loop, both halves of the if-statement would fail and no action would be taken.

AddOne is written to return true or false depending on whether the hull is modified or not, but this version of the code does not use this boolean value.

AddOne: *Cube Example.* Before discussing the routines employed by AddOne, we illustrate its functioning with the cube example. The first four vertices in the vertex list were marked by Tetrahedron: v_0, v_7, v_6, and v_5. So the first point added is v_4, and then v_3, v_2, and v_1, in that order. Let us call the initial tetrahedron P_0, and let P_i be the polytope after adding vertex v_i. The polytopes are then produced in the order P_0, P_4, P_3, P_2, and P_1. They are shown in Figures 4.14–4.18. In each figure, the next point to be added is highlighted. We will step through the construction of P_4 in detail. Refer also to Figure 4.12, which corresponds to Figure 4.15.

As is evident from Figure 4.14, v_4 can only see $f_1 = (v_0, v_7, v_5)$. The visibility calculation computes the volume of the tetrahedra formed by v_4 with faces f_0, f_3, f_2, and f_1, the four faces of the initial tetrahedron P_0, finding volumes 1000, 1000, 0, and -1000 respectively. Note that v_4 is coplanar with f_2, and f_2 is not marked visible, per our definition of visibility.

The second part of AddOne finds no edges in the interior of the visible region, since it consists solely of f_1. And it finds that each of f_1's edges,

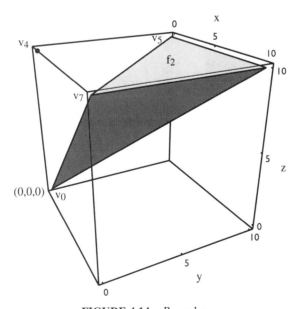

FIGURE 4.14 P_0 and v_4.

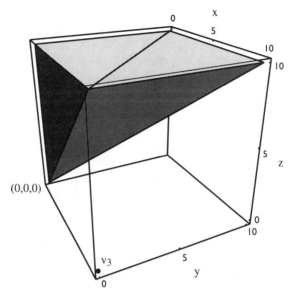

FIGURE 4.15 P_4 and v_3.

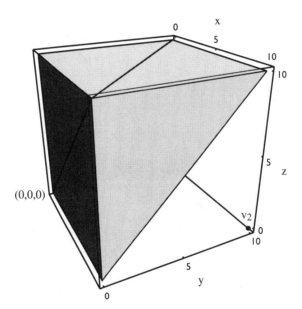

FIGURE 4.16 P_3 and v_2.

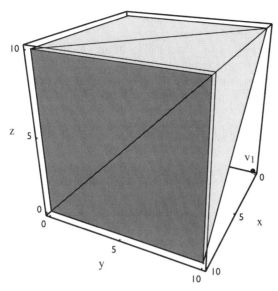

FIGURE 4.17 P_2 and v_1; origin in back.

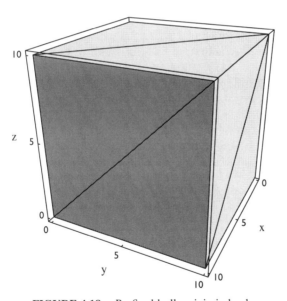

FIGURE 4.18 P_1, final hull; origin in back.

(e_0, e_4, e_3), are border edges, and so constructs three new faces with those as bases: f_4, f_5, and f_6. Initially these faces are linked into the field e->newface, permitting the old hull data structure to maintain its integrity as the cone is being added. This permits the old structure to be interrogated by MakeStructs while the new is being built. Only after the entire cone is attached are the data structures cleaned up with CleanUp.

Coplanarity Revisited. To return to the issue of coplanarity, note that if we considered f_2 visible from v_4, then two of f_2's edges (e_1 and e_5) would become boundary edges, and e_4 would be interior to the visible region. The cone would then be based on four edges rather than three. So our decision to treat coplanar faces as invisible makes the visible region, and therefore the new cone, as small as possible.

There are two reasons for treating vol == 0 faces as invisible:

1. The changes to the data structure are minimized, since, as just explained, the visible region is minimized.

2. Points that fall on a face of the old hull are discarded.

Note that if we treated zero-volume faces as visible, a point in the interior of a face would see that face, and so would end up needlessly fracturing it into new faces.

Although this treatment of visibility avoids inserting new points in the interior of old faces, it does not avoid all unnecessary coplanar points: if the interior point is encountered in the construction first, it will never be deleted later. An unfortunate consequence is that, unlike our code for Graham's two-dimensional hull algorithm in Section 3.5, the three-dimensional hull code can produce different outputs for different permutations of the same input points. Invariance with respect to permutations could be achieved by postprocessing to delete unnecessary coplanar points (Exercise 4.3.5[11]).

Two major pieces of the code remain to be explained, both managing the data structures: MakeStructs and CleanUp.

MakeStructs. Two low-level routines are used by MakeStructs for creating empty edge and face structures, MakeEdge (Code 4.18) and MakeFace (Code

```
tEdge MakeEdge( void )
{
    tEdge    e;
    NEW( e, tsEdge );
    e->adjface[0] = e->adjface[1] = e->newface = NULL;
    e->endpts[0] = e->endpts[1] = NULL;
    e->deleted = !REMOVED;
    ADD( edges, e );
    return e;
}
```

Code 4.18 MakeEdge.

```
tFaceMakeFace( void )
{
    tFace        f;
    int          i;

    NEW( f, tsFace);
    for ( i = 0; i < 3; ++i ) {
        f->edge[i] = NULL;
        f->vertex[i] = NULL;
    }
    f->visible = !VISIBLE;
    ADD( faces, f );
    return f;
}
```

Code 4.19 MakeFace.

4.19). They are straightforward, simply making the indicated structures and initializing the fields to NULL or FALSE as appropriate.

The routine MakeStructs (Code 4.20) takes an edge e and a point p as input and creates a new face spanned by e and p and two new edges between p and the endpoints of e. A pointer to the face is returned, and the created structures are linked together properly.

This is mostly straightforward, but there are two complications. First, the creation of duplicate edges must be avoided. Because we have opted not to structure the border of the visible region, the faces of the cone are constructed in an arbitrary order. Once one face of the cone and its edges have been created, subsequent faces might share two, one, or no edges with previously-created faces.

The mechanism we use to detect this is as follows. Each time an edge e_i is created with one end at p and the other at a vertex v on the old hull, a field of v's record, v->duplicate, points to e_i. For any vertex not incident to a constructed cone edge, the duplicate field is NULL. Note that each vertex is incident to at most one cone edge.

For every edge e on the border of the visible region, a new face f is always created. But new edges for f are only created if the duplicate field of the endpoints of e are NULL. If one is not NULL, the already-created cone edge pointed to by that field is used to fill the appropriate edge field of f.

The second complication in MakeStructs is the need to arrange the array elements in the vertex field of f in counterclockwise order. This is handled by the somewhat tricky routine MakeCcw. The basic idea is simple: assuming that the old hull has its faces oriented properly, make the new faces consistent with the old orientation. In particular, a cone face f can inherit the same orientation as the visible face adjacent to the edge e of the old hull that forms its base. This follows because the new face hides the old, and is in a sense a replacement for it; so it naturally assumes the same orientation.

```
tFace MakeStructs( tEdge e, tVertex p )
{
      tEdge   new_edge[2];
      tEdge   MakeEdge();
      tFace   new_face;
      tFace   MakeFace();
      int     i, j;

      /* Make two new edges (if don't already exist). */
      for ( i = 0; i < 2; ++i )
          /* If the edge exists, copy it into new - edge. */
          if ( !( new_edge[i] = e->endpts[i]->duplicate) )
{                 /* Otherwise (duplicate is NULL), MakeEdge. */
                  new_edge[i] = MakeEdge();
                  new_edge[i]->endpts[0] = e->endpts[i];
                  new_edge[i]->endpts[1] = p;
                  e->endpts[i]->duplicate = new_edge[i];
          }

      /* Make the new face. */
      new_face = MakeFace();
      new_face->edge[0] = e;
      new_face->edge[1] = new_edge[0];
      new_face->edge[2] = new_edge[1];
      MakeCcw( new_face, e, p );

      /* Set the adjacent face pointers. */
      for ( i = 0; i < 2; ++i )
      for ( j = 0; j < 2; ++j )
          /* Only one NULL link should be set to new_face. */
          if ( !new_edge[i]->adjface[j] ) {
                  new_edge[i]->adjface[j] = new_face;
                  break;
          }
      return new_face;
}
```

Code 4.20 MakeStructs.

What makes this somewhat tricky is that there is a need to orient the faces of the initial tetrahedron also. After the base face of the initial tetrahedron is created, the other three were added via calls to MakeStructs from within Tetrahedron. Clearly in this case, there is no visible face adjacent to *e*; in fact *e* has only one adjacent face at that point of the construction. In this case, we want the remaining three faces of the tetrahedron to inherit the orientation opposite to that of the base face.

```
void MakeCcw( tFace f, tEdge e, tVertex p )
{
    int        i;        /* Index */
    tFace      fi;       /* The invisible face adjacent to e */
    tEdge      s;        /* Temporary, for swapping */

    /* If this is the initial tetrahedron, then e has only one
       adjacent face, and use that for fi. Otherwise, use the
       invisible face. */
    if ( !e->adjface[1] )
            fi = e->adjface[0];
    else {
            if ( !e->adjface[0]->visible )
                    fi = e->adjface[0];
            else    fi = e->adjface[1];
    }

    /* Set vertex[0] & [1] of f to have the opposite orientation
       as do the corresponding vertices of fi. */
    /* Find the index i of e-> endpoint[1] in fi. */
    for ( i = 0; fi->vertex[i] != e->endpts[1]; ++i )
            ;
    /* Orient f opposite that of fi. */
    if ( fi->vertex[ (i+1) % 3 ] != e->endpts[0] ) {
            f->vertex[0] = e->endpts[1];
            f->vertex[1] = e->endpts[0];
    }
    else {
            f->vertex[0] = e->endpts[0];
            f->vertex[1] = e->endpts[1];
            SWAP( s, f->edge[1], f->edge[2] );
    }
    f->vertex[2] = p;
}
```

Code 4.21   MakeCcw.

We can handle both the initial tetrahedron and the generic case by arranging
for *f* to inherit the opposite orientation of the *invisible* face adjacent to *e*, and
defining this face to be the base of the tetrahedron in that special case. This
works because the endpoints of *e* appear in opposite orders in the vertex lists
of two faces adjacent to *e*. With this explanation, the functioning of MakeCcw
(Code 4.21) should be comprehensible.

CleanUp. Just prior to calling CleanUp in AddOne, the new hull has been
constructed: all the faces, edges and one new vertex are linked to each other
and to the old structures properly. However, the cone is "glued on" to the old

```
void CleanUp( void )
{
    CleanEdges();
    CleanFaces();
    CleanVertices();
}
```

Code 4.22 `CleanUp`.

structures via the `newface` fields of edges on the border of the visible region. Moreover, the portion of the old hull that is now inside the cone needs to be deleted. The purpose of `CleanUp` is to "clean up" the three data structures to represent the new hull exactly and only, and prepare the structures for the next iteration.

This task is less straightforward than one might expect. We partition the work into three natural groups (Code 4.22): cleaning up the vertex, the edge, and the face lists. However, the order in which the three are done is important. It's easiest to decide which faces are to be deleted: those marked `f->visible`. Edges to delete require an inference, made earlier and recorded in `e->delete`: both adjacent faces are visible. Vertices to delete require the most work: these vertices have no incident edges on the new hull.

We first describe `CleanFaces` (Code 4.23), which is a straight deletion of all faces marked `visible`, meaning visible from the new point just added, and

```
void CleanFaces( void )
{
    tFace       f;          /* Primary pointer into face list. */
    tFace       t;          /* Temporary pointer, for deleting. */

    while ( faces && faces->visible ) {
            f = faces;
            DELETE( faces, f );
    }
    f = faces->next;
    do {
            if ( f->visible ) {
                    t = f;
                    f = f->next;
                    DELETE( faces, t );
            }
            else f = f->next;
    } while ( f != faces );
}
```

Code 4.23 `CleanFaces`.

```
void CleanEdges( void )
{
    tEdge        e;        / * Primary index into edge list. * /
    tEdge        t;        / * Temporary edge pointer. * /

    / * Integrate the newface's into the data structure. * /
    / * Check every edge. * /
    e = edges;
    do {
                if ( e->newface ) {
                if ( e->adjface[0]->visible )
                    e->adjface[0] = e->newface;
                else    e->adjface[1] = e->newface;
                    e->newface = NULL;
                }
                e = e->next;
    } while ( e != edges );

    / * Delete any edges marked deleted. * /
    while ( edges && edges->deleted ) {
                e = edges;
                DELETE ( edges, e );
    }
    e = edges->next;
    do {
                if ( e->deleted ) {
                    t = e;
                    e = e->next;
                    DELETE( edges, t );
                }
                else e = e->next;
    } while ( e != edges );
}
```

Code 4.24 `CleanEdges`.

therefore inside the new hull. There is one minor coding feature to note. Normally our loops over all elements of a list start with the head and stop the `do-while` when the head is encountered again. However, suppose, for example, that the first two elements *A* and *B* of the `faces` list are both `visible`, and so should be deleted. Starting with `f=faces`, the element `f` = *A* is deleted, `f` is set to *B*, and the `DELETE` macro revises `faces` to point to *B* also. Now, if we used the standard loop termination `while( f != faces )`, it would appear that we are finished when in fact we are not.

This problem is skirted by repeatedly deleting the head of the list (if appropriate) and only starting the general loop when we are assured that reencountering the head of the list really does indicate proper loop termination. The same strategy is used for deletion in `CleanEdges` and `CleanVertices`.

```
void CleanVertices( void )
{
    tEdge        e;
    tVertex      v, t;

    /* Mark all vertices incident to some undeleted edge as on hull. */
    e = edges;
    do {
                e->endpts[0]->onhull = ONHULL;
                e->endpts[1]->onhull = ONHULL;
                e = e->next;
    } while (e ! = edges);

    /* Delete all vertices that have been processed but
       are not on the hull. */
    while ( vertices && vertices->mark &&
            !vertices->onhull ) {
            v = vertices;
            DELETE( vertices, v );
    }
    v = vertices->next;
    do {
                if ( v->mark && !v->onhull ) {
                    t = v;
                    v = v->next;
                    DELETE( vertices, t )
                }
                else v = v->next;
    } while ( v != vertices );

    /* Reset flags. */
    v = vertices;
    do {
                v->duplicate = NULL;
                v->onhull = !ONHULL;
                v = v->next;
    } while ( v != vertices );
}
```

Code 4.25 CleanVertices.

Recall that it is the border edges of the visible region to which the newly-added cone is attached. For each of these border edges, CleanEdges (Code 4.24) copies newface into the appropriate adjface field. The reason that CleanEdges is called prior to CleanFaces is that we need to access the visible field of the adjacent faces to decide which to overwrite. So the old faces must be around to properly integrate the new.

Second, CleanEdges deletes all edges that were previously marked for deletion (by the routine AddOne).

The vertices to delete are not flagged by any routine invoked earlier. However, we have called `CleanEdges` first so that we can infer that a vertex is strictly in the interior of the visible region if it has no incident edges: those interior edges have all been deleted by now. So in `CleanVertices` (Code 4.25) we run through the edge list, marking each vertex that is an endpoint as on the hull in the `v->onhull` field. Then a vertex loop deletes all those points already processed but not on the hull. Finally, the various flags in the vertex record are reset.

This completes the description of the code. As should be evident, there is a significant gap between the relatively straightforward algorithm, and the reality of an actual implementation. We continue discussing a few more "real" implementation issues in the next three subsections.

4.3.3. Checks

It is not feasible to hope that a program as complex as the foregoing will work correctly upon first implementation. I have spared the reader the debugging printout statements, which are turned on by a command-line flag. Another part of the code not shown is perhaps more worthy of discussion: consistency checks. Again via a command-line flag, we can invoke functions that comb through the data structures checking for various properties known to hold if all is copacetic. The current set of checks used are:

1. Face orientations: check that the endpoints of each edge occur in opposite orders in the two faces adjacent to that edge.

2. Convexity: check that each face of the hull forms a non-negative volume with each vertex of the hull.

3. Euler's relations: check that $F = 2V - 4$ (Eq. [4.5]) and $2E = 3V$.

These tests are run after each iteration. They are very slow but receiving a clean bill of health from these gives some confidence in the program.

4.3.4. Performance

The program is fundamentally quadratic, but its performance varies greatly depending on the data. We present data here for two extreme cases: random points uniformly distributed inside a cube, and random points uniformly distributed near the surface of a sphere. Figures 4.19 and 4.20 show examples for $n = 10,000$. Most of the points in a cube do not end up on the hull, whereas a large portion of the points near the sphere surface are part of the hull. In Figure 4.19, the hull has 158 vertices, so 9,842 points of the 10,000 were interior. The hull in Figure 4.20 has 2,289 vertices; the other 7,711 points were within 2% of the sphere radius of the surface. The sphere points were generated from random vectors of length $r = 100$, whose tips were then truncated to integer coordinates; about three-quarters of the lengths of these truncated vectors exceed 99.

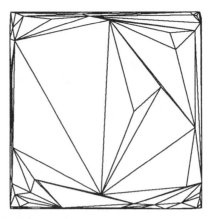

FIGURE 4.19   Hull of 10,000 points in a cube.

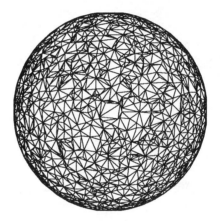

FIGURE 4.20   Hull of 10,000 points near the surface of a sphere.

Figure 4.21 shows the computation time for the two cases for various n up to 10,000. The times are in seconds on a DEC MicroVAX 3100.[18] The superlinear growth is evident in both curves.

4.3.5. Volume Overflow

All the geometry in the code just presented is concentrated in one spot: the volume computation. We have insisted on integer coordinates for the points so that we can be sure this computation is correct. Had we permitted floating-point coordinates, the comparison of the volume to zero could be in error for certain nearly coplanar quadruples of points. Now we have to face an unpleasant reality: even the integer volume computation is not certain, due to overflow! On

---

[18]This is not a fast machine by 1993 standards. The code runs in about one-third the time on a NeXTstation Turbo.

Seconds

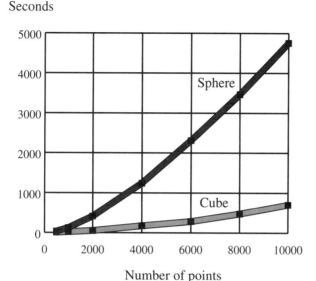

Number of points

FIGURE 4.21 Runtimes for random points in a cube and near a sphere surface.

most current machines,[19] signed integers use 32 bits, and can represent numbers from $-2^{31} = -2147483648$ to $2^{31} - 1 = 2147483647$: about $\pm$ two billion. When a computation (e.g., addition or multiplication) exceeds these bounds, the C program proceeds without a complaint: unlike division by zero, integer overflow is not detected and reported back to the C program. Rather the 32 bits are just interpreted as a normal signed integer, which usually means that numbers that exceed $2^{31} - 1$ slightly "wrap around" to negative integers.

This does not affect many programs, because the numbers used never become very large. However, our critical volume computation multiplies three coordinates together: the generic term of the computation is abc, where a, b, and c are each one of the three coordinates of various points (Eq. 4.6). Since the program will not tell the user (by crashing) when integer overflow occurs, it is important to know what is the safe "range."

This is unfortunately not a straightforward question (Exercise 4.3.5[13]), as the computation involves many terms, some of which may cancel out. The smallest coordinates with which I could make the computation err uses coordinates of only ± 512. The idea behind this example is that a regular tetrahedron maximizes its volume among all tetrahedra with fixed maximum edge length. So start with the regular tetrahedron T defined by $(1, 1, 1)$, $(1, -1, -1)$, $(-1, 1, -1)$, and $(-1, -1, 1)$, which is formed by four vertices of a cube centered on the origin. Scaled by a constant c, the volume of this tetrahedron is $16c^3$. With

---

[19]Circa 1993. Some newer machines are permitting 64-bit integer computations.

$c = 2^9 = 512$, the volume is $2^{3(9)+4} = 2^{31}$. Thus,

$$\begin{vmatrix} 512 & 512 & 512 & 1 \\ 512 & -512 & -512 & 1 \\ -512 & 512 & -512 & 1 \\ -512 & -512 & 512 & 1 \end{vmatrix} = 2^{31} = 2147483648. \tag{4.8}$$

However, `Volume6` returns the value $-2147483648 = -2^{31}$.

It is interesting to note that if all the variables of `Volume6` are changed to `double`, it produces the correct answer in this instance. The reason is that on the MicroVAX I used for the computation, `doubles` are allocated 64 bits, 57 of which are used for the mantissa. So curiously, on this machine and on several others, integer calculations can be performed more accurately with floating-point numbers! Using `doubles`, however, only shifts the precision problem elsewhere. For example, the four points $(3,0,0)$, $(0,3,0)$, $(0,0,3)$, and $(1,1,1)$ are coplanar, the fourth being the centroid of the triangle determined by the first three. Using `int` computations, `Volume6` returns the correct value of zero for this scaled version of these points:

$$\begin{vmatrix} 600003 & 0 & 0 & 1 \\ 0 & 600003 & 0 & 1 \\ 0 & 0 & 600003 & 1 \\ 200001 & 200001 & 200001 & 1 \end{vmatrix} = 0 \tag{4.9}$$

However, if `doubles` are used, the volume returned is 2! The reason is that the value of the determinant is $600003^3 - 3(600003^2)\,200001$, and the terms, which are both equal to 216003240016200027, cannot be represented exactly in 57 bits. Although the integer calculation yields the correct volume, it is correct only by accident: the intermediate calculations overflow but cancel.[20] Ultimately there is no straightforward method for avoiding the finite precision problem: if `ints` are used, we have the choice of severe limitation on the size of coordinates versus the uncertainty of unreported integer overflows; if `doubles` are used, the computation will be occasionally incorrect, without warning.

Here are several strategies for managing this fundamental problem:

1. Report integer overflows. C++ permits defining a class of integers so that overflow will be reported. Other languages also report overflows. This does not extend the range of the code, but at least the user will know when it fails.

2. Bignums. Some languages, such as LISP and Mathematica, use arbitrary precision arithmetic, often called "bignums." The problem disappears in these languages, although they are often not the most convenient to mesh with other applications. Bignum packages that supplement languages like C often incur heavy overhead.

---

[20] I appreciate the assistance of Carole Gitlin with these overflow examples.

3. Use higher precision arithmetic. Machines are now offering 64-bit integer computations, which extend the range of the volume computation to more comfortable levels (Exercise 4.3.5[13]).

4. Compare with `doubles`. Short of using a better language or a better machine, there is one technique for detecting most overflows: perform the volume computation both in `ints` and in `doubles`, and compare the results. When the floating-point result is "close" to the integer result, this usually implies that no integer overflow has occurred. When the two results differ significantly, it indicates overflow, and the user can be notified of the likely error; in this case, it makes sense to continue the hull computation based on the `double` volume.

   This method is implemented in the version of the code distributed with this book.

These issues are under debate in the community at this writing; see Fortune and Van Wyk (1993).

Exercises

1. *Explore* `chull.c` [programming]. Learn how to use `chull.c` and related routines. There are three main programs: `chull`, `sphere`, and `cube`. `sphere` n outputs *n* random points near the surface of a sphere. `cube` n outputs *n* random points inside a cube. `chull` reads points from standard input and outputs their convex hull. The output of `sphere` or `cube` may be piped directly into `chull`:

   `sphere 100 ¦ chull`

   See the README file for details of input and output formatting conventions and other relevant information.

2. *Measure time complexity* [programming]. Measure the time complexity of `chull` by timing its execution on random data produced by `sphere` and `cube`. You may use the Unix function `time`; see `man time`. Make sure you don't time the point generation routines: only time `chull`. Compare the times on your machine with those shown in Figure 4.21.

3. *Profile* [programming]. Analyze where `chull` is spending most of its time with the Unix "profiling" tools. Compile with a –p flag and then run the utility `prof`. See the manual pages.

4. *Speed up* `chull` [programming]. David Dobkin sped up my code by a factor of five in some cases with various improvements. Suggest some improvements and implement them.

5. *Distributed volume computation* [programming]. If the volume computation is viewed as area times height, some savings can be achieved by computing the area normal *a* for each face *f*, and then calculating the height of the tetrahedron by dotting a vector from the face to *p* with *a* (where *p* is the point being added to the hull). Implement this change and see how much it speeds up the code.

6. *Visibility region*. Prove that the visibility region (the region of *Q* visible from *p*) is connected (compare Exercise 4.2.2[3]). Prove that the boundary edges of the visibility region form a simple cycle (in contrast to the situation in Figure 4.7). Suggest code improvements based on this property.

7. *Criticize data structures.* Point out as many weaknesses of the data structures that you can think of. In each case, suggest alternatives.

8. *Consistency checks.* Think of a way the data structure could be incorrect that would not be detected by the consistency checks discussed in Section 4.3.3. Design a check that would catch this.

9. *Faces with many vertices.* Design a data structure that allows faces to have an arbitrary number of vertices.

10. *Distinct points.* Does the code work when not all input points are distinct?

11. *Deleting coplanar points* [programming]. Postprocess the hull data structure to delete unnecessary coplanar points.

12. *Removing common factors* (Teller) [programming]. Increase the likelihood that the volume computation will avoid overflow by removing common factors prior to the computation.

13. *Volume* int *range*

    a. For a machine with 32-bit integers, determine an integer m such that if all int coordinates are within the range $[-m, +m]$, then the value of Volume6 is correct. The example on p. 158 demonstrates that $m < 512$. Prove correctness. Is your m the largest possible?

    b. Repeat your computation for a machine with 64-bit integers.

14. *Volume and* doubles [programming]. Find an example for which the double computation of Volume6 is incorrect on your machine, and which uses coordinates whose absolute value is as small as possible.

15. *Break the code* [programming]. Find an example set of (non-coplanar) points for which the output of chull is incorrect, but where all volume computations are correct. Notify the author.

4.4. POLYHEDRAL BOUNDARY REPRESENTATIONS

Representing the boundaries of polyhedra and more general objects has developed into an important subspecialty within computer graphics, geometric modeling, and computational geometry. In this section I will sketch two representations more sophisticated than that used in Section 4.3.1. In particular, these representations do not require faces to be triangles. This immediately raises the issue of how to represent faces: can fixed-length records be used, or must we resort to variable-length lists? Our goal in this section is merely to indicate a few issues; no attempt will be made at comprehensive coverage.

4.4.1. Winged-edge Data Structure

One of the first representations developed, and still the most popular, is Baumgart's *winged-edge* representation (Baumgart, 1975). The focus of this data structure is the edge. Each vertex points to an arbitrary one of its incident edges, and each face points to an arbitrary one of its bounding edges. An edge record for e consists of eight pointers: to the two endpoints of e, v_0 and v_1; to the two faces adjacent to e, f_0 and f_1, left and right respectively of $v_0 v_1$; and to four edges (the "wings" of e): e_0^- and e_0^+, edges incident to v_0, clockwise and

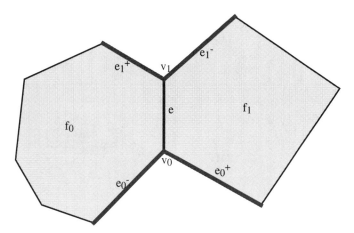

FIGURE 4.22   The winged-edge data structure.

counterclockwise of e respectively; and e_1^- and e_1^+, edges incident to v_1. See Figure 4.22. Note that all three structures are constant size, a useful feature.

As an example of the use of the data structure, the edges bounding a face f may be found by retrieving the sole edge e stored in f's record, and then following the e_1^+ edges around f until e is again encountered.

4.4.2. Quad-edge Data Structure

Guibas and Stolfi invented an alluring data structure they call the *quad-edge* structure (Guibas and Stolfi, 1985), which although more complex in the

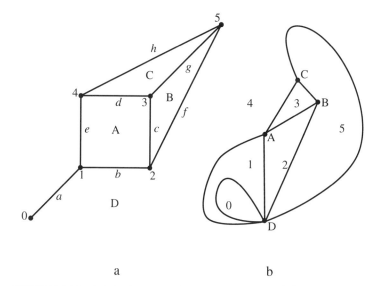

a   b

FIGURE 4.23   (*a*) A plane graph to be represented; (*b*) its dual graph.

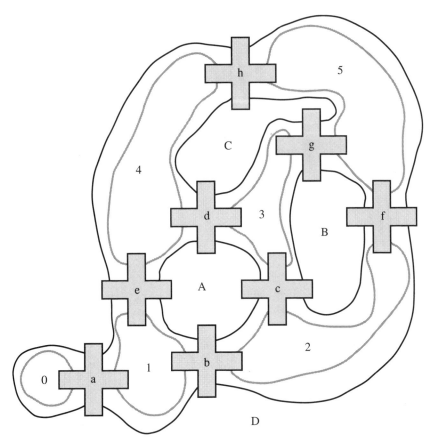

FIGURE 4.24 The quad-edge data structure for the graph in Figure 4.23. Dark cycles represent faces, and light cycles vertices.

abstract, in fact simplifies many operations and algorithms. It has the advantage of being extremely general, representing any subdivision of 2-manifolds (p. 114), permitting distinctions between the two sides of a surface, allowing the two endpoints of an edge to be the same vertex, permitting dangling edges, etc.

Each edge record is part of four circular lists: for the two endpoints, and for the two adjacent faces. Thus it contains four pointers. Additional information may be included (an above/below bit, geometric information, and so forth) depending on the application. An example is shown in Figures 4.23 and 4.24. Figure 4.23a shows a plane graph. Note that it is not a polyhedral graph (one derivable from a polyhedron) but is rather more general. There are three interior faces, A, B, and C, with D the exterior face. The eight edges are labeled $a, \ldots, h$, and the six vertices $0, \ldots, 5$. Figure 4.24 shows the corresponding quad-edge structure, with each edge record represented by a cross, the four arms corresponding to the four pointers. The face cycles are drawn with dark lines; the vertex cycles are drawn with light lines. For example, face A is the ring of edges (b, c, d, e), and vertex 3 is the ring (c, g, d). Note that the dangling edge a is modeled in a pleasingly consistent way, appearing twice on the cycle for the exterior face D.

As with the winged-edge data structure, vertices and faces have minimal representations: each is assigned to an arbitrary edge on their ring. The true representation of a vertex or face is this ring; the edge pointer just gives access to the ring.

One of the most beautiful aspects of this structure is that it encodes the dual subdivision automatically. We discussed triangulation duals in Chapter 1 (Section 1.2.3). The *dual* of a general plane graph G assigns a node to each face and an arc for each edge between adjacent faces. The "exterior face" is also assigned a node, and connects to every face with a boundary edge. This has the consequence that every vertex in G is surrounded by a cycle of face nodes in the dual, as shown in Figure 4.23b. The dual subdivision is achieved in a quad-edge structure simply by interpreting the light cycles as faces and the dark cycles as vertices in Figure 4.24: no computation is necessary! We will encounter dual graphs again in the next chapter (Section 5.2.2).

4.4.3. Exercises

1. *Winged-edge: edges incident to vertex.* Given a vertex v and a winged-edge data structure, describe how to create a sorted list of all edges incident to v.
2. *Quad-edge: enumeration of edges.* Given one edge and a quad-edge data structure, describe a method of enumerating all edges in the subdivision.

4.5.   HIGHER DIMENSIONS

Although we will not cover computational geometry in dimensions beyond three in this book, it would be remiss not even to mention this fertile and important area. This section (together with a brief discussion in Chapter 9) will constitute our nod in this direction.

It is an intellectual challenge to appreciate higher-dimensional geometry, and the reader will only get a taste here. Banchoff (1990) and Rucker (1984) are good sources for more thorough explications.

It is best to approach higher dimensions by analogy with lower dimensions, preferably attaining a running start for your intuition by examining zero-, one-, two-, and three-dimensional examples before leaping into hyperspace.

4.5.1.   Coordinates

A point on a number line can be represented by a single number: its value, or location. This can be viewed as a one-dimensional point, since the space in which it is located, the line, is one-dimensional. A point in two dimensions can be specified by two coordinates (x, y), and in three dimensions by three coordinates (x, y, z). The leap here is easy: a point in four dimensions requires

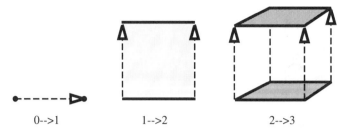

0-->1   1-->2   2-->3

FIGURE 4.25   A cube can be viewed as a square swept through the third dimension.

four coordinates for specification, say (x, y, z, t). If we think of (x, y, z) as space coordinates and t as time, the four numbers specify an event in both space and time. Besides the use of four dimensions for space-time, there are many other possible spaces of higher dimensions. Just to contrive one example, we could represent the key sartorial characteristics of a person by height, sleeve length, inseam length, and neck and waist circumferences. Then each person could be viewed as a point in a five-dimensional space: (*height, arm, leg, neck, waist*). Unfortunately, the bare consideration of coordinates yields little insight into higher-dimensional geometry. For that, we turn to the hypercube.

4.5.2. Hypercube

A zero-dimensional cube is a point. A one-dimensional cube is a line segment. A two-dimensional cube is a square. A three-dimensional cube is a normal cube. Before leaping into four dimensions, let's gather some statistics:

Dim d	Name	V_d	E_d
0	point	1	0
1	segment	2	1
2	square	4	4
3	cube	8	12
4	hypercube	16	32
d	d-cube	2^d	$2E_{d-1} + V_{d-1}$

We can view a cube in dimension d as built from two copies of cubes in dimension $d - 1$, as follows. Take a one-dimensional cube (a point) and stretch it in a second dimension, producing a two-dimensional cube, a segment. Slide a segment orthogonal to itself to sweep out a square. Raise a square perpendicular to its plane to sweep out a cube. See Figure 4.25. Now comes the leap. Start with a cube of 8 vertices and 12 edges. Sweep it into a fourth dimension, dragging new edges between the original cube's vertices and the final cube. The new object is a *hypercube*, a four-dimensional cube:[21] 16 vertices from the start

---

[21]Some authors use "hypercube" to indicate a cube in arbitrary dimensions.

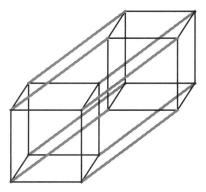

FIGURE 4.26 The edges of a hypercube. The shaded edges represent the sweep in the fourth dimension, connecting two copies of a three-dimensional cube.

and stop cubes (8 from each), and 32 edges: 12 from each, plus 8 new ones. See Figure 4.26. Note the number of edges E_d is twice the number in one lower dimension, $2E_{d-1}$, plus the number of vertices V_{d-1}.

Coordinates for the vertices of a generic hypercube can be generated conveniently by the binary digits of the first 2^d integers:

$$
\begin{aligned}
0 &\rightarrow (0,0,0,0) & 8 &\rightarrow (1,0,0,0) \\
1 &\rightarrow (0,0,0,1) & 9 &\rightarrow (1,0,0,1) \\
2 &\rightarrow (0,0,1,0) & 10 &\rightarrow (1,0,1,0) \\
3 &\rightarrow (0,0,1,1) & 11 &\rightarrow (1,0,1,1) \\
4 &\rightarrow (0,1,0,0) & 12 &\rightarrow (1,1,0,0) \\
5 &\rightarrow (0,1,0,1) & 13 &\rightarrow (1,1,0,1) \\
6 &\rightarrow (0,1,1,0) & 14 &\rightarrow (1,1,1,0) \\
7 &\rightarrow (0,1,1,1) & 15 &\rightarrow (1,1,1,1).
\end{aligned}
\tag{4.10}
$$

The hypercube is the convex hull of these 16 points.

4.5.3. Regular Polytopes

We saw how there are exactly five distinct regular polytopes in three dimensions. In four dimensions, there are precisely six regular polytopes. One is the hypercube. But there are surprises: one of the regular polytopes is known as the 600-cell: it is composed of 600 tetrahedral "facets"! It was not until the 19th century that the list of four-dimensional regular polytopes was completed, approximately 2000 years after the three-dimensional polytopes were constructed. In each dimension $d \geq 5$, there are just three regular polytopes, the generalizations of the tetrahedron, the cube, and the octahedron (see Coxeter, 1973).

4.5.4. Hull in Higher Dimensions

Much research has been invested in algorithms for constructing the convex hull of a set of points in higher dimensions. This is a problem that arises in a surprisingly wide variety of contexts. Here we touch on two. First, the probability for a certain type of program to branch one way rather than another at a conditional, can be modeled as a ratio of volumes of polytopes in a number of dimensions dependent upon the complexity of the code (Cohen and Hickey, 1979). Second, the computation of the "antipenumbra" of a convex light source (the volume of space from which some, but not all, of the light source can be seen), can be approached by computing the hull of points in five dimensions (Teller, 1992).[22] We will see another application in Section 5.7.2.

There is, unfortunately, a fundamental obstruction to obtaining efficient algorithms: the structure of the hull is so complicated that just printing it out sets a stiff lower bound on algorithms. Klee (1980) proved that the hull of n points in d dimensions can have $\Omega(n^{\lfloor d/2 \rfloor})$ facets. So in particular, the hull in $d = 4$ dimensions can have quadratic size, and no $O(n \log n)$ algorithm is possible. Nevertheless algorithms have been developed that are as efficient as possible under the circumstances (see Edelsbrunner, 1987, Chapter 8).

4.5.5. Exercises

1. *Simplices*. A *simplex* is the generalization of a triangle and tetrahedron to arbitrary dimensions. Guess how many vertices, $(d - 1)$-dimensional facets, and $(d - 2)$-dimensional "ridges" a simplex in d-dimensions has. A *ridge* is the higher-dimensional analog of an edge in three dimensions.

2. *Volume of hypersphere*. What is the volume of a unit-radius sphere in four dimensions? Try to generalize to d-dimensions. What is the limit of the volume as $d \to \infty$?

4.6. ADDITIONAL EXERCISES

1. *Diameter and width*. This is a generalization of Exercise 3.9.3[3].

   a. Construct a polytope on n vertices whose diameter (largest distance between any two points) is realized by as many distinct pairs of points as possible.

   b. Construct a polytope on n vertices that has as many distinct antipodal pairs of points as possible. *Antipodal points* are points that admit parallel planes of support: planes that touch at the points and have the hull to one side.

   c. Characterize the contacts that may realize the width of a polytope, where the *width* is the smallest distance between parallel planes of support. Each plane of support may touch a face (f), an edge (e) (but not a face), or a vertex (v) (but not an edge). Which of the six possible combinations (v, v), (v, e), (v, f), (e, e), (e, f), (f, f), can realize the width?

---

[22] The five dimensions arise when the lines containing edges of polyhedra are converted to Plücker coordinates, which represent a directed line with a six-tuple. Removing a scale factor maps these into five dimensions.

2. *G E B*. The cover of *Gödel, Escher, Bach* (Hofstadter, 1979) shows a solid piece of carved wood, which casts the letters G, E, and B as shadows in three orthogonal directions.

    a. Can all triples of letters be achieved as shadows of a solid, connected object? Make any reasonable assumptions on the shapes of the letters. If so, supply an argument. If not, exhibit triples that cannot be mutually realized.

    b. Given three orthogonal polygons, design an algorithm for computing a shape that will have those polygons as shadows, or report that no such shape exists. Keep your algorithm description at a high level, focusing on the method, not the details of implementation. Analyze your algorithm's time complexity as a function of the number of vertices n of the polygons (assume they all have about the same number of vertices).

       Discuss whether your algorithm might be modified to handle non-orthogonal polygons; it may be that it cannot.

3. *Polytope to tetrahedra*. For a polytope of V, E, and F vertices, edges, and faces, how many tetrahedra T result when it is partitioned into tetrahedra, partitioned in such a way that all edges of the tetrahedra have polytope vertices as endpoints? Is T determined by V, E, and F? If so, provide a formula; if not, provide upper and lower bounds on T.

4. *Stable polytopes*. Design an algorithm to decide if a polytope resting on a given face is stable or will fall over (cf. Exercise 1.6.8[12]).

5. *Shortest path on a cube's surface*. Design a method for finding the shortest path between two points x and y on the surface of a cube, where the path lies on the surface. This is the shortest path for a fly walking between x and y.

6. *Triangle $\cap$ cube*. When a triangle in three dimensions is intersected with the closed region bound by a cube, the result is a polygon P. This is a common computation in graphics, "clipping" a triangle to a cubical viewing space. What is the largest number of vertices P can have for any triangle?

5

Voronoi Diagrams

In this chapter, we study the Voronoi diagram, a geometric structure second in importance only to the convex hull. In a sense, a Voronoi diagram records everything one would ever want to know about proximity to a set of points (or more general objects). Often one does want to know detail about proximity: who is closest to whom, who is furthest, and so on. The concept is more than a century old, discussed in 1850 by Dirichlet and in a 1908 paper of Voronoi.[1]

We start with a series of examples to motivate the discussion, and then plunge into the details of the rich structure of the Voronoi diagram (in Sections 5.2–5.3). It is necessary to become intimately familiar with these details before algorithms can be appreciated (in Section 5.4). Finally, we reveal the beautiful connection between Voronoi diagrams and convex hulls in Section 5.7. This chapter includes only one short piece of code, in Section 5.7.4.

5.1. APPLICATIONS: PREVIEW

1. *Fire Observation Towers*

   Imagine a vast forest containing a number of fire observation towers. Each ranger is responsible for extinguishing any fire closer to her tower than to any other tower. The set of all trees for which a particular ranger is responsible constitutes the "Voronoi polygon" associated with her tower. The Voronoi diagram maps out the lines between these areas of responsibility: the spots in the forest that are equidistant from two or more towers. (A look ahead to Figure 5.5 may aid intuition.)

2. *Towers on Fire*

   Imagine now the perverse situation where all the rangers ignite their towers simultaneously, and the forest burns at a uniform rate. The fire will spread in circles centered on each tower. The points at which the fire quenches because it reaches previously consumed trees, are those points equidistant from two or more towers, which are exactly the points on the Voronoi diagram.

3. *Nearest Neighbor Clustering*

   A technique frequently employed in the field of pattern recognition is to map a set of target objects into a feature space by reducing the objects to points whose coordinates are feature measurements. The example of

---

[1]See Aurenhammer (1991) for a history.

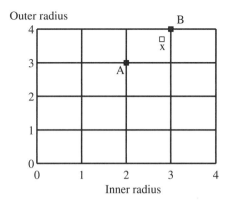

FIGURE 5.1 x is closer to B than to A.

five tailor's measurements from Section 4.5.1 can be viewed as defining such a feature space. The identity of an object of unknown affiliation then can be assigned the nearest target object in feature space.

An example will make this clearer. Suppose a parts bin includes two types of nuts A and B, A with inner and outer diameters of 2 and 3 cm respectively, and B with diameters 3 and 4 cm. Feature space is the positive quadrant of the two-dimensional Euclidean plane, positive because neither radius can be negative. A maps to the point $(2, 3)$, and B to the point $(3, 4)$.

Suppose a vision system focuses on a nut x in the bin, and measures its inner and outer radii to be 2.8 and 3.7 cm. Knowing that there are measurement inaccuracies, and that only nuts of type A and B are in the bin, which type of nut is x? It is most likely to be a B nut, because its distance to B in feature space is 0.36, whereas its distance to A is 1.06. See Figure 5.1. In other words, the nearest neighbor of x is B, because x is in B's Voronoi polygon.

If there are many types of nuts, the identification task is to locate the unknown nut x in the Voronoi diagram of the target nuts. How this can be done efficiently will be discussed in Section 5.5.1.

4. *Facility location*
Suppose you would like to locate a new grocery store in an area with several existing, competing grocery stores. Assuming uniform population density, where should the new store be located to optimize its sales? One natural method of satisfying this vague constraint is to locate the new store as far away from the old ones as possible. Even this is a bit vague; more precisely we could choose a location whose distance to the *nearest* store is as large as possible. This is equivalent to locating the new store at the center of the largest empty circle, the largest circle whose interior contains no other stores. The distance to the nearest store is then the radius of this circle.

We show in Section 5.5.3 that the center of the largest empty circle must lie on the Voronoi diagram.

5. *Path Planning*

Imagine a cluttered environment through which a robot must plan a path. In order to minimize the risk of collision, the robot would like to stay as far away from all obstacles as possible. If we restrict the question to two dimensions, and if the robot is circular, then the robot should remain at all times on the Voronoi diagram of the obstacles. If the obstacles are points (say thin poles), then this is the conventional Voronoi diagram. If the obstacles are polygons or other shapes, then a generalized version of the point Voronoi diagram determines the appropriate path.

We revisit this example in Chapter 8 (Section 8.5.2).

6. *Crystallography*

Assume a number of crystal seeds grow at a uniform, constant rate. What will be the appearance of the crystal when growth is no longer possible? It should be clear now that this is analogous to the forest fire, and that each seed will grow to a Voronoi polygon, with adjacent seed regions meeting along the Voronoi diagram. Voronoi diagrams have long been used to simulate crystal growth.[2]

The list of applications could go on and on, and we will see others in Section 5.5, but it is time to define the diagram formally.

5.2. DEFINITIONS AND BASIC PROPERTIES

Let $P = \{p_1, p_2, \ldots, p_n\}$ be a set of points in the two-dimensional Euclidean plane. These are called the *sites*. Partition the plane by assigning every point in the plane to its nearest site. All those points assigned to p_i form the *Voronoi region* $V(p_i)$.[3] $V(p_i)$ consists of all the points at least as close to p_i as to any other site:

$$V(p_i) = \left\{ x : |p_i - x| \leq |p_j - x|, \forall j \neq i \right\}. \tag{5.1}$$

Note, we have defined this set to be closed. Some points do not have a unique nearest site, or *nearest neighbor*. The set of all points that have more than one nearest neighbor form the *Voronoi diagram* $\mathscr{V}(P)$ for the set of sites.

Later we will define Voronoi diagrams for sets of objects more general than points. We first look at diagrams with just a few sites before detailing their properties for larger n.

---

[2]See Schaudt and Drysdale (1991) for recent work.

[3]This is also called a "Voronoi polygon," "Dirichlet domain," a "Thiessen polygon," or a "Wigner-Seitz region." The Voronoi region is not a polygon by our definition of "polygon," because it might be unbounded.

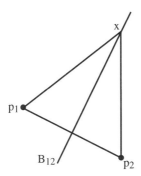

FIGURE 5.2   Two sites: $|p_1 x| = |p_2 x|$.

Two Sites

Consider just two sites, p_1 and p_2. Let $B(p_1, p_2) = B_{12}$ be the perpendicular bisector of the segment $p_1 p_2$. Then every point x on B_{12} is equidistant from p_1 and p_2. This can be seen by drawing the triangle (p_1, p_2, x) as shown in Figure 5.2. By the side-angle-side theorem of Euclid,[4] $|p_1 x| = |p_2 x|$.

Three Sites

For three sites, it is clear that away from the triangle (p_1, p_2, p_3), the diagram contains the bisectors B_{12}, B_{23}, and B_{31}. What is not so clear is what happens in the vicinity of the triangle. Again from Euclid,[5] the perpendicular bisectors of the three sides of a triangle all pass through one point, the circumcenter, the center of the unique circle that passes through the triangle's vertices. Thus, the Voronoi diagram for three points must appear as in Figure 5.3. (However, the circumcenter of a triangle is not always inside the triangle as shown.)

5.2.1. Halfplanes

The generalization beyond three points is perhaps not yet clear, but it is certainly clear that the bisectors B_{ij} will play a role. Let $H(p_i, p_j)$ be the closed halfplane with boundary B_{ij} and containing p_i. Then $H(p_i, p_j)$ can be viewed as all the points that are closer to p_i than they are to p_j. Now recall that $V(p_i)$ is the set of all points closer to p_i than to any other site: in other words, the points closer to p_i than to p_1, _and_ closer to p_i than to p_2, _and_ closer to p_i than to p_3,

---

[4]Heath (1956, I.4).
[5]Heath (1956, IV.5).

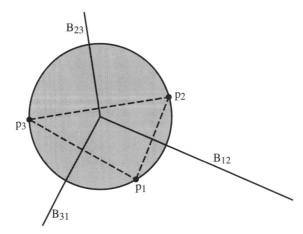

FIGURE 5.3   Three sites: bisectors meet at circumcenter.

and so on. This shows we can write this equation for $V(p_i)$:

$$V(p_i) = \bigcap_{i \neq j} H(p_i, p_j), \tag{5.2}$$

where the notation implies that the intersection is to be taken over all i and j such that $i \neq j$. Note the English conjunction "and" has been translated to set intersection.

Equation 5.2 immediately gives us an important property of Voronoi diagrams: the Voronoi regions are convex, for the intersection of any number of halfplanes is a convex set. When the regions are bounded, they are convex polygons. The edges of the Voronoi regions are called *Voronoi edges*, and the vertices are called *Voronoi vertices*. Note that a point on the interior of a Voronoi edge has two nearest sites, and a Voronoi vertex has at least three nearest sites.

Four Sites

The diagram of four points forming the corners of a rectangle is shown in Figure 5.4*a*.[6] Note the Voronoi vertex is of degree 4. Now suppose one site is moved slightly, as in Figure 5.4*b*. There is a sense in which this diagram is normal, and the one in Figure 5.4*a* is abnormal, or "degenerate." It is degenerate in that there are four cocircular points. We often will find it useful to exclude this type of degeneracy.

---

[6]This and several similar figures in this chapter were produced by the XYZ GeoBench software (Schorn 1991).

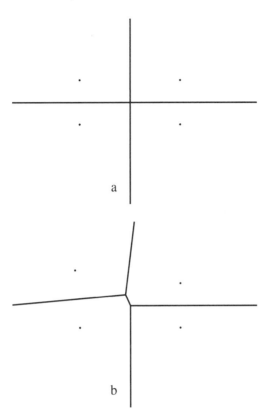

FIGURE 5.4 (*a*) Voronoi diagram of four cocircular points; (*b*) after moving upper left point.

Many Sites

A typical diagram with many sites is shown in Figure 5.5.[7] One Voronoi vertex is not shown in this figure: the two nearly horizontal rays leaving the diagram to the left are not quite parallel, and intersect at a Voronoi vertex about 50 cm left of the figure.

5.2.2. Size of Diagram

Although there are exactly n Voronoi regions for n sites, the total combinatorial size of the diagram conceivably could be quadratic in n, for any particular Voronoi region can have $\Omega(n)$ Voronoi edges (Exercise 5.3.3 [4]). We now show that this is in fact not the case, that the total size of the diagram is $O(n)$.

Let us assume for simplicity that no four points are cocircular, and therefore every Voronoi vertex is of degree three. Construct the *dual* graph G (Section

---

[7]This diagram was produced with code written by Susan Weller, John Kutcher, and Catherine Schevon.

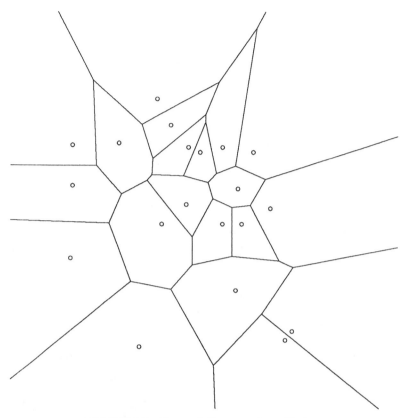

FIGURE 5.5   Voronoi diagram of $n = 20$ sites.

4.4) for a Voronoi Diagram $\mathscr{V}(P)$ as follows: the nodes of G are the sites of $\mathscr{V}(P)$, and two nodes are connected by an arc if their corresponding Voronoi polygons share a Voronoi edge (share a positive length edge).

Now observe that this is a planar graph: we can embed each node at its site, and all the arcs incident to the node can be angularly sorted the same as the polygon edges. Moreover, all the faces of G are triangles, corresponding to the degree-three Voronoi vertices. This claim will be made clearer below (Fig. 5.6).

We previously showed that Euler's formula implies that a triangulated planar graph with n vertices has $3n - 6$ edges and $2n - 4$ faces; see Section 4.1.5, Theorem 4.1.1. Since the faces of G correspond to Voronoi vertices, and the edges of G correspond to Voronoi edges (since each arc of G crosses a Voronoi edge), we have shown that the number of Voronoi vertices, edges, and faces are $O(n)$.

If we now remove the assumption that no four points are cocircular, the graph is still planar, but not necessarily triangulated. For example, the dual of the diagram shown in Figure 5.4*a* is a quadrilateral. However, such nontriangulated graphs have fewer edges and faces, so the $O(n)$ bounds continue to hold.

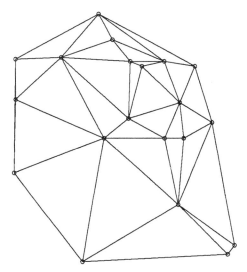

FIGURE 5.6   Delaunay triangulation for the sites in Figure 5.5.

One consequence of the $3n - 6$ edge bound is that the average number of edges of a Voronoi polygon is no more than six (Exercise 5.3.3[5]).

5.3. DELAUNAY TRIANGULATIONS

In 1934, Delaunay proved that when the dual graph is drawn with straight lines, it produces a planar triangulation of the Voronoi sites P (if no four sites are cocircular), now called the *Delaunay triangulation* $\mathscr{D}(P)$. Figure 5.6 shows the Delaunay triangulation for the Voronoi diagram in 5.5, and Figure 5.7 shows the Delaunay triangulation superimposed on the corresponding Voronoi diagram. Note that it is not immediately obvious that using straight lines in the dual would avoid crossings in the dual; the dual segment between two sites does not necessarily cross the Voronoi edge shared between their Voronoi regions, as is evident in Figure 5.7. We will not prove Delaunay's theorem now, but rather will wait until we have gathered more properties of Voronoi diagrams and Delaunay triangulations, when the proof will be easy.

5.3.1. Properties of Delaunay Triangulations

Because the Delaunay triangulation and Voronoi diagram are dual structures, each contains the same "information" in some sense, but represented in a rather different form. To gain a grasp on these complex structures, it is important to have a thorough understanding of the relationships between a Delaunay triangulation and its corresponding Voronoi diagram. We list without proof several Delaunay properties, and follow with a more substantive list of

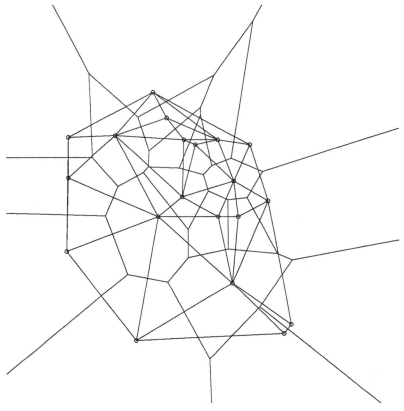

FIGURE 5.7 Delaunay triangulation and Voronoi diagram: Figures 5.5 and 5.6 together.

Voronoi properties.[8] Only the properties **D6** and **D7** have not been mentioned before. Fix a set of sites P.

D1. $\mathscr{D}(P)$ is the straight-line dual of $\mathscr{V}(P)$. This is by definition.

D2. $\mathscr{D}(P)$ is a triangulation if no four points of P are cocircular: every face is a triangle. This is Delaunay's theorem. The faces of $\mathscr{D}(P)$ are called *Delaunay triangles*.

D3. Each face (triangle) of $\mathscr{D}(P)$ corresponds to a vertex of $\mathscr{V}(P)$.

D4. Each edge of $\mathscr{D}(P)$ corresponds to an edge of $\mathscr{V}(P)$.

D5. Each node of $\mathscr{D}(P)$ corresponds to a region of $\mathscr{V}(P)$.

D6. The boundary of $\mathscr{D}(P)$ is the convex hull of the sites.

D7. The interior of each (triangle) face of $\mathscr{D}(P)$ contains no sites. (Compare **V5**.)

---

[8]Here I am following the pedagogic lead of Preparata and Shamos (1985, Section 5.5.1). In addition, some notation is borrowed from Okabe, Boots, and Sugihara (1992).

Properties **D6** and **D7** here the most interesting; they can be verified in Figures 5.6 and 5.7.

5.3.2. Properties of Voronoi Diagrams

V1. Each Voronoi region $V(p_i)$ is convex.

V2. $V(p_i)$ is unbounded iff p_i is on the convex hull of the point set. Compare property **D6**.

V3. If v is a Voronoi vertex at the junction of $V(p_1)$, $V(p_2)$, and $V(p_3)$, then v is the center of the circle $C(v)$ determined by p_1, p_2, and p_3. (This claim generalizes to Voronoi vertices of any degree.)

V4. $C(v)$ is the circumcircle for the Delaunay triangle corresponding to v.

V5. The interior of $C(v)$ contains no sites.

V6. If p_j is a nearest neighbor to p_i, then (p_i, p_j) is an edge of $\mathscr{D}(P)$.

V7. If there is some circle through p_i and p_j which contains no other sites, then (p_i, p_j) is an edge of $\mathscr{D}(P)$. The reverse also holds: for every Delaunay edge, there is some empty circle.

Property **V7** is the least intuitive, but is an important characterization of Delaunay edges, which is used in several proofs later on. This is the only property we will prove formally.

Theorem 5.3.1. ab $\in \mathscr{D}(P)$ *iff* ∃ *an empty circle through* a *and* b: *the closed disk bounded by the circle contains no sites of* P *other than* a *and* b.

Proof. One direction is easy: if ab is a Delaunay edge, then $V(a)$ and $V(b)$ share a positive-length edge $e \in \mathscr{V}(P)$. Put a circle $C(x)$ with center x on the interior of e, with radius equal to the distance to a or b. This circle is obviously empty of other sites. For were it not, if, say, site c were on or in the circle, x would be in $V(c)$ as well, but we know that x is only in $V(a)$ and $V(b)$.

The reverse implication is more subtle. Suppose there is an empty circle $C(x)$ through a and b, with center x. We aim to prove that $ab \in \mathscr{D}(P)$. Because x is equidistant from a and b, x is in the Voronoi regions of both a and b as long as no other point interferes with "nearest-neighborliness." But none does, because the circle is empty. Therefore, $x \in V(a) \cap V(b)$ (recall we defined Voronoi regions to be closed sets). Because no points are on the boundary of $C(x)$ other than a and b (by hypothesis), there must be freedom to wiggle x a bit and maintain emptiness. In particular, we can move x along B_{ab}, the bisector between a and b, and maintain emptiness while keeping the circle through a and b. See Figure 5.8. Therefore x is on a positive-length Voronoi edge (a subset of B_{ab}) shared between $V(a)$ and $V(b)$, and therefore $ab \in \mathscr{D}(P)$. □

We leave the proof of the other properties to intuition, exercises, and to Section 5.7.2.

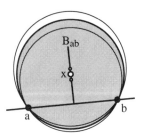

FIGURE 5.8 $C(x)$ is the shaded circle. Its center x can move along B_{ab} while remaining empty and still through a and b.

5.3.3. Exercises

1. *Regular polygon* [easy]. Describe the Voronoi diagram and Delaunay triangulation for the vertices of a regular polygon.

2. *Unbounded regions.* Prove property **V2**: $V(p_i)$ is unbounded iff p_i is on the convex hull of the point set. Do not assume the corresponding Delaunay property **D6**, but otherwise any Delaunay or Voronoi property may be employed in the proof.

3. *Nearest neighbors.* Prove property **V6**: if p_j is a nearest neighbor to p_i, then (p_i, p_j) is an edge of $\mathscr{D}(P)$. Any Delaunay or Voronoi property may be employed in the proof.

4. *High-degree Delaunay vertex.* Design a set of n points (n arbitrary), no four cocircular, such that one vertex of the Delaunay triangulation has degree $n - 1$.

5. *Average number of Voronoi polygon edges.* Prove that the number of edges in a Voronoi polygon, averaged over all Voronoi regions in any set of n points, does not exceed six (Preparata and Shamos, 1985, p. 211).

6. *Pitteway triangulations.* A triangulation of a set of points P is called a *Pitteway triangulation* (Okabe et al., 1992, p. 90) if, for each triangle $T = (a, b, c)$, every point in T has one of a, b, or c as its nearest neighbor among the points of P.

   a. Show by example that not every Delaunay triangulation is a Pitteway triangulation.

   b. Characterize those Delaunay triangulations that are Pitteway triangulations.

5.4. ALGORITHMS

The many applications of the Voronoi diagram and its inherent beauty have spurred researchers to invent a variety of algorithms to compute it. In this section, we will examine four algorithms, each rather superficially, for we will see in Section 5.7.2 that the Voronoi diagram can be computed using our convex hull code.

5.4.1. Intersection of Halfplanes

We could construct each Voronoi region separately, by intersecting $n - 1$ halfplanes according to Equation 5.2. Although it is not immediately obvious, the intersection of n halfplanes may be constructed in $O(n \log n)$ time with a divide-and-conquer algorithm. Doing this for each site would cost $O(n^2 \log n)$.

5.4.2. Incremental Construction

Suppose the Voronoi diagram $\mathscr{V}$ for k points is already constructed, and now we would like to construct the diagram $\mathscr{V}'$ after adding one more point p. Suppose p falls inside the circles associated with several Voronoi vertices, say $C(v_1),\ldots,C(v_m)$. Then these vertices of $\mathscr{V}$ cannot be vertices of $\mathscr{V}'$, for they violate the condition that Voronoi vertex circles must be empty of sites (**V5**, Section 5.3.2). It turns out that these are the *only* vertices of $\mathscr{V}$ that are not carried over to $\mathscr{V}'$. It also turns out that these vertices are all localized to one area of the diagram. These vague observations can be made precise, and form one of the cleanest algorithms for constructing the Voronoi diagram (Green and Sibson, 1977). The algorithm spends $O(n)$ time per point insertion, for a total complexity of $O(n^2)$. In spite of its quadratic complexity, this has been the most popular method of constructing the diagram; see Field (1986) for implementation details. The incremental algorithm has been revitalized recently with randomization, which we will touch upon in Chapter 9.

5.4.3. Divide and Conquer

The Voronoi diagram can be constructed with a complex divide-and-conquer algorithm in $O(n \log n)$ time, first detailed by Shamos and Hoey (1975). It was this paper that introduced the Voronoi diagram to the computer science community. This time complexity is asymptotically optimal, but the algorithm rather difficult to implement. However, it can be done with careful attention to data structures; see Guibas and Stolfi (1985).

We pass over this historically-important algorithm to focus on some exciting recent developments.

5.4.4. Fortune's Algorithm

Until the mid-1980s, most implementations for computing the Voronoi diagram used the $O(n^2)$ incremental algorithm, accepting its slower performance to avoid the complexities of the divide-and-conquer coding. In 1985, Fortune (1987) invented a clever plane-sweep algorithm that is as simple as the incremental algorithms, but has worst-case complexity of $O(n \log n)$. We will now sketch the main idea behind this algorithm.

Plane-sweep algorithms (Section 2.2.1) pass a sweep line over the plane, leaving at any time the problem solved for the portion of the plane already swept, and unsolved for the portion not yet reached. A plane-sweep algorithm for constructing the Voronoi diagram would have the diagram constructed behind the line. At first, this seems quite impossible, as Voronoi edges of a Voronoi region $\mathscr{V}(P)$ would be encountered by the sweep line L *before* L encounters the site p responsible for the region. Fortune surmounted this seeming impossibility by an extraordinarily clever idea.[9]

---

[9]My exposition relies heavily on that of Guibas and Stolfi (1988), rather than on Fortune's original paper, which explained the algorithm in a rather different manner.

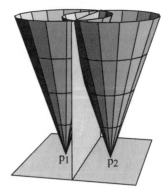

FIGURE 5.9   The curve of intersection of two cones projects to a line.

Cones

Imagine the sites in the xy-plane of a three-dimensional coordinate system. Erect over each site p a cone whose apex is at p, and whose sides slope at 45°. If the third dimension is viewed as time, the cone over p represents a circle expanding about p at unit velocity: after t units of time, its radius is t.

Now consider two nearby cones, over sites p_1 and p_2. They intersect in a curve in space. Recalling the expanding circles view of the Voronoi diagram, it should come as no surprise that this curve lies entirely in a vertical plane,[10] the plane orthogonal to the bisector of $p_1\,p_2$. (See Figure 5.9.) Thus, although the intersection is curved in three dimensions, it projects to a straight line on the xy-plane.

It is but a small step from here to the claim that if the cones over all sites are opaque, and they are viewed from $z = -\infty$, what is seen is precisely the Voronoi diagram!

Cone Slicing

We are now prepared to describe Fortune's idea. His algorithm sweeps the cones with a slanted plane π, slanted at 45° to the xy-plane. The sweep line L is the intersection of π with the xy-plane. Let us assume that L is parallel to the y-axis, and that its x-coordinate is l. See Figure 5.10. Imagine that π, as well as all the cones, are opaque, and again consider the view from $z = -\infty$.

To the $x > l$ side of L, only π is visible from below: it cuts below the xy-plane and so obscures the sites and cones. This represents the portion of the plane yet to be swept. To the $x < l$ side of L, the Voronoi diagram is visible up to the intersection of π with the right (positive x) "frontier" of cones. The intersection of π with any one cone is a parabola (a basic property of conic sections), and so the intersection of π with this right frontier projects to the xy-plane (and so appears from $z = -\infty$) as a "parabolic front," a curve composed of pieces of parabolas. See Figure 5.11. Two parabolas join at a spot

---

[10]The curve is a branch of a hyperbola, the conic section formed by intersection with a plane parallel to the axis of the cone.

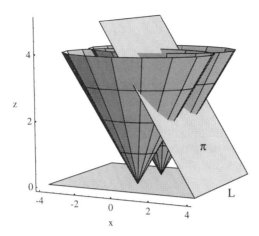

FIGURE 5.10 Cones cut by sweep plane. π and L are sweeping toward the right, $x \to \infty$

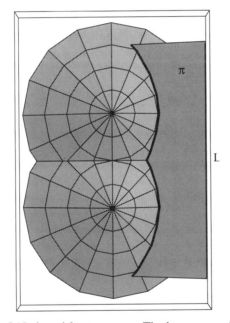

FIGURE 5.11 Figure 5.10 viewed from $z \approx -\infty$. The heavy curve is the parabolic front.

where π meets two cones. From our discussion of the intersection of two cones above, this must be at a Voronoi edge.

Parabolic Front

Now we finally can see how Fortune solved the problem of the sweep line encountering Voronoi edges prior to the generating sites: because his sweep plane π slopes at the same angle as the cone sides, L encounters a site p

exactly when π first hits the cone for p! So it is not the case that the Voronoi diagram is at all times constructed to the left of L, but it is at all times constructed *underneath* π, which means that it is constructed to the left of L up to the parabolic front, which lags L a bit.

What is maintained at all times by the algorithm is the parabolic front, whose joints trace out the Voronoi diagram over time, since these kinks all lie on Voronoi edges. Although we are by no means finished the algorithm description, we will make no attempt to detail it further here.

Finally, it should be clear that the algorithm only need store the parabolic front, which is of size $O(n)$, and is often $O(\sqrt{n})$. This is a significant advantage of Fortune's algorithm when n is large: the storage needed at any one time is often much smaller than the size of the diagram.

5.4.5. Exercises

1. $\mathscr{D}(P) \Rightarrow \mathscr{V}(P)$. Design an algorithm for computing the Voronoi diagram, given the Delaunay triangulation. Try to achieve $O(n)$ time complexity.

2. *One-dimensional Voronoi diagrams.* A one-dimensional Voronoi diagram for a set of points $P = \{p_1, \ldots, p_n\}$ on a line (say the x-axis) is a set of points $\mathscr{V}(P) = \{x_1, \ldots, x_{n-1}\}$ such that x_i is the midpoint of $p_i\, p_{i+1}$.

   Suppose you are given a set $X = \{x_1, \ldots, x_{n-1}\}$. Design criteria that will permit you to determine whether or not X is a one-dimensional Voronoi diagram of a set of points, and if so, determine P. How fast is the implied algorithm?

3. *Dynamic Voronoi diagrams.* Imagine a set of points moving on the plane, each with a fixed velocity and direction. Let $\mathscr{V}(t)$ be the Voronoi diagram of the points at time t. It is an unsolved problem to obtain tight bounds on the number of combinatorially distinct diagrams that can result over all time. Here I ask you to establish the best-known lower bound: $\Omega(n^2)$. In other words, find a set of n moving points such that $\mathscr{V}(t)$ changes its graphical structure cn^2 times for some constant c.

   No one has been able to find an example in which there are more than n^2 changes, but the best upper bound is about $O(n^3)$ (Fu and Lee, 1991) (Guibas, Mitchell, and Roos 1991).

4. *Arbitrary triangulation.* Design an algorithm to find an arbitrary triangulation of a point set P: a collection of diagonals incident to every point of P that partitions $\mathscr{H}(P)$ into triangles. The absence of the requirement that the triangulation be Delaunay permits considerable freedom in the design.

5. *Flipping algorithm.* Investigate the following proposed algorithm for constructing $\mathscr{D}(P)$. Start with an arbitrary triangulation of P. Then repeat the following procedure until $\mathscr{D}(P)$ is attained. Identify two adjacent triangles abc and cbd sharing diagonal bc, such that the quadrilateral $abcd$ is convex. If d is inside the circumcircle of abc, then delete cb and add ad. Will this work?

5.5. APPLICATIONS IN DETAIL

We will now discuss five applications of the Voronoi diagram, in uneven detail: nearest neighbors, "fat" triangulations, largest empty circles, minimum spanning trees, and traveling salesperson paths.

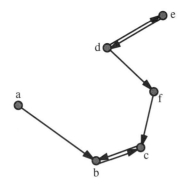

FIGURE 5.12 $a \to b$, but $b \to c$; also $d \to e$ and $d \to f$.

5.5.1. Nearest Neighbors

An application of the Voronoi diagram for nearest-neighbor clustering was mentioned in Section 5.1. That problem can be viewed as a *query* problem: which is the nearest neighbor to a query point? Another version is the *all nearest neighbors* problem: find the nearest neighbor to *each* point in a given set. This has a number of applications in a variety of fields, including biology, ecology, geography, and physics.[11]

Define the nearest neighbor relation among a set of points P as follows: b is a *nearest neighbor* of a iff $|a - b| \leq \min_{c \neq a} |a - c|$, where $c \in P$. We can write this relation $a \to b$: a nearest neighbor of a is b. Note that the definition is not symmetric with respect to the roles that a and b play, suggesting that the relation is not itself symmetric. In fact this is indeed the case: If $a \to b$, it is not necessary that $b \to a$; see Figure 5.12. In addition, note that a point can have several equally-nearest neighbors, e.g., point d in the figure.

Nearest Neighbor Queries

Given a fixed set of points P, construct the Voronoi diagram in $O(n \log n)$ time. Now for a query point q, finding a nearest neighbor of q reduces to finding in which Voronoi region(s) it falls, for the sites of those Voronoi regions are precisely its nearest neighbors. The problem of locating a point inside a partition is called *point location*. The problem has been studied heavily, and will be discussed in Chapter 7 (Section 7.6). We will see there that in this instance, $O(\log n)$ time suffices for each query.

All Nearest Neighbors

Define the *Nearest Neighbor Graph NNG* to have a node associated with each point of P, and an arc between them if one point is a nearest neighbor of the

[11]Citations in Preparata and Shamos (1985, p. 186) and Okabe et al. (1992, p. 422).

other. We have defined this to be an undirected graph, although because the relation is not symmetric, it could well be defined to be directed. We will not need the directed version here.

A succinct way to capture the essence of efficient nearest neighbor algorithms is through the following lemma.

Lemma 5.5.1. $NNG \subseteq \mathcal{D}(P)$.

I leave the proof to Exercises 5.5.6[2] and 5.5.6[3]. A brute-force algorithm for finding the nearest neighbors for each point in a set would require $O(n^2)$ time, but the above lemma lets us search only the $O(n)$ edges of the Delaunay triangulation, and therefore achieve $O(n \log n)$.

5.5.2. Triangulation Maximizing the Minimum Angle

Analyzing the structural properties of complex shapes is often accomplished by a technique called "finite element analysis." This is used, for example, by automobile manufacturers to model car bodies (Field, 1986). The domain to be studied is partitioned into "finite elements," and then the relevant differential equations modeling the structural dynamics are solved by discretizing over the partition. The stability of the numerical procedures used depends on the quality of the partition, and it so happens that Delaunay triangulations are especially good partitions. We will now discuss the sense in which Delaunay triangulations are good.

A *triangulation* of a point set S is the generalization of the object of which the Delaunay triangulation is a particular instance: a set of segments whose endpoints are in S, which only intersect each other at endpoints, and which partition the convex hull of S into triangles. For the purposes of finite element analysis, triangulations with "fat" triangles are best. One way to make this more precise is to avoid triangles with small angles. Thus, it is natural to seek a triangulation that has the largest smallest angle, that is, to maximize the smallest angle over all triangulations. This happens to be precisely the Delaunay triangulation! In fact, a somewhat stronger statement can be made, which we now describe after introducing some notation.

Let T be a triangulation of a point set S, and let its *angle sequence* $(\alpha_1, \alpha_2, \ldots, \alpha_{3t})$, be a list of the angles of the triangles, sorted from smallest to largest, with t the number of triangles in T. The number t is a constant for each S (Exercise 5.5.6[4]). We can define a relation between two triangulations of the same point set, T and T', that attempts to capture the "fatness" of the triangles. Say that $T \geq T'$ (T is fatter than T') if the angle sequence of T is lexicographically greater than the angle sequence of T': either $\alpha_1 > \alpha_1'$, or $\alpha_1 = \alpha_1'$, and $\alpha_2 > \alpha_2'$, or $\alpha_1 = \alpha_1'$ and $\alpha_2 = \alpha_2'$, and $\alpha_3 > \alpha_3'$, and so on. Edelsbrunner (1987, p. 302) proved this pleasing theorem:

Theorem 5.5.2.   *The Delaunay triangulation* $T = \mathcal{D}(P)$ *is maximal with respect to the angle-fatness relation*: $T \geq T'$ *for any other triangulation* T' *of* P.

In particular this says that the Delaunay triangulation maximizes the smallest angle.

5.5.3. Largest Empty Circle

We mentioned in Section 5.1 the problem of finding the largest empty circle among a set S of sites: the center of such a circle is a good location for a new store. Another application is mentioned by Toussaint (1983a): locate a nuclear reactor as far away from a collection of city-sites as possible. We now examine the largest empty circle problem in some detail.

The problem makes little sense unless some restriction is placed on the location of the circle center because there are always arbitrarily large empty circles outside any finite set of points. So we phrase the problem this way:

Largest Empty Circle: Find a largest empty circle whose center is in the (closed) convex hull of a set of n sites S, empty in that it contains no sites in its interior, and largest in that there is no other such circle with strictly larger radius.

Let $f(p)$ be the radius of the largest empty circle centered on point p. We are looking for a maximum of this function over all p in the hull of S, $H = \mathcal{H}(S)$. There are a seemingly infinite number of candidate points for these maxima. A common theme in computational geometry is to reduce an infinite candidate set to a small finite list and then to find these efficiently. We follow this scenario in this section, starting by arguing informally that only certain points p are true candidates for maxima of f.

Centers inside the Hull

Imagine inflating a circle from a point p in H. The radius at which this circle first bumps into and therefore includes some site of $S = \{s_1, \ldots, s_n\}$, is the value of $f(p)$. Let us temporarily assume throughout this subsection that p is strictly interior to H. If at radius $f(p)$, the circle includes just one site s_1, it should be clear that $f(p)$ cannot be a maximum of the radius function. Because if p is moved to p' along the ray $s_1 p$ (the ray from s_1 through p) away from s_1, then $f(p')$ is larger, as shown in Figure 5.13 (upper circles). Therefore p could not have been a local maximum of f, for there is a point p' in any neighborhood of p where f is larger. Note that the assumption that p is strictly interior to the hull guarantees that there is a p' as above that is also in H.

Now let us assume that at radius $f(p)$, the circle includes exactly two sites s_1 and s_2. Again $f(p)$ cannot be at a maximum: if p is moved to p' along the bisector of $s_1 s_2$ (away from $s_1 s_2$), then $f(p')$ is again larger, as shown in Figure 5.13 (lower circles). Another way to see this is via the intersection of site-centered cones, discussed in Section 5.4.4. The curve of intersection of two such cones (Figure 5.9) represents the distance from the sites for points on the bisector. Since the curve is an upward hyperbola branch, no interior point of the bisector is a local maximum: the distance increases in one direction or the other.

It is only when the circle includes three sites that $f(p)$ could be at a maximum. If the three sites "straddle" the center p, in the sense that they span

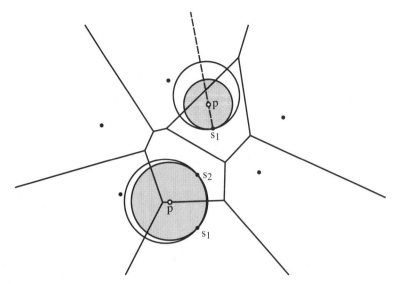

FIGURE 5.13   Center in interior, circle through one (upper) or two (lower) sites.

more than a semicircle (as in Figure 5.3), then motion of p in any direction results in moving p closer to some site, and thus decreasing $f(p)$. We have now established this fact:

Lemma 5.5.3.   *If the center* p *of a largest empty circle is strictly interior to the hull of the sites* $\mathscr{H}(\mathrm{S})$, *then* p *must be coincident with a Voronoi vertex.*

Note that it is not necessarily true that every Voronoi vertex represents a local maximum of $f(p)$ (Exercise 5.5.6[5]).

Centers on the Hull
Now let us consider circle centers p directly on the hull $\mathscr{H}(S)$. The reason our earlier arguments do not apply is that moving p to p' might move outside of the hull, and our problem specification restricted centers to the hull. We now argue even more informally than above that a maximal circle must include two sites.

Suppose $f(p)$ is a maximum with p on H and the circle includes just one site s_1. First, it cannot be that p is at a vertex of H, for the vertices of H are all sites themselves, and this would imply that $f(p) = 0$. So p is on the interior of an edge h of H. Then moving p one way or the other along h must increase its distance from s_1, as shown in Figure 5.14. One can again see this intuitively by thinking of the cone apexed at s_1, sliced by a vertical plane (Figure 5.9).

If, however, the circle centered on p contains two sites s_1 and s_2, then it is possible that the direction along the bisector of the sites that increases distance is the direction that goes outside the hull. Thus, it could well be that $f(p)$ is at a local maximum. We have shown this fact:

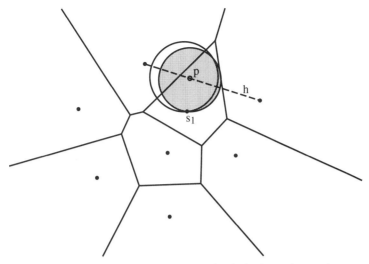

FIGURE 5.14   Center on hull edge h, circle through one site.

Algorithm: LARGEST EMPTY CIRCLE
Compute the Voronoi diagram $\mathcal{V}(S)$ of the sites S.
Compute the convex hull H.
for each Voronoi vertex v do
    if v is inside H: $v \in H$ then
        Compute radius of circle centered on v and update max.
for each Voronoi edge e do
    Compute $p = e \cap \partial H$, the intersection of e with the hull boundary.
    Compute radius of circle centered on p and update max.
Return max.

Algorithm 5.1   Largest empty circle.

Lemma 5.5.4.   *If the center* p *of a largest empty circle lies on the hull of the sites* $\mathcal{H}(S)$, *then* p *must lie on a Voronoi edge.*

Algorithm

We have now established our goal: we have found a finite set of points that are potential centers of largest empty circles: the Voronoi vertices, and the intersections between Voronoi edges and the hull of the sites. This suggests the algorithm in Algorithm 5.1, due to Toussaint (1983a).[12]

Note that not every Voronoi vertex is necessarily inside the hull (Figure 5.14), which necessitates the $v \in H$ check in the algorithm. A naive implementation of this algorithm would require quadratic time in n, but location of a Voronoi

---

[12]The main ideas go back to Shamos (1978).

FIGURE 5.15   A Euclidean Minimum Spanning Tree.

vertex in H, and intersecting a Voronoi edge with e, can both be accomplished in $O(\log n)$ time, and these efficiencies lead to an $O(n \log n)$ algorithm overall. We leave details to Exercise 5.5.6[6].

5.5.4. Minimum Spanning Tree

A *minimum spanning tree* (MST) of a set of points is a *minimum* length tree that *spans* all the points: a shortest tree whose nodes are precisely those in the set. When the length of an edge is measured by the usual Euclidean length of the segment connecting its endpoints, the tree is often called the Euclidean minimum spanning tree (EMST). Here we will only consider Euclidean lengths, and so will drop the redundant modifier. An example is shown in Figure 5.15.[13] MSTs have many applications. For example, many local area networks take the form of a tree spanning the host nodes. The MST is the network topology that minimizes total wire length, which usually minimizes both cost and time delays.

Kruskal's Algorithm
Here we will consider the problem of computing the MST of a set of points in the plane. Let us first look at the more general problem of computing the MST for a graph G. Although it is by no means obvious, a mindless greedy strategy finds the MST, based on the simple intuition that a shortest tree should be composed of the shortest edges. This suggests that such a tree can be built up incrementally by adding the shortest edge not yet explored, which also maintains tree-ness (acyclicity). This algorithm is known as Kruskal's algorithm, and dates back to 1956.[14]

Let T be the tree incrementally constructed, and let the notation $T + e$ mean the tree T union the edge e. Kruskal's algorithm is shown in Algorithm 5.2. We will not stop to prove this algorithm correct, but only claim that its complexity is dominated by the first sorting step. This requires $O(E \log E)$ time, where E is the number of edges in the graph.

---

[13]Computed by XYZ Geobench.
[14]My presentation is based on that of Albertson and Hutchinson (1988, pp. 264–268).

Algorithm: KRUSKAL'S ALGORITHM
Sort all edges of G by length: $e_1, e_2, \ldots$.
Initialize T to be empty, $i \leftarrow 1$.
while T is not spanning **do**
    if $T + e_i$ is acyclic
        then $T \leftarrow T + e_i$
    $i \leftarrow i + 1$

Algorithm 5.2   Kruskal's algorithm.

MST $\subseteq \mathscr{D}(P)$

For the MST of points in the plane, there are $\binom{n}{2}$ edges, so the complexity of the sorting step is $O(n^2 \log n)$ if carried out on the complete graph. However, recalling that the Delaunay triangulation edges record proximity information in some sense, it is reasonable to hope that only Delaunay edges ever need be used to construct a MST, and fortunately this is true, as shown by the following theorem.

Theorem 5.5.5. *A minimum spanning tree is a subset of the Delaunay triangulation*: MST $\subseteq \mathscr{D}(P)$.

Proof. We want to show that if $ab \in MST$, then $ab \in \mathscr{D}$. Assume that $ab \in MST$ and suppose to the contrary that $ab \notin \mathscr{D}$. Then we seek to derive a contradiction by showing that the supposed MST is not minimal.

Recall that if $ab \in \mathscr{D}$, then there is an empty circle through a and b (Theorem 5.3.1). So if $ab \notin \mathscr{D}$, no circle through a and b can be empty. In particular, the circle with diameter ab must have a site on or in it.

So suppose c is on or in this circle, as shown in Figure 5.16. Then $|ac| < |ab|$, and $|bc| < |ab|$; these inequalities hold even if c is on the circle, since c is distinct from a and b. Removal of ab will disconnect the tree into two trees, with a in one part T_a and b in the other, T_b. Suppose without loss of generality that c is in T_a. Remove ab and add edge bc to make a new tree, $T' = T_a + bc + $

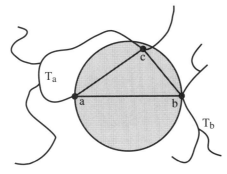

FIGURE 5.16 $T_a + bc + T_b$ is shorter than $T_a + ab + T_b$.

T_b. This tree is shorter, so the one using ab could not have been minimal. We have reached a contradiction by denying that ab is in $\mathscr{D}$, so it must be that $ab \in \mathscr{D}$.   □

This then yields an improvement on the first step of Kruskal's algorithm: first find the Delaunay triangulation in $O(n \log n)$ time, and then sort only those $O(n)$ edges, in $O(n \log n)$ time. It turns out that the remainder of Kruskal's algorithm can be implemented to run in $O(n \log n)$, so that the total complexity for finding the MST for a set of n points in the plane is $O(n \log n)$.

5.5.5. Traveling Salesperson Problem

One of the most-studied problems in computer science is the Traveling Salesperson problem: find the shortest closed path that visits every point in a given set. Such a path is called a *traveling salesperson path* (*TSP*): imagine the points as cities that the salesperson must visit in arbitrary order before returning home. This problem has tremendous practical significance, not only for that application, but because many other problems can be reduced to it. Unfortunately, the problem has been proven to be NP-hard, a technical term which means that no polynomial algorithm is known to solve it (Garey and Johnson, 1979); nor does it seem likely at this writing that one will be found. The combination of practical significance and intractability have lead to a search for effective heuristics and approximation algorithms. One of the simplest approximation algorithms is based on the Delaunay triangulation, via the Minimum Spanning Tree.

The idea is rather simple-minded, but nevertheless does a reasonable job: find the MST for the set of points, and simply follow that out and back in the manner illustrated in Figure 5.17. It should be clear that the tour constructed this way has exactly twice the length of the MST, since each edge of the tree is traversed once in each direction.

We now obtain a bound on how bad this doubled-MST tour can be. Let M be the length of a minimum spanning tree, and M_2 the length of a doubled-MST;

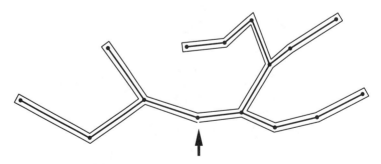

FIGURE 5.17   A tour formed by following the MST.

of course $M_2 = 2M$. Let T be the length of a traveling salesperson path, and T_1 the length of a TSP with one edge removed. Note that T_1 is a spanning tree.

The following inequalities are immediate:

$$T_1 < T$$

$$M \leq T_1$$

$$M < T$$

$$M_2 < 2T.$$

This then achieves a constant upper bound on the quality of the tour: the doubled-MST is no worse than twice the optimal TSP length.

This can be improved with various heuristics. I will sketch only the simplest such heuristic, which is based on the understandable resolve not to revisit a site twice. Traverse the doubled-MST path from the start site, with the modification that if the next site has already been visited by the path so far, skip that site and consider connecting to the next one along the doubled-MST tour. This has the effect of taking a more direct route to some sites. If we index the sites by the order in which they are visited along the doubled-MST tour, some site s_i might connect to s_j by a straight line segment in the shortcut tour, whereas in the doubled-MST tour it follows a crooked path $s_i, s_{i+1}, \ldots, s_{j-1}, s_j$. A straight path is always shorter than a crooked path (by the triangle inequality), so this heuristic can only shorten the path. An example is shown in Figure 5.18. Note that the shortened path might self-intersect.

Unfortunately this heuristic does not guarantee an improved performance, but a slight variation known as the "Christofides heuristic" does. It uses a set of segments called a "minimum Euclidean matching" as a guide to shortcutting, and can guarantee a path length no more than $(3/2) T$, that is, no more than 50% longer than the optimum. Current research (Bentley 1992) focuses on methods for getting within a few percent of optimal, but usually the performance is not guaranteed as it is for the algorithm above.

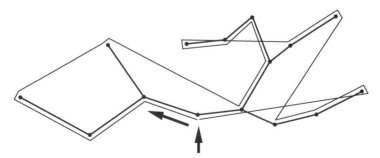

FIGURE 5.18 Shortcutting the doubled-MST tour in Figure 5.17.

5.5.6. Exercises

1. *Degree of NNG.* What is the maximum out-degree of a node of a directed Nearest Neighbor Graph (NNG) (p. 183) of n points in two dimensions? What is the maximum in-degree of a node? Demonstrate examples that achieve your answers, and try to prove they are maximum.

2. *NNG and $\mathscr{D}$* [easy]. Find an example that shows that NNG can be a proper subset of $\mathscr{D}(P)$.

3. *NNG $\subseteq \mathscr{D}$.* Prove Lemma 5.5.1: if b is a nearest neighbor of a, then $ab \in \mathscr{D}(P)$.

4. *Number of triangles in a triangulation.* Prove that the number of triangles t in any triangulation of some fixed point set S is a constant: all triangulations of S have the same t.

5. *Voronoi vertex not a local max.* Construct a set of points which has a Voronoi vertex p strictly inside the hull, such that $f(p)$ is not a local maximum, where f is the radius function defined in Section 5.5.3.

6. *Empty circle algorithm.* Detail (in pseudocode only) how to implement the empty circle algorithm Algorithm 5.1 so that its time complexity is $O(n \log n)$.

7. *Relative Neighborhood Graph.* The Relative Neighborhood Graph (RNG) of a set of points $p_1, \ldots, p_n$, is a graph whose nodes correspond to the points, and with two nodes p_i and p_j connected by an arc iff they are at least as close to each other as to any other point, that is, if

$$|p_i - p_j| \le \max_{m \neq i,j} \left\{ |p_i - p_m|, |p_j - p_m| \right\} \tag{5.3}$$

(See Jaromczyk and Toussaint, 1992.) This equation determines a "forbidden" region within which no point p_m may lie if p_i and p_j are adjacent in the RNG, not unlike Theorem 5.3.1. This region, called $Lune(p_i, p_j)$, is the intersection of two open disks centered on p_i and p_j, both of radius $|p_i - p_j|$.

   a. Design a "brute-force" algorithm to construct the RNG. Do not worry about efficiency. What is its time complexity?

   b. Prove that $RNG \subseteq \mathscr{D}(P)$: every edge of the RNG is also an edge of the Delaunay triangulation. (Compare Theorem 5.5.5.)

   c. Use (b) to design a faster algorithm.

8. *Size of Delaunay triangulation in three dimensions.* We have shown that the size of the Delaunay triangulation in two dimensions is linear, $O(n)$. Show that this does not hold in three dimensions: the size of $\mathscr{D}(P)$ can be quadratic. Define $\mathscr{D}(P)$ in three dimensions exactly analogously to the two-dimensional version: it is the dual of $\mathscr{V}(P)$, which is the locus of points that do not have a unique nearest neighbor. Let P be a point set consisting of two parts:[15]

   a. $n/2$ points uniformly distributed around a circle in the xy-plane centered on the origin, and

   b. $n/2$ points uniformly distributed on the z-axis symmetrical about the origin.

   Argue that the size of $\mathscr{D}(P)$ is $\Omega(n^2)$.

9. *Size of Relative Neighborhood Graph in three dimensions.* Exercise 7 above established that $RNG \subseteq \mathscr{D}(P)$ in two dimensions, and this relationship holds in arbitrary

---

[15]This example is from Preparata and Shamos (1985, Fig. 4.3).

dimensions. It has been proved that the size of the RNG in three dimensions is $O(n^{4/3})$ (Jaromczyk and Toussaint 1992), so it is smaller than the Delaunay triangulation, but it appears that this upper bound is weak: Jaromczyk and Kowaluk (1991) conjecture that the size is $O(n)$. Settling this conjecture is an open problem.

Try to determine what the RNG is for the example in Exercise 8 above, which established that $\mathscr{D}(P)$ can be quadratic.

10. *MST ⊆ RNG*. Prove that every edge of a MST is an edge of the RNG. (Compare Theorem 5.5.5.)

11. *Furthest-point Voronoi diagram.* Define the furthest-point Voronoi diagram $\mathscr{F}(P)$ to associate each point of the plane to the site that is its "furthest neighbor": the site that is furthest away. Points with one furthest neighbor form a furthest-neighbor Voronoi region; points with two furthest neighbors form the edges of $\mathscr{F}(P)$.

   a. What is $\mathscr{F}(P)$ for two sites?

   b. What is $\mathscr{F}(P)$ for three sites?

   c. Derive some structural properties of furthest-point Voronoi diagrams, similar to the Delaunay and Voronoi properties in Sections 5.3.1 and 5.3.2.

12. *Minimum spanning circle.* Show how the furthest-point Voronoi diagram can be used to compute the smallest-radius circle that surrounds a given point set. Assume $\mathscr{F}(P)$ is available.

5.6. MEDIAL AXIS

The Voronoi diagram may be generalized in several directions, and some of these generalizations have considerable practical significance. In this section we touch on just one generalization, one of the simplest: allowing the set of sites to be an infinite set of points, in particular the continuous boundary of a polygon.

In Section 5.2 we defined the Voronoi diagram as the set of points whose nearest site is not unique: these points are equidistantly closest to two or more sites. Define the *medial axis*[16] of a polygon P to be the set of points inside P that have more than one closest point among the points of ∂P. A very similar definition can be used for an arbitrary collection of points, but here we will examine only the case where the points form the boundary of a polygon.

The medial axis of a rectangle is shown in Figure 5.19. Each point on the horizontal segment inside the rectangle is equidistant from points vertically above and below it on the top and bottom sides of the rectangle. Each point on a diagonal segment is equidistant from two adjacent sides of the rectangle, and the two endpoints of the horizontal segment are equidistant from three sides of the rectangle.

A more complex example is shown in Figure 5.20,[17] an eight-vertex convex polygon. One might guess from this example that the medial axis of a convex polygon P is a tree whose leaves are the vertices of P. This is indeed true, and is even true for nonconvex polygons. Every point of the medial axis is the center of a circle that touches the boundary in at least two points. And just as Voronoi

---

[16]This is also known as the "symmetric axis" or the "skeleton" of the polygon.

[17]The medial axis in this figure was computed by code written by Diaz (1990).

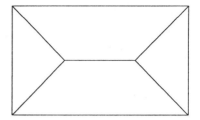

FIGURE 5.19   Medial axis of rectangle.

vertices are centers of circles touching three sites, vertices of the medial axis are centers of circles touching three distinct boundary points, as shown in Figure 5.21.

Sometimes the medial axis of P is defined as the locus of centers of *maximal circles*: circles inside P that are not themselves enclosed in any other circle inside P. The process of transforming a shape into its medial axis is sometimes called the "grassfire transformation," for if one imagines the polygon P a field of dry grass, then lighting afire the boundary of P all at once will cause the fire to burn inward at a uniform rate, and the medial axis is the set of "quench points": where fire meets fire from another direction. The connection between this analogy and the forest fires discussed in Section 5.1 should be evident.

The medial axis was introduced by Blum (1967) for studying biological shape. He viewed it as something like a skeleton (axis) that threads down the middle (median) of a shape. This is less apparent for a convex polygon than it is for nonconvex and smooth shapes, which were Blum's main interest. One can characterize a shape to a certain extent from the structure of its medial axis, and this has led to considerable interest among researchers in pattern recogni-

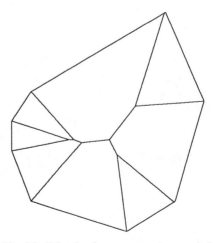

FIGURE 5.20   Medial axis of a convex polygon of eight vertices.

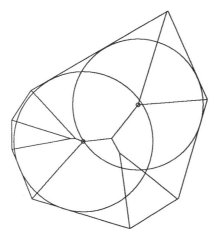

FIGURE 5.21   Circles centered on vertices touch the polygon boundary at three points.

tion and computer vision (Bookstein 1978). For example, Bookstein (1991, pp. 80–87) uses it to characterize the differences between normal mandible bones and deformed ones. The medial axis of a polygon of n vertices can be constructed in $O(n \log n)$ time (Lee 1982), and in $O(n)$ time if the polygon is convex (Aggarwal, Guibas, Saxe, and Shor 1989).

5.6.1. Exercises

1. *Medial axis of a nonconvex polygon.* Show by example that the medial axis of a nonconvex polygon can contain curved segments. What can you say about the functional form of these curves?

2. *Medial axis and Voronoi diagram.* Is there any relationship between the medial axis of a convex polygon P, and the Voronoi diagram of the vertices of P? Conjecture some aspects of this relationship and either prove them or construct counterexamples.

3. *Medial axis of a polytope.* Describe what the medial axis of a convex polytope must look like.

5.7. CONNECTION TO CONVEX HULLS

In 1986, Edelsbrunner and Seidel (1986) discovered a beautiful connection between Delaunay triangulations and convex hulls in one higher dimension.[18] I will first explain this connection between two-dimensional convex hulls and one-dimensional Delaunay triangulations (which are admittedly trivial), and then generalize to two-dimensional Delaunay triangulations and three-dimensional convex hulls. This connection will then give us an easy method for

---

[18]Their insight was based on earlier work of Brown (1979), who was the first to establish a connection to convex hulls.

computing the Delauany triangulation, and from that the Voronoi diagram, via three-dimensional hulls.

5.7.1. One-dimensional Delaunay Triangulations

We start in one dimension, where the mathematics is transparent.

Let $P = \{x_1, \ldots, x_n\}$ be a set of points on the x-axis. Clearly the one-dimensional Delaunay triangulation is simply the path connecting x_1 to x_2 to...to x_n. We will view this as a projection onto the x-axis of a set of two-dimensional points with coordinates (x_i, x_i^2). These points can be viewed as the projection of the x_i's upward to the parabola $z = x^2$. Now it is trivially true that the convex hull of these two-dimensional points project down to the one-dimensional Delaunay triangulation, as long as the "top" edge of the hull is discarded. But there is much more here than this trivial observation, which can be elucidated by considering tangents to the parabola.

The slope of the parabola $z = x^2$ at the point $x = a$ is $2a$ (because $dz/dx = 2x$). Thus the equation of the line tangent to the parabola at the point (a, a^2) is

$$z - a^2 = 2a(x - a)$$

$$z = 2ax - a^2. \tag{5.4}$$

In preparation for studying the same process in three dimensions, we now investigate the intersection between this tangent and the parabola when the tangent is translated vertically by a distance r^2. When the tangent is raised by this amount, its equation is

$$z = 2ax - a^2 + r^2. \tag{5.5}$$

Where does this line intersect the parabola? Whenever

$$z = x^2 = 2ax - a^2 + r^2$$

$$(x - a)^2 = r^2$$

$$x = a \pm r. \tag{5.6}$$

So the raised tangent intersects the parabola $\pm r$ away from a, the original point of tangency. Note that $x = a \pm r$ can be thought of as the equation of a one-dimensional circle of radius r centered on a. This is illustrated in Figure 5.22, with $a = 5$ and $r = 3$, so that the "disk" is the segment $[2, 8]$.

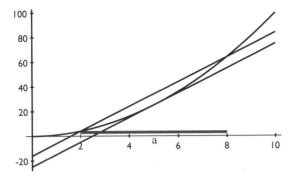

FIGURE 5.22   For $a = 5$, the tangent is $z = 10x - 25$.

5.7.2. Two-dimensional Delaunay triangulations

Now we repeat the same analysis in two dimensions.

The paraboloid is $z = x^2 + y^2$; see Figure 5.23. Take the given sites/points in the plane, and project them upward until they hit the paraboloid, that is, map every point as follows:

$$(x_i, y_i) \rightarrow (x_i, y_i, x_i^2 + y_i^2). \qquad (5.7)$$

Take the convex hull of this set of three-dimensional points; see Figure 5.24. Now discard the "top" faces of this hull: all those faces whose outward pointing normal points upward, in the sense of having a positive dot product with the z-axis vector. The result is a bottom "shell." Project this to the xy-plane. The

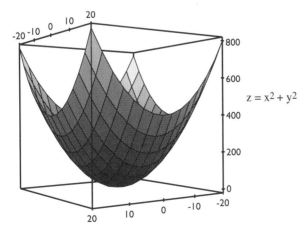

$z = x^2 + y^2$

FIGURE 5.23   The paraboloid up to which the sites are projected.

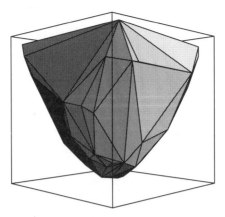

FIGURE 5.24   The convex hull of 65 points projected up to the paraboloid.

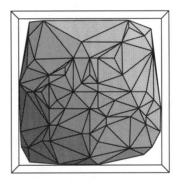

FIGURE 5.25   The paraboloid hull viewed from $z \approx -\infty$.

claim is that this is the Delaunay triangulation! See Figure 5.25.[19] We now establish this stunning connection formally.

The equation of the tangent plane above the point (a, b) is

$$z = 2ax + 2by - (a^2 + b^2). \tag{5.8}$$

(This is a direct analogy to the equation $z = 2ax - a^2$: $\partial z / \partial x = 2x$ and $\partial z / \partial y = 2y$.) Now shift this plane upward by r^2, just as we shifted the tangent line upward in the previous subsection:

$$z = 2ax + 2by - (a^2 + b^2) + r^2. \tag{5.9}$$

---

[19]Figures 5.24–5.27 were prepared by Sharmilli Ghosh and Vinita Subramanian.

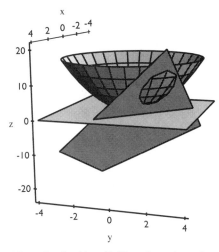

FIGURE 5.26 Plane for $(a, b) = (2, 2)$ and $r = 1$ cutting the paraboloid.

Again ask, where does this shifted plane intersect the paraboloid?

$$z = x^2 + y^2 = 2ax + 2by - (a^2 + b^2) + r^2$$

$$(x - a)^2 + (y - b)^2 = r^2. \qquad (5.10)$$

The shifted plane intersects the paraboloid in a curve (an ellipse) that projects to a circle! This is illustrated in Figures 5.26 and 5.27.

Now we reverse the viewpoint to lead us to the Delaunay triangulation. Consider the plane π through three points on the paraboloid $\triangle = (p_i, p_j, p_k)$ that form a face of the convex hull in three dimensions. This plane slices through the paraboloid. If we translate π vertically downward, at some point it will cease to intersect the paraboloid. Let us say that the last point it touches is $(a, b, a^2 + b^2)$. Then we can view π as an upwards shift of this tangent plane τ;

FIGURE 5.27 The curve of intersection in Figure 5.26 projects to a circle of radius 1 in the *xy*-plane.

call the shift amount r^2. Now it should be clear that the previous analysis applies.

Since $\triangle$ is a lower face of the hull, all of the other points of the paraboloid are above π. Since they are above π, they are more than r^2 above τ, which is r^2 below π. Therefore, these points project outside of the circle of radius r in the *xy*-plane. Therefore, the circle determined by $\triangle$ in the *xy*-plane is empty of all other sites. Therefore, it forms a Delaunay triangle. Therefore every lower triangular face of the convex hull corresponds to a Delaunay triangle. Therefore the "bottom" of the convex hull projects to the Delaunay triangulation! Again consult Figure 5.25.

Let me explain this important insight again in another way. Start with the plane τ tangent to the paraboloid above $p = (a, b)$. Its point of contact projects downward to p. Now move τ upward. The projection of its intersection with the paraboloid is an expanding circle centered on p. When τ hits a point on the paraboloid that is above a site, the expanding circle bumps into the site on the plane. Thus the circle is empty until τ reaches π, when it passes through the three sites whose projection forms the triangle hull face $\triangle$ supported by π.

A useful corollary to the above discussion is this:[20]

Corollary 5.7.1. *Four points* (x_i, y_i), $i = 1, 2, 3, 4$, *lie on a circle iff* $(x_i, y_i, x_i^2 + y_i^2)$ *lie on a plane.*

The coplanarity of these points can be checked by seeing if the volume of the tetrahedron they determine (Chapter 1, Section 1.4.9) is zero.

5.7.3. Implications

Theorem 5.7.2. *The Delaunay triangulation of a set of points in two dimensions is precisely the projection to the xy-plane of the lower convex hull of the transformed points in three dimensions, transformed by mapping upwards to the paraboloid* $z = x^2 + y^2$.

Since the convex hull in three dimensions can be computed in $O(n \log n)$ time (Section 4.2.2), this implies that the Delaunay triangulation can be computed in the same time bound. Once the Delaunay triangulation is in hand, it is relatively easy to compute the Voronoi diagram (Exercise 5.7.5[2]). This leads to another $O(n \log n)$ algorithm for constructing the Voronoi diagram.

As one might hope, this relationship between Voronoi diagrams and convex hulls in one higher dimension holds in arbitrary dimensions. Thus, the Voronoi diagram in three dimensions (which has many applications, for example in crystallography) can be constructed from a convex hull in four dimensions, and in general, the Voronoi diagram dual for a set of d-dimensional points is the projection of the "lower" hull of points in $d + 1$ dimensions.

---

[20]See Pedoe (1970, p, 146) for a proof.

5.7.4. Implementation of Delaunay Triangulation

Theorem 5.7.2 allows amazingly concise code to compute the Delaunay triangulation, if one is unconcerned about time complexity. In particular, if $O(n^4)$ is acceptable (and it rarely is), the Delaunay triangulation can be computed with less than 30 lines of C code! This is presented in Code 5.1[21] partly as a curiosity, but also to emphasize how deep understanding of geometry can lead to clean code.

The $O(n^4)$ structure of the code is evident in the four nested `for`-loops. For each triple of points (i, j, k), the program checks to see if all other points m are on or above the plane containing i, j, and k. If so, (i, j, k) are output as a Delaunay triangle. (The similarity to the two-dimensional hull algorithm in Algorithm 3.2 should be evident.) The above-plane test is performed by dotting the outward-pointing normal to the triangle, (x_n, y_n, z_n), with a vector from point i to point m.

Exercise 5.7.5[1] asks for an implementation based on the $O(n^2)$ incremental code presented in Section 4.2.3.

5.7.5. Exercises

1. $\mathcal{D}(P)$ *from hull* [programming] [easy]. Modify the convex hull code of Section 4.2.3 to input a list of two-dimensional points and output the Delaunay triangulation. Base your modifications on Theorem 5.7.2.

2. $\mathcal{D}(P) \Rightarrow \mathcal{V}(P)$ [programming]. Modify the code from the preceding exercise to compute the Voronoi diagram from the Delaunay triangulation. (See Exercise 5.5.6[1].) It will be necessary to repeatedly construct circles through three given points a, b, c. The coordinates of the center $p = (p_0, p_1)$ of this circle are:

$$p_0 = \big(b_1 a_0^2 - c_1 a_0^2 - b_1^2 a_1 + c_1^2 a_1 + b_0^2 c_1 + a_1^2 b_1$$

$$+ c_0^2 a_1 - c_1^2 b_1 - c_0^2 b_1 - b_0^2 a_1 + b_1^2 c_1 - a_1^2 c_1\big)/D \qquad (5.11)$$

$$p_1 = \big(a_0^2 c_0 + a_1^2 c_0 + b_0^2 a_0 - b_0^2 c_0 + b_1^2 a_0 - b_1^2 c_0$$

$$- a_0^2 b_0 - a_1^2 b_0 - c_0^2 a_0 + c_0^2 b_0 - c_1^2 a_0 + c_1^2 b_0\big)/D \qquad (5.12)$$

where

$$D = 2(a_1 c_0 + b_1 a_0 - b_1 c_0 - a_1 b_0 - c_1 a_0 + c_1 b_0). \qquad (5.13)$$

The radius of the circle is then:

$$r^2 = (a_0 - p_0)^2 + (a_1 - p_1)^2. \qquad (5.14)$$

Output coordinates for all the Voronoi vertices. For each finite-length Voronoi edge,

---

[21]The original (shorter!) version of this program was written by Michael McKenna in response to a class challenge for pithy code.

```
main()
{
        int x[NMAX],y[NMAX],z[NMAX];    /* input points xy,z = x² + y² */
        int n;                           /* number of input points */
        int i, j, k, m;                  /* indices of four points */
        int xn, yn, zn;                  /* outward normal to (i,j,k) */
        int flag;                        /* t if m above of (i,j,k) */

        /* Input points and compute z = x² + y². */
        scanf("%d", &n);
        for ( i=0; i<n; i++ ) {
                scanf("%d %d", &x[i], &y[i]);
                z[i]=x[i] * x[i]+y[i] * y[i];
        }

        /* For each triple (i,j,k) */
        for ( i=0; i < n-2; i++ )
        for ( j=i+1; j < n; j++ )
        for ( k=i+1; k < n; k++ )
        if ( j != k ) {
            /* Compute normal to triangle (i,j,k). */
            xn=(y[j]-y[i])*(z[k]-z[i])-(y[k]-y[i])*(z[j]-z[i]);
            yn=(x[k]-x[i])*(z[j]-z[i])-(x[j]-x[i])*(z[k]-z[i]);
            zn=(x[j]-x[i])*(y[k]-y[i])-(x[k]-x[i])*(y[j]-y[i]);

            /* Only examine faces on bottom of paraboloid: zn < 0. */
            if ( flag=(zn < 0) )
                    /* For each other point m */
                    for (m=0; m<n; m++)
                            /* Check if m above (i,j,k). */
                            flag=flag &&
                                    ((x[m]-x[i])*xn +
                                    (y[m]-y[i])*yn +
                                    (z[m]-z[i])*zn <= 0);
            if (flag)
                    printf("%d\t%d\t%d\n", i, j, k);
        }
}
```

Code 5.1 $O(n^4)$ Delaunay triangulation algorithm.

output its two endpoints (either their coordinates, or an index into your Voronoi vertex list). For each unbounded Voronoi edge-ray, output its endpoint and a vector (of arbitrary length) along the ray, oriented toward infinity.

3. *Furthest-point Voronoi diagram.* Argue that the "top" of the convex hull of the transformed points is the dual of the furthest-point Voronoi diagram. See Exercise 5.5.6[11] for a definition of this diagram. The "top" faces are those whose outward-normal has a positive z-component. Thus the view of the paraboloid hull from $z = +\infty$ shows the dual of $\mathscr{F}(P)$! See Figure 5.28.

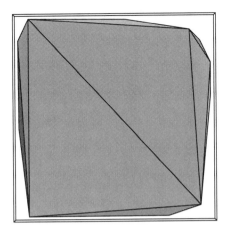

FIGURE 5.28 View of the hull in Figure 5.24 seen from $z \approx +\infty$.

4. *Circular separability.* Given two sets of planar points A and B, design an algorithm for finding (if it exists) a closed disk that encloses every point of A but excludes every point of B.

5.8. CONNECTION TO ARRANGEMENTS

We have shown how the Delauany triangulation can be derived from the paraboloid transformation, and indicated that it is then easy to obtain the Voronoi diagram. It is also possible to obtain the Voronoi diagram directly from the paraboloid transformation. Although a full understanding of this will have to await the next chapter (Section 6.6), we will sketch the connection now while the relevant equations are nearby.

5.8.1. One-dimensional Voronoi Diagrams

Consider two tangents to the parabola examined in Section 5.7.1 (Eq. 5.4), one above $x = a$ and the other above $x = b$:

$$z = 2ax - a^2$$
$$z = 2bx - b^2. \tag{5.15}$$

Where do they intersect? Solving these equations simultaneously yields:

$$2ax - a^2 = 2bx - b^2$$
$$x(2a - 2b) = a^2 - b^2$$
$$x = \frac{(a+b)(a-b)}{2(a-b)}$$
$$x = \frac{a+b}{2}. \tag{5.16}$$

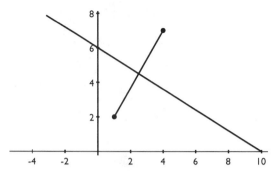

FIGURE 5.29 Bisector of $(1, 2)$ and $(4, 7)$ is $x(-6) + y(-10) = -60$, or $y = (-6/10)x + 6$.

Therefore, the intersections of adjacent tangents projects to the one-dimensional Voronoi diagram of the point set.

5.8.2. Two-dimensional Voronoi Diagrams

Consider two tangent planes to the paraboloid analyzed in Section 5.7.2 (Eq.5.8), one above (a, b) and the other above (c, d):

$$z = 2ax + 2by - (a^2 + b^2) \tag{5.17}$$

$$z = 2cx + 2dy - (c^2 + d^2). \tag{5.18}$$

Where do they intersect? Solving these equations simultaneously yields:

$$2ax + 2by - (a^2 + b^2) = 2cx + 2dy - (c^2 + d^2)$$

$$x(2a - 2c) + y(2b - 2d) = (a^2 - c^2) + (b^2 - d^2). \tag{5.19}$$

This equation is precisely the perpendicular bisector of the segment from (a, b) to (c, d). See Figure 5.29.

If we view the tangent planes from $z = +\infty$ (with the paraboloid transparent), then they would only be visible up to their first intersection. Their first intersection is the bisector between the sites that generate the tangent planes. The projection of these first intersections is precisely the Voronoi diagram!

So we have the remarkable situation that viewing the points projected onto the paraboloid from $z = -\infty$, one sees the Delaunay triangulation, and viewing the planes tangent to the paraboloid at those points from $z = +\infty$, one sees the Voronoi diagram.

Further Reading

Two surveys cover algorithms for constructing Voronoi diagrams: (Aurenhammer, 1991) and (Fortune, 1992b). The book by Okabe et al. (1992) covers applications as well as algorithms.

6

Arrangements

6.1. INTRODUCTION

Arrangements of lines (and planes) form the third important structure used in computational geometry, as important as convex hulls and Voronoi diagrams. As we glimpsed at the end of the previous chapter, and will see more clearly in Section 6.6, all three structures are intimately related. An arrangement of lines is shown in Figure 6.1. It is a collection of (infinite) lines "arranged" in the plane. These lines induce a partition of the plane into convex regions (called *cells*, or faces), segments (between line crossings), and vertices (where lines meet). It is this partition that is known as the *arrangement*. It is convenient to view the faces as open sets (not including their edges) and the edges as open segments (not including their bounding vertices), so that the dissection is a true partition: its pieces cover the plane, but the pieces are disjoint from one another, "pairwise disjoint" in the idiom preferred by mathematicians.

Arrangements may seem too abstract to have much utility, but in fact they arise in a wide variety of contexts. Here are four; more will be discussed in Section 6.7.

1. *Visibility Graphs.* Let S be a set of n disjoint segments with no three endpoints collinear. The *endpoint visibility graph* has a node for each endpoint, and an arc between endpoints x and y if the open segment (x, y) does not touch any segment in S: so x and y can see one another clearly. Usually arcs corresponding to the segments themselves are also included in the graph. This graph has application in robotics, as we will see in Chapter 8 (Section 8.2). A naive algorithm for constructing this graph has complexity $O(n^3)$: for each x and y, spend $O(n)$ time checking (x, y) against all segments. Employing arrangements leads to an $O(n^2)$ algorithm (O'Rourke, 1987, pp. 211–217).

2. *Hidden Surface Removal.* Hidden surface removal is the process of computing which surfaces in a three-dimensional scene are hidden from the viewpoint, and using this to construct a two-dimensional graphics image. The first worst-case optimal $\Theta(n^2)$ algorithm found depends on arrangements (McKenna 1987) (See Section 6.7.2).

3. *Empty Convex Polygons.* Given a set of n points in the plane, find the *largest empty convex polygon* whose vertices are drawn from S. Here "largest" means the most vertices. This problem is inspired by an unresolved question posed by Erdős: it is unknown whether every sufficiently large set of points must contain an empty hexagon (Horton

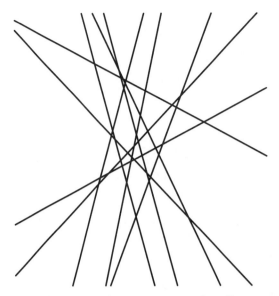

FIGURE 6.1 An arrangement of ten lines.

1983). Using arrangements, the largest empty convex polygon can be found in $O(n^3)$ time (Edelsbrunner and Guibas, 1989) (Dobkin, Edelsbrunner and Overmars, 1990).

4. *Ham Sandwich Cuts.* It is a remarkable theorem that any ham and cheese sandwich may be cut by a plane so that the two halves have precisely the same amount of bread, ham, and cheese! The two-dimensional version of this theorem states that there is always a line that simultaneously bisects two point sets. Arrangements permit finding this bisection in time linear in the size of the sets, provided they are separable by a line (Edelsbrunner 1987, Theorem 14.6) (See Section 6.7.6).

This chapter will develop the fundamentals of arrangements of lines, but will not delve deeply enough to explain all four of the above applications. Rather my goal is to sketch the essentials, and leave the remainder for Edelsbrunner (1987).[1] This chapter contains no implementations, and may be the most challenging of the book in its degree of abstraction.

6.2. COMBINATORICS OF ARRANGEMENTS

An arrangement of lines is called *simple* if every pair of lines meet in exactly one point: no three lines meet in a point, and no two lines are parallel.

---

[1] The presentation here is influenced is heavily by Edelsbrunner's.

Nonsimple arrangements are "degenerate" in some sense, and often theorems and algorithms are easiest with simple arrangements.

It is a remarkable fact that all simple arrangements on n lines have exactly the same number of vertices, edges, and faces.

Corollary 6.2.1. *In a simple arrangement of n lines, the number of vertices, edges, and faces is $V = \binom{n}{2}$, $E = n^2$, and $F = \binom{n}{2} + n + 1$, respectively, and no nonsimple arrangement exceeds these quantities.*

Proof. That the number of vertices is $\binom{n}{2}$ follows directly from the fact that in a simple arrangement, each pair of lines generates exactly one vertex. The formula for E can be proven by an easy induction. Assume any simple arrangement $\mathscr{A}$ of $n - 1$ lines has $(n - 1)^2$ edges. Insert a new line L into $\mathscr{A}$. It splits one edge on each of the $n - 1$ lines of $\mathscr{A}$ in two, and L itself is partitioned by $\mathscr{A}$ into n new edges. Thus $E = (n - 1)^2 + (n - 1) + n$, which simple algebra reveals to be n^2.

We can now derive F from Euler's formula (Theorem 4.1.1): $V - E + F = 2$. We cannot apply this directly, as it counts these quantities for plane graphs, and an arrangement $\mathscr{A}$ is not a plane graph under the usual interpretation. It is not difficult, however, to derive a graph G from $\mathscr{A}$ that captures the same quantities, as follows. Clip all the lines beyond their extreme intersections, so that they become segments. Add one new vertex, and attach the tips of every clipped line to this new vertex; see Figure 6.2. This is now a plane graph with $V + 1$ vertices, E edges, and F faces, where V, E, and F are the counts for $\mathscr{A}$. Note in particular that one face of $\mathscr{A}$ (7 in the figure) becomes the exterior face of G. Applying Euler's formula to G yields $(V + 1) - E + F = 2$, or $F = 1 + E -$

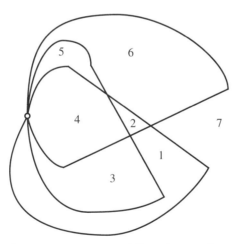

FIGURE 6.2 Converting an arrangement of lines into a plane graph with the same number of edges and faces. Here $n = 3$, and there are $\binom{3}{2} + 3 + 1 = 7$ faces.

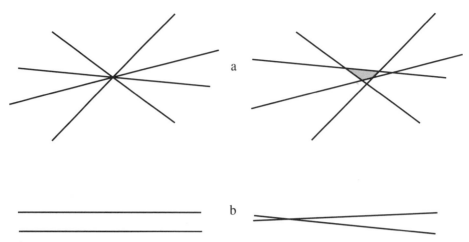

FIGURE 6.3 Perturbing the lines in a nonsimple arrangement only increases the number of vertices, edges, and faces: (a) $k > 3$ lines through a point; (b) parallel lines.

V. Now substituting in the known values of V and E yields $F = 1 + n^2 + n(n-1)/2 = (n^2 + n + 2)/2$, which is the same as the claimed formula.

Finally, we argue informally that simple arrangements are the worst case for these combinatorial quantities. If $k > 2$ lines meet at a vertex, we can "perturb" the lines slightly to break the coincidence, as shown in Figure 6.3a. This increases each of V, E, and F, as is evident from examining just the contributions of the shaded region in (a) of the figure. If two lines are parallel, then again perturbation, as in Figure 6.3b, increases V by 1, E by 2, and F by 1. Thus breaking degeneracies only increases the combinatorial complexity of an arrangement, and so a nonsimple arrangement cannot be a worst case.

What hasn't been demonstrated, but what should accord with intuition, is that all the degeneracies in an arrangement can be broken simultaneously. Establishing this formally would take us too far afield.[2] □

The important consequence of this theorem for algorithm design is that arrangements in the plane are fundamentally quadratic: V, E, and F are all $\Theta(n^2)$.

The key combinatorial property of arrangements that permits efficient construction is that no one line of an arrangement pierces cells with too many edges. The reason this is key will be made clear after we make this notion of a "zone" precise. After that, we will prove the "Zone Theorem."

6.2.1. Zone Theorem

Fix an arrangement $\mathcal{A}$ of n lines, and let L be any other line (usually not in $\mathcal{A}$). We assume for clarity that the arrangement $\mathcal{A} \cup \{L\}$ is simple. The *zone* of

[2]See (Edelsbrunner and Mucke, 1990).

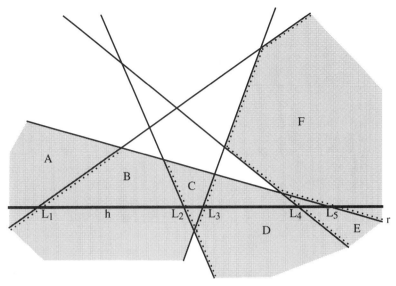

FIGURE 6.4   The zone of h is $Z(h) = \{A, B, C, D, E, F\}$; $z(h) = 2 + 4 + 3 + 4 + 2 + 4 = 19$. The lines of $\mathscr{A}$ are numbered $L_1, \ldots, L_5$.

L in $\mathscr{A}$, $Z_{\mathscr{A}}(L)$ (or just $Z(L)$ when the arrangement is clear from the context), is the set of cells (faces) intersected by L. For example, in Figure 6.4, $Z(h) = \{A, B, C, D, E, F\}$. The Zone Theorem bounds the total number of edges of these cells. Let $|C|$ be the number of edges bounding a cell/face C. In that figure, $|A| = 2$, $|B| = 4$, $|C| = 3$, $|D| = 4$, $|E| = 2$, and $|F| = 4$. The total number of edges of the cells in the zone $Z(L)$ we denote by $z(L)$; thus $z(h) = 19$ in Figure 6.4. Note that edges adjacent to two cells in the zone are counted twice in $z(L)$. Lastly, we let z_n be the maximum value of $z(L)$ over all possible lines L in all arrangements of n lines: the largest $z(L)$ could ever be as a function of n.

To look ahead to Section 6.3 quickly, we will construct an arrangement of lines incrementally, by inserting each line one after another into a growing arrangement. The complexity of this insertion will be bound above by z_n, as the edges of the zone of the inserted line will be traversed by the algorithm.

We now focus on the Zone Theorem, which claims that $z_n = O(n)$. This was first proved by Chazelle, Guibas, and Lee (1985) and Edelsbrunner, O'Rourke, and Seidel (1986)[3] and since then many alternative proofs have been found. Here I expand on a proof of Edelsbrunner et al (1991).

Theorem 6.2.2.   *The total number of edges in all the cells that intersect one line in an arrangement of* n *lines, is* O(n): *specifically,* $z_n \leq 6n$.

---

[3]Unfortunately the proof for dimensions ≥ 3 in this paper (and in Edelsbrunner, 1987) is incorrect, although the theorem is true. A correction appears in (Edelsbrunner, Seidel, and Sharir, 1991).

Proof. We will make three assumptions to simplify the exposition: the arrangement with the new line is simple, the line h whose zone we seek is horizontal, and no line is vertical. I will not take the time to justify these assumptions, since the proof is difficult enough without dealing with "special" cases. Suffice it to say that the worst case is again achieved by simple arrangements, so it is no loss of generality to assume this for an upper bound.

Because no line is vertical, it makes sense to partition the lines of each cell of $Z(h)$ into left-bounding and right-bounding edges; we will simplify these to left and right edges. Points on a *left edge* of a cell C have interior cell points immediately to their right; thus they form the left boundary of C. Right edges are those which are not left edges. Note that, by our assumption of simplicity, no line is parallel to h, and therefore the highest and lowest vertices of bounded cells C are unique, providing a clean separation between left and right edges. In Figure 6.4, the left edges of the zone cells are highlighted with dotted lines.

Since left and right edges play a symmetrical role, we need only prove that the number of left edges contributing to z_n, call this l_n, is $\leq 3n$. In Figure 6.4, there are nine left edges, and $n = 5$.

The proof is by induction. The basis of the induction is the obvious $l_0 \leq 0$: an empty arrangement has no left edges. Suppose it is true that $l_{n-1} \leq 3n - 3$. Let $\mathcal{A}$ be an arrangement of n lines satisfying our assumptions. The plan is to remove one line from $\mathcal{A}$, apply induction, and put it back. The line we choose to remove is the one whose intersection with h is rightmost: L_5 in Figure 6.4. (Note that by the assumption of simplicity, no two lines are parallel, and thus every line intersects h.) Call this rightmost line r. Let $\mathcal{A}'$ be the arrangement $\mathcal{A} - \{r\}$: $\mathcal{A}$ with r removed. It has $n - 1$ lines, and so the induction hypothesis holds. Now our goal is to show that inserting r back into $\mathcal{A}'$ can increase l_{n-1} by at most 3. The remainder of the proof establishes this, by showing that r introduces one new left edge, and splits at most two old left edges. Here "old" refers to $\mathcal{A}'$, before reinsertion of r, and "new" refers to $\mathcal{A}$, after insertion of r.

Figure 6.5 shows $\mathcal{A}'$ corresponding to $\mathcal{A}$ in Figure 6.4. We label all the cells with primes, using the same letter for obvious correspondents. Inserting $r = L_5$ splits cell G' of $\mathcal{A}'$ into cells F and E in $\mathcal{A}$, and it clips cells A', B', C', and D' to form A, B, C, and D respectively. The total effect of this insertion is complicated: for example, the number of left edges of B' and B are the same, C has one less left edge than C', and F has one more left edge than G'. What makes the situation simpler than it might first appear is that (a) we only need an upper bound on the increase, not an exact accounting, and (b) the effect on the left edges is simpler than the changes to the right edges. This latter claim results from our choice of the rightmost line to obtain a bound on the left edges, as we will see.

Because r was chosen to have the rightmost intersection with h in $\mathcal{A}$, this intersection (call it $x = r \cap h$) must lie in the rightmost cell intersected by h in $\mathcal{A}'$ (G' in Figure 6.5). r will bound the rightmost cell of $\mathcal{A}$ (F in Figure 6.4) from the left, for r contains x and the ray from x to the right must be in the rightmost cell. So, r will contain at least one new left edge. Now the key observation is that r does not contain any other left edges in $\mathcal{A}$ (note that it

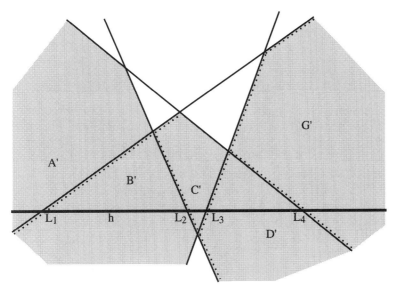

FIGURE 6.5   The arrangement $\mathscr{A}' = \mathscr{A} - \{r\}$.

does contain several new right edges in Figure 6.4). For any line α of $\mathscr{A}$ (such as L_3 in Figure 6.4) that contains more than one left edge, must be cut by a line β (such as L_4) that separates the cells α supports to the right; but then β would intersect h to the right of α. Thus α could not have the rightmost intersection with h. This explains the choice of r.

Having concluded that r contains exactly one new left edge, we need only limit the number of old left edges that r splits in two. For example, the left edge of G' in Figure 6.5 that crosses h (contained in L_4) is split by $r = L_5$ in Figure 6.4 into a left edge for E and one for F. This splitting can only happen in the rightmost cell on h in $\mathscr{A}'$, for r "clips" rather than splits all other cells that it intersects. The reason is similar to that just used above: if r splits a left edge, then the two cells supported to the right by these left edges must straddle r on h, implying that one is rightmost (since r has the rightmost intersection with h); this in turn implies that the old edge split must have been part of the rightmost cell.

So we have established that r can split only edges of the rightmost zone cell. Because this cell is convex, r can cross it at most twice (r only intersects the boundary of $G' = E + F$ once in Figure 6.4). Therefore r can split at most two old left edges. We now have our theorem: r adds one new left edge, and can split at most two old left edges, increasing l_{n-1} by at most 3, to $l_n \le 3n$. $\square$

6.2.2. Exercises

1. *Biggest zone* [difficult]. Construct a generic example that achieves the largest value of z_n that you can manage. Theorem 6.2.2 guarantees that $z_n \le 6n$, but this is not in fact achievable. (Bern, Eppstein, Plassman, and Yao 1991).

2. *Space partitions*. Derive formulae for the number of vertices, edges, faces, and cells of a simple arrangement of n planes in three-dimensional space.

6.3. INCREMENTAL ALGORITHM

We now have in place the machinery to discuss an algorithm for constructing an arrangement of lines. First we must decide on the input and output. Input is easy: any representation of the lines, such as slope and intercept, will do. Output is less clear, but I hope that after our discussion of data structures for polytope surfaces (Section 4.4) it should be evident that any of those could be used to represent an arrangement, with slight modification to account for unbounded edges. In particular, the quad-edge data structure can be used as is, since it can represent any subdivision. We will not explore representation issues, but just assume that the representation is functionally equivalent to the quad-edge data structure.

The incremental algorithm for constructing an arrangement (Algorithm 6.1) is remarkably simple. At any given stage, we have an arrangement $\mathcal{A}_{i-1}$ constructed for the first $i-1$ lines. The task is to find all the points of intersection between $\mathcal{A}_{i-1}$ and L_i, the $i-$th input line. First an intersection point x between L_i and any line of $\mathcal{A}_{i-1}$ is found in constant time. In Figure 6.6, $x = L_i \cap L_2$. Then we walk forward along the zone of L_i, $Z(L_i)$, traversing the edges of each face clockwise, repeating each cell traversal until an edge is again encountered that crosses L_i. In Figure 6.6, we traverse three edges of C before meeting the intersection between L_3 and L_i; then we traverse three edges of D; and so on as illustrated. The forward march terminates when an infinite zone edge is encountered; then the process is repeated from x backwards, traversing cell edge counterclockwise (cells B and A in the figure). Each of the steps in this traversal moves between incident or adjacent objects, and so each takes constant time. The total cost of the insertion traversal is dependent on the complexity of the zone, which as we saw in Theorem 6.2.2, is $O(n)$. Note how the structure of the arrangement is used to avoid sorting. Either after all the points of intersection with L_i have been found, or (more likely) during the traversal itself, the data structure for $\mathcal{A}_{i-1}$ is updated to that for $\mathcal{A}_i$. That this

---

Algorithm: ARRANGEMENT CONSTRUCTION
Construct $\mathcal{A}_0$, a data structure for an empty arrangement.
for each $i = 1, \ldots, n$ do
    Insert line L_i into $\mathcal{A}_{i-1}$ as follows:
        Find an intersection point x between L_i
           and some line of $\mathcal{A}_{i-1}$.
        Walk forward from x along cells in $Z(L_i)$.
        Walk backward from x along cells in $Z(L_i)$.
    Update $\mathcal{A}_{i-1}$ to $\mathcal{A}_i$.

Algorithm 6.1   Incremental construction of an arrangement.

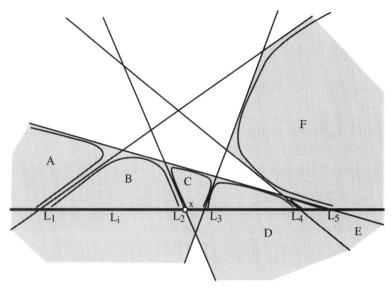

FIGURE 6.6   Inserting one line L_i into an arrangement. The curves show the path of zone traversal for discovering the vertices on L_i.

can be accomplished in $O(n)$ time we leave for Exercise 6.4.1[1]. It is clear then that the entire construction requires $O(n^2)$ time, a result first obtained by Chazelle et al. (1985) and Edelsbrunner et al. (1986):

Theorem 6.3.1.   *An arrangement of n lines in the plane may be constructed in $\Theta(n^2)$ time and space.*

Proof.   The algorithm takes $O(n^2)$ time, and as we saw in Theorem 6.2.1, the structure may be this big, so this is the best possible asymptotic bound. Storing the structure could require quadratic space in the worst case.   □

6.4.   THREE AND HIGHER DIMENSIONS

One of the most beautiful aspects of the theory of arrangements is that almost every feature carries through smoothly to higher dimensions. Although we will not discuss this topic in any detail, it is worth mentioning analogs of Theorems 6.2.1, 6.2.2, and 6.3.1:[4]

Theorem 6.4.1.   *The number of faces of any dimension in an arrangement of hyperplanes in d dimensions is $O(n^d)$, the zone of any hyperplane has total complexity $O(n^{d-1})$, and such an arrangement can be constructed in $O(n^d)$ time and space.*

[4]For proofs see Edelsbrunner (1987) and Edelsbrunner et al. (1991).

In particular, an arrangement of planes in three dimensions has complexity $O(n^3)$ and can be constructed in this time, a fact we will use in the sequel.

6.4.1. Exercises

1. *Insertion updates.* Argue that if the arrangement is represented by the quad-edge data structure, the updates caused by insertion of one new line can be effected in $O(n)$ time.

6.5. DUALITY

It may seem odd that arrangements are so useful for problems on sets of points in the plane, as in item (4) of Section 6.1. The key to this, and many applications of arrangements, is an important concept known as *duality*. The basic idea is that since lines may be specified by two numbers, lines can be associated with the *point* whose coordinates are those two numbers. For example, a line specified by $y = mx + b$ can be associated with the point (m, b). Often the space of these points is called *parameter space*, as the point coordinates are the parameters of the line. Because both the primary and the parameter space are equivalent two-dimensional spaces, it is customary (albeit confusing) to treat them as a single space whose coordinates have two interpretations. Once the mapping from lines to points is determined, it can be reversed: any point in the plane can be viewed as specifying a line when its coordinates are interpreted as, e.g., slope and intercept. Together these mappings determine a duality between points and lines: every[5] line is associated with a unique point, and every point with a unique line.

There are many different point-line duality mappings possible, depending on the conventions of the standard representation of a line. Each mapping has its advantages and disadvantages in particular contexts. We mentioned already the mapping $L:y = mx + b \Leftrightarrow p:(m, b)$, which has the advantage of tapping into our familiarity with slope and intercept. The mapping $L:ax + by = 1 \Leftrightarrow p:(a, b)$ defines what is known as *polar duality* (Coxeter and Greitzer 1967).[6] This mapping has pleasing geometric properties, some of which are explored in exercises (Exercise 6.5.3[3] and [4]). But the mapping we will use throughout this chapter is

$$L : y = 2ax - b \Leftrightarrow p : (a, b).$$

We use the symbol $\mathbb{D}$ to indicate this mapping: $\mathbb{D}(L) = p$ and $\mathbb{D}(p) = L$. Although this may seem like an odd choice for a mapping, it is often the most convenient in computational geometry, largely because of its intimate connection to the paraboloid transformation (Section 5.7.2). We now examine this connection, first informally, and then via a series of lemmas (Section 6.5.2).

---

[5]This "every" will be qualified in Lemma 6.5.2 below.

[6]The mapping $L:ax + by = -1 \Leftrightarrow p:(a, b)$ is often given the same name (Chazelle et al. 1985).

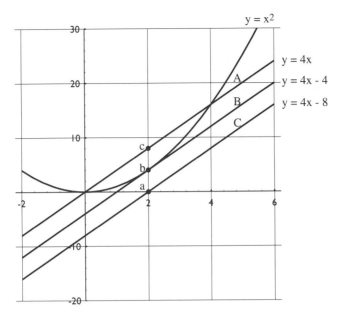

FIGURE 6.7 $\mathbb{D}(a) = A$, $\mathbb{D}(b) = B$, $\mathbb{D}(c) = C$

6.5.1. Duality mapping

The relationship between the point $p = (a, b)$ and the line $L: y = 2ax - b$ is not immediately evident. However, the similarity of L to Equation (5.15) in Section 5.8.1 should indicate a relationship to the parabola $y = x^2$. Recall that $y = 2ax - a^2$ is the tangent to this parabola at the point (a, a^2). Thus $\mathbb{D}(p)$ for $p = (a, b)$ with $b = a^2$ maps to this tangent. If $b < a^2$, then $\mathbb{D}(p)$ maps to a line parallel to this tangent but raised vertically by $(a^2 - b)$ (as we saw in Figure 5.22). If $b > a^2$, then $\mathbb{D}(p)$ maps to a parallel line shifted $(b - a^2)$ below the tangent. This is illustrated in Figure 6.7 for three points with $a = 2$, and $b \in \{0, 4, 8\}$. Here and throughout we display the points and their duals in the same space.

With this duality transformation, we can convert any set of points into an arrangement of lines, and vice versa. One reason this is often so useful is that the relationships between points are revealed more explicitly in the dual arrangement of lines.[7] Figure 6.8 shows the construction of the points dual to the ten lines shown in Figure 6.1, and Figure 6.9 displays the points alone. This example will be employed later, in Section 6.7.6.

6.5.2. Duality Properties

In this section we develop some basic properties of the duality transform, which will then be employed in later sections.

[7]This observation is due to Edelsbrunner (1987, p. 4).

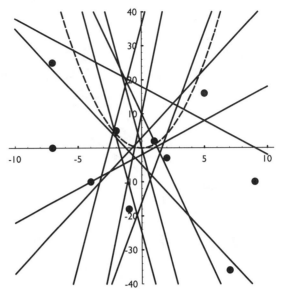

FIGURE 6.8   The duals of the lines in Figure 6.1.

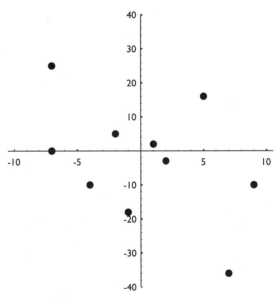

FIGURE 6.9   The points from Fig. 6.8:
$\{(-7, 25)(-7, 0), (-4, -10), (-2, 5), (-1, -18), (1, 2), (2, -3), (5, 16), (7, -36), (9, -10)\}$.

Lemma 6.5.1. $\mathbb{D}$ *is its own inverse*: $\mathbb{D}(\mathbb{D}(x)) = x$, *where* x *is either a point or a line*.

Proof. The mapping was defined to be symmetric. □

Lemma 6.5.2. $\mathbb{D}$ *is a one-to-one correspondence between all nonvertical lines and all points in the plane.*

Proof. Vertical lines cannot be represented in the form $y = 2ax - b$, and these are the only lines that cannot be so represented. □

The special cases involving vertical lines can be skirted in any given problem by rotating the lines slightly so that none is vertical. We will simply exclude vertical lines from consideration. Duality preserves point-line incidence:

Lemma 6.5.3. *Point* p *lies on line* L *iff point* $\mathbb{D}(L)$ *lies on line* $\mathbb{D}(p)$.

Proof. Let L be the line $y = 2ax - b$, and let $p = (c, d)$. Then since p lies on L, $d = 2ac - b$. $\mathbb{D}(L)$ is (a, b), and $\mathbb{D}(p)$ is the line $y = 2cx - d$. Substituting the coordinates of $\mathbb{D}(L)$ into $\mathbb{D}(p)$'s equation results in $b = 2ca - d$, which holds since this is just a rearrangement of $d = 2ac - b$. Therefore $\mathbb{D}(L)$ lies on $\mathbb{D}(p)$.
    The reverse implication follows from Lemma 6.5.1 □

The fact that two points determine a line dualizes to two lines determining a point of intersection:

Lemma 6.5.4. *Lines* L_1 *and* L_2 *intersect at point* p *iff the line* $\mathbb{D}(p)$ *passes through the two points* $\mathbb{D}(L_1)$ *and* $\mathbb{D}(L_2)$.

Proof. This follows by applying Lemma 6.5.3 twice: since p lies on L_1 and on L_2, both $\mathbb{D}(L_1)$ and $\mathbb{D}(L_2)$ lie on $\mathbb{D}(p)$. Again the reverse implication follows from Lemma 6.5.1. □

When vertical lines are excluded from consideration, points and lines can be related unambiguously as above, on, or below. The duality mapping can be seen to reverse vertical ordering, in the following sense.

Lemma 6.5.5. *If point* p *lies above line* L, *then line* $\mathbb{D}(p)$ *lies below point* $\mathbb{D}(L)$; *and symmetrically if* p *lies below* L, $\mathbb{D}(p)$ *lies above* $\mathbb{D}(L)$.

Proof. We only prove the first claim. So assume p lies above L. Let L be the line $y = 2ax - b$, and let $p = (c, d)$. Because p lies above L, the y-coordinate of p is larger than L evaluated at $x = c$: $d > 2ac - b$. $\mathbb{D}(p)$ is the line $y = 2cx - d$, and $\mathbb{D}(L) = (a, b)$. Substituting $x = a$ into $\mathbb{D}(p)$ yields a y-coordinate of $2ca - d$, which is smaller than b because $b > 2ca - d$ is just a rearrangement of $d > 2ac - b$. Thus line $\mathbb{D}(p)$ lies below point $\mathbb{D}(L)$. □

This can be seen clearly in Figure 6.7: for example, point c is above line B, and line C is below point b.

6.5.3. Exercises

1. *Collinear points* [easy]. What is the dual $\mathbb{D}$ of k collinear points?

2. *Dual of regular polygons.* Find the dual $\mathbb{D}$ of the vertices, and of the lines containing the edges, of a regular polygon centered on the origin. Start with regular polygons of just a few sides, and be sure to orient them so that no edge is vertical. What happens when the number of vertices $n \to \infty$?

3. *Polar dual properties.* Recall that the polar dual is defined by the mapping $L: ax + by = 1 \Leftrightarrow p:(a, b)$.

   a. Relate polar dual points and lines geometrically to the unit circle centered on the origin.

   b. Prove that the polar dual of a line that intersects this unit circle at points a and b, is the point p that is the intersection of the tangents to the circle at a and b.

4. *Polar dual of regular polygons.* Redo Exercise 2 above under polar duality: find the polar dual of the vertices, and of the lines containing the edges, of a regular polygon centered on the origin.

6.6. HIGHER-ORDER VORONOI DIAGRAMS

In this section we will explore the intimate connection between arrangements and Voronoi diagrams, a connection foreshadowed in Section 5.8. We will detail the relationship only for one-dimensional Voronoi diagrams, leaving the more interesting two-dimensional case largely to analogy. The focus of the connection is on objects called "higher-order Voronoi diagrams," which we will explain after developing the requisite machinery.

6.6.1. One-Dimensional Diagrams

Recall from Sections 5.8.1 that a set of points $P = \{x_1, \ldots, x_n\}$ on the x-axis are mapped to a set of lines tangent to the parabola $y = x^2$. The points of tangency are (x_i, x_i^2), directly above x_i. The equations of the tangent lines are $T_i: y = 2x_i x - x_i^2$ (Equation 5.15). Note that this tangent is precisely $\mathbb{D}((x_i, x_i^2))$. Let us choose the indices of the points so that they are sorted: $x_i < x_{i+1}$. We showed that the x-coordinate of the intersection point between two adjacent tangents is the midpoint between their generating points: the tangents for x_i and x_{i+1} intersect at $\frac{1}{2}(x_i + x_{i+1})$ (Equation 5.16). These intersections vertically project, therefore, to the one-dimensional Voronoi diagram of P, the set of midpoints for P.

Now, we consider the entire arrangement of lines formed by the n parabola tangents, as illustrated in Figure 6.10 for $P = \{-15, -3, 1, 10, 20\}$. Note that the parabola is entirely contained within one cell C of this arrangement, and it is the projection of the boundary of this cell that gives the Voronoi diagram of P:

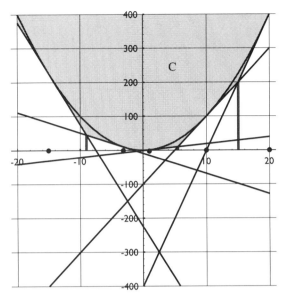

FIGURE 6.10   The parabola arrangement for $P = \{-15, -3, 1, 10, 20\}$. Cell C vertically projects to the Voronoi diagram of P, $\{-9, -1, 5\frac{1}{2}, 15\}$.

at $x = \{-9, -1, 5\frac{1}{2}, 15\}$ in Figure 6.10. It will be useful to view this in another manner, as follows. Imagine dropping down the vertical line $x = b$. The first edge of C encountered maps to the Voronoi cell (a segment on the x-axis) in which b lies.

We give yet another interpretation of this observation, already implicit in Section 5.7.1, before introducing the new connections. Let T be a line tangent to the parabola above $x = a$, so T is $y = 2ax - a^2$. We claim that the vertical distance d between the parabola and T above $x = b$ is the square of the distance between a and b. See Figure 6.11. This can be verified by a simple

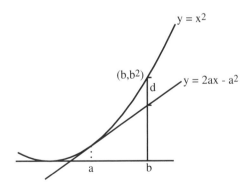

FIGURE 6.11 $d = (b - a)^2$. Here $(b - a) < 1$ so that $d < (b - a)$.

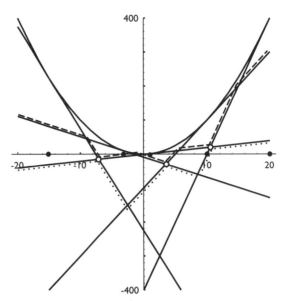

FIGURE 6.12 Dashed 2-level; dotted 3-level. Open circles indicate points of intersection between these levels. The projection of these points, $x = \{-7, 3\frac{1}{2}, 10\frac{1}{2}\}$, form the 2nd-order Voronoi diagram.

calculation: $d = b^2 - (2ab - a^2) = (b - a)^2$. The relation between this observation and the preceding one should now be clear: if, when dropping down $x = b$, T_i is encountered prior to T_j, then T_i is closer to the parabola above b than is T_j, and therefore b is closer to x_i than it is to x_j. From this discussion, we can conclude the following generalization.

Lemma 6.6.1. *The order in which the tangents are encountered moving down the vertical $x = b$ is the same as the order of closeness of b to the x_i's that generate the tangents.*

In other words, vertical sorting of the tangents corresponds to nearest-neighbor sorting.

Finally we come to the punchline. Define the *2nd-order Voronoi diagram* to partition the relevant space (in the case we are discussing, the x-axis) into regions that have the same first two nearest neighbors. Which of these neighbors is first and which second is irrelevant for this definition. Thus if a's closest neighbor is x_i and its second closest is x_j, it is in the same 2nd-order Voronoi region as a point b whose nearest neighbor is x_j and second closest is x_i. The 2nd-order diagram is implicit in those edges of the parabola arrangement composed of points that have exactly one line strictly above them vertically (and therefore two lines at or above them, since each edge is on a line). These edges comprise what is known as the *2-level* of the arrangement. The 2-level for the arrangement from Figure 6.10 is highlighted with dashes in Figure 6.12. The projections of the vertices of the 2-level partition the x-axis into cells whose points have the same first two nearest neighbors in the same order. Thus, in Figure 6.12, all $x > 15$ have $(20, 10)$ as their two nearest neighbors; all $10\frac{1}{2} < x < 15$ have $(10, 20)$ as nearest neighbors; all $5\frac{1}{2} < x < 10\frac{1}{2}$ have $(10, 1)$ as nearest neighbors; and so on. This partition of the line induced by the projection of the 2-level is finer than the 2nd-order Voronoi diagram, since in that diagram the order of the neighbors does not matter. So in Figure 6.12, all points $x > 10\frac{1}{2}$ have $\{10, 20\}$ as their set of two nearest neighbors. We now argue that the transition points for the 2nd-order Voronoi diagram are the projections of the points of intersection between the 2-level and the 3-level of the arrangement.

Define the k-level of an arrangement as the set of edges whose points have exactly $k - 1$ lines strictly above them, together with the endpoints of these edges. (Recall that arrangement edges are open segments.) We do not demand any certain number of lines above the vertices, as they might not have $k - 1$. The 3-level is hightlighted with dots in Figure 6.12. Let a be the projection of a vertex at the intersection between the 2-level and the 3-level. (These three vertices are circled in the figure.) Let the first three tangents met by the vertical line $x = a + \epsilon$ be (A, B, C) from top to bottom, where $\epsilon > 0$ is small. B is on the 2-level and C on the 3-level at this x value. Then just to the other side of a, the line $x = a - \epsilon$ meets those tangents in the order (A, C, B), for here C is on the 2-level and B on the 3-level, with B and C intersecting at $x = a$. Therefore, $x = a$ represents a change in first-two nearest neighbors from $\{A, B\}$ to $\{A, C\}$. This shows that the vertices common to the 2-level and 3-level do indeed represent 2nd-order Voronoi region transitions. It is equally clear that the other vertices of the 2-level (those not also on the 3-level) represent a switching of the order of the two nearest neighbors, without changing the set of these neighbors.

What we just argued informally holds for arbitrary k:

Theorem 6.6.2. *The points of intersection of the k- and $(k + 1)$-levels in the parabola arrangement project to the k-th order Voronoi diagram* (Edelsbrunner, 1987, p. 317).

Note that this theorem even "works" for $k = 1$: the points of intersection between the 1-level and the 2-level are precisely the vertices of the 1-level, which are the vertices of the parabola-containing cell, which project to the ordinary Voronoi diagram, which can be viewed as the 1st-order Voronoi diagram.

6.6.2. Two-Dimensional Diagrams

We will not derive any results in two dimensions, but as the reader should expect, all definitions and results from one dimension generalize exactly as one might hope. Given a set of points in the plane, construct an arrangement of planes tangent to the paraboloid above the points, as in Section 5.8.2. The Voronoi diagram is the projection of the 1-level, the edges and vertices of the cell containing the paraboloid. The k-level is an undulating "sheet" of

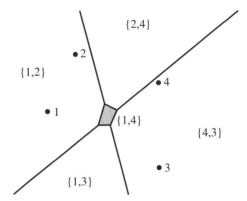

FIGURE 6.13 A 2nd-order Voronoi diagram for four points. The central shaded region's nearest neighbors are $\{1, 4\}$.

faces (and the edges and vertices in their closures). The k-th order Voronoi diagram is the projection of the intersection of the k- and $(k + 1)$-levels, which is a collection of edges and vertices. A simple 2nd-order Voronoi diagram is shown in Figure 6.13. So all the higher-order Voronoi diagrams are in a precise sense embedded in the arrangement of tangent planes.

This incidentally shows that the total complexity of all these diagrams is $O(n^3)$, since the levels are all embedded in an arrangement with complexity of $O(n^3)$ (by Theorem 6.4.1), and no face is shared between levels. It is not difficult to construct all the k-th order Voronoi diagrams, for $k = 1, \ldots, n - 1$, in time $O(n^3)$, by constructing the arrangement of planes.

6.6.3. Exercises

1. *Furthest-point Voronoi diagram.* Show that the furthest-point Voronoi diagram (Exercises 5.5.6[11]) and 5.7.3[3]) is the same as the $(n - 1)$st-order Voronoi diagram.

2. *k-th order Voronoi diagram in one dimension.* How many regions are there in a k-th order Voronoi diagram in one-dimension?

3. *Cells are convex.* Prove that the cells of a k-th order Voronoi diagram are convex.

4. *Bisector bounding more than one cell.* Demonstrate by example that a bisector of two points might bound two non-adjacent cells of a k-th order Voronoi diagram.

5. *k-levels.* Prove that the k-level in a simple arrangement of lines is a polygonal chain that separates the plane into two parts.

6.7. APPLICATIONS

6.7.1. k-Nearest Neighbors

In the same way that the Voronoi diagram can be used to find the nearest neighbor of a query point (Section 5.1 and 5.5.1), the k-th order Voronoi

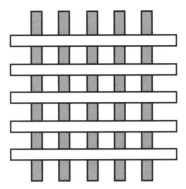

FIGURE 6.14 A grid of crossed rectangles establishes an $\Omega(n^2)$ lower bound on output complexity.

diagram can be used to find the k-nearest neighbors of a query point. This is used for what is called the "k-nearest neighbors decision rule": classify an unknown into the class most heavily represented among its k nearest neighbors.[8] The k-nearest neighbors are also useful for facility location, information retrieval, and surface interpolation. See Okabe et al. (1992) for further applications and references.

6.7.2. Hidden Surface Removal

Surely there is no geometric computation performed more frequently today than hidden surface removal, as it is the basis of all three-dimensional computer graphics, which is the basis of many television advertisements and movie special effects. The task is to take a set of flat, opaque, colored polygons in three-dimensional space and produce an image or "scene" of their appearance from a particular viewpoint. Often the polygons are linked into a surface, and the occluded portions of the surface are "hidden" and must be "removed" from the final scene.

Let n be the total number of vertices of the input polygons. One can see that the complexity of the output scene can be $\Omega(n^2)$: a grid of vertical rectangles obscuring horizontal rectangles leads to $> \frac{1}{16}n^2$ scene vertices as shown in Figure 6.14. If we demand a list of polygons as output, no algorithm can beat quadratic time in the worst case. Many algorithms achieved $O(n^2 \log n)$, only $O(\log n)$ time slower than optimal, by including an $O(n \log n)$ sorting at some juncture (Sutherland, Sproull, and Shumacker, 1974); but an optimal algorithm remained elusive for years. The theory of arrangements finally led to a worst-case optimal $O(n^2)$ algorithm (due to McKenna (1987)), which I will now sketch.

[8]See Devijver and Kittler (1982) and Mizoguchi and Kakusho (1978).

First, assume the polygons do not interpenetrate in space: their interiors are disjoint, although they may share boundary points. Second, assume the viewpoint is infinitely far from the polygons, so that all lines of sight are parallel, and we do not have to deal with the complications of perspective. Although not immediately obvious, any scene with a finite viewpoint can be transformed to one with the eye at infinity, so this is no loss of generality.[9] Let the eye be at $(0, 0, +\infty)$, so the "viewplane" is the xy-plane, $z = 0$. It is convenient to add one large "background" polygon below all the others so that all lines-of-sight hit some polygon.

The first step is to project every edge of the input polygons to the xy-plane (by discarding the z-coordinates of their endpoints). This is known as *orthographic* projection (in contrast to perspective projection). Next extend each edge to the line that contains it. The result is an arrangement $\mathscr{A}$ of n lines in the xy-plane, which can be constructed in $O(n^2)$ time by Theorem 6.3.1. Now the task is to decide, for each cell of $\mathscr{A}$, which polygon in space among those whose projection contains it, is highest, and therefore closest to the eye. Knowing this permits the cells to be "painted" appropriately according to the color of the polygon (and according to its orientation if shading is desired). Note that each cell has a unique foremost polygon.

A naive algorithm would require $O(n^3)$ time: for each of the $O(n^2)$ cells, compute the height for each of the $O(n)$ polygons. The challenge is to spend only constant time per cell.

McKenna's algorithm employs a topological sweep of the arrangement, a generalization of plane sweep (Section 2.2.1) introduced by Edelsbrunner and Guibas (1989). Rather than sweep a vertical line over the arrangement, we sweep a vertical "pseudoline" L, a curve that intersects each line of $\mathscr{A}$ exactly once, at which point it crosses it bottom to top. The advantage of making the sweep line "bendable" is that it is then unnecessary to spend $O(\log n)$ time in priority-queue lookup to determine which vertex is the next to be swept. Rather an unordered collection of "sweepable" vertices can be maintained: those incident to two edges adjacent among those crossed by L. In Figure 6.15, vertex v is sweepable because two edges of the cell C crossed by L are incident to it.

The data structures maintained by the algorithm, besides the fixed arrangement, include the list of *active* cells and edges crossed by L (such as the shaded cell in the figure), and for each active cell C, a list of all the polygons whose projection contain C in the xy-plane, sorted by z-depth. Note these lists are only maintained for active cells, of which there are always precisely $n + 1$ (since L crosses all n lines). Clearly these lists provide enough information to determine the foremost polygon for every cell of $\mathscr{A}$. I will not provide a detailed accounting of the algorithm actions as L sweeps over a vertex, but rather just mention one feature of the algorithm. As a vertex is swept, old cells "die" and new cells become active, but their lists of containing polygons are either the same or nearly the same. This "coherence" can be exploited to inherit enough information across a swept vertex to keep the updating cost to constant time per

---

[9]See, for example, Foley, van Dam, Feiner, and Hughes (1990, pp. 268–271).

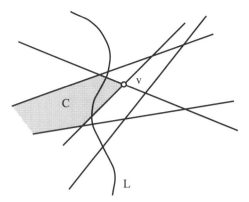

FIGURE 6.15 Vertex v is sweepable.

cell, amortized over all cells of $\mathscr{A}$. The result is a hidden surface algorithm that is $O(n^2)$ in the worst case.

This is not, however, the "best" hidden surface algorithm in practice because it *always* takes $\Omega(n^2)$ time and space, whereas most realistic scenes have much smaller complexity. Since it is not uncommon for n to be as large as 10^6 for high-quality graphics, it is important to avoid quadratic time when possible. Algorithms whose performance is sensitive to the output scene complexity are called *output-size sensitive* hidden surface algorithms, and are a topic of considerable current research (Dorward 1991).

6.7.3. Aspect Graphs

In the late 1970's, researchers in computer vision introduced the notion of an "aspect graph" to aid image recognition (Koenderink and van Doorn, 1976, 1979). The idea is to store all the "characteristic views" an object can present to a viewer, and compare these against what is actually seen. For a polyhedral object, a characteristic view is determined by combinatorial equivalence: two viewpoints see the same *aspect* of the polyhedron if the image has the same combinatorial structure, that is, the (labeled) plane graph induced by the projection of the visible faces of the polyhedron on the viewplane is the same. The *visual space partition* (VSP) is a partition of all space exterior to an object into connected regions or cells of constant aspect. Finally, the *aspect graph* is the dual of the VSP (dual in the sense used in Sections 1.2.3 and 4.4.2), with a node for every region and an arc connecting regions that share a face.

Arrangements provide a clean framework for understanding VSP's (and therefore aspect graphs) for convex polyhedra, an important special case. For a polytope P, the VSP is precisely the arrangement formed by planes containing the faces of P (Plantinga and Dyer, 1990). For example, consider this arrangement for a cube. It partitions space into 26 unbounded regions, as shown in Figure 6.16: six rectangular cylinders based on the cube faces, eight octants, one

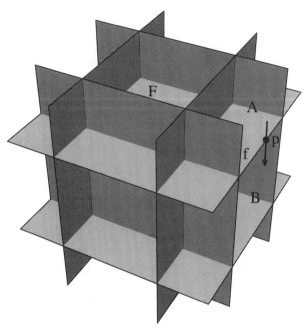

FIGURE 6.16   The arrangement of planes containing the faces of a cube. p can see F from cell A but not from cell B.

incident to each vertex, and twelve "wedges," one incident to each edge of the cube. Consider the view of the cube from a point p that moves from one cell A, across a face f of the arrangement, to an adjacent cell B, as illustrated in the figure. Suppose from cell A the cube face F in whose plane the arrangement face f lies is visible. Then, when p is on f, it views F edge-on, and when p is in cell B, F is no longer visible. So f indeed represents a transition in the aspect.

From Theorem 6.4.1 we obtain immediately that the VSP of a convex polytope of n vertices has size $O(n^3)$ and can be constructed in $O(n^3)$ time. The aspect graph is then available by traversing the representation of the VSP.

6.7.4. Smallest Polytope Shadow

Consider the problem of finding the smallest area shadow a given polytope P can cast orthogonally on a plane from a light source at infinity. This problem was first investigated by McKenna and Seidel (1985) (McKenna, 1989), who gave a solution based on arrangements. I will sketch their employment of arrangements, without explaining their solution in full.

The primary insight is the same as the basis of aspect graphs: the combinatorial structure of the shadow projection changes when the lightsource crosses a plane containing a face of P. What makes this problem different from the VSP construction is that the viewpoint/lightsource is at infinity, so the projection is

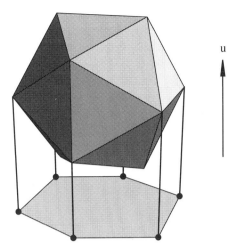

FIGURE 6.17 The shadow of a polytope from light at infinity is a convex polygon.

orthographic rather than perspective. From a viewpoint infinitely far away, P in effect shrinks to a point, and all the face planes include that point. This intuition suggests the following approach.

Let π_f be the plane parallel to face f of P that passes through the origin. Let $\mathscr{A}$ be the arrangement of planes formed by π_f for all f of P. $\mathscr{A}$ cuts up space into unbounded cones apexed at the origin. Any vector u representing the direction of lightrays falls inside some cone. The cone determines the combinatorial equivalence class of the view from infinity in the direction u, and therefore the combinatorial structure of the shadow on a plane orthogonal to u. See Figure 6.17.

Although the combinatorial structure of the shadow is constant for any direction vector within one cone, the area of the shadow is not constant. McKenna and Seidel proved, however, that the minimum area is achieved along some edge of $\mathscr{A}$, that is, along a direction determined by the intersection of two face planes. Although $\mathscr{A}$ is an arrangement of planes, and therefore has size $O(n^3)$ by Theorem 6.4.1, it is highly degenerate since all planes include the origin. In fact, it only has size $O(n^2)$, as the following argument shows.

Intersect $\mathscr{A}$ with a plane π parallel to the xy-plane, say $\pi : z = 1$. It should be clear that $\mathscr{A} \cap \pi = \mathscr{A}'$ is itself an arrangement of lines. Any direction vector u maps to the point on π that is the intersection of π with the line containing u. Thus, all the viewpoints at infinity are in one-to-one correspondence with points in the two-dimensional arrangement $\mathscr{A}'$, which has complexity $O(n^2)$. Finally, a viewpoint that achieves minimum area corresponds to a vertex of $\mathscr{A}'$, a claim proved in McKenna and Seidel (1985).

We now have an algorithm. Construct $\mathscr{A}'$ in $O(n^2)$ time (there is no need to construct $\mathscr{A}$). For each of its $O(n^2)$ vertices, compute the area of the shadow on the plane orthogonal to the direction determined by the vertex. Return the smallest area.

What remains is computing the shadow area from each vertex of $\mathscr{A}'$, and this is the part I will not explain. There is a clever method of avoiding recomputing the area at each vertex, which achieves constant time per vertex, thereby yielding $O(n^2)$ time overall (Exercise 6.7.5[1]).

6.7.5. Exercises

1. *Area calculation*.

   a. Let N be an *area normal*, a vector normal to a face F, whose length is the area of F. Let u be the viewing direction. Show that the area of the projection of F onto a plane orthogonal to u is $N \cdot u$.

   b. Let N_i be area normals for faces F_i. Show that the area of the projection of all the F_i is $(\Sigma N_i) \cdot u$.

   c. Use (b) to show how to compute the area of the polytope shadow from the direction determined by each vertex of $\mathscr{A}'$.

2. *Maximum area shadow*. Find the maximum area shadow for a unit cube, projected onto a plane orthogonal to the lightrays.

6.7.6. Ham Sandwich Cuts

We will now explore the beautiful manner in which arrangements can be used to find ham sandwich cuts for separated sets of points, as mentioned in Section 6.1. Define a *bisector* of a set of points to be a line that has at most half the points strictly to each side. We will restrict our attention for simplicity to points in general position (no three on a line). In addition, we will assume our sets each have an odd number of points; so a bisector of a set passes through (at least) one point (Exercise 6.7.7[1]) asks for a removal of this restriction).

Consider first bisectors of a single set A of n points. Under our assumptions above, a set will never have only vertical bisectors, so we can safely ignore them. Dualize the points of A by the mapping $\mathbb{D}$ discussed in Section 6.5, producing an arrangement $\mathscr{A}$ of n lines. We now argue that all the bisectors of A dualize precisely to the *median level* $M_{\mathscr{A}}$ of $\mathscr{A}$. The median level is the collection of edges of $\mathscr{A}$ (and their connecting vertices) whose points have exactly $(n-1)/2$ lines strictly above them vertically (and the same number below). For by Lemma 6.5.5, a point $p \in M_{\mathscr{A}}$ dualizes to a line $\mathbb{D}(p)$ that has the same number of points below it as p has lines above it. Since p has $(n-1)/2$ lines above it by definition of the median level, $\mathbb{D}(p)$ has $(n-1)/2$ points of A below it: i.e., $\mathbb{D}(p)$ bisects A. Thus, $\mathbb{D}(p)$ is a bisector iff $p \in M_{\mathscr{A}}$.

Lemma 6.7.1. *The bisectors of a set of points dualize to the median level of the dual arrangement of lines.*

By this lemma, a line that is a ham sandwich cut for A and B must dualize to a point that lies on both $M_{\mathscr{A}}$, and $M_{\mathscr{B}}$ (where $\mathscr{B}$ is the arrangement dual to B). Thus all ham sandwich cuts can be found by intersecting the median levels of the two sets.

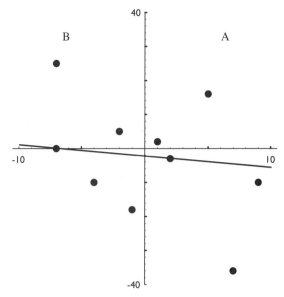

FIGURE 6.18 Two sets of five points each (from Figure 6.9): *A* right of the *y*-axis, and *B* left. The line shown is a ham sandwich cut: it bisects both *A* and *B*.

These two levels can intersect in a complicated way, but the situation is simpler if the two sets are separable by a line (as they often are in applications). Let A' and B' be two sets separable by a line. Then by a suitable translation and rotation, they can be transformed to sets A and B separated by the y-axis (A right and B left). See Figure 6.18 for an example. Now apply the dual mapping $\mathbb{D}$ to both. The lines in arrangement $\mathscr{A}$ all have positive slope, as shown in Figure 6.19, whereas the lines in B all have negative slope, as shown in Figure 6.20.

Because $M_{\mathscr{A}}$ is composed of subsegments of positively sloped lines, it is strictly monotonically increasing; similarly, $M_{\mathscr{B}}$ is strictly monotonically decreasing. (Both are drawn shaded in Figures 6.19 and 6.20.) Therefore they intersect in a single point: the ham sandwich cut is unique. Figure 6.21 shows they intersect at $\left(-\frac{1}{6}, 2\frac{1}{3}\right)$, and indeed the line $y = 2(-\frac{1}{6})x - \frac{7}{3}$ is the ham sandwich cut for those two point sets shown in Figure 6.18.

It turns out that this intersection point can be found without constructing the entirety of either arrangement, in only $O(n+m)$ time for sets of n and m points! The algorithm is rather intricate, and I will not explain it here. See Edelsbrunner (1987, pp. 336–345).

6.7.7. Exercises

1. *Even number of points* [easy]. Using the definition of a bisector, argue that the cases where *A* and/or *B* have an even number of points, can be reduced to sets with an odd number of points.

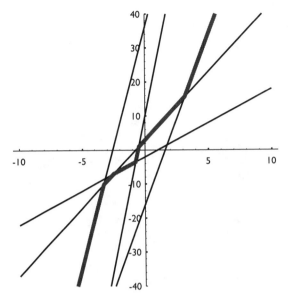

FIGURE 6.19   The duals of the points with $x > 0$ (set A in Figure 6.18) all have positive slope.

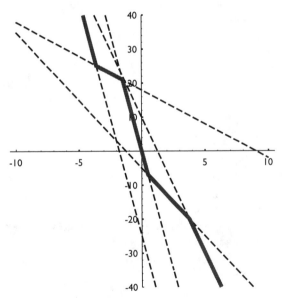

FIGURE 6.20   The duals of the points with $x < 0$ (set B in Figure 6.18) all have negative slope.

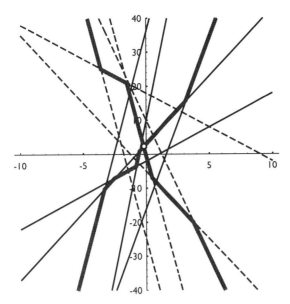

FIGURE 6.21 $\mathscr{A}$ and $\mathscr{B}$ together. The intersection of their median levels is at $(-\frac{1}{6}, 2\frac{1}{3})$.

2. *Size of median level.* Let A be the following set of points. Draw three rays from the origin separated by $2\pi/3 = 120°$. Place $n/3$ points equally-spaced along each ray. Compute the number of edges in the median level of the arrangement formed by the duals of the points of A.

3. *Bisection program* [programming]. Write a program to find one bisector of a given set of points in the plane. Make no assumptions about the points aside from distinctness.

6.8. ADDITIONAL EXERCISES

1. *Centerpoints.* A point x is called a "centerpoint" of a set of n points P if every halfplane that includes x also includes a large proportion of the points of P (in a sense to be made precise momentarily). The point x is not necessarily in P. A centerpoint is "central" to P in the sense that capturing it with a halfplane necessarily captures a large portion of P. The technical definition is that x is a *centerpoint* if no open halfplane that avoids x includes more than $2/3n$ points of P (Edelsbrunner, 1987, p. 64).

   a. Verify that every set of $n = 4$ points has a centerpoint by exploring "all" configurations of four points.

   b. Interpret the claim that every finite set of points has a centerpoint in terms of levels in arrangements.

   c. Suggest an algorithm for finding a centerpoint based on (b).

2. *Minimum area triangle.* Design an algorithm for finding a minimum area triangle whose vertices are selected from a set of n points P in the plane. Try to beat the brute-force $O(n^3)$ algorithm.

3. *Voracious circle points.* Given a set of n points $P = \{p_1, \dots, p_n\}$, define $\mu(p_i, p_j)$ as the fewest points of P contained in any closed disk that contains both p_i and p_j. Call a pair of points *voracious circle points* (Diaz, 1990) if they maximize μ over all pairs of points in P. Call this maximum $M(P) = \max_{p_i, p_j \in P} \mu(p_i, p_j)$.

   (a) Determine $M(P)$ for all sets P of $n = 3$ points.

   (b) Determine $M(P)$ for all sets P of $n = 4$ points.

   (c) Prove that, if there is a disk D that includes p_i and p_j and k other points of P, there is a disk $D' \subseteq D$ whose boundary includes p_i and p_j, and which encloses $\leq k$ points of P.

   (d) Use (c) to design an algorithm to compute $\mu(p_i, p_j)$ for a fixed p_i and p_j.

   (e) Use (d) to design an algorithm to find a pair of voracious circle points.

4. *Four-section.* A *four-section* of a point set P is a pair of lines such that the number of points in each of the open wedges formed by these lines is no more than $\lceil n/4 \rceil$.

   (a) Argue that every finite point set has a four-section.

   (b) Design an algorithm to find a four-section.

5. *Orthogonal four-section.* Design an algorithm to find a four-section of a point set such that the two sectioning lines are orthogonal (Diaz, 1990).

7

Search and Intersection

7.1. INTRODUCTION

In this chapter, we examine several problems that can be loosely classified as involving search or intersection (or both). This is a vast, well-developed topic, and I make no attempt at systematic coverage. We first consider two relatively easy problems on convex polygons: determining whether a point is in a polygon (Section 7.2) and finding an extreme point of a convex polygon (Section 7.3); implementations of both are presented. Then, we explore the problem of computing the intersection between two convex polygons. This is still not too difficult, but the provided implementation is delicate (Section 7.4). All of these problems are elementary, especially in comparison to the material in the previous chapter.

The jewel in this chapter is an algorithm to find extreme points of a polytope in any given query direction (Section 7.5). This leads naturally to planar point location (Section 7.6), an important topic on which we only touch.

7.2. POINT IN POLYGON

Every time a mouse is clicked inside a shape on a workstation screen, an instance of the point-in-polygon problem is solved: Given a fixed polygon P and a query point q, is $q \in P$? Although the hardware of a particular machine may permit solutions that avoid geometry, we consider the problem here from the computational geometry viewpoint.

If P is convex, the obvious method is to perform a LeftOn test (Code 1.5) for each edge of the polygon. We used this technique in the two-dimensional incremental hull algorithm in Chapter 3 (Section 3.7). This can be improved to $O(\log n)$, but we leave this to Exercise 7.2.3[1].

The more interesting case is when P is nonconvex. Two rather different methods for solving this problem have become popular: counting ray crossings, and computing "winding" numbers. These are the topics of the next two subsections.

7.2.1. Ray crossings

Draw a ray r from q in an arbitrary direction (say, in the $+x$ direction) and count the number of intersections of r with ∂P. The point q is in or out of P if the number of crossings is odd or even, respectively. For example, suppose there

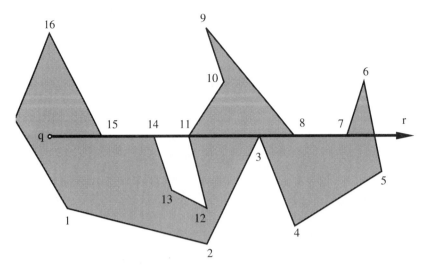

FIGURE 7.1   Degenerate intersections of ray with the boundary of *P*.

are three crossings, and you imagine traveling backward along *r* from infinity to *q*. The first crossing penetrates to the interior of *P*, the second moves to the exterior, and the third and last returns to the interior. Therefore, $q \in P$.

In spite of the simplicity of this idea, implementation is fragile due to the necessity of handling special-case intersections of *r* with ∂P, as shown in Figure 7.1: the ray may hit a vertex, or be collinear with an edge. There is also the possibility that *q* lies directly on ∂P, in which case we would like to conclude that $q \in P$ (because *P* is closed). Note that even the traditional assumption that no three polygon vertices are collinear will not exclude all these "degenerate" cases.

Fix *r* to be horizontal to the right. One method of eliminating most of the difficulties is to require that for an edge *e* to count as a *crossing* of *r*, one of *e*'s endpoints must be strictly above *r*, and the other endpoint on or below. This convention implies that edge $(10, 11)$ in Figure 7.1 crosses *r*, but edge $(11, 12)$ does not. Thus the path $(10, 11, 12)$ contributes just one crossing, as is appropriate. Vertex 3 does not increment the crossing counter, because both $(2, 3)$ and $(3, 4)$ do not cross *r*. Edges collinear with *r*, such as $(14, 15)$ and $(7, 8)$, do not count as crossing. Before revealing what this convention leaves unresolved, we turn to simple code (Code 7.1) implementing the idea.

The code first translates the entire polygon so that *q* becomes the origin and *r* coincides with the positive *x*-axis. This step is unnecessary but makes the code more transparent.[1] In a loop over all edges $e = (i - 1, i)$, it checks whether *e* "straddles" the *x*-axis according to the definition above. If *e* straddles, then the *x*-coordinate of the intersection of *e* with $y = 0$ is computed via a straightfor-

---

[1]Note that as written the code will overwrite the polygon coordinates with the shifted coordinates, a side effect rarely desired.

```
#define DIM     2
#define X       0
#define Y       1
bool    InPoly( tPointi q, tPolygoni P, int n )
{
        int     i, i1;              /* point index; i1 = i-1 mod n */
        int     d;                  /* dimension index */
        double  x;                  /* x intersection of e with ray */
        int     crossings = 0;      /* number of edge / ray crossings */

        /* Shift so that q is the origin. */
        for( i = 0; i < n; i++ ) {
                for( d = 0; d < DIM; d++ )
                        P[i][d] = P[i][d] - q[d];
        }
        /* For each edge e = (i-1,i), see if crosses ray. */
        for( i = 0; i < n; i++ ) {
                i1 = ( i + n - 1 )
                /* if e straddles the x-axis... */
                if( ( ( P[i] [Y] > 0 ) && ( P[i1][Y] <= 0 ) ) ||
                    ( ( P[i1][Y] > 0 ) && ( P[i] [Y] <= 0 ) ) ) {
                        /* e straddles ray, so compute intersection with ray. */
                        x = (P[i][X] *  P[i1][Y] - P[i1][X] *  P[i][Y])
                                / (double)(P[i1][Y] - P[i][Y]);
                        /* crosses ray if strictly positive intersection. */
                        if (x > 0) crossings++;
                }
        }
        /* q inside if an odd number of crossings. */
        if( (crossings % 2) == 1 )
                return TRUE;
        else    return FALSE;
}
```

Code 7.1 `InPoly`. Typedefs in Code 1.1 and 1.2.

ward formula obtained by solving for x in the equation

$$y - y_{i-1} = (x - x_{i-1})(y_i - y_{i-1})/(x_i - x_{i-1}) \qquad (7.1)$$

and setting $y = 0$; here (x_{i-1}, y_{i-1}) and (x_i, y_i) are the endpoints of e. Note that x is `double` in the code; this dependence on a floating-point calculation can be eliminated (Exercise 7.2.3[2]), but we will leave it to keep attention focused on the algorithm. A crossing is counted whenever the intersection is strictly to the right of the origin. When run on the example in Figure 7.1, `InPoly` finds five crossings with edges $(5,6)$, $(6,7)$, $(8,9)$, $(10,11)$, and $(15,16)$, correctly concluding that $q \in P$.

FIGURE 7.2   Points on L and B are considered inside; those on R and T are not.

There is a flaw to this code (aside from the floating-point calculation): although it returns the correct answer for any point strictly interior to P, it does not handle the points on ∂P consistently. If q is moved horizontally to the $(0, 1)$ edge in Figure 7.1, InPoly returns TRUE, but if q is placed at vertex 15, it returns FALSE. The behavior of this code is perhaps clearer if the polygon is a square S aligned with the coordinate axes; call its edges L, R, B, and T, as in Figure 7.2. For $q \in L$, only R counts as a crossing (the $L \cap r$ intersection is at $x = 0$), and $q \in S$. However, for $q \in R$, there are no crossings, so $q \notin S$. For $q \in B$, again R counts as a crossing; except for $q \in T$, there are again no crossings. So points on L and B are considered inside S by InPoly, but points on R and T are not. Although this inconsistent treatment of points on the polygon boundary is dissatisfying from a purist's point of view, workers in graphics often prefer this behavior, because in a partition of a region into many polygons, every point will be "in" exactly one polygon.[2] The code could be modified to return TRUE for every point in the closed polygon by addition of a supplementary $q \in \partial P$ test that uses the techniques employed in Between (Code 1.8).

7.2.2. Winding number

A completely different method of determining whether or not a point is in a polygon is based on the "winding number." Imagine you are standing at point q. While watching a point p completely traverse ∂P counterclockwise, pivot so that you always face toward p. If $q \in P$, you would turn a full circle, 2π radians, whereas if $q \notin P$, your total angular turn would be exactly zero (with the usual convention: counterclockwise turns are positive, clockwise turns negative). This is easy to see if P is convex, and I hope at least intuitively believable when P is arbitrary: after all, you return to your starting orientation, so the total turn must be a whole number of revolutions. See Figure 7.3. We will not pause to prove this claim. The *winding number*[3] of q with respect to P is the number of

---

[2] Haines (1992).

[3] See (Chinn and Steenrod, 1966, pp. 84–86); also used in (Foley et al., 1990, p. 965).

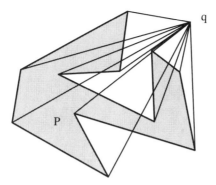

FIGURE 7.3   Exterior points have winding number 0: a total angular turn of 0.

revolutions ∂P makes about q: the total signed angular turn (call it ω) divided by 2π.

We now discuss some details of the computation, stopping short of providing explicit code (Exercise 7.2.3[4]). The basic routine required is the angle subtended by a polygon edge from the point q. Let $v_i = P[i] - q$, as shown in Figure 7.4. We can find the angle θ_i either from the dot or the cross product: $v_i \cdot v_{i+1} = |v_i||v_{i+1}|\cos\theta_i$, and $v_i \times v_{i+1} = |v_i||v_{i+1}|\sin\theta_i$. We already have code for the cross product: `Area2( q, P[i], P[i+1] )` from Chapter 1 (Code 1.3) is precisely the desired cross product. One must then divide out the lengths of the vectors, compute the arcsine, and sum the angles over all i (Exercise 7.2.3[3]).

One of the attractive features of this method is that, with little extra effort, the case when q lies on ∂P also could be distinguished. If q lies on the interior of an edge, the angle sum is $\omega = \pi$, and if q is coincident with a vertex, ω is the internal angle at that vertex. Mitigating this attractiveness, however, is the reality of floating-point calculations: ω will often not be exactly 0 or 2π, because of round-off error. To avoid confusing the case when $\omega = 0$ with the case where q is at a very sharp vertex, it makes sense to check for q equal to a

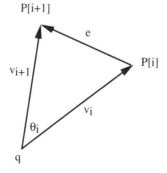

FIGURE 7.4 θ_i is the angle subtended by e from q.

vertex in a separate loop, which can be done with exact integer comparisons for integer coordinates.

Although the winding-number algorithm is appealing, its dependence on floating-point computations, and trigonometric computations in particular, makes it significantly slower (on standard hardware) than the ray-crossing algorithm, in spite of the fact that both are $O(n)$: an implementation comparison showed it to be more than 20 times slower (Haines, 1992)! This incidentally demonstrates the danger of thoughtlessly absorbing constants in the big-Oh notation.

Finally, we mention that the same basic idea works for determining if a point q is in a (perhaps nonconvex) polyhedron P. A notion of signed "solid angle" can be defined for the apex q of the tetrahedron formed by q and a triangle face of P. Summing these angles over all faces of P yields 4π if $q \in P$, and zero if $q \notin P$.

7.2.3. Exercises

1. *Point in convex polygon.* Design an algorithm to determine in $O(\log n)$ time if a point is inside a convex polygon.

2. *Integer ray crossing* [programming]. Modify `InPoly` (Code 7.1) to avoid the sole floating-point calculation.

3. *Angle sum* [programming].
   a. Develop code for computing the angle sum. Pay particular attention to the range of angles returned by the `asin` library function, remembering that all counterclockwise turns must be positive angles, and clockwise turns negative angles. Decide what should be done when $|v_i| = 0$ or $|v_{i+1}| = 0$.
   b. Compare the method in (a) with computing the difference of two `atan2`'s, and decide which is "better."

4. *Implementation of angle code* [programming]. Implement the winding number algorithm, and test on as many degenerate cases as you can think of. Compare its performance to the ray-crossing code (Code 7.1).

5. *Point in cube.* Define an appropriate notion of solid angle, and verify that the sum of these angles from the centroid of a cube is 4π.

7.3. EXTREME POINT OF CONVEX POLYGON

It is frequently necessary to find a boundary point of a convex polygon extreme in a certain direction. For example, the smallest box enclosing a polygon, where the box sides are aligned with the coordinate axes, can be constructed from extreme points in the four compass directions. Although often this computation is performed by a simple $O(n)$ scan of all vertices, it is not surprising that a minor variant of binary search will accomplish the same goal in $O(\log n)$ time. In this section we will first sketch such a search algorithm to find a highest

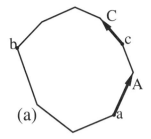
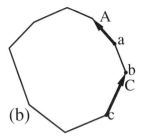

FIGURE 7.5   (*a*) [*a*, *b*] is replaced by [*c*, *b*]; (*b*) [*a*, *b*] is replaced by [*a*, *c*].

point, and then discuss a slightly more general implementation. Even though the implementation is easy, it is not without subtleties.

Let the *n* polygon vertices be P[0],...,P[n-1]. Suppose at some point of the search we know a highest vertex is counterclockwise between indices *a* and *b*. So if *a* < *b*, one of P[a],P[a+1],...,P[b-1],P[b] is a highest vertex. For this rough sketch, we will not worry over wraparound through index 0, nor will we be concerned with the possibility that two vertices are equally highest.

The main idea is to use the directed edges of the polygon to decide how to halve the search interval. Let *c* be an index strictly between *a* and *b*. Assume that the edge *A* after P[a] points upward. Then if the edge *C* after P[c] also points upward, the situation is as illustrated in Fig. 7.5: the interval [*a*, *b*] is shortened to either [*c*, *b*] or [*a*, *c*] depending on whether P[c] is higher or lower than P[a]. A similar shortening occurs if *A* points downward. This halving process is repeated until the edge after *c* points down and the edge before it points up. The pseudocode in Algorithm 7.1 shows the basic structure. Two points are worthy of note. First, the tests are not completely detailed in this pseudocode; in particular, the situation in Fig. 7.5 is relegated to "other combinations." Second, we have not detailed the loop termination conditions.

Algorithm: HIGHEST POINT OF CONVEX POLYGON
Initialize *a* and *b*.
repeat forever
      c ← index midway from *a* to *b*.
      if P[c] is locally highest then return *c*
      if *A* points up and *C* points down
            then *b* ← *c*
      else if *A* points down and *C* points up
            then *a* ← *c*
      else Handle other *A*/*C* combinations.

Algorithm 7.1   Highest point of convex polygon.

```
int     Midway( int a, int b, int n )
{
        if (a < b) return ( a + b ) / 2;
        else        return ( ( a + b + n ) / 2 ) % n;
}
```

Code 7.2 MidWay.

7.3.1. Implementation

We generalize the preceding algorithm slightly to find the extreme in an arbitrary direction, specified by a vector u. This does not complicate the code much; what complexity there is lies in a precise handling of the indices.

Let us tackle the first problem: how to find an index midway between a and b. We assume the points are ordered in a counterclockwise traversal of the polygon's boundary, and we require at all times that an extreme vertex be counterclockwise between a and b, an index interval we indicate by $[a, b]$. We interpret $[a, a]$ as representing the entire boundary of P, as this will ease initializing the algorithm.

If $a < b$, then $(a + b)/2$ is midway. Note that if $b = a + 1$, then $(a + b)/2 = a$, due to truncation. If $a \geq b$, the interval $[a, b]$ includes 0, and the formula $(a + b)/2$ no longer works. For example, let $n = 10$, $a = 7$, and $b = 3$. Here $[7, 3] = (7, 8, 9, 0, 1, 2, 3)$, and the midpoint is 0. This can be computed by shifting b by n so that it is again larger than a, and taking the result mod n: $((a + b + n)/2) \mod n$. In our example, $((7 + 3 + 10)/2) \mod 10 = 0$. Note that if $a \geq b$ and $b = (a + 1) \mod n$, then again the computation yields a, which is the same behavior as when $a < b$: when a and b are adjacent, the midpoint is a.

This gives us the midway function in Code 7.2.

Note what this function yields for the midpoint of $[a, a]$: $(a + n/2) \mod n$, halfway around from a, which is consistent with interpreting $[a, a]$ as all of ∂P.

We are now prepared to present the search code in Code 7.3. We first discuss the interval-halving code. Assume A points up, i.e., $\text{Dot}(u, A) > 0$. Then if C points down, the extreme is in the interval $[a, c]$. If C points up, the situation is as in Fig. 7.5, and the new interval is $[a, c]$ or $[b, c]$ if $P[a]$ is higher or lower than $P[c]$ respectively. This relationship is encoded in the variable y, which again uses dot-products with u to generalize the notion of "height." The logic for A pointing down is analogous. There are two remaining subtleties: how to handle zero dot products, and the stopping conditions.

Loop Termination Conditions

If during the search, c indexes the unique extreme vertex, then $u \cdot C < 0$ and $u \cdot B > 0$, where B is the edge vector before c. This is the normal stopping condition. If the extreme in either $\pm u$ is achieved by one or more edges, then it may be that A and/or C may point neither up nor down. Because we assume the polygon is oriented counterclockwise, an edge pointing directly left of u must be a $+u$ extreme. These are detected in the code by dotting with u_r, the

```
int  Extreme( tPointi u, tPolygoni P, int n )
{
     int      a,a1, b;/* [a,b] includes extreme; a1=a+1. */
     int      c, c1;  /* index midway; c1 is c +- 1. */
     tPointi A, C, B;/* edge vectors after a, after c, before c. */
     int      Adot, Cdot, Bdot;    /* dots with u. */
     int      y;      /* height difference: P[a] - P[c] in dir. u */
     tPointi ur;      /* u rotated cw by pi/2 */

     ur[0] = u[1];    ur[1] = -u[0];  a = 0;  b = 0;
     do {   c = Midway( a, b, n );
            /* Compute basic vectors and dots. */
            a1 = ( a + 1 ) % n;         SubVec( P[a1], P[a], A );
            c1 = ( c + 1 ) % n;         SubVec( P[c1], P[c], C );
            c1 = ( c + ( n-1 ) ) % n;   SubVec( P[c], P[c1], B );
            Adot =Dot( u, A ); Cdot = Dot( u, C ); Bdot = Dot ( u, B );
            y = Dot( u, P[a] ) - Dot( u, P[c] );

            /* Termination conditions */
            if ( (Adot == 0) && (Dot( ur, A ) < 0) ) /* A points left */
                    return  a;
            if ( (Cdot == 0) && (Dot( ur, C ) < 0) ) /* C points left */
                    return c;
            if ( (Cdot < 0) && (Bdot > 0) ) /* normal case */
                    return  c;
            if (a == c) {    /* b = a+1 */
                    if (Adot > 0) return  b;
                    else               return  a;
            }
            /* Halving interval */
            if ( (Adot >= 0) && (Cdot <= 0) )
                    b = c;            /* new: (a,c) */
            else if ( (Adot <= 0) && (Cdot >= 0) )
                    a = c;            /* new: (c,b) */
            else if ( (Adot > 0) && (Cdot > 0) ) {
                    if ( y > 0 ) b = c;   /* new: (a,c) */
                    else            a = c;} /* new: (c,b) */
            else if ( (Adot < 0) && (Cdot < 0) ) {
                    if ( y < 0 ) b = c;   /* new: (a,c) */
                    else            a = c;} /* new: (c,b) */
     }
     while  ( TRUE );

}
```

Code 7.3 Extreme.

$90°$ degree clockwise rotation of u. Consider, for example, the polygon in Fig. 7.6 with $u = (0, 1)$ and $u_r = (1, 0)$. The $[a, b]$ intervals considered by the algorithm are: $[0, 0]$ and $[5, 0]$, at which point $c = 7$ is computed as the midpoint. Now $C = (-6, 0)$, $u \cdot C = 0$ and $u_r \cdot C = -6 < 0$, so c is returned. The $u \cdot A = 0$ case is handled similarly. Thenceforth it is known that a zero dot product with u indicates a $-u$ extreme.

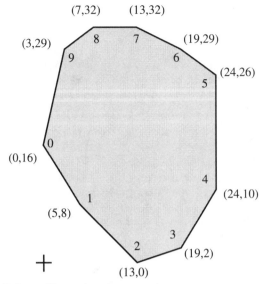

FIGURE 7.6   Polygon illustrating the operation of the extreme finding algorithm.

Unfortunately we cannot be guaranteed that c will ever hit an extreme vertex, due to the truncation in `Midway` when $b = a + 1$. This always truncates clockwise, which can block a last needed counterclockwise step. The presented code deals with this by capturing the $c = a$ case specially, and returning b when $u \cdot A > 0$. An example of this is again shown by the polygon in Fig. 7.6, except now with $u = (-1, 0)$. The sequence of index intervals $[a, b]$ is $[0, 0]$, $[5, 0]$, $[7, 0]$, $[8, 0]$, and $[9, 0]$, at which point $c = 9$ and $u \cdot A = (-1, 0) \cdot (-3, -13) = 3 > 0$, and $b = 0$ is returned.

7.3.2. Exercises

1. *Collinear points.* What does `Extreme` do when three or more consecutive vertices of the polygon are collinear? Will it work in all cases?

2. *Degenerate polygons.* Will `Extreme` work for a "polygon" that consists of just two vertices, that is, a segment?

3. *Stabbing a convex polygon.* Design an algorithm for finding the intersection of a convex polygon P of n vertices with a line L. This is often called a "stabbing" problem for obvious reasons. Achieve $O(\log n)$ time.

4. *Line-polygon distance.* Design an algorithm to determine the distance between an arbitrary polygon P of n vertices and a query line L. Define the distance to be

$$\min_{x, y} \{|x - y| : x \in P, y \in L\},$$

where x and y are points. Try to achieve $O(\log n)$ per query after preprocessing.

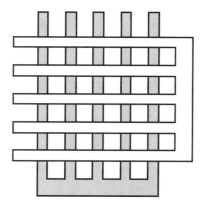

FIGURE 7.7   The intersection of two polygons can have quadratic complexity.

7.4. INTERSECTION OF CONVEX POLYGONS

The intersection of two arbitrary polygons of n and m vertices can have quadratic complexity, $\Omega(nm)$: the intersection of the polygons in Figure 7.7 is 25 squares. But the intersection of two convex polygons has only linear complexity, $O(n + m)$. Intersection of convex polygons is a key component of a number of algorithms, including determining whether two sets of points are separable by a line, and for solving two-variable linear programming problems (Shamos, 1978). The first linear algorithm was found by Shamos (1978), and since then a variety of different algorithms have been developed, all achieving $O(n + m)$ time complexity. This section describes one that I developed with three undergraduates, an amalgamation of their solutions to a homework assignment (O'Rourke, Chien, Olson, and Naddor, 1982). I feel it is the simplest algorithm available, but this is hardly an objective opinion.

The basic idea of the algorithm is straightforward, but the translation of the idea into code is delicate (as is often the case). Assume the boundaries of the two polygons P and Q are oriented counterclockwise as usual, and let A and B be directed edges on each. The algorithm has A and B "chasing" one another, adjusting their speeds so that they meet at every crossing of ∂P and ∂Q. The basic structure is as shown in Algorithm 7.2. A "movie" of the algorithm in action is shown in Figure 7.8.[4] The edges A and B are shown as vectors in the figure. The key is clearly the rules for advancing A and B, to which we now turn.

Let a be the index of the head of A, and b the head of B. If B "aims toward" the line containing A but does not cross it (as do all the solid vectors in Figure 7.9), we want to advance B to "close in" on a possible intersection with A. This is the essence of the advance rules. The situations in the figure can be captured as follows. Let $H(A)$ be the (closed) halfplane to the left of A. I will use the notation "$A \times B > 0$" to mean that the z-coordinate of the cross

---

[4]This figure was inspired by the animation of this algorithm provided in XYZ GeoBench.

Algorithm: INTERSECTION OF CONVEX POLYGONS
Choose A and B arbitrarily.
repeat
    if A intersects B then
        Check for termination.
        Update an *inside* flag.
    Advance either A or B,
        depending on geometric conditions.
until iterations $> 2(n + m)$
Handle $P \cap Q = \varnothing$ and $P \subseteq Q$ and $P \supseteq Q$ cases.

Algorithm 7.2   Intersection of convex polygons.

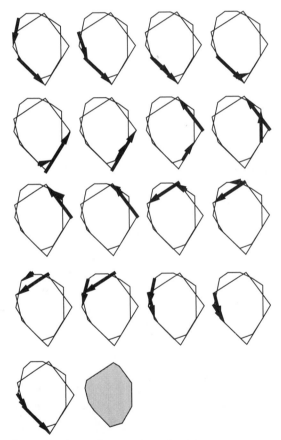

FIGURE 7.8 Snapshots of polygon intersection algorithm, sequenced left to right, top to bottom. This example is explored in more detail in Section 7.4.3.

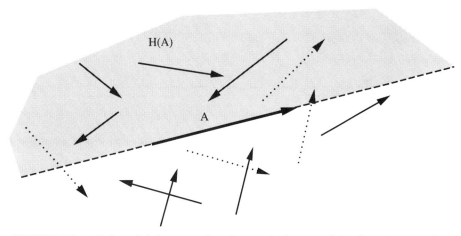

FIGURE 7.9   All the solid B vectors "aim" toward A; none of the dotted vectors do.

product is > 0 (recall this means that the shortest turn of A into B is counterclockwise).

$$\text{if } A \times B > 0 \text{ and } b \notin H(A), \text{ or}$$

$$\text{if } A \times B < 0 \text{ and } b \in H(A),$$

then advance B.

(Let us ignore for the moment collinearities of $P[a]$ with B or $P[b]$ with A.) A similar rule applies with the roles of A and B reversed (recall that $B \times A = -A \times B$):

$$\text{if } A \times B < 0 \text{ and } a \notin H(B), \text{ or}$$

$$\text{if } A \times B > 0 \text{ and } a \in H(B),$$

then advance A.

If both vectors aim toward each other, either may be advanced. When neither A nor B aim toward the other, we advance whichever is outside the halfplane of the other, or either if they are both outside. It takes some thought to realize that if both $a \in H(B)$ and $b \in H(A)$, then one must aim toward the other; so the above rules cover all cases. The cases may be organized in the following table.

$A \times B$	$a \in H(B)$	$b \in H(A)$	Advance rule
> 0	T	T	A
> 0	T	F	A or B
> 0	F	T	A
> 0	F	F	B
< 0	T	T	B
< 0	T	F	B
< 0	F	T	A or B
< 0	F	F	A

These rules are realized by the following condensation, which exploits the freedom in the entries that are arbitrary.

$A \times B$	Halfplane condition	Advance rule
> 0	$b \in H(A)$	A
> 0	$b \notin H(A)$	B
< 0	$a \in H(B)$	B
< 0	$a \notin H(B)$	A

These are the advance rules we use below.

7.4.1. Implementation

It only remains to settle the "degenerate" cases to get code. We will not argue these details here; they require some care. We choose $H(A)$ and $H(B)$ to be open, and capture collinearities in a separate section of code. Recognizing that $a \in H(B)$ is `Left ( Q[b1], Q[b], P[a] )`, with $b1 = (b - 1) \bmod n$, and $A \times B$ is `Area2( O, A, B )`, where O is the origin, we arrive at the code shown in Code 7.4 and Code 7.5. The main outlines of the pseudocode are followed, but with many added details. The main routine `ConvexIntersect` calls two utility routines `InOut` and `Advance`, plus a function to compute segment intersection, `Intersection`. This later function will be described in the section following.

There are an unfortunate number of local variables in `ConvexIntersect`, but most are straightforward. Two require some explanation. First, the variable `inflag` is an enumerated type that keeps track of which polygon is currently "inside." Before the first intersection, its value is `Unknown`.

```
typedef enum { Pin, Qin, Unknown }      tInFlag;
```

Second, the variables aa and ba count the number of advances on each polygon. These are used for terminating the do—while: the loop runs until both polygon boundaries have been completely traversed. Every intersection causes the

```
void      ConvexIntersect( tPolygoni P, tPolygoni Q, int n, int m )
                                /* P has n vertices, Q has m vertices. */
{
          int       a, b;           /* indices on P and Q (resp.) */
          int       a1, b1;         /* a-1, b-1 (resp.) */
          tPointi A, B;             /* directed edges on P and Q (resp.) */
          int       cross;          /* A x B */
          bool      bHA, aHB;       /* b in H(A); a in H(b). */
          tPointi Origin = {0,0};   /* (0,0) */
          tPointd p;                /* double point of intersection */
          tInFlag inflag;           /* {Pin, Qin, Unknown}:
                                       which polygon is known to be inside */
          int i;                    /* loop counter */
          int       aa, ba;         /* # advances on a & b indices
                                       (from first intersection) */

          /* Initialize variables. */
          a = 0; b = 0; aa = 0; ba = 0;
          i = 0;
          inflag = Unknown;
   /* ...continued... */
```

Code 7.4 `ConvexIntersect`, part a.

`inflag` to be toggled in `InOut` (Code 7.6) between `Pin` and `Qin`, which is then used to decide (via the boolean `inside`) whether to print out the vertex just passed in the `Advance` routine (Code 7.7). If `inflag` remains Unknown throughout a cycling of the counters, we know ∂P and ∂Q do not cross, and either they do not intersect, or one contains the other.

7.4.2. Intersection of Segments

In Chapter 1 (Section 1.5) we spent some time developing code that detects intersection between two segments (`Intersect`, Code 1.9) for use in triangulation, but we never bothered to *compute* the point of intersection. It was not needed in the triangulation algorithm, and it would have forced us to leave the comfortable world of integer coordinates. Fortunately, it is not difficult to compute the intersection point, and the necessary floating-point calculations are not as problematical here as they sometimes are.

Although the computation could be simplified a bit by employing the boolean `Intersect` from Chapter 1, we opt here for an independent calculation. Let the two segments have endpoints a and b and c and d, and let L_{ab} and L_{cd} be the lines containing the two segments. A common method of computing the point of intersection is to solve slope-intercept equations for L_{ab} and L_{cd} simultaneously:[5] two equations in two unknowns (the x and y coordinates of the point of intersection). Instead, we will use a parametric representation of the two segments, as the meaning of the variables seems more intuitive.

Let $A = b - a$, and $C = d - c$; these vectors point along the segments. Any point on the line L_{ab} can be represented as the vector sum $p(s) = a + sA$, which

```
/ * ...continued... * /
   do {
        / * Computations of key variables. * /
        a1 = (a + n - 1) % n;
        b1 = (b + m - 1) % m;
        SubVec( P[a], P[a1], A );
        SubVec( Q[b], Q[b1], B );
        cross = Area2( Origin, A, B );
        bHA = Left ( P[a1], P[a], Q[b] );
        aHB = Left ( Q[b1], Q[b], P[a] );
        / * If A & B intersect, update inflag. * /
        if ( Intersection( P[a1], P[a], Q[b1], Q[b], p ) ) {
            if ( inflag == Unknown )
                    aa = ba = 0;
            inflag = InOut( p, inflag, aHB, bHA );
        }
        / * Advance rules. * /
        if ( (cross == 0) && !bHA && !aHB ) {
            if ( inflag == Pin )
                b = Advance( b, &ba, m, inflag == Qin, Q[b] );
            else
                a = Advance( a, &aa, n, inflag == Pin, P[a] );
        }
        else if ( cross >= 0 )
            if ( bHA )
                a = Advance( a, &aa, n, inflag == Pin, P[a] );
            else {
                b = Advance( b, &ba, m, inflag == Qin, Q[b] );
            }
        else   / * if ( cross < 0 ) * /  {
            if ( aHB )
                b = Advance( b, &ba, m, inflag == Qin, Q[b] );
            else
                a = Advance( a, &aa, n, inflag == Pin, P[a] );
        }
   / * Quit when both adv. indices have cycled, or one has cycled twice. * /
   } while ( ((aa < n) || (ba < m)) && (aa < 2*n) && (ba < 2*m) );
   / * Deal with special cases: not implemented here. * /
   if ( inflag == Unknown )
        printf("The boundaries of P and Q do not cross:\n");
}
```

Code 7.5 `ConvexIntersect`, part b.

```
/*
    Prints out the double point of intersection, and toggles in / out flag.
*/
tInFlag InOut( tPointd p, tInFlag inflag, bool aHB, bool bHA )
  {
          PrintPointd( p ); putchar( '\n ');

          /* Update inflag. */
          if ( aHB )
                  return Pin;
          else if ( bHA )
                  return Qin;
          else    return inflag;

  }
```

Code 7.6   InOut.

```
/*
                Advances and prints out an inside vertex if appropriate.
*/
int     Advance( int a, int *aa, int n, bool inside,
                  tPointi v )
  {
          if ( inside ) {
                  PrintPoint( v ); putchar( '\n ');
          }
          (*aa)++;
          return (a+1) % n;
  }
```

Code 7.7   Advance.

takes us to a point a on L_{ab}, and then moves some distance along the line by scaling A by s. See Figure 7.10. The variable s is called the *parameter* of this equation. Consider the values obtained for $s = 0$, $s = 1$, and $s = 1/2$: $p(0) = a$, $p(1) = a + A = a + b - a = b$, and $p(1/2) = (a + b)/2$. These examples demonstrate that $p(s)$ for $s \in [0, 1]$ represents all the points on the segment ab, with the value of s representing the fraction of the distance between the endpoints; in particular, the extremes of s yield the endpoints.

We can similarly represent the points on the second segment by $q(t) = c + tC$, $t \in [0, 1]$. A point of intersection between the segments is then specified by values of s and t that make $p(s)$ equal to $q(t)$: $a + sA = c + tC$. This vector equation is also two equations in two unknowns: the x and y equations, both

---

[5]See Berger (1986, pp. 332–335) for example.

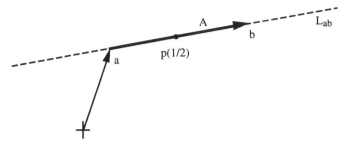

FIGURE 7.10 $p(s) = a + sA$; $p(1/2) = a + (1/2)A$ is shown.

with s and t as unknowns. With our usual convention of subscripts 0 and 1 indicating x and y coordinates, its solution is

$$s = [a_0(d_1 - c_1) + c_0(a_1 - d_1) + d_0(c_1 - a_1)]/D \qquad (7.2)$$

$$t = -[a_0(c_1 - b_1) + b_0(a_1 - c_1) + c_0(b_1 - a_1)]/D \qquad (7.3)$$

$$D = a_0(d_1 - c_1) + b_0(c_1 - d_1) + d_0(b_1 - a_1) + c_0(a_1 - b_1). \qquad (7.4)$$

Division by zero is a possibility in these equations. The denominator D happens to be zero iff the two lines are parallel, a claim left to Exercise 7.4.4[1]. Some parallel segments involve intersection, and some do not, as we detailed in Chapter 1 (Section 1.5.4). For our immediate purposes, we can consider any pair of parallel segments not to intersect, since the code (Code 7.8) is mainly concerned with detecting switches in which polygon boundary is inside and which outside. Note that the point p returned is of type `double tPointd`.

7.4.3. Example

In this section, we show the output of the code on the example shown in Figure 7.11. The code produces the following output for these polygons.

```
( 5.00, 8.00)
(13.00, 0.00)
(19,2)
(24,10)
(24.00,21.33)
(17.80,29.60)
(14.67,31.17)
( 1.62,23.01)
( 0.72,19.12)
( 2.50,12.00)
```

Figure 7.8 shows the progression of A and B for this example.

```
bool Intersection( tPointi a, tPointi b, tPointi c, tPointi d,
tPointd p )
{
    double s, t;   /* The two parameters of the parametric eqns. */
    double denom;  /* Denominator of solutions. */
    denom =
            a[0] * ( d[1] - c[1] ) +
            b[0] * ( c[1] - d[1] ) +
            d[0] * ( b[1] - a[1] ) +
            c[0] * ( a[1] - b[1] );

    /* If denom is zero, then the line segments are parallel. */
    /* In this case, return false even though the segments might overlap. */
    if (denom == 0.0)
            return FALSE;
    s = (
            a[0] * ( d[1] - c[1] ) +
            c[0] * ( a[1] - d[1] ) +
            d[0] * ( c[1] - a[1] )
        ) / denom;
    t = -(
            a[0] * ( c[1] - b[1] ) +
            b[0] * ( a[1] - c[1] ) +
            c[0] * ( b[1] - a[1] )
        ) / denom;
    p[0] = a[0] + s * ( b[0] - a[0] );
    p[1] = a[1] + s * ( b[1] - a[1] );

    if (    (0.0 <= s) && (s <= 1.0) &&
            (0.0 <= t) && (t <= 1.0)
        )
            return TRUE;
    else    return FALSE;
}
```

Code 7.8 Intersection.

The alternation between integers and reals in the output reflects whether the point is a vertex (and printed in `Advance`) or a computed intersection point (and printed in `InOut`). Although not evident from this example, degeneracies can cause points to be output more than once, sometimes both as vertices and as intersection points. Such duplicate points could wreak havoc with another program that expects all polygon vertices to be distinct. Although it is not difficult to suppress output of duplicates (Exercise 7.4.4[2]), this raises the integer versus float problem directly. For it will be necessary to decide, e.g., if the integer 5 is equal to the floating-point number 5.00, where this later number is computed with doubles in `Intersection`. Any conversion between floats

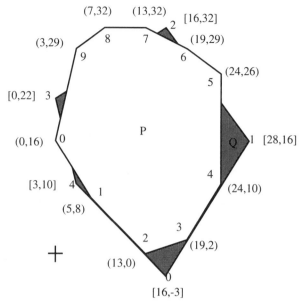

FIGURE 7.11   *P* is in front; *Q* is behind. *P*'s vertex coordinates are in parentheses; *Q*'s in brackets.

and integers is subject to round-off error, and might result in deciding that 5 != 5.00; use of a "fuzz" factor will inevitably accept some distinct points as equal. The only foolproof method of circumventing these difficulties is to represent the intersection point coordinates as rationals: ratios of integers (Exercise 7.4.4[4]). As this would make the code unpleasantly complex, we will leave matters as they stand.

7.4.4. Exercises

1. *Denominator.* Prove that the denom in Intersection (Code 7.8) is zero iff *ab* is parallel to *cd*.

2. *Duplicate points* [programming]. Modify the code to suppress the output of duplicate points. Do not concern yourself with the float versus integer problem discussed above, but rather just compare ints and doubles with ==, which will force a conversion to doubles.

   Once you have your code working, try to find a case that will break it. This may be quite difficult, and even impossible on some machines.

3. *Loop termination* (Schorn) [programming]. Modify the code so that loop termination depends on cycling past the first output vertex, rather than on the loop counters aadv and badv. Test your code on the two triangles (3, 4), (6, 4), (4, 7) and (4, 7), (2, 5), (6, 2).

4. *Degeneracies.* Run the code by hand on examples with the following types of degeneracies:

   a. A vertex of *P* lies on the interior of an edge of *Q*.

   b. Two vertices of *P* and *Q* coincide.

   c. Two edges of *P* and *Q* are collinear and overlap, but neither includes the other.

5. *Rationals*

  a. Discuss (but do not implement) how the point of intersection could be represented as an exact rational, a ratio of two integers.

  b. Design a boolean function that determines if two such rationals are equal. Note that, e.g., $2/6 = 127131/381393$.

  c. [programming] Implement the rational equal function.

7.5. EXTREMAL POLYTOPE QUERIES

The problem of finding an extreme point of a polytope is much more difficult than the two-dimensional version discussed in Section 7.3. There is no direct counterpart to the one-dimensional search we used on the boundary chain of the convex polygon: the two-dimensional surface of a polytope provides too much freedom in the search direction. Nevertheless, Kirkpatrick (1983) invented a breathtakingly beautiful search structure that permits the problem to be solved in $O(\log n)$ query time, asymptotically the same as in two dimensions (although we will see the constant of proportionality is larger).

7.5.1. Sketch of Idea

The key idea is to form a sequence of simpler and simpler polytopes nested within the original given polytope P.[6] The innermost polytope is a tetrahedron or triangle, and there are $O(\log n)$ polytopes altogether. Construction of the hierarchy of polytopes can be done in $O(n)$ time, and storing all of them only uses $O(n)$ space. Once they are constructed, extremal queries can be answered in $O(\log n)$ time. Note that although this matches the time complexity for finding extreme points of convex polygons, the polygons did not require preprocessing (although even to read such a polygon into memory requires $O(n)$ time, which can be considered a crude form of preprocessing).

An extremal query is answered by first finding the extreme for the innermost polytope, and using that to work outward through the hierarchy toward P. Let the sequence of nested polytopes be $P = P_0, P_1, P_2, \ldots, P_k$, where P_k is the innermost, and let a_i be the extreme point for polytope P_i. We first find the extreme point a_k of P_k by comparing its three or four vertices. Knowing a_k (and some other information) will give us a small set of candidate vertices of P_{k-1} to check for extremality. This yields a_{k-1}, and from that we find a_{k-2}, and so on. It will turn out that the work to move from one polytope to the next in the hierarchy is constant. Because $k = O(\log n)$, the total time to find a_0 is also $O(\log n)$. We now proceed to detail the search structure and the algorithm.

7.5.2. Independent Sets

Recall that the edges and vertices of a polytope form a planar graph (Section 4.1.4); Figure 7.12*a* shows the graph for an icosahedron, Figure 7.13, an example we will use to illustrate ideas throughout this section. Kirkpatrick's key

---

[6]This sequence is often called the Dobkin-Kirkpatrick hierarchy; see Dobkin and Kirkpatrick (1990).

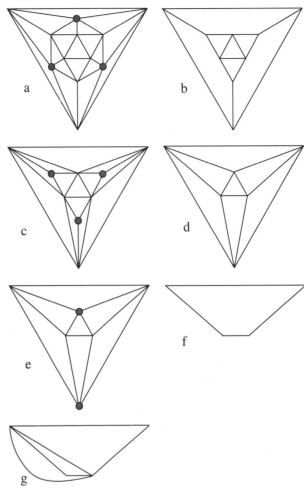

FIGURE 7.12 The graph of the vertices and edges of an icosahedron. Marked nodes form independent sets. (*a*) original graph of P_0; (*b*) after deletion of independent set; (*c*) after retriangulation: the graph of P_1; (*d*) after deletion; (*e*) after retriangulation (same as [d]): the graph of P_2; (*f*) after deletion; (*g*) after retriangulation: the graph of P_3.

idea depends on the graph theory notion of an "independent set." A set of nodes I of a graph G is called an *independent set* if no two nodes in I are adjacent in G: so they are "spread out" in a sense. Such an independent set is marked in Figure 7.12*a*. This set of three nodes is in fact a *maximum independent set* for this graph, in that there are no four nodes forming an independent set. It is important for Kirpatrick's scheme that planar graphs have "large" independent sets composed entirely of vertices of "small" degree (i.e., a small number of adjacent nodes); these vague qualifiers will be made precise later.

FIGURE 7.13   Icosahedron, P_0 (Figure 7.12a).

The construction of P_1, the first polytope nested inside $P = P_0$, proceeds as follows. An independent set of vertices for P_0 is found as in Figure 7.12a. These vertices and all their incident edges are deleted from the graph. The result is shown in Figure 7.12b. Because the vertices are independent, each deletion produces one new face in the graph. In Figure 7.12b, each deletion produces a pentagon (which looks like a quadrilateral because two edges are collinear). Next, these faces are triangulated; see Figure 7.12c. In our case, we can triangulate them arbitrarily; more on this later. The geometric equivalent to this operation on polytopes is to delete the vertices in the independent set and take the convex hull of the remaining vertices. This produces polytope P_1, which is clearly nested inside P_0, since it is the hull of a subset of P_0's vertices. Figure 7.14 shows P_1 corresponding to the graph in Figure 7.12c. Note the pentagons (two of which are visible in the figure) are composed of three coplanar triangles. In general, the vertices adjacent to a deleted independent vertex will not be coplanar; they are in this instance because of the symmetry of the icosahedron. It is the coplanarity and convexity of the face that permitted us to triangulate it

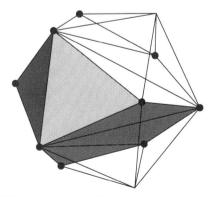

FIGURE 7.14 P_1: 9 vertices, 14 faces (Figure 7.12c).

FIGURE 7.15 P_2: an octahedron (Figure 7.12*e*).

arbitrarily. In general, we would have to take the hull of the vertices around the boundary of the new face to construct the triangulation.

Now the process is repeated to construct P_2. A set of independent vertices of P_1 are identified, as marked in Figure 7.12*c*. These are deleted, producing the graph shown in Figure 7.12*d*. It so happens that this time, the deletion produces only triangle faces, so no further triangulation is needed. Figure 7.12*d* is the "Schlegel" diagram of an octahedron: the corresponding polytope P_2 is a (nonregular) octahedron, as shown in Figure 7.15.

The process is repeated one more time. An independent set of size two is identified in Figure 7.12*e*. Deletion produces the graph in Figure 7.12*f*. Triangulation of the two quadrilateral faces (one of which is exterior) produces Figure 7.12*g*, which is the graph of a tetrahedron. Figure 7.16 displays this tetrahedron, which, again because of the symmetry of the icosahedron, consists of four coplanar points.

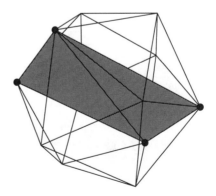

FIGURE 7.16 P_3: a flat tetrahedron (Figure 7.12*g*).

7.5.3. Independent Sets: Properties and Algorithm

To achieve a nested polytope hierarchy with the right properties, the independent sets cannot be chosen arbitrarily. Fortunately, it is easy to obtain the appropriate properties, as Kirkpatrick showed for arbitrary planar graphs (Kirkpatrick, 1983). The arguments are slightly easier for polytope graphs; here I follow the presentation of Edelsbrunner (1987).

To achieve only $O(\log n)$ polytopes, it suffices to delete a constant fraction of the vertices at each step. For suppose we can find an independent set of cn vertices on any polytope of n vertices, for $c < 1$. Then at each step, we reduce the vertices by a factor of $(1 - c)$, so after k steps, we will have $n(1 - c)^k$ vertices. This quantity reaches four when k is a particular value:

$$n(1 - c)^k = 4$$

$$\log n + k \log (1 - c) = 2$$

$$k = \frac{\log n}{-\log (1 - c)} - \frac{2}{-\log (1 - c)}. \tag{7.5}$$

Since $(1 - c) < 1$, $-\log(1 - c) > 0$, and the right hand side of Equation 7.5 is a positive constant times $\log n$, minus another constant; so it is $O(\log n)$. For example, for $n = 2^{20} \approx 10^6$, and $c = 1/10$, $k = 118$. So our goal is to show that every polytope graph has an independent set of size cn for some $c < 1$.

The most natural method of finding an independent set is iterate the following "greedy" procedure: choose a vertex of lowest degree that is not adjacent to any other vertices previously chosen. The intuition is that low-degree vertices "kill" as few other vertex candidates as possible. Although this simple-minded algorithm will not necessarily find a maximum independent set, it turns out to be sufficient for our purposes. We can even loosen it up a bit to chose any vertex whose degree is not too high: this avoids a search for a vertex of lowest degree. In particular, we use Algorithm 7.3. It is clear that this

---

Algorithm: INDEPENDENT SET
Input: a graph G.
Output: an independent set I.
$I \leftarrow \varnothing$
Mark all nodes of G of degree ≥ 9.
while some nodes remain unmarked do
    Choose an unmarked node v.
    Mark v and all the neighbors of v.
    $I \leftarrow I \cup \{v\}$.

Algorithm 7.3 Independent set.

algorithm produces an independent set, and runs in $O(n)$ time on a planar graph of n nodes. What is not so clear is that it produces a "large" independent set. This is established in the following theorem of Edelsbrunner (1987, Theorem 9.8).

Theorem 7.5.1. *An independent set* I *of a polytope graph* G *of* n *vertices produced by Algorithm 7.3 has size at least* n/18.

In terms of our previous notation, the theorem claims the constant $c = 1/18$ is achieved by Algorithm 7.3.

Proof. The key to the proof is Euler's formula, $V - E + F = 2$. We established in Chapter 4 (Section 4.1.5, Equation 4.4) that this formula implies that the number of edges of a polytope graph is bounded above by $3V - 6$: $E \leq 3n - 6$. We now use this to obtain an upper bound on the sum Σ of the degrees of all the nodes of G. This sum double-counts every edge of G, since each edge has two endpoints. Thus, $\Sigma \leq 6n - 12$.

Now this bound on the sum of degrees immediately implies that there must be numerous nodes with small degrees. For if all nodes had high degree, the sum of their degrees would exceed this bound. Quantitatively, there must be at least $n/2$ vertices of degree ≤ 8. For suppose the contrary: there are more than $n/2$ nodes of degree ≥ 9. The sum of the degrees of just these nodes is $\geq 9n/2$. The other nodes must each have degree ≥ 3. Let us assume that n is even, to simplify the calculations. The smallest value of Σ would occur when only half the nodes have high degree, and the other half have the lowest degree possible. Therefore,

$$\Sigma \geq 9n/2 + 3n/2 = 6n. \tag{7.6}$$

This contradicts the upper bound of $6n - 12$ we established above. For n odd, a similar contradiction is obtained (Exercise 7.5.6[2]). Therefore, we have established that at least half the nodes of G have degree ≤ 8, and so are candidates for the independent set constructed by Algorithm 7.3. It remains to show that the algorithm selects a "large" number of these candidates.

Every time the algorithm chooses a node v, it marks v and all of v's neighbors. The worst that could happen is that (a) all of these nodes it marks were previously unmarked, and (b) v has the highest degree possible, 8. Let m be the number of unmarked nodes of G of degree ≤ 8. An example may make the relationships clearer: suppose $m = 90$. A node v is chosen, and in the worst case, 8 unmarked nodes are marked. This reduces m by 9, to 81. Again a node is chosen among these 81, and again in the worst case, m is reduced by 9. It should be clear that at least $1/9$ of m nodes will be added to the independent set I; so with $m = 90$, $|I| \geq 10$.

Now since we showed above that $m \geq n/2$, $|I| \geq n/18$, and thus we have established that Algorithm 7.3 always produces an independent set at least $1/18$ the size of the original graph. $\qquad\square$

Algorithm: NESTED POLYTOPE HIERARCHY
Input: a polytope P.
Output: an $O(\log n)$ hierarchy of nested polytopes, $P = P_0, P_1, \ldots, P_k$
$i \leftarrow 0;\ P_0 \leftarrow P$.
while $|P_i| > 4$ do
  Apply Algorithm 7.3 to identify an independent set I of P_i.
  Initialize P_{i+1} to P_i
  for each vertex $v \in I$ do
    Delete v from P_{i+1}.
    Retriangulate the hole by constructing the hull of $N(v)$.
    Link each new face of P_{i+1} to v.
  Link unchanged faces of P_{i+1} to P_i.

Algorithm 7.4 Nested polytope hierarchy.

With $c = 1/18$, the number of nested polytopes is (by Equation 7.5) less than $12.13 \log n$. This constant of proportionality leaves much to be desired, but always choosing the unmarked node of smallest degree improves c to $1/7$ (Edelsbrunner, 1987, Problem 9.9[d]) and the log constant to 4.50.

7.5.4. Construction of Nested Polytope Hierarchy

We now detail the construction of the hierarchy. In the pseudocode shown in Algorithm 7.4, $N(v)$ is the set of neighbors of v: all the vertices adjacent to v.

Space Requirements
We have already established that the polytope hierarchy has height $O(\log n)$. At first, it might seem that the time and space required to construct the hierarchy would be $O(n \log n)$, linear per level, but in fact the total is linear because of the constant fractional reduction between levels of the hierarchy. In particular, with $c = 1/18$, each polytope has at most $17/18$ as many vertices as its "parent." So the total size is no more than

$$n\left[(17/18) + (17/18)^2 + (17/18)^3 + \cdots \right].$$

Although the sum of powers of $(1 - c)$ has only k terms, it is easier to obtain an upper bound by letting it run to infinity. Then it is the familiar geometric series, with sum

$$\frac{1}{1 - (1 - c)} = \frac{1}{c} = 18.$$

Therefore, the total storage required is at most $18n = O(n)$. Similarly the construction time is $O(n)$, although this needs some argument, not provided here.

Retriangulating Holes

We mentioned earlier that when a vertex v is deleted from P_i, the resulting hole must be triangulated appropriately to produce P_{i+1}. In general, the neighbors $N(v)$ of v will not be coplanar, and so an arbitrary triangulation will not suffice. We need to compute the convex hull of $N(v)$, and use the "outer faces" of this hull to provide the triangulation. In practice, we might recompute the entire hull at each step to construct P_{i+1} from P_i, but this would lead to $O(n \log n)$ time complexity. Observe that $|N(v)| \leq 8$, because v had degree ≤ 8. This means that each hole can be patched with triangles in constant time. The total number of hole patches necessary for the entire hierarchy construction is no more than a constant times the number of vertices deleted, which is $O(n)$.

Linking Polytopes

It is necessary to connect the polytopes in adjacent positions of the hierarchy with data structure links to aid the search. Because the vertices removed at each step of the hierarchy construction form an independent set, the relationships between vertices, edges, and faces of two adjacent polytopes are unambiguous. We will not go into details here (see Edelsbrunner [1987, pp. 199–200]), but rather will just assume that any reasonable link we need is available.

7.5.5. Extreme Point Algorithm

Now, we apply the hierarchy to answer extreme point queries. We will explain the algorithm as if we are seeking the highest point of the polytope, a vertex with largest z-coordinate, but the process works for an extreme in any direction u in an analogous fashion. The algorithm was first detailed by Edelsbrunner and Maurer (1985); see also Edelsbrunner (1987, Section 9.5.3).

Let a_i be a highest point of polytope P_i. To keep the presentation simple, we will assume that a_i is unique for each i. The essence of the algorithm is to find the highest point a_k of P_k, the innermost polytope, by brute-force search, and then use a_k to help find a_{k-1}, use this to find a_{k-2}, and so on until a_0 is found, which is the highest point of $P_0 = P$, the original polytope. This process can be viewed as raising a plane π orthogonal to the z-axis from a_k, to a_{k-1}, and so on to a_0. Because the polytopes are nested, this plane only moves upward. An example is shown in Figure 7.17.[7] Here the innermost polytope, a triangle, is not shown.

The key to the algorithm is the relationship between a_{i+1} and a_i. We condense this relationship into two lemmas, Lemmas 7.5.2 and 7.5.3 below. The first is perhaps easiest to see if we imagine π moving downward, from a_i to a_{i+1}.

Lemma 7.5.2. *Let* a_i *and* a_{i+1} *be uniquely highest vertices of* P_i *and* P_{i+1}. *Then either* $a_i = a_{i+1}$, *or* a_{i+1} *is the highest among the vertices adjacent to* a_i.

---

[7]This figure was constructed by Michelle Maurer.

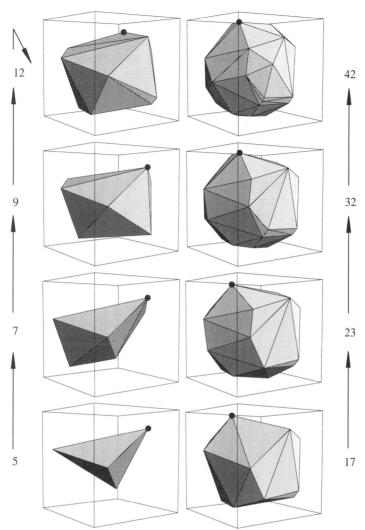

FIGURE 7.17   Polytope hierarchy with highest vertices marked, and number of vertices noted to the side. Box dimensions are ± 100. The highest vertex has z coordinate 63, 63, 63, 77, 92, 92, 94, 94, moving up the hierarchy.

Proof. We consider two cases. First, suppose that a_i is a vertex of both P_i and P_{i+1}. Because $P_i \supset P_{i+1}$, no vertex of P_{i+1} can be higher than the highest of P_i, and therefore the highest vertex a_{i+1} of P_{i+1} must in this case be a_i.

Second, suppose a_i is one of the vertices deleted in the construction of P_{i+1}. Let b_{i+1} be the highest vertex of P_{i+1} among those adjacent to a_i in P_i. The claim of the lemma is that b_{i+1} is the highest vertex of P_{i+1}.

Consider the cone of faces incident to a_i in P_i; see Figure 7.18. Call the infinite extension of this cone C. By the convexity of P_i, $C \supset P_i$, and by nesting,

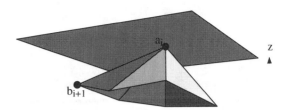

FIGURE 7.18   Highest point a_i of P_i.

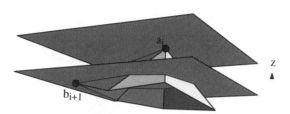

FIGURE 7.19   Highest point $b_{i+1} = a_{i+1}$ of P_{i+1}.

$C \supset P_i \supset P_{i+1}$. Thus, $a_{i+1} \in C$. Now no vertex of P_{i+1} can be located in the umbrella-shaped region under a_i, $U = C - P_{i+1}$. So a_{i+1} must lie in the other part of C, $C - U$, which is necessarily below the height of b_{i+1}, as Figure 7.19 makes clear. Therefore, $b_{i+1} = a_{i+1}$.   □

An immediate corollary of this lemma is that a_i is either identical to a_{i+1}, or it is adjacent to it. It might seem this gives us the "hook" we need to move from a_{i+1} to a_i, but in fact this is not enough. We have no bound on the number of vertices adjacent to a_{i+1}, so if we search them all for a_i the algorithm will work correctly, but it will have time complexity $O(n)$ rather than the $O(\log n)$ we desire. We need a more specific hook from a_{i+1} to a_i.

Extreme Edges

If one projects P_{i+1} onto a plane orthogonal to π, say the xz-plane, π becomes a line and P_{i+1} becomes a convex polygon P'_{i+1}, as shown in Figure 7.20. Let primes denote objects projected to the xz-plane. Define L_{i+1} and R_{i+1} as the two edges of P_{i+1} that project to the two edges of P'_{i+1} incident to a'_{i+1}, as illustrated.

Now define the "umbrella parents," or just *parents*, of an edge e of P_{i+1} to be the vertices of P_i from which it derives, in the the following sense. If e is an edge of P_{i+1} but not of P_i, it sits "under" some vertex v of P_i whose umbrella of incident faces was deleted to produce P_{i+1}; this v is the (sole) parent of e. (This is most evident in Figure 7.14, where the two diagonals of the upper pentagonal face sit under a vertex of degree five.) If e is an edge of both P_{i+1}

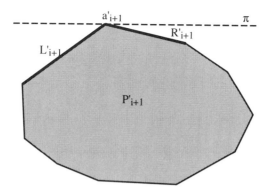

FIGURE 7.20   Definition of extreme edges L_{i+1} and R_{i+1}; The z-axis is vertical.

and P_i, then its parents are the two vertices of P_i at the tips of the two triangle faces adjacent to e (which may or may not be vertices of P_{i+1}).

Now the key lemma is this:

Lemma 7.5.3.   *Let* a_i *and* a_{i+1} *be uniquely highest vertices of* P_i *and* P_{i+1}. *Then, either* $a_i = a_{i+1}$, *or* a_i *is the highest among the parents of the extreme edges* L_{i+1} *and* R_{i+1}.

Before discussing why this might be true, let us explore its consequences. If we have both the extreme vertex a_{i+1} of P_{i+1}, and the extreme edges L_{i+1} and R_{i+1}, we can find the extreme vertex a_i of P_i by examining the (at most) five candidates provided by the lemma. If we can then find the new extreme edges L_i and R_i of P_i in constant time, we have achieved one full step up the hierarchy in constant time, which will result in $O(\log n)$ overall.

How can the extreme edges be computed once a_i is known? There are two cases to consider:

1. $a_i \neq a_{i+1}$. Here, surprisingly, we can use a brute-force search for the extreme edges. The reason is that such a search will have time complexity dependent on the degree of a_i, which, when we *first* encounter it in the hierarchy of polytopes, is an independent vertex chosen for deletion in the hierarchy construction, and therefore has degree ≤ 8.

2. $a_i = a_{i+1}$. Here a brute-force search is not appropriate, because if we move through a series of levels of the hierarchy without the extreme vertex changing, its degree can grow larger and larger by "accretion" of edges: we are only guaranteed a degree ≤ 8 on first encounter. This accretion is evident in the three innermost polytopes of the hierarchy in Figure 7.17. Fortunately, the new extreme edges are "close" to the old: L_i is either L_{i+1}, or it is adjacent to a parent of L_{i+1}; and similarly for R_i. I will not justify this claim (Exercise 7.5.6[3]).

So in both cases the new extreme edges can be found in constant time. Now, we justify Lemma 7.5.3.

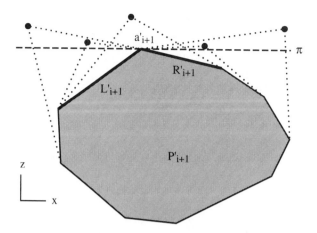

FIGURE 7.21   Potential locations for a_i' and tangents shown dotted.

Proof. Suppose $a_i \neq a_{i+1}$. Then a_i is above π. Of course, the projection of P_i onto the the xz-plane is a convex polygon P_i' that encloses the projection P_{i+1}'. (Recall primes indicate projected objects.) If possible locations for a_i' are considered, as in Figure 7.21, it becomes clear that a_i must "sit over" one or both of the extreme edges L_{i+1} and R_{i+1}. This is the intuition behind the lemma.

Now why are the dotted connections from a_i' in the figure reasonable possibilities? First, recall that all the vertices adjacent to a_i in P_i are also vertices of P_{i+1}. So, the edges in the projection emanate from a_i' and terminate in P_{i+1}' below π. Second, $P_i \supset \mathrm{conv}\{a_i \cup P_{i+1}\}$, so the two tangents through a_i' supporting P_{i+1}' are in P_i'. Third, there can be no edges from a_i' "outside of" these tangents, because such edges could not terminate in P_{i+1}'. Thus the

---

Algorithm: EXTREME POINT OF A POLYTOPE
Input: a polytope P, and a direction vector u.
Output: the vertex a of P extreme in the u direction.
Construct the hierarchy of nested polytopes, $P = P_0, P_1, \ldots, P_k$,
    by running Algorithm 7.4.
    $a_k \leftarrow$ the vertex of P_k extreme in the u direction.
Compute L_k and R_k.
for $i = k - 1, k - 2, \ldots, 1, 0$ do
    $a_i \leftarrow$ the extreme vertex among a_{i+1}
        and the parents of L_{i+1} and R_{i+1}.
    if $a_i \neq a_{i+1}$ then
        for all edges incident to a_i do
            Save extreme edges L_i and R_i.
    else ($a_i = a_{i+1}$) Compute L_i from L_{i+1} etc.

Algorithm 7.5   Extreme point of a polytope.

boundary of P_i' includes the a_i' tangents, and Figure 7.21 is an accurate depiction. Since it is clear that the a_i' tangents must encompass at least one of the extreme edge of P_{i+1}', and that a_i is a parent of this edge, we have established the lemma.   □

We can summarize the algorithm in the pseudocode shown in Algorithm 7.5. From Lemmas 7.5.2 and 7.5.3, and from Exercise 7.5.6[3], this algorithm will work correctly, so the only issue remaining is its time complexity. We have ensured that the work done at each level of the algorithm is constant. This then establishes the query time of the algorithm: $O(\log n)$ levels of the hierarchy are searched, and the work at each level is a constant. Modulo the details we have ignored, we have established the following theorem.

Theorem 7.5.4.   *After* $O(n)$ *time and space preprocessing, polytope extreme-point queries can be answered in* $O(\log n)$ *time each.*

7.5.6. Exercises

1. *Innermost polytope* [easy]. Why cannot the innermost polytope of the hierarchy have ≥ 5 vertices?

2. *n odd*. In the proof of Theorem 7.5.1, we only covered the n even case. Follow the argument for n odd, and show the conclusion still holds.

3. $a_i = a_{i+1}$. Argue that if $a_i = a_{i+1}$ in Algorithm 7.5, L_i is either L_{i+1}, or it is adjacent to a parent of L_{i+1}. Show how these facts permit L_{i+1} to be found in constant time in this case.

4. *Nested polygon hierarchy*. Develop a method of constructing a hierarchy of $O(\log n)$ convex polygons nested inside a given convex polygon of n vertices. Use this to design an extreme-point algorithm that achieves $O(\log n)$ query time.

5. *The constant c* [easy]. Compute the average constant c for the example in Figure 7.17, and using this, calculate k from Equation 7.5.

6. *Implementation of independent set algorithm* [programming]. Write a program to find an independent set in a given graph using Algorithm 7.3.

7. *Nested polytope implementation* [programming]. Use the convex hull code from Chapter 4, and the independent set code from the previous exercise, to find a polytope nested inside the hull of n points. Test it on randomly generated hulls, and compute the average fractional size of the independent sets. Compare this against the $c = 1/18$ constant established in Theorem 7.5.1, and try to explain any difference.

8. *Plane-polyhedron distance*. Design an algorithm to determine the distance between an arbitrary polyhedron P of n vertices and a query plane π. Define the distance to be

$$\min_{x, y} \{|x - y| : x \in P, y \in \pi\},$$

where x and y are points. Try to achieve $O(\log n)$ per query after preprocessing. Compare Exercise 7.3.2[4].

9. *Finger probing a polytope* (Skiena, 1992). Develop an algorithm for "probing" a polytope P that contains the origin, with a directed line L through the origin. Each

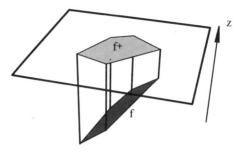

FIGURE 7.22 Face f of the polytope projects up to face f^+ of the upper planar subdivision.

probe is to return the first face of P hit by L moving in from infinity. Try to achieve $O(\log n)$ query time, by dualizing P and L with the polar dual discussed in Chapter 6 (Exercise 6.5.3[3]).

10. *Circumscribed hierarchies*
    a. Define an $O(\log n)$ hierarchy of polygons surrounding a convex polygon, with properties similar to the inscribed hierarchy.
    b. Define an $O(\log n)$ hierarchy of polytopes surrounding a given polytope.
    c. Suggest applications for these circumscribed hierarchies.

7.6. PLANAR POINT LOCATION

7.6.1. Applications

One of the most fundamental of geometric searches is locating a point in a subdivision of the plane, known as the *planar point location* problem. We have already encountered this need in searching Voronoi diagrams to find nearest neighbors (Chapter 5, Section 5.5.1) or searching the k-th order Voronoi diagram to find the k-nearest neighbors (Chapter 6, Section 6.7.1).

Another common application of planar point location is determining if a query point is inside a given polytope. Although we already mentioned a method for solving the point-in-polytope problem in Section 7.2, that method is "single-shot," and not efficient for the situation where the polytope is fixed, and repeatedly queried for different points. The connection between this problem, and planar point location, can be seen via projection.[8] Suppose the given polytope P sits on the xy-plane, and let P^+ be the set of all faces of P whose outward normal has a nonnegative upward component, that is, whose z component is ≥ 0. These are the faces visible from $z = +\infty$. Let P^- be the set of all the other faces, whose normals point down. Project P^- onto the $z = 0$ plane, and project P^+ onto the $z = h$ plane, where h is the height of P. This results in

---

[8]Suggested in (Edelsbrunner, 1987, Exercise 11.5).

two subdivisions on these two planes; call them S^+ and S^-. Now, given any query point q, project it up and down and locate it in both subdivisions. Suppose it projects into face f^+ of S^+. Then this selects out a vertical "prism" as shown in Figure 7.22. It is then easy to decide whether q is above or below f in this prism. If it is above f, $q \notin P$. If below, the process is repeated on the lower subdivision. $q \in P$ iff it is below the face of P provided by the search in S^+, and above the face of P provided by the search in S^-.

7.6.2. Independent Set Algorithm

The reader may have realized already that Kirkpatrick's search structure, presented in Section 7.5, provides a solution to the planar point location problem. Indeed, this was his original motivation (Kirkpatrick, 1983). The only complication is that a general planar subdivision may have general polygonal faces, which need to be triangulated by a polygon triangulation algorithm. After that step, we can proceed as with the polytope hierarchy, except that each hole produced by a vertex deletion should be retriangulated by a polygon triangulation algorithm. As with the polytope case, however, this retriangulation only takes constant time per hole, since the holes have at most eight vertices.

Theorem 7.6.1. *A polygonal planar subdivision of* n *vertices can be preprocessed in* O(n) *time and space so that point location queries can be answered in* O(log n) *time.*

7.6.3. Monotone Subdivisions

Although Kirkpatrick's search structure in some sense settles the planar point location problem, it was neither the first algorithm to achieve those bounds nor the most recent. An early algorithm by Dobkin and Lipton (1976) uses quadratic space but is very simple and achieves a much better query constant: queries can be performed with $2 \log n$ comparisons. Lipton and Tarjan (1980) were the first to achieve $O(n)$ preprocessing with $O(\log n)$ query time, but their algorithm is impractically complex. Kirkpatrick's algorithm is elegant and ideal for polytope problems, but its high query constant make it unattractive for general planar subdivision search.

One of the most popular methods of performing planar point location depends on *monotone subdivisions*. A subdivision is monotone if every face is monotone, say with respect to the horizontal. A face is *monotone* if it meets every vertical line in a connected set: either a point or a segment (see Section 2.1). Many commonly encountered subdivisions are monotone: triangulations, and any convex subdivision such as a Voronoi diagram or a k-th order Voronoi diagram or an arrangement of lines. Those subdivisions that are not monotone can be further partitioned (by, e.g., triangulating each face) to produce a monotone subdivision. The utility of these subdivisions was recognized by Lee and Preparata (1977), and they have been studied intensively ever since.

We now sketch roughly some of the main ideas behind monotone subdivision search. Define a *separator* in a monotone subdivision as a connected collection

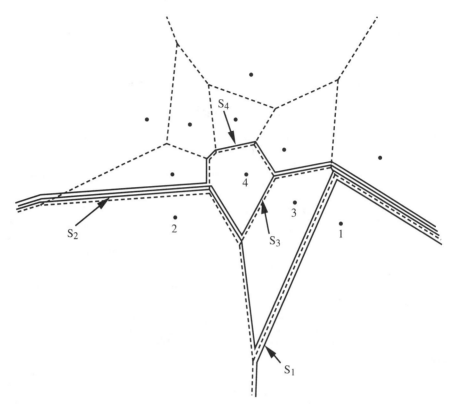

FIGURE 7.23   Separators in a monotone subdivision: $S_1 < S_2 < S_3 < S_4$.

of edges of the subdivision that meet every vertical line exactly once. These are monotone chains that separate the subdivision into two parts: above and below.

The main idea is to find a collection of separators that partition the subdivision into "horizontal" strips. Then a double binary search is performed: a vertical search on these strips to locate the query point between two separators, and a horizontal search to locate it within one strip.

An example is shown in Figure 7.23. The subdivision is a Voronoi diagram, which is of course monotone. Four separators are shown. S_1 is the lowest, having only the Voronoi cell C_1 for point 1 below it. S_2 is the next highest, having C_2 and C_1 below it. Note that S_2 is above S_1 throughout their lengths. Similarly, S_3 is above C_3, and S_4 is above C_4. This process could be continued, finding a collection of separators $S_1, S_2, \ldots, S_m$ that can be considered sorted vertically, with each pair of adjacent separators having one cell of the subdivision sandwiched between them.

Consider the problem of deciding whether a query point q is above or below some particular separator S_i. This can be accomplished via a horizontal binary search on the x-coordinates of the vertices of S_i and the x-coordinate of q, because S_i is monotone with respect to the x-axis. Once the projection of q on the x-axis is located between two endpoints of an edge e of S_i, it can be tested for above or below e. Since any S_i has $O(n)$ edges, the query "Is q above or below S_i?" can be answered in $O(\log n)$ time.

Now, this query can be used repeatedly to perform a binary search on the collection of separators. First, ask if q is above or below $S_{m/2}$. If it is below, query its relation to $S_{m/4}$; if above, query $S_{3m/4}$, and so on. This binary search will take $O(\log m)$ steps, each of which costs $O(\log n)$. Since $m = O(n)$, the total query time is $O(\log^2 n)$.

Of course this is asymptotically worse than what is achieved in Theorem 7.6.1. Moreover, it could require quadratic space to store the separators, because of the high degree of shared edges, as is evident in Figure 7.23. However, the algorithm is attractively simple, and it can be improved in both query time and space requirements to achieve the same asymptotic complexities as claimed in Theorem 7.6.1. These improvements are by no means straightforward and awaited the inventions of topological sorting and fractional cascading (Chazelle and Guibas, 1986*a*, Chazelle and Guibas, 1986*b*), among other ideas. See Edelsbrunner (1987, Chapter 11) for a thorough presentation.

Planar point location remains an active area of research. Not only does there remain room for improvement on the basic problem discussed here, but also two important related problems are very much in flux at this writing: (1) "dynamic" planar point location, where the subdivision changes, for example, by insertions or deletions of Voronoi sites, and (2) point location in subdivisions of three-dimensional and higher spaces.

7.7. ADDITIONAL EXERCISES

1. *Detection of intersection of convex polygons.* Develop an algorithm for reporting whether or not two convex polygons of n and m vertices intersect. Try to achieve $O(\log(n + m))$ time. (Chazelle and Dobkin, 1987).

2. *Interval trees.* Preprocess a set of n intervals I with integer endpoints so that they can be efficiently queried. Consider three types of queries (the preprocessing need not be the same for all three):
   a. Is x in some interval in I?
   b. Within how many intervals of I does x lie?
   c. Does the interval $[a, b]$ intersect any interval of I?

3. *Length of union of intervals.* Design an algorithm to find the total length covered by the union of n intervals.

4. *Empty circle queries* (Goodrich). Given a set S of n points in the plane, sketch a good method for constructing an efficient data structure to quickly answer empty circle queries. An *empty circle query* for a query point q asks for the largest circle that has q as its center and does not contain any point of S in its interior.

5. *Cops and robbers* (Goodrich). Suppose you are given two sets of n points in the plane, P and R. The points in P represent "police officers," and the points in R represent "robbers." A point q in the plane is *safe* if it is inside the triangle formed by three points in P. A point q in the plane is *robbed* if it is not safe and is inside the triangle formed by three points in R. A point q is *suspect* if it is neither safe nor robbed. Describe an efficient data structure to determine, for any query point q, whether q is safe, robbed, or suspect.

8

Motion Planning

8.1. INTRODUCTION

The burgeoning field of robotics has inspired the exploration of a collection of problems in computational geometry loosely called "motion planning" problems, or more specifically "algorithmic motion planning" problems. As usual, details are abstracted away from a real-life application to produce mathematically "cleaner" versions of the problem. If the abstraction is performed intelligently, the theoretical explorations have practical import. This happily has been the case with motion planning.

8.1.1. Problem Specification

The primary paradigm we examine in this chapter assumes a fixed environment of impenetrable obstacles, usually polygons and polyhedra in two and three dimensions, respectively. Within this environment is the "robot" R, a movable object with some prespecified geometric characteristics: it may be a point, a line segment, a convex polygon, a hinged object, and so on. The robot is at some initial position s ($s$tart), and the task is to plan motions that will move it to some specified final position t ($t$erminus), such that throughout the motion, collision between the robot and all obstacles is avoided. A *collision* occurs when a point of the robot coincides with an interior point of an obstacle. Note that sliding contact with the boundary of the obstacles does not constitute a collision. A collision-avoiding path is called a *free path*.[1] Often there are restrictions on the type of motions permitted. Within this general class of problems, we consider three specific questions, each asking for more information than the preceding:

1. Decision question: Does there exist a free path for R from s to t?
2. Path construction: Find a free path for R from s to t.
3. Shortest path: Find the shortest free path for R from s to t.

A solution to (3) solves (2), which in turn solves (1). So the decision question is the easiest, although in practice it is usually answered by finding some path,

---

[1] Most authors follow Schwartz and Sharir (1983*a*) in calling this a *semi-free path*, using "free path" to imply no boundary contact (e.g., Latombe, 1991, p. 10). We will not require the distinction.

thereby solving (2).[2] We will see, however, an example in Section 8.6 where the decision question is much simpler than actually finding a path.

The sense in which a path is "shortest" is not always clear. If the robot is a circle, it is clear. However, suppose the robot is a line segment that is permitted to rotate (Section 8.5). Then several definitions of "shortest" are conceivable, and once one is selected, it is extremely difficult to find a shortest path.

8.1.2. Outline

We only consider shortest paths for the simplest problem instance: when the robot is a point (Section 8.2). We then examine two of the better-understood motion planning problems: translating a convex polygon (Section 8.4) and moving a "ladder": a line segment (Section 8.5). Next, we study moving a hinged robot "arm" (Section 8.6). This section includes the code to position an *n*-link arm to reach a specified hand location. Finally, we look at the fascinating problem of separating interlocking puzzle pieces (Section 8.7).

8.2. SHORTEST PATHS

In this section, we examine the problem of finding a shortest path between two given points, s and t, amidst a collection of disjoint polygonal obstacles with a total of n vertices. An example is shown in Figure 8.1: path A is shorter than path B and is in fact the unique shortest path connecting s and t and avoiding the interior of all obstacles. We assume that s and t are not interior to any polygon, which, together with the assumption of obstacle disjointness, implies that there is always some path; so the problem is to find the best one.

8.2.1. Visibility Graphs

A usual first step in optimizing over an infinite set of possibilities (and there are infinite number of paths between s and t) is to reduce the set to a finite list of *bona fide* candidates. This is achieved, in this instance, by the observation that a shortest path comprises segments whose endpoints are either s, t, or vertices of the polygons. Since s and t "act like" polygon vertices in this sense, it simplifies the discussion if we treat s and t as point polygons of one vertex each. Then, the observation can be strengthened to this statement:

Lemma 8.2.1. *A shortest path is a subpath of the visibility graph of the vertices of the obstacle polygons.*

Visibility graphs were mentioned in Chapter 6 (Section 6.1). A *visibility graph* of a set of polygons is a graph whose nodes correspond to vertices of the polygons and whose arcs correspond to vertices x and y that can "see" one another, in

---

[2] Problem 2 is sometimes called the "Find-Path" problem (Brooks, 1983).

FIGURE 8.1 *A* is the shortest path from *s* to *t*.

the sense that the segment *xy* does not meet the interior of any polygon. Note that *xy* may intersect the boundaries of the polygons, so that, for example, the edges of the polygons are in the visibility graph. This is the same notion of visibility used in Chapter 1 (Section 1.1.2), except now exterior to the polygons. The visibility graph for the polygons in Figure 8.1 is shown in Figure 8.2.

Lemma 8.2.1 can be justified in three steps:

1. The path is polygonal. Suppose to the contrary that the path contains a curved section *C*. It cannot be the case that all of *C* lies along polygonal boundaries, as these boundaries are not curved. So there must be a convex subsection of *C* that does not touch any polygon and that can be shortcut by a straight segment, contradicting the assumption that the path is shortest.

2. The turning points of the path are at polygon vertices: any turn in "free space" can be shortcut.

3. The segments of the path are visibility edges. This follows from the definition of visibility and the definition of what constitutes a free path.

Since the visibility graph is finite, this lemma establishes that there are only a finite number of candidate paths from *s* to *t* to search. However, the number of paths in the graph might be exponential in *n*, and we will need further analysis before we have a practical algorithm. First, we briefly consider constructing the visibility graph.

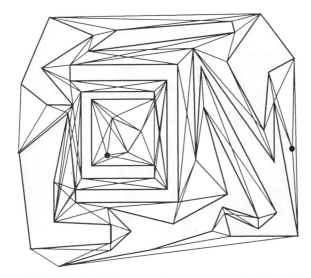

FIGURE 8.2 Visibility graph for the example in Figure 8.1.

8.2.2. Constructing the Visibility Graph

Constructing the visibility graph for a set of polygons is a fascinating problem with many applications, and it has been studied extensively. It would be a distraction from our main focus on motion planning to explain this, however, so we will make just a few remarks.

Finding visibility graph edges is nearly identical to finding polygon diagonals, the only differences being inessential: several polygons versus just one, exterior versus interior visibility. An $O(n^3)$ algorithm is immediate: for each vertex x, for each vertex y, check xy against every edge. The graph can have a quadratic number of edges, so $\Omega(n^2)$ is a lower bound on any algorithm. We mentioned in Section 6.1 that use of arrangements leads to an optimal $O(n^2)$ algorithm (O'Rourke, 1987, Chapter 8). After a long pursuit, an output-size sensitive algorithm was found by Ghosh and Mount (1991): $O(n \log n + E)$ for a graph with E edges. Of course $E = O(n^2)$, but often (as in Figure 8.2), E is much smaller than $\binom{n}{2}$.

8.2.3. Dijkstra's Algorithm

Assuming we have the visibility graph constructed and stored in some convenient data structure, the next question, and one on which we will concentrate, is how to find a shortest path in this graph. This is an instance of a problem studied in graph theory: finding a shortest path in a weighted graph. In our case, the "weights" on the edges of the graph are the lengths of those edges, the Euclidean distances between the endpoints. A gem of an algorithm for this problem was found by Dijkstra (1959). I will start explaining the key idea on a small example before turning to implementation details.

Spreading Paint

Consider the portion of a visibility graph shown in Figure 8.3; not all visibility edges are included to reduce clutter. Imagine pouring paint on the source node s, and suppose the visibility edges are thin pipes of the same diameter so that the paint spreads evenly along all visibility edges at a uniform rate, one unit of length per unit of time. The first vertex of the visibility graph to be hit by paint is a, shown in Figure 8.3a. Its distance of 1.93 to s is the shortest length of all

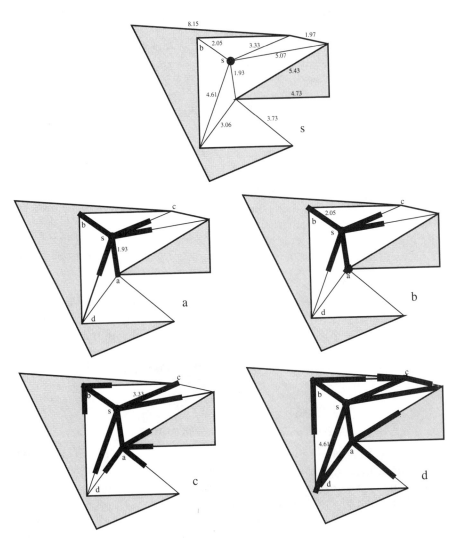

FIGURE 8.3 At the start s, and after vertices a, b, c, and d are reached respectively.

visibility edges incident to s. After just another 0.12 time units, vertex b is hit (part b of the figure), and the paint has crept a bit further along all other paths. At time 3.33, vertex c is hit, and at time 4.61, vertex d is reached, and so on.

The idea of Dijkstra's algorithm is to simulate this paint-spreading process. Then, when the destination t is reached by the paint, the simulated time gives the length of the shortest path. By storing information at each node indicating from which direction paint first reached it, it is possible to work backward and find the complete shortest path to any node. This is roughly equivalent to tagging each paint molecule with its path so far, so that when the first molecule reaches t, its path is known.

Algorithm

Let G be the visibility graph. Dijkstra's algorithm avoids a continuous simulation of the paint creeping down each visibility edge and recognizes that discrete steps suffice. The algorithm maintains a tree $T \subset G$ rooted at s that spans all those nodes so far reached by paint: the discrete paint frontier. At each step, the edges incident to every node of T are examined, and one edge is added to T that (a) reaches a node x outside of T: $x \in G - T$, and (b) such that the distance to x from s is shortest among all nodes satisfying (a). The point of (b) is to ensure that x is the next node to be reached by paint.

Consider the step of the algorithm after Figure 8.3b. Nodes s, a, and b have been reached by paint, so $T = \{sa, sb\}$. Now, all edges incident to these three nodes are examined, and their lengths added to the shortest distance to the nodes. So, the edge ad has length 3.06, yielding a distance $1.93 + 3.06 = 4.99$ from s. Edge sc has length 3.33, yielding a distance $0 + 3.33 = 3.33$ from s. One can see that sc is the appropriate edge to add to T.

We can state Dijkstra's algorithm succinctly: see Algorithm 8.1.

Algorithm: DIJKSTRA'S ALGORITHM
$T \leftarrow \{s\}$
while $t \notin T$ do
     Find an edge $e \in G - T$ that augments T to reach a node x
          whose distance from s is minimum
     $T \leftarrow T + e$

Algorithm 8.1 Dijkstra's shortest path algorithm

Time Complexity

Analyzing the time complexity of Dijkstra's algorithm is an interesting exercise in the analysis of algorithms,[3] but a little off from our interests here. So, we will just sketch some issues and leave a full analysis as an exercise.

---

[3]See, e.g., Albertson and Hutchinson (1988, pp. 390–394) or Chartrand and Oellermann (1993, p. 106).

The while loop cannot execute more than n times, as each edge added to T reaches a new node, and there are n nodes total. The number of candidate edges to examine for each step of the loop is potentially $O(n^2)$, since a visibility graph can have a quadratic number of edges. This gives a crude bound of $O(n^3)$. One can see, however, that it is wasteful to examine these edges afresh at each iteration, and in fact the algorithm can be implemented to run in $O(n^2)$ time (Exercise 8.2.4[2]). Together with the $O(n^2)$ construction of the visibility graph, this gives the following theorem.

Theorem 8.2.2. *A shortest path for a point moving among polygon obstacles with a total of n vertices, can be found in $O(n^2)$ time and space.*

8.2.4. Exercises

1. *Strengthen visibility graph lemma*? Can Lemma 8.2.1 be strengthened to say that a shortest path never includes a reflex vertex of a polygon?

2. *Complexity of Dijkstra's algorithm.* Show that Dijkstra's algorithm can be implemented to run in $O(n^2)$ time.

3. *Disk obstacles.* Design and analyze an algorithm for finding a shortest path for a point amidst n disjoint disk obstacles.

4. *Visibility graph* [programming]. Write a program to construct the visibility graph for a set of polygons. Just implement the brute-force $O(n^3)$ algorithm. Use as much of the triangulation code from Chapter 1 as possible.

5. *Number of shortest paths.* For polygon obstacles with a total of n vertices (not counting s and t), what is the largest number of equal-length shortest paths possible?

6. *Unit disks* [(b) open].

    a. Suppose that all obstacles are unit disks, disjoint as usual. Must a shortest path between s and t be monotonic with respect to the segment st?

    b. Design a subquadratic algorithm for finding a shortest path in the presence of unit disks.

7. *Shortest path in a polygon* (Guibas, Hershberger, Leven, Sharir, and Tarjan, 1987). Design an algorithm to find a shortest path between two points inside a polygon. Try to beat $O(n^2)$.

8.3. MOVING A DISK

We now commence our study of motion planning algorithms where the goal is to find any path (if one exists), rather than a shortest path. We proceed in three increasingly complex stages: moving a disk, translating a convex polygon (Section 8.4), and moving a segment with rotation (Section 8.5). Only in this latter section will we consider a variety of approaches.

Suppose the robot R is a disk centered on s, and the goal is to move it so that it becomes centered on t, while never penetrating an obstacle. As before, the

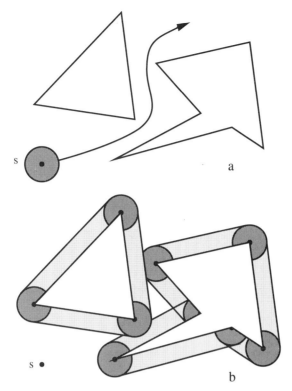

FIGURE 8.4 Enlarging a polygon by a disk: (*a*) a non-free path; (*b*) expanded obstacles.

obstacles are disjoint polygons. The path shown in Figure 8.4a is not a free path, as the robot is too wide to fit through the indicated channel. There is a useful way to view the problem that makes it obvious that this path is not free; and this view extends nicely to more complicated situations. Let r be a reference point on the moving disk R, say its center. Then, r cannot get too close to any particular polygon P: in fact, r cannot move closer than the disk radius ρ to P. This suggests that we consider an "expanded" obstacle P' for the purposes of moving the point r, expanded by ρ. Effectively, we shrink the robot to a point and grow the obstacles by ρ, thereby reducing the problem to moving a point among obstacles.

What does the enlarged P' look like for any given P? Its boundary can be obtained by tracing out what happens to r when the disk is moved around the boundary of P, tracking ∂P. This is illustrated in Figure 8.4b. It should be clear that if r stays outside of P', R will not intersect P; and if r is inside P', then R must intersect P. Figure 8.4b now makes it quite clear that the path in Figure 8.4a is not possible, as the grown obstacles overlap in the channel.

Our description of P' is somewhat vague. We can be more precise by using the notion of the "Minkowski sum" of two point sets.

8.3.1. Minkowski Sum

Let A and B be two sets of points in the plane. If we establish a coordinate system, the points can be viewed as vectors in that coordinate system. Define the *sum* of A and B in the most natural manner possible: $A + B = \{x + y \mid x \in A, y \in B\}$, where $x + y$ is vector sum of the two points. This is known as the *Minkowski sum* of A and B. It will be a little easier to grasp the meaning of this abstract idea by considering the Minkowski sum of a point x and a set B: $x + B = \{x + y \mid y \in B\}$. This is just a copy of B translated by the vector x, for each point y of B is moved by x. So $A + B = \bigcup_{x \in A}(x + B)$ is the union of copies of B, one for each $x \in A$. Now, suppose A is a polygon P, and B is a disk R centered on the origin. Then $P + R$ can be viewed as many copies of R, translated by x for all $x \in P$. Since R is centered on the origin, $x + R$ will be centered on x. So $P + R$ amounts to placing a copy of R centered on top of every point of P. Now, it should be clear that $P + R$ is precisely the expanded region P'.

Let us examine the expansion of the triangle obstacle in Figure 8.4b. A copy of R is placed at each vertex of the triangle when x is a vertex, and when x lies on an edge, the tangents between these vertex disks are generated. For x interior to the triangle, $x + R$ lies inside P'.

8.3.2. Conceptual Algorithm

We return now to the problem of moving a disk among polygonal obstacles. We will sketch a conceptual algorithm, but will not provide details. First, grow every obstacle by the disk R by constructing the Minkowski sum with R. We have not described how the grown obstacles can be constructed algorithmically; this issue we defer to the next section. Second, form the union of the grown obstacles. Again, we do not discuss how this can be done; it is not trivial. If t, the destination, is in a different "component" of the plane than is s, there is no free path from s to t. If they are in the same component, there is a path, and the shortest path can be found by modifying the visibility graph to include the appropriate arcs of the circles. We will not describe this algorithm any further, but it can be accomplished all in $O(n^2 \log n)$ time (Chew, 1985).

8.4. TRANSLATING A CONVEX POLYGON

When the robot is a convex polygon, we come to a serious complication: rotation of the robot might be necessary to move from one location to another. We will defer consideration of rotation until Section 8.5. Here, we restrict the motion to translations only.

The task is still more complicated than moving a disk, but fortunately the idea of growing obstacles by Minkowski sums still works. We explain the basic idea with an example before discussing algorithmic details.

8.4.1. Minkowski Sum Example

Let the robot R be a square, and choose the reference point r to be its lower left corner. Consider a polygon P such as the pentagon shown in Figure 8.5. As R moves around ∂P, r traces out the boundary of P', an expanded obstacle that defines the region of the plane where r cannot penetrate. Note that the situation is somewhat different from that with a disk, since we chose the reference point at a corner of R: P grows by a different amount along each edge. For example, along edge e_0, P and P' match, since it is possible for r to touch e_0. The offset of P' from edges e_1 and e_4 of P is different: the width of R horizontally from e_1, and the height of R vertically from e_4. In addition, note what happens near the reflex vertex: if we trace the complete lengths of the two edges incident to it, r traces out a self-crossing path, whose "outside" nevertheless precisely represents the physical limits of R's approach to P.

8.4.2. Minkowski Subtraction

With R a disk, we argued that $P' = P + R$, but that clearly will not work in Figure 8.5: for example, $P + R$ will "stick out" beyond edge e_0 of P, but P' does not. The appropriate computation is rather to take the Minkowski sum of P with a reflection of R through the reference point r. Since r is the origin for the purposes of the Minkowski sum formulation, this reflected version of R is simply $-R$, where every point of R is negated. Now we can see that P' in Figure 8.5 is $P + (-R) = P - R$. Note that because a disk is centrally symmetric

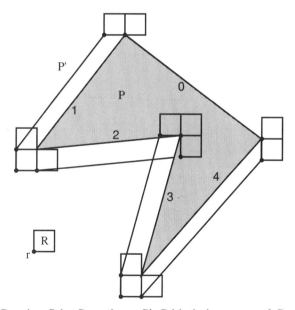

FIGURE 8.5 Growing P by R produces P'. Critical placements of R near the vertices of P are shown.

about its center, $R = -R$, so this new formulation is consistent with our presentation in the previous section. Because Minkowski subtraction is just addition of a reflected region, we will continue to call it Minkowski addition.[4] We formalize our discussion with a slightly more general claim.[5]

Theorem 8.4.1. *Let* R *be a region* (*the robot*) *containing the origin, and* r $\in$ R *be a reference point at the origin. Let* P *be an obstacle. Then the region* P' = P $-$ R *is the set of points forbidden to* r *in the sense that:*

1. *If* R *is translated so that* r *is strictly interior to* P', *then* R *penetrates* P.
2. *If* R *is translated so that* r *lies on* ∂P', *then* ∂R *touches* ∂P.
3. *If* R *is translated so that* r *is strictly exterior to* P', *then* R$\cap$P = $\varnothing$.

This is slightly more general in that neither R nor P need be convex, nor must they even be polygons. We continue to assume in this section that both are polygons, and R is convex.

8.4.3. Constructing the Minkowski Sum

We now sketch a method for constructing the Minkowski sum of two polygons. To keep focused on motion planning, rather than on the fascinating problems it engenders, full details are not provided, but rather relegated to the exercises.

We continue to use the example started in Figure 8.5. Figure 8.6b shows $P' = P - R$, with edges of P labeled $0, \ldots, 4$, edges of $-R$ labeled $a, \ldots, d$, both according to counterclockwise traversals, and edges of P' labeled among $\{0, 1, 2, 3, 4, a, b, c, d\}$ according to which edge of P or $-R$ "generates" it. Thus, when R scrapes along edge 2 of P, the reference point r traces out a parallel edge of P' we label 2, and when R scrapes along c vertically at the vertex at the intersection of edges 1 and 2 of P, we label that edge of P' c, also.

Note that we have labeled the entire self-intersecting polygonal path τ that "bounds" P', including edges in the vicinity of the reflex vertex that are inside P'. It is easiest to approach P' by first constructing τ, which is sometimes called the *convolution* of P and $-R$ (Guibas, Ramshaw, and Stolfi, 1983).

The pattern of labels of the edges of τ can be neatly understood from a "star" diagram of the edge vectors of P and R', shown in Figure 8.6a. If we think of P as large and R as small, as in our running example, then roughly speaking τ has edges corresponding to those of P, interspersed with some edges of $-R$. Indeed, one can see that the sequence of labels for τ, $(0, b, 1, c, d, 2, a, b, 3, c, d, 4, a)$, includes $(0, 1, 2, 3, 4)$ as a subsequence. The star diagram gives a mechanism for predicting the interspersed labels of $-R$.

Consider each edge a vector directed according to a counterclockwise traversal, and move them all to a common origin, as shown in Figure 8.6a. Call this arrangement of edge vectors the *star diagram*. Now, starting with 0, circle

---

[4]Also the term "Minkowski subtraction" is sometimes used for another concept (Guggenheimer, 1977).
[5]This seems to have been used first by Jarvis (1983).

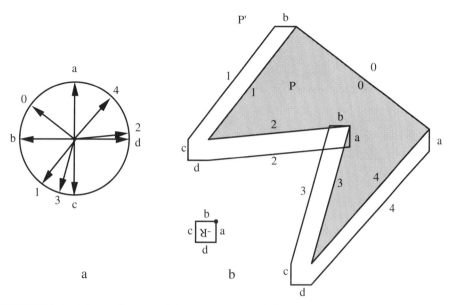

FIGURE 8.6 (*a*) star diagram of the edge vectors; (*b*) convolution edges labeled with *P* or −*R* labels.

around the star counterclockwise. Between the indices i and $i + 1$ of P edges, write down all the indices of $-R$ encountered. Thus, between 0 and 1, b is encountered, yielding the subsequence $(0, b, 1)$. Between 1 and 2, c and d are encountered, yielding the subsequence $(1, c, d, 2)$. Continuing in this manner, we generate the entire sequence for τ by the time 0 is reached again.

From τ, we must then construct P', another interesting problem we do not explore (Guibas, et al., 1983). Although the details are not clear, it at least should be clear that a determinant procedure exists for constructing P' from P and R. We jump now to a statement of the complexity of computing $P - R$ under a variety of convexity assumptions:

Theorem 8.4.2. *If* P *has* n *vertices, and* R *has a fixed (constant) number of vertices, then the Minkowski sum* P − R *can be constructed in these time complexities:*

R	P	Size of Sum	Time Complexity
convex	convex	$O(n)$	$O(n)$
convex	nonconvex	$O(n)$	$O(n^2 \log n)$
nonconvex	nonconvex	$O(n^2)$	$O(n^2 \log n)$

These results were obtained by Guibas et. al. (1983), Toussaint (1983*b*), Sharir (1987), and Kaul, O'Connor, and Srinivasan (1991). Note, we view the size of the robot to be some fixed constant number of vertices, and only report

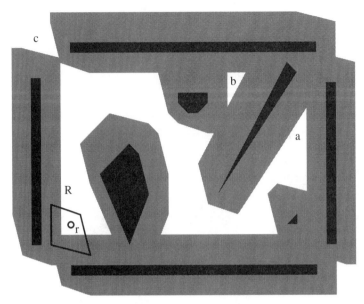

FIGURE 8.7 Robot R with reference point and origin r shown in lower left corner. Dark polygons are obstacles. The grown obstacles, each the Minkowski sum with $-R$, are shown lightly shaded.

complexities with respect to n, the number of vertices of the obstacle polygon. Exercises 8.4.5[4–6] explore complexities as a function of the number of robot vertices.

8.4.4. Conceptual Algorithm

Again we will only provide a rough sketch of an algorithm for planning the motion of a convex polygon R. Let the obstacles be $P_1, P_2, \ldots, P_m$ with a total of n vertices. The algorithm consists of four steps:

1. Grow all obstacles: $P_i' = P_i - R$.
2. Form their union $P' = \bigcup_i P_i'$.
3. Find the component containing s and t.
4. Find a path between s and t in that component.

Figure 8.7 illustrates the process with a quadrilateral robot R and eight obstacles (dark shading). Note that in this example, the free space has three connected components, containing the points a, b, and c. From the initial robot position shown, a is reachable, but both b and c are unreachable. Thus, deciding whether or not a goal position t is reachable from s is reduced to determining whether s and t are in the same connected component of the free space, and planning a path for the robot reduces to finding a path for the reference point within this component.

All four of the above steps present interesting algorithmic issues, none of which we explore here. In light of the apparent intricacy of the scheme, it is a testimony to the many researchers who worked on aspects of this problem that Kedem and Sharir (1990) were able to achieve the remarkable complexity of $n \log n$:

Theorem 8.4.3. *Finding a series of translations that move a convex polygonal robot between given start and termination positions, avoiding polygonal obstacles with a total of n vertices, can be accomplished in $O(n \log n)$ time. More precisely, if the robot has k vertices, the complexity is $O(kn \log(kn))$.*

8.4.5. Exercises

1. *Sum of square and triangle* [easy]. What is the largest number of edges the Minkowski sum of a square and a triangle can have?

2. *Star diagram*.

   a. Detail the algorithm suggested for computing the Minkowski sum of a convex R and a convex P, using the star diagram, and prove that it works.

   b. Extend the analysis in (a) to cover a convex R and a nonconvex P.

3. *Convex-convex convolution* [programming]. Write a program to compute the Minkowski sum of two convex polygons.

4. *Convex-convex* [easy]. Prove that the Minkowski sum of two convex polygons R and P of k and n vertices, respectively, can have $\Omega(k + n)$ vertices.

5. *Convex-nonconvex*. Prove that the Minkowski sum of a convex polygon R and a (perhaps nonconvex) polygon P of k and n vertices, respectively, can have $\Omega(kn)$ vertices.

6. *Nonconvex-nonconvex*. Prove that the Minkowski sum of two (perhaps nonconvex) polygons R and P of k and n vertices respectively, can have $\Omega(k^2n^2)$ vertices.

7. *Union of convex regions* [difficult] What is the largest possible number of vertices of the union of m convex polygons with a total of n vertices? Express your answer as a function of n and m.

   a. First guess an upper bound, supported with examples.

   b. Prove your bound. (Kedem, Livne, Pach, and Sharir, 1986)

8.5. MOVING A LADDER

The most complicated rigid-robot motion planning problem we consider is moving a line segment robot among polygonal obstacles. The segment is often called a *ladder* (or sometimes a *rod*). What makes this complicated is that, in contrast with the previous sections, here we allow rotation.

Rotation gives the ladder three "degrees of freedom" in its motion: two of translation (e.g., horizontal and vertical), and one of rotation. This means that it is not possible to transform a general instance of this problem to that of a point moving in two dimensions (as we did in the previous two sections), since such a point has two degrees of freedom. However, it is possible to reduce any ladder problem to a motion planning problem of a point robot moving in a three-dimensional obstacle space. The beautiful idea that permits this transformation was first annunciated by Lozano-Pérez and Wesley (1979). We will explain it with the simple example shown in Figure 8.8*a*. The ladder *L* is initially horizontal; we would like it to follow the path indicated in (a). But it can only do so by rotation. Figure 8.8*b* grows the obstacles by the Minkowski sum of the objects with the horizontal ladder, as described in the previous section. That *C* grows to overlap *A* and *B* clearly shows that *L* cannot pass through the channel without rotating. Part *c* of the figure shows the grown obstacles when the ladder is rotated by 30°, and in part *d* the ladder is rotated 60°. In *d* the vertical channel between *A* and *C* has opened up, while the horizontal channel between *A* and *B* has closed. These figures show that the ladder can follow a

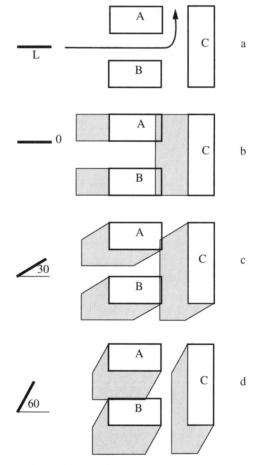

FIGURE 8.8 Rotating the ladder permits it to pass between *A* and *B* and move up, following the path indicated in *a*. *b–d* show the grown obstacles for $\theta = 0, 30°, 60°$, with the ladder reference its left endpoint.

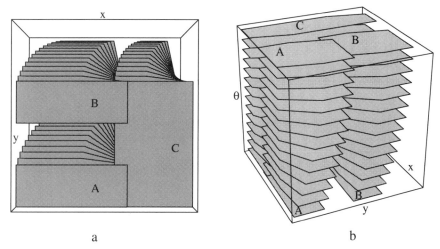

FIGURE 8.9 (*a*) View from underneath the stacks of grown obstacles, with the bottom corresponding to $\theta = 0$, Figure 8.7*b*. (*b*) Front view of same stacks; θ varies from 0 at the bottom of the box to 75° on top.

path indicated in *a*, by moving between *A* and *B* with little or no rotation and then by rotating counterclockwise 60° or more before moving vertically.

Now imagine stacking all the grown obstacles for all possible rotation values θ, all in parallel planes, as depicted in Figure 8.9. Each point (x, y, θ) in this space represents a position of the reference point of the ladder; the plane on which it lies represents the rotation θ. Thus, we have achieved what was claimed above: we have transformed the problem of moving a ladder in two dimensions, to an equivalent problem of moving a point in three dimensions. This three-dimensional space is known as the *configuration space* for the robot/ladder.

Although perhaps not evident from Figure 8.9, the obstacles are not polyhedral. In each θ-plane they are polygonal, but they twist along the θ direction, producing complex shapes. The space in which the reference point is free to move is called the *free space*. Were you standing at the start position *s* in this space, you would see a cavernous chamber with twisted walls. There is a path for the ladder iff *t* is in the same connected component of the free space as is *s*.

It should be evident that there is nothing special about a ladder: we could as well obtain a configuration space for an arbitrary polygonal robot among polygonal obstacles, by the same technique. Indeed, the basic idea extends to three-dimensional robots and obstacles, and even to jointed robots.

Constructing a representation for a configuration space, and then finding a path inside of it, is a challenging task. However, its importance has fostered intense research, and these configuration spaces are indeed constructed, sometimes in as high as six-dimensional space, and then navigated to construct paths for the corresponding robot. Lozano-Pérez (1983) contains a general discussion, and Brost (1991) contains some stunning images of various configuration spaces.

We now sketch two different methods for solving motion planning problems by finding a free path through configuration space. Although both methods are quite general, we only discuss the case of moving a ladder.

8.5.1. Cell Decomposition

The first general method invented for solving motion planning problems was the *cell decomposition* method, developed in a remarkable series of five papers by Schwartz and Sharir, the "piano movers" papers.[6] These papers established that a wide variety of motion planning problems can be solved with polynomial-time algorithms, with the exact complexity depending on the details of the problem. Here, I outline roughly their technique applied to the ladder problem, as detailed by Leven and Sharir (1987).

Definition of a Cell

The essence of the cell decomposition approach is to partition the unruly configuration space into a finite number of well-behaved "cells" and to determine a path in the space by finding a path between cells. Consider the environment shown in Figure 8.10: it consists of two triangle obstacles and a bounding (open) polygonal wall. The ladder L is horizontal, with its reference point to the left, at the arrow head. For the moment we only look at a single orientation of L, horizontal as shown. A cell is a connected region within the free space of the appropriate configuration space. Because we have fixed the ladder's orientation, the configuration space is just the plane, and the free space is what remains after growing the obstacles by the Minkowski sum with the ladder. To get a precise definition of a cell, we assign labels to every obstacle edge,[7] as is done in the figure; we use the label ∞ to represent a "surrounding" edge infinitely far away. Suppose we place the ladder's reference point at a point x not on the same horizontal as any vertex. Then, moving L horizontally forward (left) will cause it to bump into some (one) obstacle edge eventually, as will moving it backward (right). Label the point x with this pair of edge labels. A *cell* is a collection of free points all with the same forward/backward label pairs. In Figure 8.10, cell A has labels $(3,2)$; cell B has labels $(3,8)$; cell C has labels $(1,9)$; and no cell has labels $(3,6)$ because there are no free points between those two edges.

Connectivity Graph G_θ

In the cell decomposition approach, the cell structure is represented with a graph, the *connectivity graph* G_θ. The subscript indicates that this graph captures the structure for a particular orientation of the ladder θ. The nodes of G_θ are the cells, and two nodes are connected by an arc if the cells touch: if their boundaries share at least one point. So G_θ is something like the duals consid-

---

[6]Schwartz and Sharir (1983a), Schwartz and Sharir (1983b), Schwartz and Sharir (1983c), Sharir and Ariel-Sheffi (1984), Schwartz and Sharir (1984). All five are collected in Hopcroft, Schwartz, and Sharir (1987).

[7]Also labels should be assigned to the vertices, but we will ignore this minor complication here. See Leven and Sharir (1987).

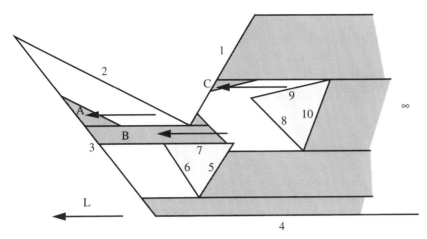

FIGURE 8.10 Cell decomposition, ladder horizontal. Integer labels index edges.

ered in Chapter 1 (Section 1.2.3) and Chapter 4 (Section 4.4). Note that G_0 corresponding to the cells in Figure 8.10 will be disconnected: there is no path in G_0 between cells A and C.

The importance of this graph is that motion planning within a cell is trivial, so that a path in the graph can be easily converted into a path for the ladder. Moreover, the ladder can only move from one cell to another if there exists a path in the graph between these cells.

Critical Orientations

Now we incorporate rotation in a manner similar to the plane-stacking idea used previously. If we rotate the ladder slightly, the connectivity graph for the obstacles in Figure 8.9 normally will not change: all the cells will change shape, but they will remain and will maintain their cell adjacencies. However, when the rotation exceeds some *critical orientation* θ^*, the combinatorial structure of G_{θ^*} will be different from that of G_0.

The $\theta = 0$ orientation shown in Figure 8.9 is critical because there are obstacle edges parallel to L. Thus a slight rotation of L counterclockwise about its reference point will create a $(7, 8)$ cell, and a $(4, \infty)$ cell. Further rotation to the orientation of obstacle edge e_9 causes cell C to disappear, since no points any longer have label $(1, 9)$. The cell decomposition at this orientation is shown in Figure 8.10.

As the reader might guess, critical orientations all involve the alignment of the ladder with either edges of obstacles or two obstacle vertices. Thus, there are at most $O(n^2)$ critical orientations.

Connectivity graph G

Now the idea is to form one grand connectivity graph G that incorporates the information in all the G_θ graphs. We extend the definition of a cell to represent regions of the three-dimensional configuration space, all of whose points have

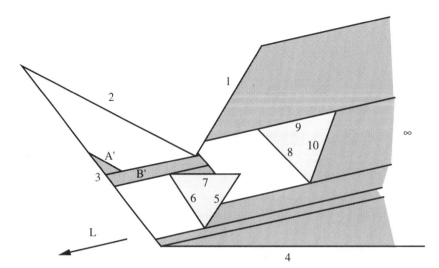

FIGURE 8.11   Cell decomposition, ladder tilted.

the same forward/backward label pairs. This amounts to stacking the cells for
fixed orientations on top of one another in the θ direction. Thus, the points in
cell A in Figure 8.10 are in the same three-dimensional cell as the points in cell
A' in Figure 8.11. Each distinct three-dimensional cell is a node of G, and again
two nodes are connected by an arc if their cells touch.

G may be constructed by building G_0, initializing $G \leftarrow G_0$, and then moving
through all critical orientations in sorted order, modifying G_θ along the way,
and incorporating the changes into G. We will not present any details (see
Leven and Sharir (1987)), but the reader should see that construction of G is
possible.

Again motion planning within a single cell represented by a node of G is not
difficult, and moving between touching cells is also not difficult. For example,
one could move from the interior of a cell to its boundary, and then move along
the boundary to a point shared with an adjacent cell. So the problem of motion
planning is reduced to a graph problem: finding a path between the node
corresponding to the cell containing s, to the node corresponding to the cell
containing t. If there is no such path in G, there is no path for the ladder, and if
there is a path in G, it can be used as a guide for planning the motion of the
ladder.

8.5.2. Retraction

A rather different but no less general technique for solving motion planning
problems is the *retraction* method of Ó'Dúnlaing and Yap (1985). Here, we
sketch the idea applied to moving a ladder; details are in Ó'Dúnlaing, Sharir,
and Yap (1986) and Ó'Dúnlaing, Sharir, and Yap (1987).

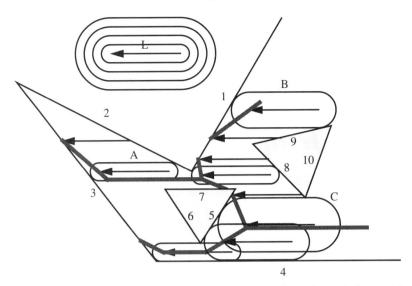

FIGURE 8.12 Voronoi diagram for a ladder. *A*, *B*, and *C* mark particular positions of the ladder.

Voronoi Diagram

The essence of retraction is to construct a "Voronoi diagram" for the ladder, and then "retract" from *s* and *t* to this diagram, and perform path planning within the "network" of the diagram. First, we explain what a Voronoi diagram means in this context.

Recall from Chapter 5 (Section 5.2) that points on the edges of a Voronoi diagram are "equidistant" from at least two sites (vertices of the diagram are equidistant from at least three sites). For a fixed orientation of the ladder *L*, we define the Voronoi diagram of the obstacles with respect to *L* to be the set of free points *x* such that, when the ladder's reference point is placed at *x*, *L* is equidistant from at least two obstacle points.

We must define distance to *L*. The distance of a point *p* to *L* is the minimum length of any line segment from *p* to a point on *L*. Just as the points at distance *r* from a point form a circle, the points a distance *r* from *L* form a "racetrack": an oval formed by two edges parallel to *L* connected by half circles. Nested racetracks are shown in Figure 8.12 surrounding *L*. The same figure shows the Voronoi diagram as shaded lines, together with several sample ladder positions. For example, in position *A*, *L* is equidistant from e_3 and e_2; in position *B*, it is equidistant from e_1 and e_9; in position *C*, it is equidistant from e_5 and the vertex common to e_8 and e_{10}. We can see that the diagram is disconnected: there is no path from *A* to *B*.

This diagram has the pleasant property that, when moving *L* so that its reference point stays on diagram edges, it prudently places *L* as far from nearby obstacles as possible, since all these positions are equidistant from two or more obstacle points. This is a very useful feature for a robot who is trying to avoid collisions with obstacles.

From here, the strategy should sound familiar. We imagine stacking Voronoi diagrams for each value of θ orthogonal to the θ axis, thereby forming a Voronoi diagram for all of configuration space. One can see that the diagram consists of twisted "sheets" formed by the stacking of edges, and "ribs," where two sheets meet, formed by the stacking of vertices.

Retraction

Again the problem will be reduced to a graph search but in a rather different manner than in the cell decomposition approach. The ribs between Voronoi sheets form a network of curves on the Voronoi diagram in configuration space. These curves form a graph N in the natural manner: interpret each curve as an arc, and the point where two or more curves meet as a node.

The final step involves two *retractions* of the start and termination points s and t: the first retraction maps these points to the Voronoi surface, and the second maps from there to the network. Let s' and t' be these retracted points on the network. Then, there is a path for the ladder from s to t iff there is a path in the network from s' to t', which can be determined by searching the graph N.

8.5.3. Complexity

So far, we have said little about the complexity of planning motion for a ladder. Rather than attempt to analyze the complexity of the above incompletely-specified algorithms, we will sketch a short history of the complexities obtained for moving a ladder in two and in three dimensions, which illustrates, if nothing else, the doggedness of the community's pursuit.

The two-dimensional problem, which we have been discussing in this section, has received considerable attention, serving as something of a test bed for algorithmic ideas. The first solution was obtained in the first piano movers paper, and subsequently there were a variety of improvements (not all of which are reflected in the asymptotic time complexity). I showed that there are configurations of obstacles that force any solution path to have a quadratic number of distinct "moves," establishing a lower bound on any algorithm that prints them out. This lower bound was finally reached in 1990. The time complexities are shown in the table below.

Authors	Time Complexity
Schwartz and Sharir (1983*a*)	$O(n^5)$
Ó'Dúnlaing, et. al (1987)	$O(n^2 \log n \log^* n)$
Leven and Sharir (1987)	$O(n^2 \log n)$
Sifrony and Sharir (1987)	$O(n^2 \log n)$
Vegter (1990)	$O(n^2)$
O'Rourke (1985*b*)	$\Omega(n^2)$

We have not discussed the problem of moving a ladder in three dimensions, among polyhedral obstacles. It is of course much more complicated, leading to a five-dimensional configuration space. Again, the first algorithm was achieved by cell decomposition, with a formidable time complexity. The fastest algorithm to date employs Canny's "roadmap" algorithm, which is another general technique for solving motion planning problems. In this instance, there remains at this writing a gap with the best lower bound.

Authors	Time Complexity
Schwartz and Sharir (1984)	$O(n^{11})$
Ke and O'Rourke (1987)	$O(n^6 \log n)$
Canny (1987)	$O(n^5 \log n)$
Ke and O'Rourke (1988)	$\Omega(n^4)$

The strongest general result on motion planning is that of Canny (1987):

Theorem 8.5.1. *Any motion planning problem in which the robot has* d *degrees of motion freedom, can be solved in* $O(n^d \log n)$ *time.*

Although this is the best general result, specific problem instances have asymptotically faster algorithms. For example, a ladder in two dimensions has three degrees of freedom, and Canny's result implies there is an $O(n^3 \log n)$ algorithm; but we have already seen this has been improved by a factor of $n \log n$.

8.5.4. Exercises

1. *Shape of cells.* For moving a ladder in two dimensions via the cell decomposition approach (Section 8.5.1), prove or disprove the following:

   a. Every cell represented by a node of G_θ is convex.

   b. Every cell represented by a node of G is convex.

2. *Ladder Voronoi diagrams.* Prove or disprove that the ladder Voronoi diagram for a fixed orientation of the ladder consists of straight segments only.

3. $\Omega(n^2)$ *connected components.* Construct an example that establishes that the connectivity graph G for moving a ladder can have $\Omega(n^2)$ distinct components.

4. *Worst chair through a doorway* [open]. Let a *doorway* be a vertical line, say coinciding with the y-axis, with the open segment from $y = 0$ to $y = 1$ removed. A polygon is said to *fit through the doorway*, if there is a continuous motion that moves it from the left of the doorway to the right without the interior of the polygon ever intersecting the rays above and below the doorway: from $y = 1$ upward and from $y = 0$ downward. In this problem you are to concoct a class of polygons of n vertices that all fit through the doorway but require a large number of distinct moves to pass through the doorway. For this to make sense, we need to define what constitutes a "move."

   Fix a reference point r in the polygon. Then any continuous motion of the polygon can be viewed as a continuous translation of and rotation about r, continuous with respect to a time parameter t. Thus, a motion of the polygon can be represented by

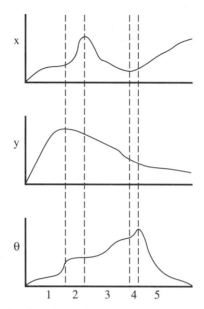

FIGURE 8.13   Motion functions of time. This motion counts as five "moves."

three functions $x(t)$, $y(t)$, and $\theta(t)$ specifying the translation of r, and the rotation about r.

Imagine plotting these functions with respect to time; see Figure 8.13. We consider a *move* to encompass a maximal interval of time during which all three functions are monotonic, either increasing or decreasing. The task is to find polygons that require the most moves under this definition, with respect to the number of polygon vertices. These are the shapes that are the most difficult in some sense to move through a doorway.

The "worst" polygons I know of require $n/2$ moves (Jones and O'Rourke, 1990), but the only upper bound is $O(n^2)$ (Yap, 1987*b*). Either find a generic example that forces more than a linear number of moves, or prove a smaller upper bound. Even improving on the fraction $1/2$ would be interesting.

8.6. ROBOT ARM MOTION

Problem Definition

A subfield of motion planning of considerable practical interest is planning the motion of an anchored "robot arm." In this section, we will examine a particularly simple instance, the planar multilink arm. This is a chain of fixed-length segments, the *links* L_i, $i = 1, \ldots, n$, connected at *joints* J_i, $i = 0, \ldots, n$. J_0 is anchored to the origin, sometimes called the "shoulder" of the arm. J_i for $0 < i < n$ is the joint between L_i and L_{i+1}. J_n is the tip of L_n, sometimes called the "hand." See Figure 8.14.

We will need notation for various quantities associated with a given robot arm. We let ℓ_i be the length of link L_i, and j_i be the angle at joint J_i, measured counterclockwise between L_i and L_{i+1}, treated as vectors from J_{i-1}

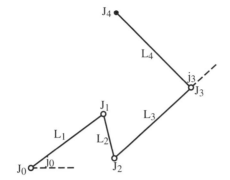

FIGURE 8.14 Notation for a multilink arm.

to J_i and from J_i to J_{i+1} respectively. j_0 is measured from the positive x-axis; j_n is undefined. An *arm A* is specified by its list of link lengths: $(\ell_1, \ldots, \ell_n)$.

We will explore a particularly simple version of the general problem, simple in two respects:

1. We place no restriction on the joint angles. In particular, the arm may self-intersect.

2. We consider the plane to be empty: there are no obstacles.

With these restrictions, we study the *reachability* problem: given n link lengths ℓ_i defining an arm A, and a point in the plane p, determine if A can reach p, and if so, find a set of joint angles that establish $J_n = p$. It will turn out that deciding whether p is reachable (the decision question) is easy, but computing joint angles that realize a solution is more challenging.

History

The algorithmic issues for robot arm motion were first explored in a paper by Hopcroft, Joseph, and Whitesides (1985). They established that the problem with no obstacles (the one studied in this section) is easy, the problem with arbitrary obstacles is hard (the technical term is "NP-hard"), but the problem with the arm confined inside a circle is tractable (polynomial). Since then, a number of other researchers have improved on their circle-confined algorithm (Kantabutra and Kosaraju, 1986), or obtained similar algorithms for different obstacle environments (Kantabutra, 1991*b*; 1991*a*; Kutcher, 1992). See Whitesides (1991) for a general discussion.

8.6.1. Reachability: Decision[8]

What is the set of points reachable by a multilink arm? The answer is surprisingly easy: it is always an origin-centered annulus, the closed set of points

---

[8]The preliminary form of the material in Sections 8.6.1 and 8.6.2 was developed in collaboration with J. Cannon, S. Ghosh, C. Johnston, S. Jones (Dorward), V. Subramanian, and S. Wyman, in a class at Smith College during the spring of 1990. I also benefited from invaluable feedback from a series of lectures I gave at the Faculty Advancement in Mathematics workshop on geometry 1992 (sponsored by COMAP with funding from NSF.)

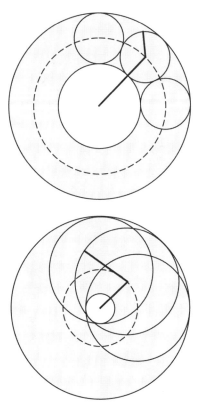

FIGURE 8.15   Reachable region for a two-link arm: (*a*) $\ell_1 > \ell_2$. (*b*) $\ell_1 < \ell_2$.

between two concentric circles. We establish this in Lemma 8.6.1 below, and then proceed to determine in Theorem 8.6.3 the inner and outer radii r_i and r_o of the annulus as a function of the link lengths.

Reachability Region
The region reachable by a one-link arm is a circle centered on the origin, which is a annulus with equal inner and outer radii.

Let $A = (\ell_1, \ell_2)$ be a two-link arm. If $\ell_1 \geq \ell_2$, the reachability region is clearly an annulus with outer radius $r_o = \ell_1 + \ell_2$ and inner radius $r_i = \ell_1 - \ell_2$. See Figure 8.15a. If $\ell_1 = \ell_2, r_i = 0$ and the annulus is a disk of radius r_o.

When $\ell_1 < \ell_2$, the situation is perhaps not so clear, but, as Figure 8.15b shows, the result is again an annulus with $r_o = \ell_1 + \ell_2$ but with $r = \ell_2 - \ell_1$ (or, as it will sometimes be convenient to write, $r_i = |\ell_1 - \ell_2|$).

It is revealing to view the two-link reachablility region as the Minkowski sum of two circles (see Section 8.3.1): on each point on the circle C_1 of radius ℓ_1, center a circle of radius ℓ_2. Thus, the sum of two origin-centered circles is an origin-centered annulus.

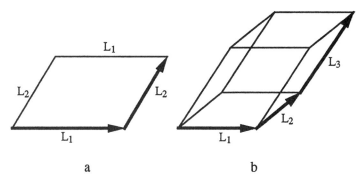

FIGURE 8.16   Parallelograms for (*a*) two links, and (*b*) three links show that the order of the links does not affect reachability.

Moreover, it should now be clear that the sum of an annulus and a circle, both origin-centered, is again an origin-centered annulus. Thus, we have:

Lemma 8.6.1.   *The reachability region for an* n*-link arm is an annulus centered on the origin (shoulder).*

Annulus Radii

Although it is clear that the outer radius of the annulus in Lemma 8.6.1 is obtained by stretching all the links out straight, $r_o = \sum_{i=1}^{n} \ell_i$, the inner radius is not so obvious. We now turn to computing r_i.

Whether or not $r_i > 0$, depends on the relation between the length of the longest link and the lengths of the other links. In particular, $r_i > 0$ iff the longest link is longer than all the other link lengths combined. This is perhaps easiest to see if the longest link is the first link in the arm. We will now show how to view matters this way without loss of generality.

Lemma 8.6.2.   *The region of reachability for an arm is independent of the order in which the links are arranged.*

Proof. This follows from the commutativity of vector addition. Consider, for example, a configuration of a particular two-link arm, as shown in Figure 8.16*a*. The other two sides of the parallelogram clearly reach the same endpoint.[9] The same holds true for a three-link arm, as shown in Figure 8.16*b*, and indeed for an *n*-link arm.   □

We therefore concentrate, without loss of generality, on arms whose first link L_1 is longest. For these arms, it is should be clear from Figure 8.17 that

----

[9]This proof idea is from Dettmers, Doraiswamy, Gorini, and Toy (1992).

FIGURE 8.17 $r_i = \ell_1 - (\ell_2 + \ell_3 + \ell_4)$.

$r_i = \ell_1 - \Sigma_{i=2}^{n} \ell_i$, as long as this sum is positive, and $r_i = 0$ otherwise. We can now summarize our findings, first stated by Hopcroft et al., (1985).[10]

Theorem 8.6.3.   *The reachability region for an* n-*link arm is an origin-centered annulus with outer radius* $r_o = \Sigma_{i=1}^{n} \ell_i$ *and inner radius* $r_i = 0$ *if the longest link length* ℓ_M *is less than half the total length of the links, and* $r_i = \ell_M - \Sigma_{i \neq M} \ell_i$ *otherwise.*

It is an immediate corollary of this theorem that we can decide reachability in $O(n)$ time: find ℓ_M and compute r_o and r_i; then p is reachable iff $r_i \leq |p| \leq r_o$. The theorem, however, gives no hint how to find a configuration that reaches a given point. We now turn to this question.

8.6.1. Reachability: Construction

At first blush, it is not evident how to find a configuration for an *n*-link arm to reach a point within its reachability region. In some sense, there are too many solutions, and methods that attempt to explore methodically all potential solutions can become mired in exponentially-many possibilities. For example, trying to delimit the angle ranges at each joint within which solutions lie, quickly fractures into an exponential number of ranges.

Exploiting the weak requirement that just some one solution is desired, leads to much more efficient algorithms. We examine the two- and three-link problems before jumping to the *n*-link case.

Two-link Reachability
Determining the shoulder angle j_0 for a one-link arm to reach a point on its circle is trivial. Solving a two-link problem is not much more difficult. Let p be the point to be reached. Simply intersect the circle C_1 of radius ℓ_1 centered on the origin (J_0), with the circle C_2 of radius ℓ_2 centered on p. In general, there will be two solutions, but there could be zero, one, two, or an infinite number, depending on how the circles intersect, as shown in Figure 8.18. We will discuss implementing this intersection in Section 8.6.3.

Three-link Reachability
Our general approach will be to reduce multilink problems to two-link problems. Let $A_3 = (\ell_1, \ell_2, \ell_3)$. We know from Lemma 8.6.1 the reachability region

---

[10]They offer no proof in their paper. They remark, incidentally, that the theorem clearly holds in three dimensions as well.

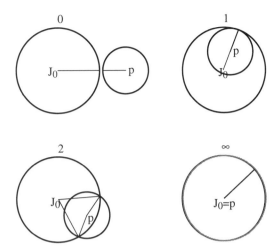

FIGURE 8.18   Two-link reachability: number of solutions shown.

for $A_2 = (\ell_1, \ell_2)$ is an annulus; call it R. Note that all points of the boundary ∂R of R represent configurations of A_2 which are extreme in that either the arms are aligned or antialigned: $j_1 = 0$ or $j_1 = \pi$. In these positions, A_2 acts like a single link of length $\ell_1 + \ell_2$ or $|\ell_1 - \ell_2|$, respectively.

Now examine how the circle C of radius ℓ_3, centered on $p = J_3$, intersects R. Our goal is to reduce three-link solutions to alignments of two links, so that they may be viewed as two-link solutions. We distinguish two cases, depending on whether or not $\partial R \cap C = \varnothing$.

1. Case 1: $\partial R \cap C \neq \varnothing$. (Figure 8.19*a,b*.)

   In this case, the problem can be reduced to a two-link problem by aligning (*a*) or antialigning (*b*) L_1 and L_2. Of course, there are in general infinitely many other solutions, but we restrict ourselves to seeking just one. It will be convenient to avoid antialignment of links, so we analyze Figure 8.19*b* a bit closer.

   Let $\partial R = I \cup O$, where I is the inner and O the outer boundary of the annulus. If $O \cap C = \varnothing$ and $I \cap C \neq \varnothing$ as in Figure 8.19*b*, we can choose a circle C_2 of radius ℓ_2 tangent to C, which permits reaching p by alignment of L_2 and L_3 rather than antialignment of L_1 and L_2. See Figure 8.20.

2. Case 2: $\partial R \cap C = \varnothing$.

   Two further cases can be distinguished here, depending on whether or not C encloses the origin J_0.

   (a) C does not enclose J_0. (Figure 8.19*c*.)

   We claim that again it is possible to find a solution with two links aligned. Let C_2 be a circle of radius ℓ_2 in the annulus R and tangent to C. Then, L_2 and L_3 can be aligned (in a manner similar to Figure 8.20), which again reduces the problem to two links.

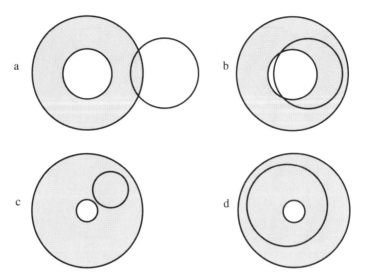

FIGURE 8.19   Three-link reachability. The shaded annulus is R; the other circle is C.

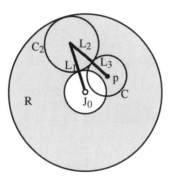

FIGURE 8.20   Aligning links L_2 and L_3 when $C \cap I \neq \varnothing$.

(b) C does enclose J_0. (Figure 8.19d.)

Here there is no solution in which two links align (or antialign), dashing hopes that every three-link problem can be solved by such alignments. There is another feature of this situation that makes it easy to solve nevertheless: there is a solution for every value of j_0! To see this, choose j_0 arbitrarily and draw a circle C_2 centered on J_1. Because C is in the annulus R and encloses the origin, it must enclose I, the inner boundary of R. Since C_2 connects the inner to the outer boundary of R, it must cross C somewhere. That crossing provides a solution for an arbitrary j_0.

Thus, we can reduce this case to two-links after all: choose j_0 arbitrarily, say $j_0 = 0$, and then solve the resulting two-link problem.

We summarize in a lemma:

Lemma 8.6.4.   *Every three-link problem may be solved by one of the following three two-link problems:*

  1. $(\ell_1 + \ell_2, \ell_3)$.
  2. $(\ell_1, \ell_2 + \ell_3)$.
  3. $j_0 = 0$ and (ℓ_2, ℓ_3).

Proof. Figure 8.19a corresponds to (1), Figure 8.19b and Figure 8.20, and Figure 8.19c correspond to (2), and Figure 8.19d corresponds to (3).   □

n-Link Reachability

Linear Algorithm for n-*link Reachability.* Reexamine Figure 8.19, but now imagining the annulus R representing $n - 1$ links of an n-link arm A, with the circle C of radius ℓ_n, centered on p. Since we are assuming A can reach the target point, we know $R \cap C$ is nonempty. Indeed, the possibilities for intersection are just those illustrated in Figure 8.19. This suggests the following recursive procedure[11] for determining a configuration for an n-link arm to reach a given reachable point p.

  1. Case 1: $\partial R \cap C \neq \varnothing$. (Figure 8.19$a$,$b$.)
     Choose one of the (in general) two points of intersection t.
  2. Case 2: $R \supseteq C$. (Figure 8.19c,d.)
     Choose any point t on C, say the point furthest from J_0.

In either case, recursively find a configuration for $A_{n-1} = (\ell_1, \ldots, \ell_{n-1})$ to reach t. Append the last link L_n to this solution to connect t to p (recall C is centered on p). The base of the recursion can be our previously outlined solution to the three-link problem.

Because the cases in Figure 8.19 are exhaustive, this procedure is guaranteed to find a solution (if one exists). That it requires only $O(n)$ time follows from the fact that reducing n by 1 is accomplished in constant time, by intersecting C with O and with I, where $\partial R = I \cup O$.

This then achieves our goal: given a point p to reach and a list of link lengths specifying the arm, first determine if p is reachable with Theorem 8.6.3, and if it is, find a configuration via this recursive procedure.

Two Kinks. Although it is not possible to improve on the asymptotic time complexity of $O(n)$, for it takes that long just to sum the link lengths, there is in fact a significant conceptual simplification possible. One hint is provided by the simplicity of the solution obtained in Case 1 of the above algorithm: the first $n - 1$ links are straightened out if $p \in O$, and they are "kinked" only at the joints on either end of the longest link if $p \in I$. This latter claim follows from the formula for r_i: all links "oppose" L_M (the longest link) to reach a point on

[11]Suggested by Carl Lee.

the inner annulus radius. So, the arm need not have many kinks in Case 1, and in Case 2, p could lie anywhere on C, suggesting that this freedom might be exploited to avoid kinks.

In fact, it is a remarkable theorem that if an n-link arm can reach a point, it can do so with only two kinked joints![12] Moreover, which two joints can be easily determined. The implication of this is that any n-link problem can be directly reduced to one three-link problem! We now proceed to prove this.

Theorem 8.6.5 (Two Kinks). *If an* n-*link arm* A *can reach a point, it can reach it with at most two joints "kinked": only two joints among* $J_1, \ldots, J_{n-1}$ *have nonzero angles. The two joints may be chosen to be those at either end of the "median link": the link* L_m *such that* $\sum_{i=1}^{m-1} \ell_i$ *is less than or equal to half the total length of the links, but* $\sum_{i=1}^{m} \ell_i$ *is more than half.*

Proof.[13] The strategy of the proof is to modify the arm A by "freezing" all but the two indicated joints, and showing that the resulting new arm A' has the same reachability region. A joint is "frozen" by fixing its angle to 0. Note that since r_o depends only on the sum of the link lengths (Theorem 8.6.3), such freezing leaves r_o fixed. So, the onus of the proof is to show that r_i is also unaltered.

Let ℓ be the total length of the links. We partition the work into two cases, depending on whether or not $r_i = 0$.

1. Case $r_i > 0$. (Figure 8.21a.)
   Recall from Theorem 8.6.3 that r_i is nonzero only when the longest link L_M exceeds the length of the remaining links. Then, it must be that $\ell_M > \ell/2$. Therefore, $L_M = L_m$, regardless of where it appears in the sequence of links: because L_M is so long, it covers the midpoint of the lengths under any shift in the sequence.
       Now because $L_m = L_M$ and $\ell_M > \sum_{i \neq M} \ell_i$, if we freeze all joints except those at the endpoints of L_M to form a new arm A', we do not change the fact that L_M is the longest link. (In Figure 8.21a, the longest link length is six in both A and A'.) Since r_i depends only on ℓ and ℓ_M by Theorem 8.6.3 again, A' has the same reachability region as A.

2. Case $r_i = 0$. (Figure 8.21b.)
   In this case, we know from Theorem 8.6.3 that the longest link L_M is $\leq \ell/2$, since $\ell_M \leq \sum_{i \neq M} \ell_i$. Let L_m be the median link and freeze all joints before and after L_m, forming arm A'. This might change which link is longest; in Figure 8.21b, the longest link length is six in A and eight in A'. Note that the new longest link L'_M cannot exceed $\ell/2$ in length: since L_m straddles the midpoint of the lengths, both what precedes it and what follows it must be $\leq \ell/2$. Since r_i is only nonzero when the longest link exceeds $\ell/2$, we are assured that r_i is still zero. Therefore, the reachability region of A' is the same as that of A. □

[12] This result is implicit in the work of Kutcher (1992, pp. 191–193) and of Lenhart and Whitesides (1992). Both works prove stronger results.

[13] This proof was suggested by the participants of the 1992 FAIM workshop on geometry.

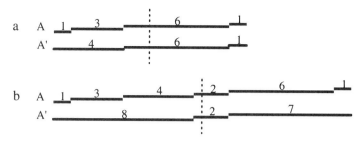

FIGURE 8.21   Two-kinks theorem, with links shown staggered for clarity: (*a*) $\ell/2 = 5.5$, $r_i = 1 > 0$, longest link is the median link; (*b*) $\ell/2 = 8.5$, $r_i = 0$, median link is not the longest link.

Algorithm. The two-kinks theorem gives us an alternative $O(n)$ algorithm, where the only part that depends on n is summing the lengths of the n links: after that the algorithm is constant-time. So, if we count the number of circle-intersection tests performed, the recursive algorithm requires $O(n)$ of these, whereas the two-kinks algorithm only needs $O(1)$. For after identifying L_m, the problem is reduced to a single three-link problem, which is reduced by Lemma 8.6.4 to three two-link problems, each of which performs one circle-intersection test.

8.6.2. Implementation

The implementation of the just-described algorithm is relatively straightforward, although intersecting two circles requires some care. We first describe the top-level procedures before plunging into the circle-intersection detail.

The link lengths are stored in an integer array. Throughout the code we stick to integers until we are forced to use `doubles`, as of course we will be (for circle intersection). This isolates problems that might arise from floating-point calculations. The main routine and data structures are as shown in Code 8.1.

```
int      linklen[NLINKS];      / * link lengths * /
int      nlinks;               / * number of links * /
tPointi  target;               / * target point * /

main( )
{
        ReadTarget( target );
        nlinks = ReadLinks( );

        if ( !Solven( nlinks ) )
          printf("Solven: no solutions!\n");
}
```

Code 8.1 `main`.

```
bool      Solven( int nlinks )
{
          int     i;
          int     m;               /* index of median link */
          int     l1, l2, l3;      /* length of links between kinks */
          int     totlength;       /* total length of all links */
          int     halflength;      /* floor of half of total */

          /* Compute total & half length. */
          totlength = 0;
          for ( i = 0; i < nlinks; i++ )
                  totlength += linklen[i];
          halflength = totlength / 2;


          /* Find median link. */
          l1 = 0;
          for ( m = 0; m < nlinks; m++ ) {
                  if ( (l1 + linklen[m]) > halflength)
                          break;
                  l1 += linklen[m];
          }

          l2 = linklen[m];
          l3 = totlength - l1 - l2;
          if ( Solve3( l1, l2, l3, target ) )
                  return TRUE;
          else return FALSE;
          }
```

Code 8.2 Solven.

The code invokes a cascade of function calls, each reducing the problem to a simpler problem: Solven → Solve3 → Solve2 → TwoCircles → TwoCircles0a → TwoCircles0b → TwoCircles00. The three Solvex routines are boolean functions, returning TRUE iff the target is reachable. The four TwoCirclesx routines compute the number circle intersections, and one point of intersection p. This point is passed back up as J to Solve3, which prints out the solution. We now describe each of the main functions.

The Solven procedure (Code 8.2) identifies the median link, and calls Solve3 with the joints fore and aft of it frozen. Solve3 (Code 8.3) follows Lemma 8.6.4, calling Solve2 as many as three times. Only the last call results in two kinked joints. Solve2 (Code 8.4) simply arranges the arguments for TwoCircles, which intersects two circles.

Intersection of Two Circles

Two circles can clearly be intersected in constant time, so the only issues are practical. Let the two circles C_1 and C_2 have centers $c_i = (a_i, b_i)$ and radii r_i,

```
bool  Solve3( int l1, int l2, int l3, tPointi target )
{
      tPointd Jk;         / * coords of kinked joint returned by Solve2 * /
      tPointi J1;         / * Joint1 on x-axis * /
      tPointi Ttarget;    / * translated target * /

      if ( Solve2( l1 + l2, l3, target, Jk ) ) {
            printf("Solve3: link1=%d, link2=%d, joint=",
                  l1 + l2, l3);
            PrintPointd( Jk );
            return TRUE;
      }
      else if ( Solve2( l1, l2 + l3, target, Jk ) ) {
            printf("Solve3: link1=%d, link2=%d, joint=",
                  l1, l2 + l3);
            PrintPointd( Jk );
            return TRUE;
      }
      else { / * pin J0 to 0. * /
            / * Shift so J1 is origin. * /
            J1[X] = l1; J1[Y] = 0;
            SubVec( target, J1, Ttarget );
            if ( Solve2( l2, l3, Ttarget, Jk ) ) {
                  / * Shift solution back to origin. * /
                  Jk[X] += l1;
                  printf("Solve3: link1 = %, link2 = %, \
link3 = %, \
                        joints=", l1, l2, l3);
                  PrintPointi( J1 );
                  PrintPointd( Jk );
                  return TRUE;
            }
            else    return FALSE;
      }
}
```

Code 8.3 Solve3.

```
bool  Solve2( int l1, int l2, tPointi target, tPointd J )
{
      tPointi c1 = {0,0};     / * center of circle 1 * /
      int nsoln;              / * # of solns: 0, 1, 2, 3(infinite) * /

      nsoln = TwoCircles( c1, l1, target, l2, J );
      return nsoln != 0;
}
```

Code 8.4 Solve2.

```
/*
        TwoCircles finds the intersection points between two circles.
        This is the general routine, no assumptions. One intersection
        point is placed in p, and the number of solutions is returned.
*/
int   TwoCircles( tPointi c1, int r1, tPointi c2, int r2,
                  tPointd p)
{
        tPointi c;

        SubVec( c2, c1, c );
        return TwoCircles0( r1, c, r2, p );
}
```

Code 8.5   TwoCircles. `SubVec` is in Code 3.13.

$i = 1, 2$. Since the equation of a circle is a quadratic equation, on the basis of general algebraic principles,[14] we can expect there to be no more than four intersections. In fact, there can be no more than two intersections because of the special form of the equations. Of course, there can also be zero, one, or an infinite number of intersections, as previously shown in Figure 8.18. The first task is to distinguish these cases, the second to solve the generic two-intersection case.

It will simplify matters considerably to arrange the circles conveniently with respect to the coordinate system. It will be no loss of generality to assume that $c_1 = (0,0)$ and $c_2 = (a_2, 0)$. The sole function of TwoCircles (Code 8.5) is to ensure half of this by translating so that $c_1 = (0,0)$ and calling TwoCircles0a.

TwoCircles0a (Code 8.6) handles all the special cases. Continuing our resolve to stick with integers until forced to floating-point numbers, we detect all special cases in integers. This is possible because we assumed the target point has integer coordinates. Computing $(r_1 + r_2)^2$ and $(r_1 - r_2)^2$ and comparing against the square of the distance to c_2, permits detection of the zero-, one-, and infinite-intersections cases. In the one-intersection cases, we know the point of intersection is at distance r_1 from the origin, a fraction of the way to c_2. For example, if $r_1 = 10$, $r_2 = 15$, and $c_2 = (-3, -4)$, then $(r_1 - r_2)^2 = 25 = |c_2|^2$, and the fraction $f = 10/-5 = -2$ is used to compute the intersection point $p = f \cdot c_2 = (6, 8)$.

If no special case holds, then TwoCircles0a calls TwoCircles0b (Code 8.7). This routine ensures the second half of convenient arrangement within a coordinate system by placing c_2 on the x-axis. It rotates c_2 so that it lies on the x-axis, calls TwoCircles00 to solve the problem in this rotated coordinate system, and rotates back. Rotation is performed by the standard

---

[14] Bezout's Theorem: the number of proper intersections between two plane curves of algebraic degree m and n is at most mn.

```
/ *     TwoCircles0a assumes that the first circle is centered
        on the origin. It handles all the special cases, returning
        the number of intersection points: 0, 1, 2, 3 (inf).
* /
int     TwoCircles0a( int r1, tPointi c2, int r2, tPointd p )
{
        int     dc2;                    / * dist to center 2 squared * /
        int     rplus2, rminus2;        / * (r1 + / − r2)² * /
        double  f;                      / * fraction along c2 for nsoln = 1 * /

        dc2 = Length2( c2 );
        rplus2 = (r1 + r2) * (r1 + r2);
        rminus2 = (r1 - r2) * (r1 - r2);

        / * No solution if c2 out of reach + or − . * /
        if ( ( dc2 > rplus2 ) || ( dc2 < rminus2 ) )
                return 0;

        / * One solution if c2 just reached. * /
        / * Then solution is r1-of-the-way (f) to c2. * /
        if ( dc2 == rplus2 ) {
                f = r1 / (double)(r1 + r2);
                p[X] = f * c2[X];       p[Y] = f * c2[Y];
                return 1;
        }
        if ( dc2 == rminus2 ) {
                if ( rminus2 == 0 ) { / * Circles coincide. * /
                        p[X] = r1;      p[Y] = 0;
                        return 3;
                }
                f = r1 / (double)(r1 - r2);
                p[X] = f * c2[X];       p[Y] = f * c2[Y];
                return 1;
        }

        / * Two intersections. * /
        return TwoCircles0b( r1, c2, r2, p );
}
```

Code 8.6 `TwoCircles0a`. `Length2` is in Code 3.15.

method, well-known in graphics:[15] multiplying the point q by the rotation matrix R:

$$\begin{bmatrix} p_0 \\ p_1 \end{bmatrix} = \begin{bmatrix} \cos\theta & -\sin\theta \\ \sin\theta & \cos\theta \end{bmatrix} \cdot \begin{bmatrix} q_0 \\ q_1 \end{bmatrix}.$$

---

[15]See, e.g., Foley, et. al. (1990, p. 203).

```
/*
        TwoCircles0b also assumes that the first circle is centered
        on the origin. It rotates c2 to lie on the x-axis.
*/
int     TwoCircles0b( int r1, tPointi c2, int r2, tPointd p )
{
        double  a2;                /* center of 2nd circle when rotated to x-axis
*/
        tPointd q;                 /* one solution when c2 on x-axis */
        double  cost, sint;        /* sine and cosine of angle of c2 */

        /* Rotate c2 to a2 on x-axis. */
        a2 = sqrt( (double) Length2( c2 ) );
        cost = c2[X] / a2;
        sint = c2[Y] / a2;

        TwoCircles00( r1, a2, r2, q );

        /* Rotate back */
        p[X] = cost * q[X] + -sint q[Y];
        p[Y] = sint * q[X] + cost q[Y];

        return 2;
}
```

Code 8.7 TwoCircles0b.

Finally, TwoCircles00 (Code 8.8) performs the generic two-intersections computation. The task is to solve these two equations simultaneously:

$$x^2 + y^2 = r_1^2$$

$$(x - a_2)^2 + y^2 = r_2^2.$$

```
/*
        TwoCircles00 assume circle one is origin-centered, and
        that the center of the second circle is at (a2,0).
*/
void    TwoCircles00( int r1, double a2, int r2, tPointd p )
{
        /* Two intersections (only one returned in p). */
        p[X] = ( a2 + ( r1*r1 - r2*r2 ) / a2 ) / 2;
        p[Y] = sqrt( r1*r1 - p[X]*p[X] );
}
```

Code 8.8 TwoCircles00.

Solving the first equation for y^2 and substituting into the second yields $(x - a_2)^2 + r_1^2 - x^2 = r_2^2$, which can be solved for x:

$$x = \frac{1}{2}\left(a_2 + \frac{r_1^2 - r_2^2}{a_2}\right).$$

Note that $a_2 \neq 0$ because we have already eliminated the no-solutions and infinite-solutions cases. From x we solve for y by substituting back into one of the circle equations. The two solutions have the same x coordinate and one y-coordinate the negative of the other. This is the advantage of working in a convenient coordinate system. The remaining utility routines necessary to make working code are straightforward and not shown.

It is unfortunately typical of computational geometry code that a large portion of the effort is spent dispensing of the special cases. In this case, the actual circle intersection is performed in two lines of code but preceded by many other lines arranging that those two lines work correctly.

Example
Consider a four-link arm, with link lengths 10, 1, 4, and 9, respectively, with the goal to reach back to the shoulder, $(0,0)$. `Solven` computes the total length to be 24, and identifies the third link as the median link. It then calls `Solve3(11,4,9)`. This in turn calls `Solve2(15,9)` and `Solve2(11,13)`, both of which fail. We then fall into the third case of the three-link lemma (Lemma 8.6.4): the first joint is fixed at $j_0 = 0$ and `Solve2(4,9)` is called, this time trying to reach $(-11,0)$. This succeeds, returning two solutions, one of which is shown in Figure 8.22.

8.6.3. Exercises

1. *Turning a polygon inside-out.* Imagine a polygon whose edges are rigid links, and whose vertices are joints. "To turn a polygon inside out is to convert it by a continuous motion in the plane to the polygon that is the mirror image (with respect to some arbitrary line in the plane) of the original one" (Lenhart and Whitesides, 1991). Here, the intent is to permit intermediate figures to be self-crossing polygons. Can this be done for every polygon? If so, prove it. If not, find conditions that guarantee configuration inversion.

2. *Division by zero* [programming]. Establish under what conditions division by zero can occur in `TwoCircles0a` (Code 8.6), `TwoCircles0b` (Code 8.7), or `TwoCircles00` (Code 8.8). Do there exist inputs that will force the code to realize these conditions? Test your conclusions on the code.

3. *Reachability region with pole(s).* Decide what is the reachability region of a two-link arm if there are impenetrable obstacles in the plane, for example poles through which the arm may not pass. In particular, consider the following obstacles:

   a. A single point.

   b. Two points.

   c. One disk.

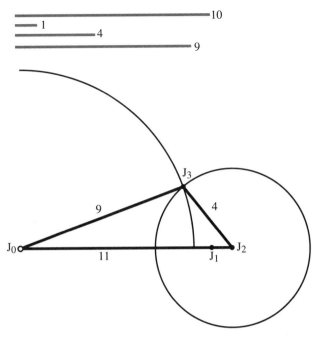

FIGURE 8.22 A four-link example: $A = (10, 1, 4, 9)$. The intersection shown is at $(8.45, 3.09)$ with respect to J_0.

4. *Line tracking*. Define a continuous motion of an arm to be *line tracking* if the hand moves along a straight line (Whitesides, 1991).

    a. Can a two-link arm track a line? Can it track every line?

    b. Can a three-link arm track a line? Can it track every line?

5. *Joint constraints*. Suppose that each joint is only free to move within a certain angular range, $\pm \theta_i$ for j_i.

    a. What is the reachability region of a joint-constrained two-link arm?

    b. What is the reachability region of a joint-constrained three-link arm?

8.7. SEPARABILITY

A number of applications in robotics, circuit layout, and graphics have led to research on a variety of "separability" problems, where objects are to be separated from one another without collision. A typical instance of this problem models the situation faced by movers emptying a house of its contents. Given a collection of disjoint polygons in the plane, may each be moved "to infinity" without disturbing the others? Of course, the motion must be a continuous motion in the plane. Collision avoidance is the same concept as used in the robot motion planning problems: two polygons collide if they share an interior point. Moving "to infinity" means moving arbitrarily far away. Often constraints

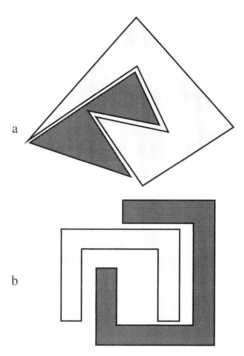

FIGURE 8.23   (*a*) Inseparable polygons; (*b*) inseparable by translations, but separable using rotations.

are placed on the types of movement permitted: for example, translation only. As we will see, it is also important to specify whether only one polygon can move at a time or can several move simultaneously. In this section, we dip into this area just enough to suggest its richness.[16]

8.7.1. Varieties of Separability

Not all collections of polygons are separable, even with no restriction on allowable motions: Figure 8.23*a* shows two interlocked polygons that are inseparable (without lifting one into the third dimension!). Some sets of polygons are separable if rotation is permitted but inseparable via translation only, as are the pair in Figure 8.23*b*.

If only one polygon may be moved at a time, during which time all others stay fixed, it may be that a set of polygons are separable, but only with a huge number of motions. Figure 8.24[17] shows an instance where the configuration is separable by moving A and B alternately to the right, freeing Q to move up and right. The number of moves to get A and B out depends on the gap δ with

[16]See (Toussaint, 1985*b*) for a survey.
[17]Fig. 3.1 from Chazelle, Ottmann, Soisalon-Soininen, and Wood (1984).

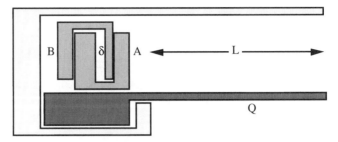

FIGURE 8.24 The number of one-at-a-time moves needed to separate this collection is proportional to L/δ.

respect to the length L: the number of moves is at least L/δ, which can be made arbitrarily large independent of n, the number of vertices. This example hardly seems to demonstrate that the problem is truly difficult, however: it is easy to separate this collection of polygons if two may be moved simultaneously; and even when only one is moved at a time, no polygon has to move a "large" total distance (large with respect to, for example, the diameter of the hull of the original configuration). Nevertheless, we will see that the separability problem is indeed "hard" in these senses.

8.7.2. Separability by Translation

The earliest, and still perhaps the prettiest result on separability, was obtained by Guibas and Yao (1983). They proved that a collection of convex polygons can be separated under the following motion conditions:

1. Translation: all motions are translations.
2. Unidirectional: all translations are in the same (arbitrary) direction.
3. Moved once: each polygon is moved only once.
4. One-at-a-time: only one polygon is moved at a time.

These are severe restrictions, and many otherwise separable polygons are inseparable under them: for example, the pair of polygons in Figure 8.25 are inseparable along the direction u. However, convex polygons (or curved convex shapes, for that matter) are separable under these conditions and along any direction. If the reader finds this intuitively obvious, it may prove a jolt to learn that convex objects in three dimensions are not always separable under these conditions (Exercise 8.7.5[1]).

Application

The work of Guibas and Yao (1983) was motivated by the then-new technology of windows on workstations. Some of these workstations have a hardware instruction that copies a block of screen memory from one location to another.

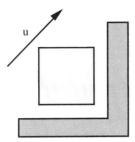

FIGURE 8.25   Inseparable along *u*.

Shifting several windows with this instruction without overwriting memory can be solved by moving each according to a separability ordering.

Separating segments

We start with a special case, which we will soon see suffices to encompass the general case: separating a set of disjoint segments. Let the direction in which the segments are to be separated be the positive *x*-direction; we can choose this without any loss of generality. It should be clear that if we can identify one segment in any collection that can be moved horizontally rightward without colliding with any other, the segments are separable along that direction. For after we move that one to infinity, we have a smaller instance of the same problem, and we can identify another that can be moved, and so on.

Imagine illuminating the segments from $x = +\infty$, as depicted in Figure 8.26. Our question becomes: Must there always be one segment completely illuminated?

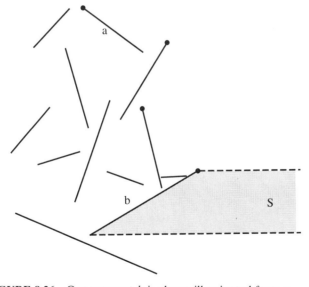

FIGURE 8.26   One segment *b* is always illuminated from $x = +\infty$.

Lemma 8.7.1.   *In any collection of disjoint line segments, there is always at least one that is completely illuminated from* x $= +\infty$.

Proof. We first examine the subset U of segments whose upper endpoint is illuminated, that is, a horizontal rightward ray from their upper endpoint does not hit any segment. Certainly U is not empty: consider the segments whose upper endpoint is highest. If there is just one, it is in U. If there are several tied for highest, the one with the rightmost upper endpoint is in U (segment a in Figure 8.26).

As the figure shows, this rightmost highest segment is not necessarily completely illuminated: a is blocked from below. However, our claim is that the segment b in U with the lowest upper endpoint is completely illuminated. Let S be the infinite strip to the right of b. Because the upper endpoint of b is visible from $x = +\infty$, if any portion of S is blocked by a segment c, the upper endpoint of c must lie in S. Then, the highest upper endpoint of all the segments blocking S must be illuminated, contradicting our assumption that b has the lowest illuminated upper endpoint.   □

Separating Convex Polygons
The problem for convex polygons is now solved by the simple observation that the region swept by the right boundary of a convex shape C moving horizontally is a subset the region swept by a line segment s between a highest and a lowest point of C see (Figure 8.27). Therefore, a schedule for separating such vertically spanning segments for a set of convex shapes will suffice to separate the shapes.

Complexity
Computing a separating order for a set of convex shapes is similar to sorting them along the direction of separation, so it should not be surprising that it can be accomplished in $O(n \log n)$ time. We will not prove this result of Guibas and Yao (1983).

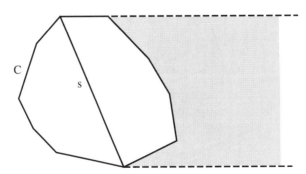

FIGURE 8.27   The region swept by C is a subset of the region swept by s.

Theorem 8.7.2. *Any set of* n *convex shapes in the plane may be separated via translations all parallel to any given fixed direction, with each shape moving once only. An ordering for moving them can be computed in* $O(n \log n)$ *time.*

8.7.3. Reduction from Partition

Having considered an "easy" instance of separability, we now demonstrate in this and the next subsection that general separability problems are "hard" in some sense. Proving hardness can be done by proving a lower bound on the problem, as we did in Chapter 3 (Section 3.6) by reduction from a known hard problem. Recall that the idea is to show that, if we could solve our problem B quickly, we could solve some problem A quickly, where A is known to be difficult. This then establishes that B is at least as difficult as A: A has been *reduced to B*.

The separation problem B we examine allows only translation and movement of polygons one-at-a-time, but each translation can be in a different direction, and each polygon can be moved several times. The known difficult problem A is the *partition* problem: given a collection S of integers, decide whether or not it may be partitioned into two parts whose sums are equal. For example, if $S = \{1, 3, 3, 5, 6\}$, the answer to the partition question is YES since $1 + 3 + 5 = 3 + 6$ but for the set $\{1, 3, 3, 5, 10\}$, the answer is NO. Although this may not seem like a very difficult problem, no one has been able to think of a way to solve it that is significantly better than examining every possible partition of S. Because there are 2^n possible partitions for a set of n elements, this is a very slow algorithm: it requires time exponential in n, and so is effectively useless for, as an example, $n = 100$. Moreover, the partition problem has been shown to be "NP-complete," which means that it is among a large class of apparently intractable problems.[18]

Given any instance of the partition problem, we construct a separability problem that can be solved iff the partition problem can. The construction is illustrated in Figure 8.28 for the set $\{1, 3, 3, 5, 6\}$.[19] It consists of blocks of height 1 and widths corresponding to each element of S. Let Σ be the sum of all the numbers in S. The piece Q in the figure can be moved down and right iff the blocks can be packed to the left within the $(\Sigma/2) \times 2$ rectangle of empty "storage" space. This can be done iff S can be partitioned into two equal parts.

This proves that this version of the separation is at least as difficult as the partition problem: in the technical argot, separation is "NP-hard."

8.7.4. Mimicking the Towers of Hanoi

Although we have shown that separation is hard, note that separating the partition configuration does not require many moves: it may take considerable

---

[18] As of 1993, however, it has not been proven that even the NP-complete problems are truly hard. This is the famous $P = NP$ question. See Garey and Johnson (1979).

[19] Based on Fig. 4.1 of Chazelle, et. al. (1984).

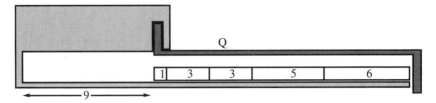

FIGURE 8.28 Q can be moved to infinity iff the partition problem can be solved.

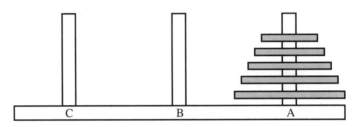

FIGURE 8.29 Towers of Hanoi, side view.

off-line thought, but the actual moves, once known, are easy. Separation can be effected by moving each block just once. We conclude with an example whose solution is not difficult to find, but which requires some pieces to be moved an exponential number of times. Again we restrict motions to be translations and allow polygons to be moved more than once but always one-at-a-time.

It is based on the well-known "Towers of Hanoi" puzzle. In this puzzle, disks of various radii are stacked on one of three pegs, sorted with largest on bottom and smallest on top; see Figure 8.29. The task is to move the disks one by one from peg A to peg B, using peg C whenever convenient, such that at all times not more than one disk is "in the air" (not on a peg), and no disk is ever placed on top of one of smaller radius. This "sorted at all times" condition forces many moves: $2^n - 1$ moves are required to move n disks from A to B (Rawlins, 1992, p. 14–26).

A clever separation instance that mimics the Towers of Hanoi puzzle was suggested by Chazelle, et. al. (1984). The disks are simulated by n U-shaped polygons each of height h and thickness 1, which may nest snugly inside one another to form a stack $n + h$ tall; see Figure 8.30a. Any stack not sorted by size must be at least $n + 2h$ tall, as shown in b of the figure. By choosing h to be much larger than n, we can ensure that a sorted stack is much more compact than an unsorted stack.

The separation puzzle is shown in Figure 8.31.[20] The three rectangular "wells" labeled A, B, and C correspond to the three pegs. The polygon Q can be slid right and down only when A is empty. A can only be emptied by moving

---

[20]Based on Fig. 4.2 of Chazelle, et. al. (1984).

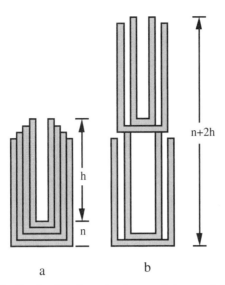

FIGURE 8.30   Stack of U-shaped polygons: (*a*) nested, (*b*) unsorted.

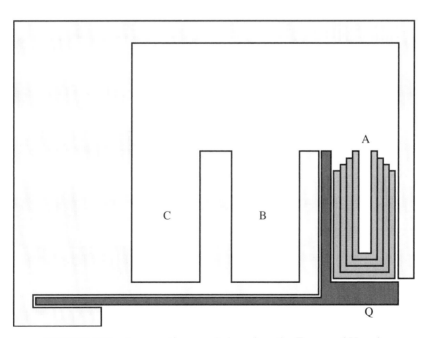

FIGURE 8.31   A separation puzzle based on the Towers of Hanoi.

the n U's into wells B and C, and because of the inefficiency of unsorted stacking, this can only be done by nearly mimicking the Tower of Hanoi moves, nearly in that it is possible to violate sorting once per column, but not more. It still requires an exponential number of moves for each U before Q can be separated.

8.7.5. Exercises

1. *Separating in three dimensions.* Find a set of convex polyhedra in three dimensions that cannot be separated à la Guibas and Yao (1983) (Section 8.7.2) in some direction.

2. *Separating spheres.* Prove or disprove that a collection of disjoint spheres in three dimensions may be separated one-at-a-time by translations parallel to any given direction.

3. *Nondisjoint segments.* Can Lemma 8.7.1 be extended to nondisjoint segments of this type: a collection of segments whose interiors are disjoint, but which may touch with the endpoint of one lying on another? The interior of a segment is the segment without its endpoints. A special case here is the edges of a polygon.

4. *Lower bound.* Show that $\Omega(n \log n)$ is a lower bound on computing the separating order for a disjoint set of line segments.

5. *Partition.* Strengthen the partition reduction to the case when each piece is permitted just a single translation.

6. *Hanoi improvements.*
   a. Exactly how many moves does it take to separate the configuration of polygons in Figure 8.31? Define a move as any continuous translation of one piece (not necessarily along a straight line).
   b. Prove that the puzzle in Figure 8.31 (for general n) requires an exponential number of moves, by proving an exponential lower bound on the number of moves required.
   c. Modify the structure of the puzzle so that the moves more closely mimic the Tower of Hanoi moves, requiring at least $2^n - 1$ moves of the n U's to clear A.
   d. Can the puzzle be modified so that it still requires an exponential number of moves even when any number of polygons may be moved simultaneously?

7. *Star polygons* (Toussaint, 1985*b*). Recall from Chapter 1 (Exercise 1.1.4[5]) that a *star polygon* is one visible from a point in its interior.
   a. Does there always exist a single translation in some direction that will separate two star polygons? If not, provide a counterexample. If so, provide a proof.
   b. Answer the questions in (a) for three star polygons.

8. *Monotone polygons* (Toussaint, 1985*b*). Recall from Chapter 2 (Section 2.1) that a *strictly monotone polygon* is one whose boundary meets every line parallel to some direction u in at most two points.
   a. Show that two strictly monotone polygons, monotone perhaps with respect to different directions, are always separable by a single translation.
   b. Design an algorithm for finding a direction that separates them.
   c. Do your results change if the polygons are monotone, but not strictly monotone, that is, if the polygon boundaries meet every line parallel to some direction in at most two connected sets (where these sets can now be line segments)?

9

Additional Topics

This text has neither covered the majority of computational geometry, nor even all the most important topics. To give some hint at (and pointers to) what lies beyond, I list in this postscript a somewhat random collection of topics not covered.

9.1. TOPICS NOT COVERED

Motion Planning
It goes without saying that my coverage of each topic in this book is a mere surface scratch, but this is especially true of motion planning. Five surveys demonstrate the extent of the work in this area: Yap (1987*a*), Schwartz and Sharir (1988), Sharir (1989), Schwartz and Sharir (1990), and Hwang and Ahuja (1992). One especially important area I didn't mention is motion planning that incorporates aspects of the kinematics and dynamics of the robot's motion; see, for example, the work of Donald (1988). This material (and much else) is given thorough coverage in the recent book by Latombe (1991). Other new areas include motion planning in an environment where the obstacles move (perhaps on a factory floor), coordinating the motion of several robots (say, two robot arms), analyses of stable grasps and firm grips for robot hands, and recognition of objects via tactile sensing (Skiena, 1992).

Pattern Recognition
Pattern recognition, the art of recognizing shapes and patterns from a variety of forms of data, has had a significant influence on computational geometry, largely through the promotion of Toussaint: (Toussaint, 1980, 1986). One example is the Relative Neighborhood Graph, which was mentioned in Chapter 5 (Exercise 5.5.6[7]) as a subgraph of the Delaunay triangulation: study of this and related graphs has stimulated fascinating work (Jaromczyk and Toussaint, 1992). Another lively area is geometric clustering, grouping points into clusters, usually in high dimensional spaces; see Asano, Bhattacharya, Keil, and Yao (1988); and Capoyleas, Rote, and Woeginger (1991).

Graphics
Computer graphics has long been a source of inspiration for computational geometry. Hidden surface removal has already been discussed in Chapter 6 (Section 6.1), but there are many other equally rich problems posed by the

exacting needs of graphics: ray tracing (Schmitt, Müller, and Leister, 1988), spatial partitions (Samet, 1990*a* and 1990*b*), efficient data structures, and decomposition of polygons and polyhedra. See Overmars (1988*b*) and Dobkin (1992) for surveys.

Robustness

As the field of computational geometry matures, attention has increasingly turned toward the practical issues surrounding "robust computation": algorithms that truly work. As we have seen at several locations throughout this text, geometric computations are especially prone to failure in "degenerate" cases, or succumb to problems caused by round-off of floating-point calculations. Researchers are reexamining long-solved problems such as computing the Delaunay triangulation, but with the goal of finding algorithms which are guaranteed to be numerically stable. The work of Fortune (1992*a*), Milenkovic (Fortune and Milenkovic, 1991), and Sugihara and Iri (1992) is in this vein.

Randomized Algorithms

Perhaps the most exciting recent development in computational geometry is the realization that "randomized" algorithms are often superior to "deterministic" algorithms, both theoretically and in practice. Although there is a long tradition in the analysis of algorithms of studying "average case" behavior of algorithms, randomized algorithms are a relatively recent development. These algorithms, sometimes called "Las Vegas" algorithms, use randomization within the algorithm (via a random number generator) to achieve fast expected behavior.

This approach has achieved the fastest practical algorithm for computing the convex hull of n points in three dimensions. As we mentioned in Chapter 4, this is an instance where the only asymptotically optimal algorithm, achieving $O(n \log n)$, is rather complex to implement (Section 4.2.2). So often the $O(n^2)$ incremental algorithm is employed in practice. Clarkson and Shor (1989) showed that by randomizing the incremental algorithm appropriately and supplementing it with a few simple data structures, the incremental algorithm has expected time of $O(n \log n)$. This expected behavior is independent of the input, which is how this differs from a good average-case algorithm: the latter algorithms run fast on the "average" input but could run slowly on some especially nasty inputs. Randomized algorithms could perform poorly on any input, but this would take an especially unlucky string of random numbers; so, they run fast on all inputs with high probability. In all these algorithms, the probability of running fast can be increased arbitrarily close to certainty by appropriate parameter choices.

Most of computational geometry can be revisited with randomization, as is evidenced by the text of Mulmuley (1994). See Clarkson (1992) for a survey.

Parallel Computation

Surely the future belongs to parallel computers, and there has been a substantial effort to reexamine all geometric algorithms for implementation on a variety of parallel computers. Not only has this work been fruitful in its own right, but the additional scrutiny has led to several improvements in conventional sequential algorithms. See Atallah (1992) for a survey.

Range Searching

Considerable work has been done in the area of "range searching," an area with extensive practical applications. One form of this problem is as follows. Given a set of n points in d-dimensional space, preprocess them so that queries requesting all points within a multidimensional box can be answered efficiently (Overmars, 1988*a*). This may seem abstract until one realizes that a data base, for example, student records, can be viewed as specifying points in a multidimensional space: age, sex, major, grade point average, and so forth. Then a query might be: which seniors with a humanities major have a GPA exceeding 3.9? There are also more geometric versions of the problem (Chazelle and Preparata, 1986), and curiously these are now relevant to the recent work on machine learning (Shapire, 1991).

Dynamic Data Structures

Most data change over time: they are "dynamic." Consider, for example, animating a graphics scene: each frame is slightly different from the one before, and recomputing the hidden surfaces from scratch for each frame is wasteful. Even fixed data can lead to a need for dynamic data structures, as the incremental convex hull algorithm demonstrates. Designing data structures that efficiently incorporate insertions, deletions, and other alterations is a fertile  area with connections to all aspects of data structures. See Chiang and Tamassia (1992) for a survey.

Discrete and Combinatorial Geometry

One of the richest influxes to computational geometry is from the pure mathematics concerned with discrete geometry and geometrical combinatorics. This connection is amply documented in Edelsbrunner (1987), which includes an especially thorough coverage of multidimensional geometry.

One exciting development in this area is the discovery by Sharir (1988) that the complexity of many geometric algorithms depends on a function $\alpha(n)$, the extremely slow-growing inverse of Ackermann's function. Ackermann's function grows very rapidly, and its inverse grows correspondingly slowly, so slowly that even for $n = 10^{100}$, $\alpha(n) = 4$. The unexpected appearance in geometry algorithms of Ackermann's function, which is commonplace only in recursion theory, is due to its role in "Davenport-Schinzel sequences." These are strings from a finite alphabet with certain substrings restricted. Counting these sequences under various restrictions has been pursued in combinatorics for its own sake, but it turns out that many geometric algorithms, motion planning algorithms in particular, are dependent on these sequences. For example, the current fastest algorithm for finding a sequence of translations (if they exist) for separating two polygons with a total of n vertices, has complexity $O(n^2\alpha(n^2) \log^2 n)$ (Pollack, Sharir, and Sifrony, 1987). Because $\alpha(n) \le 5$ for all n that might be encountered in this universe, the complexity is effectively $O(n^2 \log^2 n)$.

9.2. GENERAL SOURCES

Four texts on computational geometry predate this one, and all go further in several directions: Mehlhorn (1984), Preparata and Shamos (1985), and Edelsbrunner (1987); the new text of Mulmuley (1994) was mentioned above. Slightly more research-oriented information can be obtained from various survey papers: Dobkin and Souvaine (1987), O'Rourke (1988), Dobkin (1988), Toussaint (1989), Graham and Yao (1990), Mitchell and Suri (1993), and Fortune (1993).

Of course the latest research is appearing in conference proceedings and journals, especially the *Proceedings of the ACM Symposium on Computational Geometry* and the three journals *Discrete and Computational Geometry* (Springer), *Computational Geometry and Applications* (World Scientific), and *Computational Geometry: Theory and Applications* (Elsevier).

Enjoy!

Bibliography

Abellanas, M., García, J., Hernández, M., Hurtado, F. and Serra, F., Onion polygonizations, in *Proc. 4th Canad. Conf. Comput. Geom.*, St. John's, Newfoundland, pp. 127–131, 1992.

Aggarwal, A., Guibas, L., Saxe, J., Shor, P., A linear-time algorithm for computing the Voronoi diagram of a convex polygon, *Disc. Comp. Geom.* **4**(6), 591–604, 1989.

Aho, A. V., Hopcroft, J. E., Ullman, J. D., *Data Structures and Algorithms*, Addison-Wesley, Reading Mass, 1983.

Akl, S. G. and Toussaint, G. T., A fast convex hull algorithm, *Inform. Process. Lett.* **7**(5), 219–222, 1978.

Albertson, M. O. and Hutchinson, J. P., *Discrete Mathematics with Algorithms*, John Wiley and Sons, New York, 1988.

Anderson, K. R., A reevaluation of an efficient algorithm for determining the convex hull of a finite planar set, *Inform. Process. Lett.* **7**, 53–55, 1978.

Asano, T., Bhattacharya, B., Keil, J. M., Yao, F., Clustering algorithms based on minimum and maximum spanning trees, in *Proc. 4th Annu. ACM Sympos. Comput. Geom.*, pp. 252–257, 1988.

Atallah, M. J., Parallel techniques for computational geometry, *Proc. of the IEEE* **80**(9), 1435–1448, 1992.

Aurenhammer, F., Voronoi diagrams: A survey of a fundamental data structure, *ACM Comput. Surveys* **23**, 345–405, 1991.

Banchoff, T. F., *Beyond the Third Dimension: Geometry, Computer Graphics, and Higher Dimensions*, Scientific American Library, 1990.

Bass, L. J. and Schubert, S. R., On finding the disc of minimum radius containing a given set of points, *Math. Comput.* **12**, 712–714, 1967.

Batchelor, B. G., Hierarchical shape description based upon convex hulls of concavities, *J. Cybernetics* **10**, 205–210, 1980.

Baumgart, B. G., A polyhedron representation for computer vision, in *Proc. AFIPS Natl. Comput. Conf.*, Vol. 44, pp. 589–596, 1975.

Bentley, J. L., Fast algorithms for geometric traveling salesman problems, *ORSA J. Comput.* **4**(4), 387–411, 1992.

Berger, M., *Computer Graphics with Pascal*, Benjamin/Cummings, 1986.

Bern, M., Eppstein, D., Plassman, P., Yao, F., Horizon theorems for lines and polygons, in Goodman, J., Pollack, R., Steiger, W., eds., *Discrete and Computa-*

tional Geometry: *Papers from the DIMACS Special Year*, in *DIMACS Series in Discrete Mathematics and Theoretical Computer Science*, Vol. 6, Amer. Math. Soc., pp. 45–66, 1991.

Blum, H., A transformation for extracting new descriptors of shape, in Wathen-Dunn, W., ed., *Models for the Perception of Speech and Visual Form*, MIT Press, pp. 362–380, 1967.

Bookstein, F. L., *The Measurement of Biological Shape and Shape Change*, Lecture Notes in Biomathematics 24, Springer-Verlag, Berlin, 1978.

Bookstein, F. L., *Morphometric Tools for Landmark Data*, Cambridge University Press, Cambridge, 1991.

Brooks, R. A., Solving the Find-Path problem by good representation of free space, *IEEE Trans. Syst. Man Cybern.* **SMC-13**(3), 190–197, 1983.

Brost, R., Analysis and planning of planar manipulation tasks, PhD thesis, Carnegie Mellon University. CMU-CS-91-149, 1991.

Brown, K., Voronoi diagrams from convex hulls, *IPL* **9**, 223–228, 1979.

Buck, R. C. and Buck, E. F., *Advanced Calculus*, McGraw-Hill, New York, 1965.

Canny, J., *The Complexity of Robot Motion Planning*, MIT Press, Cambridge, MA, 1987.

Capoyleas, V., Rote, G., Woeginger, G., Geometric clusterings, *J. Algor.* **12**, 341–356, 1991.

Chand, D. R. and Kapur, S. S., An algorithm for convex polytopes, *J. ACM* **17**, 78–86, 1970.

Chartrand, G. and Oellermann, O. R., *Applied and Algorithmic Graph Theory*, McGraw-Hill, New York, 1993.

Chazelle, B., Computational geometry and convexity, Report CMU-CS-80-150, Dept. Comput. Sci., Carnegie-Mellon Univ., Pittsburgh, PA. PhD thesis from Yale University, 1980.

Chazelle, B., Triangulating a simple polygon in linear time, *Disc. Comp. Geom.* **6**, 485–524, 1991.

Chazelle, B. and Dobkin, D. P., Optimal convex decompositions, in Toussaint, G. T., ed., *Computational Geometry*, North-Holland, Amsterdam, Netherlands, pp. 63–133, 1985.

Chazelle, B. and Dobkin, D. P., Intersection of convex objects in two and three dimensions, *J. ACM* **34**, 1–27, 1987.

Chazelle, B. and Guibas, L. J., Fractional cascading: I. A data structuring technique, *Algorith.*, **1**, 133–162, 1986a.

Chazelle, B. and Guibas, L. J., Fractional cascading: II. Applications, *Algorith.* **1**, 163–191, 1986b.

Chazelle, B. and Incerpi, J., Triangulation and shape complexity, *ACM Trans. Graph.* **3**, 135–152, 1984.

Chazelle, B. and Preparata, F. P., Halfspace range search: an algorithmic application of *k*-sets, *Disc. Comp. Geom.* **1**, 83–93, 1986.

Chazelle, B., Guibas, L. J., Lee, D. T., The power of geometric duality, *BIT* **25**, 76–90, 1985.

Chazelle, B., Ottmann, T. A., Soisalon-Soininen, E., Wood, D., The complexity and decidability of SEPARATION, in *Proc. 11th Internat. Colloq. Automat. Lang. Program.*, in *Lecture Notes in Computer Science*, Vol. 172, Springer-Verlag, pp. 119–127, 1984.

Chew, L. P., Planning the shortest path for a disc in $O(n^2 \log n)$ time, in *Proc. 1st Annu. ACM Sympos. Comp. Geom.*, pp. 214–220, 1985.

Chiang, Y.-J. and Tamassia, R., Dynamic algorithms in computational geometry, *Proc. IEEE* **80**(9), 1412–1434, 1992.

Chinn, W. G. and Steenrod, N. E., *First Concepts of Topology: The Geometry of Mappings of Segments, Curves, Circles, and Disks*, Math. Assoc. Amer., Washington, D.C., 1966.

Chvátal, V., A combinatorial theorem in plane geometry, *J. Combin. Theory Ser. B* **18**, 39–41, 1975.

Clarkson, K. L., Randomized geometric algorithms, in Du, D.-Z. and Hwang, F. eds., *Computing in Euclidean Geometry*, in *Lecture Notes Series on Computing*, Vol. 1, World Scientific, pp. 117–162, 1992.

Clarkson, K. L. and Shor, P. W., Applications of random sampling in computational geometry, II, *Disc. Comp. Geom.* **4**, 387–421, 1989.

Clarkson, K., Tarjan, R. E., Van Wyk, C. J., A fast Las Vegas algorithm for triangulating a simple polygon, *Disc. Comp. Geom.* **4**, 423–432, 1980.

Cohen, J. and Hickey, T., Two algorithms for determining volumes of convex polyhedra, *J. ACM* **26**, 401–414, 1979.

Cormen, T. H., Leiserson, C. E., Rivest, R. L., *Introduction to Algorithms*, MIT Press, Cambridge, Mass., 1990.

Coxeter, H. S. M., *Regular Polytopes*, 2nd ed., Dover, New York, 1973.

Coxeter, H. S. M. and Greitzer, S. L., *Geometry Revisited*, Math. Assoc. Amer., Washington, D. C., 1967.

Day, A. M., Implementation of an algorithm to find the convex hull of a set of 3-d points, *ACM Trans. Graph.* **9**(1), 105–132, 1990.

Dettmers, R., Doraiswamy, I., Gorini, C., Toy, C., Where can a robot reach?, COMAP Module, 1992.

Devijver, P. A., and Kittler, J., *Pattern Recognition: A Statistical Approach*, Prentice-Hall, Inc., N.J., 1982.

Diaz, M., Algorithms for balanced partitioning of polygons and point sets, PhD thesis, Johns Hopkins, 1990.

Dijkstra, E. W., A note on two problems in connexion with graphs, *Numer. Mathem.* **1**, 269–271, 1959.

Dobkin, D. P., Computational geometry: then and now, in Earnshaw, R. A., ed., *Theoretical Foundations of Computer Graphics and CAD*, *NATO ASI*, Vol. F40, Springer-Verlag, pp. 71–109, 1988.

Dobkin, D. P., Computational geometry and computer graphics, *Proc. IEEE* **80**(9), 1400–1411, 1992.

Dobkin, D. P. and Kirkpatrick, D. G., Determining the separation of preprocessed polyhedra—a unified approach, in *Proc. 17th Internat. Colloq. Automata Lang. Program.*, in *Lecture Notes in Computer Science*, Vol. 443, Springer-Verlag, pp. 400–413, 1990.

Dobkin, D. P. and Lipton, R. J., Multidimensional searching problems, *SIAM J. Comp.* **5**, 181–186, 1976.

Dobkin, D. P. and Souvaine, D. L., Computational geometry: a user's guide, in Schwartz, J. T. and Yap, C.-K., eds., *Advances in Robotics* 1: *Algorithmic and Geometric Aspects of Robotics*, Lawrence Erlbaum Associates, Hillsdale, N.J., pp. 43–93, 1987.

Dobkin, D. P., Edelsbrunner, H. and Overmars, M. H., Searching for empty convex polygons, *Algorith.* **5**, 561–571, 1990.

Donald, B. R., A geometric approach to error detection and recovery for robot motion planning with uncertainty, *Artif. Intell.* **37**(1-3), 223–271, 1988.

Dorward, S. E., A survey of object-space hidden surface removal, *Internat. J. Comput. Geom. Appl.* **4**(3), 325–362, 1994.

Edelsbrunner, H., Computing the extreme distances between two convex polygons, *J. Algor.* **6**, 213–224, 1985.

Edelsbrunner, H., *Algorithms in Combinatorial Geometry*, Springer-Verlag, Berlin, Germany, 1987.

Edelsbrunner, H. and Guibas, L., Topologically sweeping an arrangement, *J. Comp. Syst. Sci.* **38**, 165–194, 1989. Corrigendum in 42 (1991), 249–251.

Edelsbrunner, H. and Maurer, H. A., Finding extreme points in three dimensions and solving the post-office problem in the plane, *Inform. Process. Lett.* **21**, 39–47, 1985.

Edelsbrunner, H. and Mücke, E. P., Simulation of simplicity: a technique to cope with degenerate cases in geometric algorithms, *ACM Trans. Graph.* **9**, 66–104, 1990.

Edelsbrunner, H. and Seidel, R., Voronoi diagrams and arrangements, *Disc. Comp. Geom.* **1**, 25–44, 1986.

Edelsbrunner, H., O'Rourke, J., Seidel, R., Constructing arrangements of lines and hyperplanes with applications, *SIAM J. Comput.* **15**(2), 341–363, 1986.

Edelsbrunner, H., Seidel, R., Sharir, M., On the zone theorem for hyperplane arrangements, *SIAM J. Comp.* **22**(2), 418–429, 1993.

Feng, H. Y. F. and Pavlidis, T., Decomposition of polygons into simpler components: feature generation for syntactic pattern recognition, *IEEE Trans. Comp.* **C-24**, 636–650, 1975.

Field, D., Implementing Watson's algorithm in three dimensions, in *Proc. 2nd Annu. Symp. Comput. Geom.*, ACM, pp. 246–259, 1986.

Fisk, S., A short proof of Chvátal's watchman theorem, *J. Combin. Theory Ser. B* **24**, 374, 1978.

Foley, J. D., van Dam, A., Feiner, S. K., Hughes, J. F., *Computer Graphics: Principles and Practice*, Addison-Wesley, Reading, MA., 1990.

Fortune, S., A sweepline algorithm for Voronoi diagrams, *Algorith.* **2**, 153–174, 1987.

Fortune, S., Numerical stability of algorithms for 2D Delaunay triangulations and Voronoi diagrams, in *Proc. 8th Annu. ACM Sympos. Comput. Geom.*, pp. 83–92, 1992a.

Fortune, S., Voronoi diagrams and Delaunay triangulations, in Du, D.-Z. and Hwang, F. eds., *Computing in Euclidean Geometry, Lecture Notes Series on Computing*, Vol. 1, World Scientific, pp. 193–234, 1992b.

Fortune, S., Progress in computational geometry, in Martin, R., ed., *Directions in Geometric Computing*, Information Geometers, Winchester, England, 81–128, 1993.

Fortune, S. and Milenkovic, V., Numerical stability of algorithms for line arrangements, in *Proc. 7th Annu. ACM Sympos. Comput. Geom.*, pp. 334–341, 1991.

Fortune, S. and van Wijk, C., Efficient exact arithmetic for computational geometry, in *Proc. 9th Annu. ACM Sympos. Comput. Geom.*, pp. 163–172, 1993.

Fournier, A. and Montuno, D. Y., Triangulating simple polygons and equivalent problems, *ACM Trans. Graphics* **3**, 153–174, 1984.

Fu, J.-J. and Lee, R. C. T., Voronoi diagrams of moving points in the plane, *Internat. J. Comp. Geom. Appl.* **1**(1), 23–32, 1991.

Garey, M. and Johnson, D., *Computers and Intractability: A Guide to the Theory of NP-Completeness*, Freeman, 1979.

Garey, M. R., Johnson, D. S., Preparata, F. P., Tarjan, R. E., Triangulating a simple polygon, *Inform. Proc. Lett.* **7**, 175–179, 1978.

Ghosh, S. K. and Mount, D. M., An output-sensitive algorithm for computing visibility graphs, *SIAM J. Comput.* **20**(5), 888–910, 1991.

Giblin, P. J., *Graphs, Surfaces and Homology: An Introduction to Algebraic Topology*, Chapman and Hall, 1977.

Graham, R. L., Personal communication, 1992.

Graham, R. L. and Yao, F., A whirlwind tour of computational geometry, *Amer. Math. Monthly* **97**(8), 687–701, 1990.

Graham, R. L., An efficient algorithm for determining the convex hull of a finite planar set, *Inform. Process. Lett.* **1**, 132–133, 1972.

Green, P. and Sibson, R., Computing Dirichlet tesselations in the plane, *Comp. J.* **21**, 168–173, 1977.

Greene, D. H., The decomposition of polygons in convex parts, in Preparata, F. P., ed., *Advances in Computing Research*, JAI Press, pp. 235–259, 1983.

Gries, D. and Stojmenović, I., A note on Graham's convex hull algorithm, *Inform. Process. Lett.* **25**, 323–327, 1987.

Guggenheimer, H. W., *Applicable Geometry: Global and Local Convexity*, R. E. Krieger, Huntington, N.Y., 1977.

Guibas, L. J. and Stolfi, J., Primitives for the manipulation of general subdivisions and the computation of Voronoi diagrams, *ACM Trans. Graph.* **4**, 74–123, 1985.

Guibas, L. J. and Stolfi, J., Ruler, compass, and computer: the design and analysis of geometric algorithms, in Earnshaw, R. A. ed., *Theoretical Foundations of Computer Graphics and CAD*, in *NATO ASI*, Vol. F40, Springer-Verlag, pp. 111–165, 1988.

Guibas, L. J. and Yao, F. F., On translating a set of rectangles, in Preparata, F. P., ed., *Computational Geometry*, in *Advances in Computing Research*, Vol. 1, JAI Press, London, England, pp. 61–77, 1983.

Guibas, L. J., Hershberger, J., Leven, D., Sharir, M., Tarjan, R. E., Linear-time algorithms for visibility and shortest path problem *s* inside triangulated simple polygons, *Algorith.* **2**, 209–233, 1987.

Guibas, L. J., Ramshaw, L., Stolfi, J., A kinetic framework for computational geometry, in *Proc. 24th Annu. IEEE Sympos. Found. Comput. Sci.*, pp. 100–111, 1983.

Guibas, L., Mitchell, J. S. B., Roos, T., Voronoi diagrams of moving points in the plane, in Schmidt, G. and Berghammer, R., eds., *Proc. 17th Internat. Workshop Graph-Theoret. Concepts Comput. Sci.*, in *Lecture Notes in Computer Science*, Vol. 570, Springer-Verlag, pp. 113–125, 1991.

Haines, E., In a posting to the Usenet newsgroup Comp.graphics, 1992.

Haines, E., Point in polygon strategies, in *Graphics Gems IV*, ed. P. S. Heckbert, Academic Press, Boston, 24–46, 1994.

Halmos, P. R., *I Want to be a Mathematician*, Springer-Verlag, 1985.

Heath, T. L., *Euclid: The Elements*, Dover, 1956.

Henle, M., *A Combinatorial Introduction to Topology*, W. H. Freeman, pp. 79–81, 1979.

Hertel, S. and Mehlhorn, K., Fast triangulation of simple polygons, in *Proc. 4th Internat. Conf. Found. Comput. Theory*, in *Lectur Notes in Computer Science*, Vol. 158, pp. 207–218, 1983.

Hoffmann, C., *Geometric and Solid Modeling*, Morgan Kaufmann, San Mateo, California, 1989.

Hofstadter, D. R., *Gödel, Escher, Bach: An Eternal Golden Braid*, Basic Books, 1979.

→ Honsberger, R., *Mathematical Gems II*, Math. Assoc. Amer., pp. 104–110, 1976. *Art gallery theorem's origin reported here. See footnote 6 on pg. 3.*

Hopcroft, J. E., Schwartz, J. T., Sharir, M., *Planning, Geometry, and Complexity of Robot Motion*, Ablex Publishing, Norwood, N.J., 1987.

Hopcroft, J., Joseph, D., Whitesides, S., On the movement of robot arms in 2-dimensional bounded regions, *SIAM J. Comp.* **14**(2), 315–333, 1985. Also in *Planning, Geometry, and Complexity of Robot Motion*, Schwartz, J. T., Sharir, M., Hopcroft, J., eds., Ablex, 1987, 304–329, 1985.

Horton, J. D., Sets with no empty convex 7-gons, *Canad. Math. Bull.* **26**, 482–484, 1983.

Hwang, Y. K. and Ahuja, N., Gross motion planning—a survey, *ACM Comput. Surveys* **24**(3), 219–291, 1993.

Jaromczyk, J. Q. and Kowaluk, M., Constructing the relative neighborhood graph in 3-dimensional space, *Discrete. Appl. Math.* **31**, 181–192, 1991.

Jaromczyk, J. Q. and Toussaint, G. T., Relative neighborhood graphs and their relatives, *Proc. IEEE* **80**(9), 1502–1517, 1992.

Jarvis, R. A., Growing polyhedral obstacles for planning collision-free paths, *Aust. Comput. J.* **15**(3), 103–111, 1983.

Jones, S. and O'Rourke, J., A note on moving a chair through a doorway, *Algor. Rev.* **1**(3), 139–149, 1990.

Kallay, M., The complexity of incremental convex hull algorithms in R^d, *Inform. Process. Lett.* **19**, 197, 1984.

Kantabutra, V., Motion of a short-linked robot arm in a square, *Disc. Comp. Geom.*, **7**, 69–76, 1992.

Kantabutra, V., Reaching a point with an unanchored robot arm in a square, *Algorith.* (In Press).

Kantabutra, V. and Kosaraju, S. R., New algorithms for multilink robot arms, *J. Comp. Syst. Sci.*, **32**(1), 136–153, 1986.

Kaul, A., O'Connor, M. A., Srinivasan, V., Computing Minkowski sums of regular polygons, in *Proc. 3rd Canad. Conf. Comput. Geom.*, pp. 74–77, 1991.

Ke, Y. and O'Rourke, J., An algorithm for moving a ladder in three dimensions, Technical Report JHU-87/17, Dept. Comput. Sci., Johns Hopkins Univ., Baltimore, MD., 1987.

Ke, Y. and O'Rourke, J., Lower bounds on moving a ladder in two and three dimensions, *Disc. Comput. Geom.* **3**, 197–217, 1988.

Kedem, K. and Sharir, M., An efficient motion planning algorithm for a convex rigid polygonal object in 2-dimensional polygonal space, *Disc. Comp. Geom.* **5**, 43–75, 1990.

Kedem, K., Livne, R., Pach, J., Sharir, M., On the union of Jordan regions and collision-free translational motion amidst polygonal obstacles, *Disc. Comp. Geom.* **1**, 59–71, 1986.

Keil, J. M., Decomposing a polygon into simpler components, *SIAM J. Comp.* **14**, 799–817, 1985.

Kirkpatrick, D. G., Optimal search in planar subdivisions, *SIAM J. Comp.* **12**, 28–35, 1983.

Kirkpatrick, D., Klawe, M., Tarjan, R., Polygon triangulation in $O(n \log\log n)$ time with simple data structures, in *Proc. 6th Annu. Symp. Comp. Geom.*, ACM, pp. 34–43, 1990.

Klee, V., On the complexity of d-dimensional Voronoi diagrams, *Archiv. Mathem.*, **34**, 75–80, 1980.

Knuth, D. E., Sorting and searching, in *The Art of Computer Programming*, Vol. 3, Addison Wesley, Reading, MA., 1973.

Koenderink, J. J., *Solid Shape*, MIT Press, 1990.

Koenderink, J. J. and van Doorn, A. J., The singularities of the visual mapping, *Biol. Cyb.* **24**, 51–59, 1976.

Koenderink, J. J. and van Doorn, A. J., The internal representation of solid shape with respect to vision, *Biol. Cyb.* **32**, 211–216, 1979.

Kutcher, J., Coordinated motion planning of planar linkages, PhD thesis, Johns Hopkins University, 1992.

Lakatos, I., *Proofs and Refutations*: *The Logic of Mathematical Discovery*, Cambridge, 1976.

Latombe, J.-C., *Robot Motion Planning*, Kluwer Academic Publishers, Boston, 1991.

Lay, S. R., *Convex Sets and Their Applications*, Wiley, New York, 1982.

Lee, D. T., Medial axis transformation of a planar shape, *IEEE Trans. PAMI* **4**, 363–369, 1982.

Lee, D. T. and Preparata, F. P., Location of a point in a planar subdivision and its applications, *SIAM J. Comp.* **6**, 594–606, 1977.

Lenhart, W. J. and Whitesides, S. H., Turning a polygon inside-out, in *Proc. 3rd Canad. Conf. Comput. Geom.*, pp. 66–69, 1991.

Lenhart, W. J. and Whitesides, S. H., Reconfiguration with line tracking motions, in *Proc. 4th Canad. Conf. Comput. Geom.*, pp. 198–203, 1992.

Lennes, N. J., Theorems on the simple finite polygon and polyhedron, *Amer. J. Math.* **33**, 37–62, 1911.

Leven, D. and Sharir, M., An efficient and simple motion planning algorithm for a ladder moving in two-dimensional space amidst polygonal barriers, *J. Algor.*, **8**, 192–215, 1987.

Lipton, R. J. and Tarjan, R. E., Applications of a planar separator theorem, *SIAM J. Comp.* **9**, 615–627, 1980.

Lozano-Pérez, T., Spatial planning: A configuration space approach, *IEEE Trans. Comput.* **C-32**, 108–120, 1983.

Lozano-Pérez, T. and Wesley, M. A., An algorithm for planning collision-free paths among polyhedral obstacles, *Commun. ACM* **22**, 560–570, 1979.

Malkevitch, J., Milestones in the history of polyhedra, in Senechal, M. and Fleck, G., eds., *Shaping Space: A Polyhedral Approach*, Birkhäuser, pp. 80–92, 1988.

McKenna, M., Worst-case optimal hidden-surface removal, *ACM Trans. Graph.* **6**, 19–28, 1987.

McKenna, M., Applications of arrangements to geometric problems in higher dimensions, PhD thesis, Johns Hopkins University, 1989.

McKenna, M. and Seidel, R., Finding the optimal shadows of a convex polytope, in *Proc. 1st Annu. ACM Symp. Comp. Geom.*, pp. 24–28, 1985.

Mehlhorn, K., Multi-dimensional searching and computational geometry, *Data Structures and Algorithms*, Vol. 3, Springer-Verlag, Berlin, Germany.

Meister, G. H., Polygons have ears, *Amer. Math Mon.* **82**, 648–651, 1975.

Mendelson, B., *Introduction to Topology*, 3rd ed., Dover, New York, 1990.

Mitchell, J. S. B. and Suri, S., A survey of computational geometry, in Ball, M., Magnant, T., Monma, C., Nemhauser, G., eds., *Handbook of Operations Research and Management Sciences*, Vol. 5, Elsevier, New York, (In Press).

Mizoguchi, R. and Kakusho, O., Hierarchical clustering algorithms based on k-nearest neighbors, in *4th Internat. Joint Conf. on Pattern Recogn.*, pp. 314–316, 1978.

Modayur, B., Problem posted on Usenet newsgroup Sci.math, 1991.

Mortenson, M. E., *Geometric Modeling*, John Wiley and Sons, New York, 1985.

Mulmuley, K., *Computational Geometry: An Introduction through Randomized Algorithms*, Prentice Hall, New York, 1994.

Nievergelt, J. and Preparata, F. P., Plane sweeping algorithms for intersecting geometric figures, *Commun. ACM* **25**, 739–747, 1982.

Ó'Dúnlaing, C. and Yap, C. K., A "retraction" method for planning the motion of a disk, *J. Algor.*, **6**, 104–111, 1985.

Ó'Dúnlaing, C., Sharir, M., Yap, C. K., Generalized Voronoi diagrams for moving a ladder, I: topological analysis, *Commun. Pure Appl. Math.* **39**, 423–483, 1980.

Ó'Dúnlaing, C., Sharir, M., Yap, C. K., Generalized Voronoi diagrams for moving a ladder, II: efficient construction of the diagram, *Algorith.* **2**, 27–59, 1987.

Okabe, A., Boots, B., Sugihara, K., *Spatial Tessellations: Concepts and Applications of Voronoi Diagrams*, John Wiley, Chichester, England, 1992.

O'Rourke, J., An on-line algorithm for fitting straight lines between data ranges, *Commum. ACM* **24**, 574–578, 1981.

O'Rourke, J., Finding minimal enclosing boxes, *Intern. J. Comp. Inform. Sci.* **14**, 183–199, 1985a.

O'Rourke, J., A lower bound on moving a ladder, Report JHU/EECS-85/20, Dept. Comput. Sci., Johns Hopkins Univ., Baltimore, MD., 1985b.

O'Rourke, J., *Art Gallery Theorems and Algorithms*, Oxford University Press, New York, 1987.

O'Rourke, J., Computational geometry, *Annu. Rev. Comp. Sci.* **3**, 389–411, 1988.

O'Rourke, J., Chien, C.-B., Olson, T., Naddor, D., A new linear algorithm for intersecting convex polygons, *Comput. Graph. Image Process.* **19**, 384–391, 1982.

Overmars, M. H., Efficient data structures for range searching on a grid, *J. Algor.* **9**, 254–275, 1988a.

Overmars, M. H., Geometric data structures for computer graphics: an overview, in Earnshaw, R. A., ed., *Theoretical Foundations of Computer Graphics and CAD*, NATO ASI, Vol. F40, Springer-Verlag, pp. 21–49, 1988b.

Pedoe, D., *Geometry: A Comprehensive Course*, Dover, 1970.

Plantinga, H. and Dyer, C. R., Visibility, occlusion, and the aspect graph, *Int. J. Comput. Vis.* **5**(2), 137–160, 1990.

Pollack, R., Sharir, M., Sifrony, S., Separating two simple polygons by a sequence of translations, *Disc. Comp. Geom.* **3**(2), 123–136, 1987.

Preparata, F. P. and Hong, S. J., Convex hulls of finite sets of points in two and three dimensions, *Commun. ACM* **20**, 87–93, 1977.

Preparata, F. P. and Shamos, M. I., *Computational Geometry: an Introduction*, Springer-Verlag, New York, 1985. Corrected and expanded second printing, 1988.

Rawlins, G. J. E., *Compared to What? An Introduction to the Analysis of Algorithms*, W. H. Freeman, New York, 1992.

Rucker, R., *The Fourth Dimension: Toward a Geometry of Higher Reality*, Houghton Mifflin, 1984.

Samet, H., *Applications of Spatial Data Structures*, Addison Wesley, Reading, Mass., 1990a.

Samet, H., *The Design and Analysis of Spatial Data Structures*, Addison Wesley, Reading, Mass., 1990b.

Schaudt, B. and Drysdale, R. L., Multiplicatively weighted crystal growth Voronoi diagrams, in *Proc. 7th Annu. Symp. Comp. Geom.* ACM, pp. 214–223, 1991.

Schmitt, A., Müller, H., Leister, W., Ray tracing algorithms: theory and practice, in Earnshaw, R. A., ed., *Theoretical Foundations of Computer Graphics and CAD*, NATO ASI, Vol. F40, Springer-Verlag, pp. 997–1030, 1988.

Schorn, P., The XYZ GeoBench: A programming environment for geometric algorithms, in *Lecture Notes in Computer Science 553*, Springer-Verlag, pp. 187–202, 1991.

Schwartz, J. T. and Sharir, M., On the "piano movers" problem I: the case of a two-dimensional rigid polygonal body moving amidst polygonal barriers, *Commun. Pure Appl. Math.* **36**, 345–398, 1983a.

Schwartz, J. T. and Sharir, M., On the "piano movers" problem II: general techniques for computing topological properties of real algebraic manifolds, *Adv. Appl. Math.* **4**, 298–351, 1983b.

Schwartz, J. T. and Sharir, M., On the "piano movers" problem III: coordinating the motion of several independent bodies: the special case of circular bodies moving amidst polygonal barriers, *Internat. J. Rob. Res.* **2**(3), 46–75, 1983c.

Schwartz, J. T. and Sharir, M., On the "piano movers" problem V: the case of a rod moving in three-dimensional space amidst polyhedral obstacles, *Commun. Pure Appl. Math.*, 1984.

Schwartz, J. T. and Sharir, M., A survey of motion planning and related geometric algorithms, *Artif. Intell.* **37**, 157–169, 1988.

Schwartz, J. T. and Sharir, M., Algorithmic motion planning in robotics, in van Leeuwen, J., ed., *Algorithms and Complexity, Handbook of Theoretical Computer Science*, Vol. A, Elsevier, Amsterdam, pp. 391–430, 1990.

Sedgewick, R., *Algorithms in C++*, Addison Wesley, Reading, Mass., 1992.

Seidel, R., Output-size sensitive algorithms for constructive problems in computational geometry, PhD thesis, Report TR 86-784, Dept. Comput. Sci., Cornell Univ., Ithaca, N.Y., 1986.

Shamos, M. and Hoey, D., Closest point problems, in *Proc. 16th. Annu. IEEE Sympos. Found. Comput. Sci.*, pp. 151–162, 1975.

Shamos, M. I., Computational geometry, PhD thesis, UMI #7819047, Yale University, New Haven, CT., 1978.

Shapire, R. E., *The Design and Analysis of Efficient Learning Algorithms*, The MIT Press, Cambridge, Mass., 1991.

Sharir, M., Efficient algorithms for planning purely translational collision-free motion in two and three dimensions, in *Proc. IEEE Internat. Conf. Robot. Autom.*, pp. 1326–1331, 1987.

Sharir, M., Davenport-Schinzel sequences and their geometric applications, in Earnshaw, R. A., ed., *Theoretical Foundations of Computer Graphics and CAD*, NATO ASI, Vol. F40, Springer-Verlag, pp. 253–278, 1988.

Sharir, M., Algorithmic motion planning in robotics, *Comp.* **22**, 9–20, 1989.

Sharir, M. and Ariel-Sheffi, E., On the "piano movers" problem IV: various decomposable two-dimensional motion planning problems, *Commun. Pure Appl. Math.* **37**, 479–493, 1984.

Shermer, T., Recent results in art galleries, *Proc. IEEE* **80**(9), 1384–1399, 1992.

Sifrony, S. and Sharir, M., A new efficient motion-planning algorithm for a rod in two-dimensional polygonal space, *Algorith.* **2**, 367–402, 1987.

Skiena, S. S., Interactive reconstruction via geometric probing, *Proc. IEEE* **80**(9), 1364–1383, 1992.

Subramaniyam, R. V. and Diwan, A. A., A counterexample for the sufficiency of edge guards in star polygons, *Inform. Process. Lett.* **40**, 97–99, 1991.

Sugihara, K. and Iri, M., Construction of the Voronoi diagram for "one million" generators in single-precision arithmetic, *Proc. IEEE* **80**(9), 1502–1517, 1992.

Sutherland, I. E., Sproull, R. F., Shumacker, R. A., A characterization of ten hidden surface algorithms, *ACM Comput. Surv.* **6**, 1–55, 1974.

Tarjan, R. E. and van Wyk, C. J., An O (n log log n)-time algorithm for triangulating a simple polygon, *SIAM J. Comp.* **17**(1), 143–178, 1988.

Teller, S. J., Computing the antipenumbra of an area light source, *Comp. Graph.* **26**, 139–148, 1992.

Toussaint, G. T., Pattern recognition and geometrical complexity, in *Proc. 5th Internat. Conf. Pattern Recogn.*, pp. 1324–1347, 1980.

Toussaint, G. T., Computing largest empty circles with location constraints, *Int. J. Comput. Info. Sci.* **12**(5), 347–358, 1983a.

Toussaint, G. T., Solving geometric problems with the "rotating calipers", in *Proc. IEEE MELECON 83*, Athens, Greece, pp. A10.02/1–4, 1983b.

Toussaint, G. T., A historical note on convex hull finding algorithms, *Patt. Recogn. Lett.* **3**, 21–28, 1985a.

Toussaint, G. T., Movable separability of sets, in Toussaint, G. T., ed., *Computational Geometry*, North-Holland, Amsterdam, Netherlands, pp. 335–375, 1985b.

Toussaint, G. T., New results in computational geometry relevant to pattern recognition in practice, in Gelsema, E. S. and Kanal, L. N., eds., *Pattern Recognition in Practice II*, North-Holland, Amsterdam, Netherlands, pp. 135–146, 1986.

Toussaint, G. T., Computational geometry: recent developments, in Earnshaw, R. A. and Wyvill, B., eds., *New Advances in Computer Graphics*, Springer-Verlag, N.Y. pp. 23–51, 1989.

Toussaint, G. T., An output-sensitive polygon triangulation algorithm, in *Proc. of the 8th Internat. Conf. on Computer Graphics*, pp. 443–446, 1990.

Vegter, G., The visibility diagram: a data structure for visibility problems and motion planning, in *Proc. 2nd Scand. Workshop Algorithm Theory*, *Lecture Notes in Computer Science*, Vol. 447, Springer-Verlag, pp. 97–110, 1990.

Whitesides, S., Algorithmic issues in the geometry of planar linkages, *Aust. Comput. J.* **24**(2), 42–51, 1991.

Winter, D. T., Personal communication, in response to a post on the Usenet newsgroup Comp.lang.c, 1991.

Yap, C.-K., Algorithmic motion planning, in Schwartz, J. T. and Yap, C.-K., eds., *Advances in Robotics 1*: *Algorithmic and Geometric Aspects of Robotics*, Lawrence Erlbaum Associates, Hillsdale, N.J., pp. 95–143, 1987a.

Yap, C.-K., How to move a chair through a door, *IEEE J. Rob. Autom.*, **RA-3**(3), 172–181, 1987b.

Index

Princeton U-Store, NJ
Sat 6 Dec 1997
$23.16 with 20% discount
+ 1.39 tax ($28.95 list)